Teach Yourself in 24 Hours

Sams Te
book **W9-CTK-002**
in a proven step-by-step approach that works for you. In just 24 sessions of one hour or less, you will tackle every task you need to get the results you want. Let our experienced authors present the most accurate information to get you reliable answers—fast!

Emacs

The keyboard quick reference card at the bottom of this tearcard is meant to be attached above the function keys of your keyboard. The card bindings on this side are merely examples to get you started binding keys. On the other side of this tear card, you will find an empty keyboard quick reference card, on which you should create your own keybindings.

Follow these steps to activate the bindings on the following sample reference card:

1. Create the directory `~/Emacs/Configurations` and copy the file `/usr/share/emacs-lisp/refcard/refcard.el` from the CD to this directory.

2. In your `~/.emacs` file, include the following line:

   ```
   (load "~/Emacs/Configurations/refcard.el")
   ```

   (Windows users should refer to Chapter 2 for information about the location of the home directory.)

			Open Rectangle	Load Tag File			
Meta			Open Rectangle	Load Tag File			
Control		Delete Matching Lines	Insert String in Rectangle	Tags Apropos		Refontify Buffer	Toggle Truncate
Shift		Delete Non-matching Lines	Yank Rectangle	Tag Replace		(Un)set Mark	Redo
	Help	List Matching Lines	Kill Rectangle	Tag Search		Rotate Mark	Undo
	F1	F2	F3	F4		F5	F6

TABLE 2 CONTINUED

PATTERN	REGULAR EXPRESSION	COMMENTS
*.txt	.*\.txt	The star represents a number of characters in the pattern. It is replaced with .* in regular expressions (that is, dot star). The dot that separates the star and txt is always special for regular expressions, so it needs to be prepended with a slash.
file?.txt	file.\.txt	A question mark represents a single character in the pattern. It is translated to a dot.
file0[1-6].txt	file0[1-6]\.txt	This pattern represents the text file01.txt, file02.txt, …, file06.txt.
file{AB,CDE,F}	file\(AB\¦CDE\¦F\)	This pattern represents the text fileAB, fileCDE, or fileF.

TABLE 3 FUNCTIONS CONCERNING MACROS

DEFAULT DESCRIPTION	FUNCTION NAME	KEYBINDINGS
C-x (	start-kbd-macro	Start recording a macro. If you give it a numerical prefix (C-u), you instead continue the previous macro recorded.
C-x)	end-kbd-macro	Stop recording a macro.
C-x e	call-last-kbd-macro	Execute the macro recently defined.
M-x	name-last-kbd-macro	Give a name to the most recently defined macro.
M-x	sams-apply-macro-on-region	Run a macro on a region until point is outside the region after an iteration.
C-x q	(kbd-macro-query)	Make the macro ask the user for permission to continue. Given a numerical prefix (C-u), the macro instead enters recursive editing, which lets you type some text before the macro continues.
C-x k	edit-kbd-macro	This asks you for a keyboard macro to edit and places you in a buffer with the macro in a readable form.
M-C-c	exit-recursive-edit	When the macro pauses for your editing (that is, in recursive-edit), pressing M-C-c continues the macro.

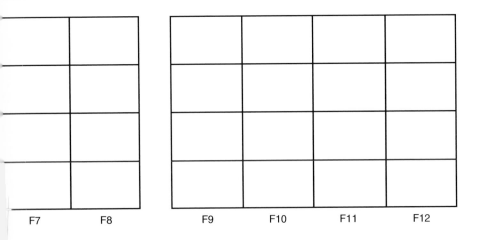

F7   F8   F9   F10   F11   F12

3. On the CD, the keyboard quick reference card is located as LaTeX source code and as RTF (RTF can be used in Microsoft Windows programs such as Microsoft Word or Corel WordPerfect). The following files exist:

   - `refcard.tex`—an empty reference card in LaTeX
   - `refcard-example.tex`—the sample reference card
   - `refcard.rtf` and `refcard-example.rtf`—reference cards in RTF
   - `refcard.ps` and `refcard.pdf`—empty reference cards in PostScript and PDF (this is the emergency file, in case you don't have access to a program that can print RTF or translate LaTeX files)

   These are all located in the directory `/usr/share/emacs-lisp/refcard/` on the CD. For a description on how to make a paper copy of them, see the top of each of the files.

It is, of course, not enough for Emacs that you attach a piece of paper to the keyboard; you must also tell it about the keybinding. To create your own bindings for the function keys, simply edit the file `refcard.el` that you have installed here. You can do this by inserting a line similar to the following into your `.emacs` file:

```
(global-set-key [(control f6)] 'sams-toggle-truncate)
```

This line tells Emacs that pressing Ctrl, holding it down, and pressing the F6 key causes Emacs to invoke the function `sams-toggle-truncate`. (Please note the single quote before the word `sams`.)

More information on the keyboard quick reference card is available in Hour 1 in the "The Keyboard Quick Reference Card" section.

Flyspell-Mode					
Ispell Buffer	List Bookmark	Compile			
Ispell Region	Set Bookmark	Macro on Region			
Ispell Word	Goto Bookmark	Goto Line			
F7	F8	F9	F10	F11	F12

TABLE 1   REGULAR EXPRESSION SYMBOLS

SYMBOL	MEANING	SYMBOL	MEANING
REPEATERS		**POSITIONS**	
*	Repeats the previous regular expression any number of times (including zero times)	^	Matches the beginning of the line or string
+	Repeats the previous regular expression any number of times (at least one time)	$	Matches the end of the line or string
		\<	Matches the beginning of a word
		\>	Matches the end of a word
?	The previous regular expression matches zero or one time	**SPECIAL CHARACTERS**	
GROUPING AND CHARACTER GROUPS		.	Matches any character
\(...\)	Groups the text for later reference or just to overcome precedence problems	\w	Matches any character from a word (in most cases equivalent to [0-9a-zA-Z])
[...]	Matches any of the characters within the group (but only one character; if you need to match a number, combine this with *, +, or ?)	\W	Matches any character not from a word ([^0-9a-zA-Z])
[^...]	Matches any character not in this group		

TABLE 2   CONVERSION FROM PATTERNS TO REGULAR EXPRESSIONS

PATTERN	REGULAR EXPRESSION	COMMENTS
file42	file42	This pattern does not contain any of the special characters listed here.
file.txt	file\.txt	The dot is one of the special characters, therefore it must be prepended with a slash.

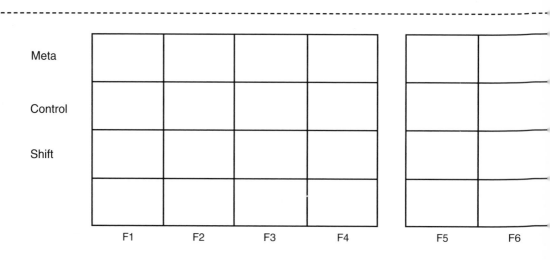

	F1	F2	F3	F4		F5	F6
Meta							
Control							
Shift							

Jesper Pedersen
Jari Aalto
Charles Curley
Eric Ludlam
Larry Ayers

SAMS
Teach Yourself

Emacs

in 24 Hours

SAMS

A Division of Macmillan Computer Publishing
201 West 103rd Street, Indianapolis, Indiana 46290

Sams Teach Yourself Emacs in 24 Hours

Copyright © 1999 by Sams Publishing

International Standard Book Number: 0-672-31594-7

Library of Congress Catalog Card Number: 98-83136

Printed in the United States of America

First Printing: April 1999

01   00   99   4   3   2

Trademarks

Warning and Disclaimer

EXECUTIVE EDITOR
Jeff Koch

ACQUISITIONS EDITOR
Gretchen Ganser

DEVELOPMENT EDITOR
Maureen A. McDaniel

MANAGING EDITOR
Brice Gosnell

PROJECT EDITOR
Natalie Harris

COPY EDITOR
Michael Dietsch

INDEXER
Rebecca Salerno

PROOFREADER
Benjamin Berg

TECHNICAL EDITORS
Jari Aalto
Jon Konrath

INTERIOR DESIGN
Gary Adair

COVER DESIGN
Aren Howell

LAYOUT TECHNICIANS
Brandon Allen
Timothy Osborn
Stacey Richwine-DeRome
Staci Somers

Contents at a Glance

Contents

Dedication

This book is dedicated to all those people who have worked very hard to make Emacs and all its extensions available.

Acknowledgments

First of all, a huge thank you should go to the people at Macmillan, especially Gretchen Ganser, Maureen McDaniel, and Tracy Williams. They have all encouraged me very much and helped me as well as they could throughout this book.

Next, a huge thank you should go to Jari Aalto with whom I have discussed much of the content of the book and to Charles Curley who has ensured that the subjects presented are correct in Microsoft Windows.

Thank yous should also be said to Eric M. Ludlam, Larry Ayers, and Jon Konrath who worked on the book by writing the chapters my deadline didn't permit me to write myself, and doing technical editing.

A huge thank you should go to Lars Magne Ingebrigtsen (the maintainer of Gnus) and Christoph Wedler (the author of the template package, and much more) for being very kind and helpful during my writing about their valuable extensions.

The people behind GNU Emacs and XEmacs, and all those thousands of people who have made extensions to Emacs (and shared it with the rest of the world) deserve a very big round of applause! Without your work, this book would never have existed and we would all still use vi.

Finally my beautiful girlfriend Anne Helene should be thanked for keeping up with me during the three months it took to write this book. Thank you; you have been very supportive!

Did I forget anyone? Thank you to all of you who inspired me to write this book or came with comments and criticism on it.

About the Authors

JESPER KJAER PEDERSEN was born and has lived all his life in Denmark. Currently he lives in the city of H. C. Andersen together with his girlfriend Anne Helene, who studies communication at Odense University. In September 1998, he got his master's degree in computer science from Odense University.

Jesper has always been very fond of computers, but, in contrast to many others, he'd rather make the computer work for him and make it easier for others than play games. Examples of this are this book on Emacs and the open source software program called The Dotfile Generator, which he created. Jesper has used UNIX since early 1990, when he started at the university, and has used Linux on his computer since 1994. Jesper is the founder and chairman of the local Linux user group at Funen.

While Jesper studied at the university, he also worked as a student programmer, where he maintained the UNIX system (especially the Emacs installation) and wrote The Dotfile Generator. The idea for The Dotfile Generator came from users who asked questions regarding their Emacs setup. Nowadays, the Emacs module is outdated because Emacs itself offers customization using graphical widgets. You can still use The Dotfile Generator to configure several other programs, including Procmail, tcsh, and Bash. In his spare time, when he's not in front of his computer, he enjoys doing jujitsu and listening to music from the '80s. In the future, you might expect to see much more work done on The Dotfile Generator or a book on Emacs extensions. You can get more information about Jesper or The Dotfile Generator from `http://www.imada.ou.dk/~blackie`.

JARI AALTO, a software engineer with Nokia Telecommunications, is an experienced Emacs user who has helped develop numerous Emacs packages, including 60 of his own. He is currently developing an Emacs tool set, Tiny-Tools. Jari maintains several book-like documents such as the Procmail Tips page. He is also a veteran UNIX shell, Modula, Pascal, C, C++, awk, and Perl programmer whose modules can be found from `http://www.cpan.org`.

When Jari is not hacking away with Emacs, he enjoys ballroom dancing and passionate Argentine tango. For his listening pleasure and weekend relaxation, he plays flamenco with his guitar.

CHARLES CURLEY lives in the western part of the US, where he rides herd on two horses, two dogs, a cat, and several computers that run Linux, Windows NT, and Windows 95. He uses Emacs on all of them (well, all the computers, anyway). He has been programming and otherwise playing with computers for 20 years. Much to his surprise, he frequently gets someone to pay him to do it. Groups that have encouraged him this way include the Jet Propulsion Laboratory, Colorado Memory Systems, Alpha Technologies, Hewlett-Packard, Maxtor, and an obscure operating systems company in Redmond, Washington, which is trying very hard to compete with Linux (at least that's what it said in its defense at the antitrust trial). He also worked briefly at Weyerhaeuser, but gave up trying to port Emacs to a tree.

He co-authored a book about TCP/IP administration on Windows NT and has published articles on the Forth programming language. This makes him one of the very few geeks who can write both software and actual human language.

Eric Ludlam is a software engineer at The MathWorks, Inc. where he has taught classes for beginning and advanced Emacs users. He has authored several tools included in Emacs for the Free Software Foundation, such as gtalk, Speedbar, and checkdoc. He has over five years of experience in GNU-related projects.

Eric lives in Massachusetts with his Emacs-using wife, Amy, and two Emacs-abusing cats. His current passion is building replicas of medieval siege engines, such as trebuchets, for use in pumpkin-throwing competitions and high school physics demonstrations.

Larry Ayers lives on a small farm in northeast Missouri with his wife and teenage son and daughter. He operates a portable sawmill, does general woodworking, raises sheep and shiitake mushrooms, and does computer consulting from time to time.

Larry discovered GNU software several years ago and has used Emacs and Linux ever since. When he's not beta-testing software he enjoys playing the fiddle and guitar. During the warmer months he spends time identifying and propagating rare prairie plants.

Tell Us What You Think!

As the reader of this book, *you* are our most important critic and commentator. We value your opinion and want to know what we're doing right, what we could do better, what areas you'd like to see us publish in, and any other words of wisdom you're willing to pass our way.

As an associate publisher for Sams, I welcome your comments. You can fax, email, or write me directly to let me know what you did or didn't like about this book—as well as what we can do to make our books stronger.

Please note that I cannot help you with technical problems related to the topic of this book, and that due to the high volume of mail I receive, I might not be able to reply to every message.

When you write, please be sure to include this book's title and author as well as your name and phone or fax number. I will carefully review your comments and share them with the author and editors who worked on the book.

Fax:	317.581.4770
Email:	opsys@mcp.com
Mail:	Associate Publisher
	Sams
	201 West 103rd Street
	Indianapolis, IN 46290 USA

Introduction

There is no doubt that Emacs is the most powerful text editor available! Unfortunately Emacs has quite a reputation for being difficult to learn and hard to use. With this book this will not be true for you, for the following reasons:

- The book is organized in a way that makes it possible for you, within just a few hours, to learn enough for your daily work with Emacs.

- The focus in this book is on usability, rather than on obscure features that only a few people need. Thus several extensions to Emacs are discussed (including on-the-fly spell-checking, file templates, and major modes for editing LaTeX, HTML, C, C++, and Java).

- In Hour 1, "Introduction to Emacs," you will learn how to bind functions to the function keys (F1, F2, F3...F12). The CD-ROM accompanying this book contains a keyboard quick reference card, which you may edit to include your customizations. This way, you do not need to learn difficult keybindings.

Accompanying the book is a CD-ROM with many extensions to Emacs that you can play with in your spare time. Using these extensions, you can customize Emacs in even more ways than those described in the pages of this book.

The CD also contains a file with features that might seem like they are missing in Emacs, when you read the book. Often these features are not missing; to avoid discussing details that are too technical, however, a fix has been made to ensure that the topics are as easily understandable as possible. (This file is discussed in Hour 1.)

The focus in the book is on using Emacs with a graphical interface, either X Window or Microsoft Windows. Thus no time will be wasted on discussing how to make Emacs work when you have a monitor that displays only 25 lines with 80 characters each.

 Text within several figures throughout this book is excerpted from *The Hitchhiker's Guide to the Galaxy* by Douglas Adams.

Which Version and Flavor Does the Book Cover?

The book covers the two major flavors of Emacs, namely GNU Emacs and XEmacs. The focus is on Emacs version 20, but in many places notes are given on differences and incompatibilities with Emacs version 19.

GNU Emacs is a bit faster than XEmacs; on the other hand, XEmacs is more graphically oriented than GNU Emacs. Whichever you choose depends on your personal preferences. Fortunately, you can shift from one to the other or even use both at the same time. They share the same configuration file and, in the first chapter, you will be taught how to make them coexist. Any major differences that exist between them will be pointed out in the book.

Keybindings

By default Emacs uses three different modifiers: Shift, Control (Ctrl), and Meta (or Alt). Whenever you must press a key you are instructed in the following way:

Press C-a (beginning-of-line) to go to the beginning of the line.

First you are instructed which keys to press, and then you are told which function this is associated with. This enables you to bind the function to one of the function keys, and thus use that function key in the future instead.

The following conventions are used for keybindings:

- C-F1—In this example, you press the Control key, hold it down while you press the F1 key, and then release both.
- M-F1—Press the Meta key (which might be labeled Alt on your keyboard). Hold it down and press F1, and release both.
- S-F1—Press and hold the Shift key, press F1, and then release.
- S-C-M-F1 or C-M-S-F1, and so on—Sometimes it is necessary to press more than one modifier; the order in which you press them is not important. Thus in the above, press and hold Shift, Ctrl, and Meta while pressing F1, and release all of the keys.

If your keyboard does not have the Meta or the Alt key, then press the Escape (Esc) key instead. Thus to press M-F1, press the Esc key, release it, and press the F1 key. Likewise to press C-M-F1, press the escape key, release it, and press and hold Ctrl while pressing F1.

Conventions Used in This Book

This book uses the following typeface conventions:

- All code in the listings appears in monospace.
- Many code-related terms within the text also appear in monospace.

- Placeholders in code appear in *italic monospace*.
- When a line of code is too long to fit on one line of this book, it is broken at a convenient place and continued to the next line. A code continuation character (➥) precedes the continuation of a line of code. (You should type a line of code that has this character as one long line without breaking it.)

Special design features enhance the text material:

Notes explain interesting or important points that can help you understand Emacs concepts and techniques.

Tips provide information to help you in real-world situations. Tips often offer shortcuts or information to make tasks easier or faster.

Cautions provide information about detrimental performance issues or dangerous errors. Pay careful attention to Cautions.

Windows Notes provide Windows-specific information about Emacs. These Windows Notes inform you when Emacs for Windows 95/98/NT differs from GNU Emacs or XEmacs.

PART I
Getting Started

Hour

HOUR 1

Introduction to Emacs

You have now started your journey into the world's most powerful editor. To make you understand the power of Emacs, this hour begins by listing some of the features of Emacs; with each feature, a short description or an example is given to show the power of the given feature.

The power of Emacs is split over thousands of functions. Some of them are bound to the keys of the keyboard, whereas others are not. All modern keyboards have a row of twelve function keys, which you can use to make your own personal keybindings. This will hopefully make it possible for you to get the most out of Emacs. A customizable quick reference card, which is described in the section "The Keyboard Quick Reference Card," is shipped with the book.

This hour also discusses the basics of configuring Emacs.

Windows NT and Windows 95/98 users will find that Emacs is one of the few editors that runs on both Windows and other operating systems. You will learn a lot more about Emacs on Windows, including how to install it, in Hour 2, "Using Emacs in Microsoft Windows." But don't skip ahead; there is much to learn here.

Overview of Emacs Features

Emacs is the most powerful editor in the world. If you understand the basic ideas behind how it works, you will find that you can do almost anything from within Emacs. Some users love to do all their work from within Emacs (for example, reading and sending mail and news, managing files and directories, and—of course—editing files). Others tend to use it for a more limited set of needs. This section gives you an introduction to the capabilities of Emacs. You might find that you never use some of the features (some people do not want to take the time to learn to use Emacs for email, for example). The important thing is that you are aware of what Emacs can do in case you later have the need to use it.

Working with Many Files in Different Windows at the Same Time

Emacs makes it possible for you to edit several files at the same time. Some of them might be visible, whereas others might be temporarily hidden. This can be seen in Figure 1.1, which shows two top-level windows.

FIGURE 1.1

Emacs has the capability to edit several files at once.

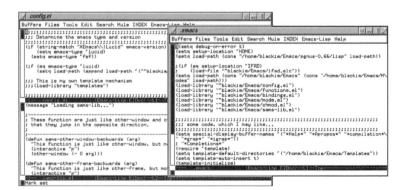

1

Editing several files is especially useful when you write computer programs that are split over several files. You can, for example, look at the definition of a function in one file while you edit its use in another file.

Editing multiple files is described in Hour 6, "Editing Several Files at Once."

Editing Files on Different Hosts

Besides editing a file that is located on your local hard disk, Emacs also makes it possible for you to edit files that are located on other machines. This is very useful because you do not need to log in to the other machine to edit the file. (If you cannot see how this is useful, just imagine that your specially configured Emacs setup is not available on the other machine.) You can edit files that are located on other machines by downloading the file to your local hard disk using the FTP program; when you save the file, it is uploaded to the remote file again.

Another advantage of this feature is that you can FTP to your own machine as a different user (for example, as the superuser), and then edit files on your local machine as another user. You can do this without having to log in as another user and use his Emacs setup.

This process is described in Hour 4, "Basic Editing."

Customizable Keyboards and Functions

Emacs has thousands of user-accessible functions for doing all kind of things. Many of these functions are intended for the user to invoke from the keyboard. Given the limited number of keys on the keyboard, however, not every one of these functions is accessible by pressing a few keys. But you can configure the keyboard just the way you like it. In the next section you will learn how to bind functions to the keys labeled F1–F12. In Hour 23, "Binding Keys and Creating Menus," you will learn how to bind functions to any key on the keyboard.

Another—even more important—way in which Emacs can be configured is through user options. User options are used to configure the behavior of functions in minor predefined ways. An example of this is the behavior that occurs when you press the arrow down key on the last line of a file. What does Emacs do in this situation? There are two answers to this question:

- Emacs might ring the bell to indicate that you are at the last line of the file, and that it is therefore not possible to move down one line.

- Emacs might add a blank line to your file and move down to this line.

Which answer you like is totally a matter of user preference; some might like the first solution, whereas others might like the second. Using user options, you can tell Emacs which of these solutions you like; just insert an appropriate line in the .emacs file that is located in your home directory.

Finally, Emacs can be extended by writing Lisp files. These Lisp files can vary in size from a few lines to several megabytes. The GNU news reader that is described in Hours 20, "Gnus Basics," and 21, "Advanced Gnus," is an example of the latter.

Writing extensions in Lisp is beyond the scope of this book. However, in Hour 22, "Learning Lisp Basics," you will learn the basics of Lisp. This will make you capable of configuring Emacs, but it can also serve as a step toward learning Lisp so that you can later develop your own functions.

Lots of Additional Third-Party Extensions

 As was mentioned previously, Emacs can be extended using Lisp functions. Many people have done so, and they have shared the functions with the rest of us. This means that there are thousands of extensions for Emacs. Some merely change a bit about Emacs's behavior in certain situations, whereas others add brand new features to Emacs. Examples include new major modes for editing specific files (such as HTML), on-the-fly spell-checking, loading templates for new files, and interfacing to different programs (such as diff). Many of these extensions are described throughout the book, and several of them are located on the CD. In Hour 24, "Installing Emacs Add-Ons," you will learn how to install new packages.

Undo and Recovery

Emacs has functions that make it capable of erasing large chunks of text with just a few keystrokes. Therefore, it is of significant importance to note that Emacs has a very powerful undo mechanism. Like some of the more modern editors and word processors, Emacs is not limited to undoing only the latest command; instead, you can undo many hours of work, step by step.

Although Emacs very seldom crashes (this book is written in Emacs, and it has not crashed even once during this writing!), other circumstances make it necessary for Emacs to have a high level of security. This makes it possible for you to recover when your window manager, your operating system, or something else crashes.

Emacs works with two levels of security:

- Whenever you start editing a new file, Emacs saves the original to a backup file; therefore, you can return to the file as it was before you started editing it.

- Emacs saves the files that you are editing, at regular intervals, to a copy that you can recover in case a crash occurs.

The undo and recovery mechanism is described in Hour 6.

Editing Modes

Emacs has several predefined modes for editing specific types of files (called major modes); examples of these include major modes for C, C++, Java, LaTeX, Perl, Python, Lisp, HTML, SGML, and many more.

These major modes configure Emacs to know a bit about the type of text that you edit. This can help you indent your text in fancy ways (mostly for programming modes), highlight keywords and other constructions using colors, and move around (for example, you can easily go to the beginning of a function or to the beginning of the sentence, depending on the type of text you are editing). Editing modes for LaTeX, HTML, C, C++, and Java are described in Hours 17, "Editing LaTeX and HTML Files," and 18, "Editing C, C++, and Java Files." These hours will provide you with enough understanding to make it easy for you to learn the major modes for the language that you most often use.

Making the Text More Readable Using Colors

Today's monitors have the capability to show text in different colors, fonts, and shapes. Emacs uses this capability to make the text more readable. From the major mode you are using, Emacs knows enough about your text to show keywords in one face, comments in another, text literals in a third, and so on. An example of this can be seen in Figure 1.2.

FIGURE 1.2

Emacs highlights text so that you can get an better overview.

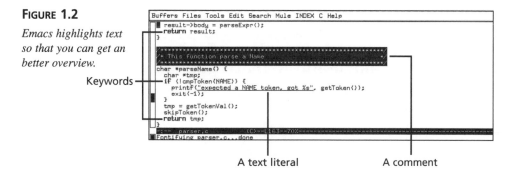

Keywords

A text literal   A comment

In Hour 12, "Visible Editing Utilities," this is described in detail.

Spell-Checking

One of the major advantages of a computer is its capability to help you spell-check your documents. Emacs, of course, can also do this. There are two different ways in which you can do this, depending on your personal preferences:

- You can spell-check the entire document when you are finished writing it.
- You can spell-check it on-the-fly. Then, whenever you have written a word, it is spell-checked; if it is misspelled, the word is highlighted.

In Figure 1.3 you can see the Emacs interface to spell-checking (when it is done for a whole document). In the beginning, you might think that this interface seems old-fashioned; as you get used to Emacs, however, you will find that it is very pleasant that you do not have to use the mouse for spell-checking.

Suggestions for alternatives

FIGURE 1.3

The Emacs interface to spell-checking.

Misspelled word

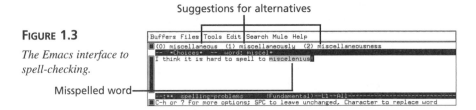

Furthermore, you can ask Emacs to replace some misspelled words for you as you type them. For example, you can have *teh* replaced with *the* automatically. Emacs does not do this unless you ask for it, however. It is important to realize that Emacs never does such things behind your back.

The tools that are used for spell-checking are described in Hour 11, "Editing Utilities."

Search and Search-and-Replace Capabilities

If you think carefully, you might realize that you often search for things in files. For example, you might find yourself

- Searching for a literal string in your current file.
- Searching for a given function in any of the C files of your current programming project.
- Searching for all header lines in your current HTML file.
- Searching for the file in which the words *Dotfile Generator* appear.

The Emacs function for searching that is the most frequently used is the one that searches for text in your current file (incremental search). You invoke it by pressing C-s

1

and then typing the text for which you want to search. Emacs then advances through the text, looking for each character you type—therefore, it is always located at a match for the text that you have typed so far. This is a very powerful way of searching a file because you seldom need to type many characters of the words for which you are searching before you arrive at the correct location. Figure 1.4 shows an example of an incremental search.

FIGURE 1.4

Incremental search.

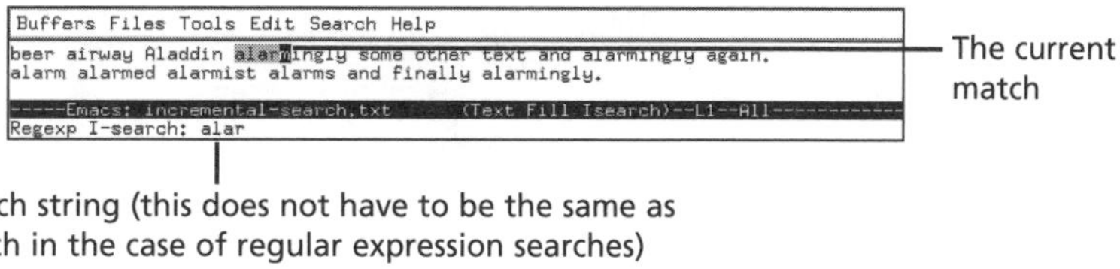

```
Buffers Files Tools Edit Search Help
beer airway Aladdin alarmingly some other text and alarmingly again.
alarm alarmed alarmist alarms and finally alarmingly.
-----Emacs: incremental-search.txt      (Text Fill Isearch)--L1--All----------
Regexp I-search: alar
```

The current match

The current search string (this does not have to be the same as the current match in the case of regular expression searches)

Besides searching for text in a single file, Emacs can also search in all the files of a given project, or even in all the files in a given directory tree.

Apart from searching for ordinary text strings, Emacs can also search using regular expressions. A regular expression is a kind of a pattern that describes some properties for which to search. For example, using a regular expression you can search for

- Lines starting with a space, or empty lines
- Occurrences of the word *the*, but not *then* or *aesthetic*
- The word UserX, UserY, or UserZ, and nothing else (for example not UserA).

Searching for text in a single file is described in Hour 7, "Searching for Text in a Buffer," searching for text in several files is described in Hour 8, "Searching for Text in Multiple Files," and regular expressions are described in Hour 9, "Regular Expressions."

Having said *searching*, one must also say *search-and-replace*. The Emacs capability to perform a search-and-replace is as powerful as its capability to search. Search-and-replace is also described in Hours 7–9.

Compiling and Debugging Programs from Within Emacs

The Emacs editor has been used for many years by programmers; it is therefore especially useful for programming. From within Emacs you can compile and debug programs. Therefore, Emacs can be seen as a fully capable programming environment. The main advantage of this is that you have the same capabilities when compiling and debugging as you have when you write your programs, or even when you write letters to your uncle. (That is, you use the same tools to search for text, insert text, cut and paste, and so on.)

In Figure 1.5 you can see Emacs at work, compiling a program; Figure 1.6 shows a debugging session.

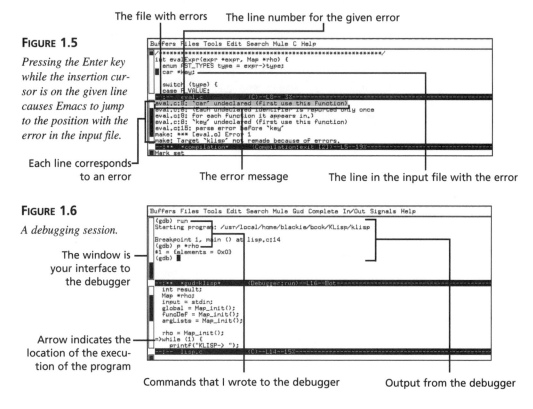

FIGURE 1.5

Pressing the Enter key while the insertion cursor is on the given line causes Emacs to jump to the position with the error in the input file.

The file with errors

The line number for the given error

Each line corresponds to an error

The error message

The line in the input file with the error

FIGURE 1.6

A debugging session.

The window is your interface to the debugger

Arrow indicates the location of the execution of the program

Commands that I wrote to the debugger

Output from the debugger

Powerful Macros

Emacs is very good at making you use your energy to write text rather than to perform trivial, monotonous editing tasks. Emacs accomplishes this through the use of powerful macros. Think of a macro as a recording mechanism, where you can tell Emacs to record your coming keystrokes; you can later execute these keystrokes simply by telling Emacs to retype them. This, however, is not the whole truth about macros...

Although the concept of macros might sound like no big deal, it most certainly is a big deal. If you are aware of your typing, you will find many places in which you perform the same editing tasks over and over again.

The following examples show instances in which a macro might speed up things up. If you don't think that any of the tasks are made much easier with a macro, just imagine that you have to do them several times in a row, or hundreds of times each and every day:

- Removing ^M at the end of every line in the whole file.
- Changing the dictionary that is used for spelling to British.
- Inserting a template for letter heads, and querying for each entry.

Macros are described in Hour 13, "Macros."

Folding and Hiding Text

When you are working with huge files that contain documents or even programs, you are often faced with the need to have an overview. If writing a book, for example, you might need to see which chapters exist; when you have seen that, you might want to focus on one of the chapters, and then see which sections are included in that particular chapter. Emacs can help you get such an overview by collapsing all the text of a chapter into three dots and showing only the chapter headings. Likewise, it might show only the section headers for a chapter, and so on. In Figure 1.7 you can see the file for this chapter, where all the subsections are hidden except for this section.

Only the heading for this subsection is shown.

FIGURE 1.7

Getting an overview of the text.

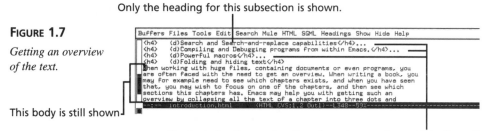

This body is still shown

The body for these subsections have been collapsed into these three

Overviews are discussed in Hour 15, "Getting an Overview of a File."

Reading/Composing Mail and News

I am assuming that you are not new to computers, so you are probably used to writing email. After you have learned to love Emacs for its editing capabilities, you might find that you often say to yourself, "I wish my mail program did the following editing task as well as Emacs does," or "Gosh, I wish I had Emacs's powerful macros at hand right now." You can, of course, tell most email programs to use Emacs to edit your messages—but that is not a very pleasant solution because it takes some time for Emacs to start up, and the interaction will never be the way that you want it. Well, how about switching to Emacs, and using it for *all* your mailing needs? The mail reader that is presented in this book is called Gnus. It is, without a doubt, the most powerful mail reader available; and if that is not enough, think about having all Emacs's features (that is, incremental search, macros, and on-the-fly spell-checking) available with your mail program. Furthermore, Gnus is also a news reader, so you can use the same interface for handling news that you use for handling email. Well, what are you waiting for?!

Gnus is described in Hours 20 and 21.

Extra Help Using the Info System

Built into Emacs is a hyper-reference system that is similar to the World Wide Web, but that is intended for manuals. This system is called the info system. There are two main differences between the info system and the World Wide Web, however. First, no references point outside your computer; you are only referred inside the document or to other documents that are located on your system. Therefore, you do not have to be online to read these manuals. The second difference is that because all the text resides on your local computer, Emacs is capable of searching through all the pages that belong to a single document.

Much information can be found in the info pages. The two most important ones are the Emacs reference manual (which contains much of the same information that is found in this book, but that is in the form of a reference manual and that doesn't have many of the extensions) and the Emacs Lisp reference manual. This manual describes the Emacs Lisp programming language, in which extensions to Emacs are written. Figure 1.8 shows a sample info page.

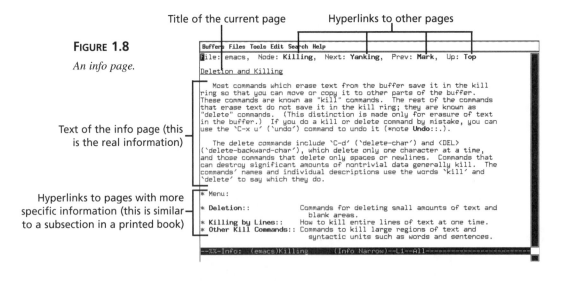

FIGURE 1.8

An info page.

The Keyboard Quick Reference Card

Emacs has thousands of different functions for doing almost anything that is possible with a computer. Many of these are available from the keyboard. The most important functions are easily available (for example, search forward is bound to C-s), but others are bound to hard-to-remember keys (for example, C-x r b for Jump to Bookmark). Functions that the developers of Emacs have found are even less likely to be used, or that come with extra packages, are not bound to keys. Examples of this include Search in multiple files using tags and Spell-check buffer.

The functions that are either not bound to a key or that are bound to keys that are difficult to remember can be bound to the function keys that are available on any new keyboards.

 The CD contains a keyboard quick reference card that can be printed out and attached to the keyboard. You need to modify this quick reference card to include the functions that you find most interesting and useful. In Figure 1.9 you can see a sample quick reference card.

FIGURE 1.9

The keyboard quick reference card that is available on the CD.

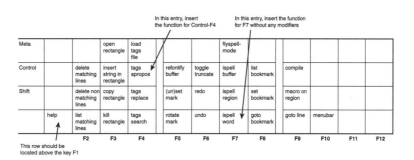

	(F1)	F2	F3	F4	F5	F6	F7	F8	F9	F10	F11	F12
Meta			open rectangle	load tags file			flyspell-mode					
Control		delete matching lines	insert string in rectangle	tags apropos	refontify buffer	toggle truncate	ispell buffer	list bookmark	compile			
Shift		delete non matching lines	copy rectangle	tags replace	(un)set mark	redo	ispell region	set bookmark	macro on region			
	help	list matching lines	kill rectangle	tags search	rotate mark	undo	ispell word	goto bookmark	goto line	menubar		

In this entry, insert the function for Control-F4

In this entry, insert the function for F7 without any modifiers

This row should be located above the key F1

It is, of course, not enough for Emacs that you attach a piece of paper to the keyboard; you must also tell it about the keybinding. You can do this by inserting a line similar to the following into your .emacs file:

```
(global-set-key [(control f6)] 'sams-toggle-truncate)
```

This line tells Emacs that pressing Ctrl, holding it down, and pressing the key labeled F6 causes Emacs to invoke the function sams-toggle-truncate. Please note the single quote before the word sams.

Throughout this book, function names are given whenever a function is discussed. This way, you can easily bind any of the function keys without a modifier, or with Ctrl, Shift, or Meta as the modifier.

The following information is available on the CD.

 This is a sample Lisp file with the bindings from my setup; here you can see examples of binding any of the twelve function keys:

```
/usr/share/emacs-lisp/refcard/refcard.el
```

The following is the keyboard quick reference card for UNIX users. It is made in LaTeX. At the top of the file there is a description of how to print it out. If you have LaTeX installed on your system, you can probably make your own quick reference card without knowing anything about LaTeX:

```
/usr/share/emacs-lisp/refcard/refcard.tex
```

The following is a sample of my personal setup. Some of the functions that are described on my quick reference card are not even mentioned in this book, nor are they available on the CD, so this is to only be used as an example of how to use the keyboard quick reference card:

```
/usr/share/emacs-lisp/refcard/refcard-example.tex
```

This is the keyboard quick reference card for Windows users. It is in RTF, which means that MS Word, WordPerfect, and a number of other Windows programs can read it:

```
/usr/share/emacs-lisp/refcard/refcard.rtf
```

The following is my setup in RTF. Once again, please note that this is only an example:

```
/usr/share/emacs-lisp/refcard/refcard-example.rtf
```

This is an empty quick reference card, to be used for an emergency—in case, for example, you do not have the appropriate tools to edit the other quick reference cards. Simply print these out and write on them with a pen or pencil:

```
refcard.ps and refcard.pdf
```

A Note on Configuring Emacs

You most certainly know now that Emacs is very configurable. You can configure Emacs by inserting Lisp code into the file called .emacs, which is located in your home directory. But don't panic. Throughout this book, you are told every detail about what is to be inserted—you do not have to learn a single line of Lisp.

In the next hour, "Using Emacs in Microsoft Windows," you will be told the exact location of the .emacs file in Windows because, unlike with UNIX, there is no home directory. You might already want to take a look at the section called "Home" or make a mark in the book at this point so that you can get back and insert the lines that follow.

Throughout this book, you will be told about different extensions to Emacs that are not shipped with Emacs. These extensions are located on the CD as Lisp files. Copy the Lisp files that you would like to use into a directory on your hard disk. One extension is very important—it contain lots of functions that are described throughout this book. Therefore, you need to start right; that is, you need to let Emacs know about this extension.

Setting Up Emacs for This Book

Windows users, you should defer this step until after you read Hour 2. You will make some decisions there that will affect what you do here.

This task tells you how to get Emacs ready for this book. If you do not perform this task, much of the information in this book will not work for you. Follow these steps:

1. Make a directory, called Emacs, in your home directory. This directory contains all the Lisp files that you want to add to your Emacs setup.

2. Copy the file /usr/share/emacs-lisp/sams/sams-lib.el from the CD to this directory.

3. Insert the following lines into your .emacs file:
   ```
   (setq load-path (cons "~/Emacs" load-path))
   (require 'sams-lib)
   ```
   You might need to change ~/Emacs to the correct location of the directory. You can also copy the file /usr/share/emacs-lisp/refcard/refcard.el into this directory, and then modify this file for your keybindings. In this case, insert the following line into your .emacs file (after you have entered the preceding lines).
   ```
   (load "refcard")
   ```

These steps ensure that whenever one of the functions from sams-lib.el is described, you do not need to do anything special to load it.

Using Different Emacs

This book covers both GNU Emacs and XEmacs; furthermore, GNU Emacs is covered for Windows as well. The Emacs version that is focused on is version 20, and incompatibilities with Emacs 19 are pointed out. All in all, this book covers quite a few different combinations. Something special might need to be done for GNU Emacs version 19, whereas other things need to be done for Emacs under Windows.

Throughout this book I will tell you to insert code into your `.emacs` file, in case you need a given feature in, for example, GNU Emacs. In these cases, you need to make a clause around the lines to ensure that the given line is only interpreted by GNU Emacs. Several predicates are defined in `sams-lib.el`, which describe the setup that you are using (see Table 1.1).

TABLE 1.1   PREDICATES FOR SETUP TESTING

Name	Meaning
`sams-Emacs-20-p`	This predicate is true if your current Emacs is version 20
`sams-Emacs-19-p`	This predicate is true if your current Emacs is version 19
`sams-UNIX-p`	This predicate is true if your Emacs is running under UNIX
`sams-Windows-p`	This predicate is true if your current Emacs is running under Windows
`sams-GNU-Emacs-p`	This predicate is true if your current Emacs is GNU Emacs
`sams-XEmacs-p`	This predicate is true if your current Emacs is XEmacs

If I suggest, for example, that you insert the line `(require 'customize)` in GNU Emacs version 19, you should take one of the following actions:

- If you are not using GNU Emacs version 19, do nothing.
- If you are only using GNU Emacs version 19, no other versions of GNU Emacs, and never XEmacs, just insert the line as is into your `.emacs` file
- If you use GNU Emacs version 19, but you also use other versions or XEmacs, insert the following code into your `.emacs` file:

```
(if (and sams-Gnu-Emacs-p sams-Emacs-19-p)
    (progn
      (require 'customize)
))
```

Even though you only use one flavor and one version of Emacs on one system, you might still consider inserting the text to ensure that everything
works correctly, in case you ever try another combination of these parameters (that is, another version: XEmacs instead of GNU Emacs, or Emacs in
Windows instead of only in UNIX).

The parentheses say that (and sams-GNU-Emacs-p sams-Emacs-19-p) is the predicate
that selects the correct conditions. This is a Lisp expression; because you haven't learned
Lisp yet, however, Table 1.2 shows you a few different examples of such predicates (that
is, alternatives to (and ...) in the preceding code.)

TABLE 1.2   A FEW COMBINED TESTS

Test	Description
`sams-GNU-Emacs-p`	If you only test on one thing, you do not need the parentheses around this test.
`(or sams-XEmacs-p` `sams-Windows-p)`	This is true if you use either XEmacs or Emacs in Windows.
`(and sams-GNU-Emacs-p` `sams-Emacs-19-p)`	This is true if you use GNU Emacs, version 19.

`(or sams-GNU-Emacs-p`
`(and sams-XEmacs-p`
`sams-Emacs-20-p))`
	This is true if you use either GNU Emacs or XEmacs version 20.

`(not (and sams-`
`GNU-Emacs-p sams-`
`Emacs-19-p))`
	This is true if the current Emacs is anything other than GNU Emacs version 19.

Any number of lines can be dropped in place of (require 'customize). Therefore, as a
final example, I suggest that you insert the following lines if you use GNU Emacs in
UNIX:

```
(message "Loading bla bla...")
(require 'bla)
(message "Loading bla bla...Done")
```

In your .emacs file, this would look like:

```
(if (and sams-GNU-Emacs-p sams-Windows-p)
    (progn
       (message "Loading bla bla...")
       (require 'bla)
       (message "Loading bla bla...Done")
))
```

Summary

You have now been introduced to Emacs, and you have learned the basics that are necessary to get the most out of this book. If you are using Windows, you need to get a bit more information about setting up and installing Emacs under Windows; otherwise, you are now ready to learn about the most powerful and configurable editor available. Believe me, when you get started, the only time that you will want to put this book down is to try it out for real using Emacs.

Hour **2**

Using Emacs in Microsoft Windows

This hour is for users of NT Emacs on Microsoft's operating systems: Windows NT—including Windows 2000—Windows 95, and its successor, Windows 98. This hour covers acquiring and installing NT Emacs, some common problems, and where to go for help. If you don't use Emacs on Windows, you can skip this hour.

What Is NT Emacs?

NT Emacs is a port of GNU Emacs to Win32. Although Emacs runs on a great many operating systems, its native environment is UNIX. A *port* simply means taking the source code for Emacs on one operating system, moving it to another, and adjusting the source to reflect the differences between the old operating system and the new one.

Did I say "simply"? It isn't simple at all. To give one little example, the scrollbars operate quite differently on X Window (the GUI commonly found on UNIX) than on Windows. So the people who ported Emacs to Windows had to write code to handle those differences. Then, to maintain Emacs's portability, they folded those changes back into the source for Emacs, so that the source for Emacs will compile on any computer to which Emacs has been ported. The result is that, having learned Emacs on any one computer, you should be able to use it on any other computer it runs on. Not only that, but any elisp code you write on any one computer should run on any other computer that has Emacs running on it.

In case you are wondering, the scrollbars (and other widgets and GUI artifacts) operate as Windows scrollbars, not X scrollbars.

What Version Do I Need?

Because NT Emacs is a difficult port from UNIX, it depends on a small team of integrators to verify that each revision of Emacs also works correctly on Win32. Due to this difference, and the occasional rewrite of NT code, the latest version of NT Emacs can be behind the latest version of UNIX Emacs.

The exact version you run doesn't really matter all that much, unless you need some specific feature not found in earlier versions. Emacs, like most open source software, evolves gradually, rather than lurching from major version to major version like some commercial products. If you want crossplatform portability, try to keep the major version numbers the same, but don't worry too much about the minor version numbers. So you'll work on NT with 20.3.1, but if you have 20.4 or 20.5, you should not see too many differences.

Requirements

NT Emacs is known to run on NT version 3.51 SP 5 and up, and Windows 95 and up. A reasonable installation of NT Emacs should not unduly burden a machine with 32MB of memory and a 150Mhz Pentium processor. Chances are if you need the power of Emacs you are running other tools that require at least as powerful a machine.

You need about 30MB of disk space for the binary-only distribution and various add-ons, and at least 60MB during the initial unpacking process.

If you are on Windows NT, you need to have administrator privileges for the installation. Log out now and log in again as administrator if you don't already have administrator privileges.

Where to Get NT Emacs

The easiest place to get NT Emacs is the CD-ROM that comes with this book. It includes NT Emacs version 20.3.1. See Appendix A, "Installing Functions and Packages from the CD," for more information on installing Windows NT Emacs from the CD-ROM.

There is also a live filesystem on the CD-ROM. It runs on Win32 for Intel i386 or later processors. You can install that without taking up any room on your hard drives. However, it will be slow—because CD-ROM drives tend to be slower than hard drives— and hog your CD-ROM drive. So I would recommend the live version of NT Emacs for testing the waters. If you like NT Emacs, you can install the whole thing on your hard drive.

FAQs

The NT Emacs Web site at `http://www.cs.washington.edu/homes/voelker/ntemacs.html` is also the best place to go for questions and answers about NT Emacs.

A copy of the FAQ is included on the CD-ROM. You can load this into your Web browser and search it for useful topics. You can also use it as a jumping-off point for other NT Emacs–related Web sites. That should save you a lot of typing. However, do check the Internet copy from time to time. It will be more current that the CD-ROM copy.

The FAQ also has instructions on how to join the NT Emacs email list. You can meet other NT Emacs users and trade tips and solutions to problems.

Needed Directories

The first things to do are to make a few adjustments in your system. You need `home`, `bin`, and `gnu` directories.

If you work with both Windows NT and a version of UNIX (or Linux), you might think about partially duplicating the UNIX file structure on your NT machine. Then you know where everything is, and you can move more easily from one to the other. For example, on Red Hat Linux, the Emacs executable is typically found at `/usr/bin/emacs`. The rest of the distribution is found under `/usr/share/emacs`. Home directories are found under `/home`. Each user has a private directory for executables, called `bin`, under his or her home directory. If you duplicate that structure on your Win32 computer, you have one fewer thing to remember when you shift from one computer to another.

If you plan to install the Cygwin utilities (also on the CD-ROM) you should duplicate the UNIX file structure because many UNIX utilities assume that file structure.

home

You should have a personal, or home, directory somewhere. Emacs does not require a separate directory, but it is a good idea. Emacs looks for your personal startup information in the home directory. It lets you keep personal files (such as your .emacs configuration file, your spelling dictionary file, and so on) all in one place, separate from system and application software such as Emacs itself. This is a convenience on a single-user system, but it is essential when two or more people share a machine.

> Use your .emacs file to customize Emacs as covered in Hour 1, "Introduction to Emacs." I will mention it again later in this hour. UNIX considers a filename with a leading period to be a hidden file, so it is .emacs on UNIX. Early versions of NT Emacs used a filename of _Emacs, so you will see that filename in email and documentation occasionally. Either one works, but .emacs ports handily to and from UNIX, so it is preferable.
>
> In fact, all your Emacs data files can be used on UNIX as well as on NT, so if you use both NT and UNIX, you can port back and forth.

On NT 4.0 and Windows 2000, each user has a profile directory, which might be important if you share your computer with another person. On NT 4.0, it is under $WINDIR$\Profiles\<*your login*>, where <*your login*> is your NT login name. $WINDIR$ is typically c:\winnt40, but that can vary. Under the login, there is a directory, PERSONAL, which is a good place to make your home directory. For Windows 2000, $WINDIR might be C:\WINNT50. On Windows 95/98, multiuser login profiles are usually found under C:\WINDOWS\Profiles.

Your home directory is a convenient personal spot to put files you edit often because it is easy to get to. You can specify the home directory in Emacs by typing ~/ (or ~\, Emacs doesn't care). So you can specify your .emacs file with ~/.emacs. If you share your computer with other people, placing your home directory in your profile directory lets each person have his or her own .emacs, diary, and other files.

> While I'm at it, let me offer a short digression on command-line syntax. UNIX uses the forward slash (/) to separate directory names in paths. Win32 uses backward slashes (\). UNIX specifies command-line options with a dash or hyphen (-). Windows and its predecessor MS-DOS use both forward slashes (/) and hyphens (-) to indicate command-line options. Because the hyphen command-line option is common to both environments, I use the hyphen for command-line options. So grep -i foo * runs identically on

both Windows NT and Linux. Because Emacs accepts either slash in a path, I find myself using either, but mostly I use the UNIX forward slash. This is because I use Linux a lot, and on Windows NT I often use the Cygnus port of Bash.

Also, in elisp source code, as in C source, forward slashes are escape characters. So in an elisp string such as //server/deskjet, back slashes must be doubled. Forward slashes are more readable.

If you aren't on a multiuser system, you can put your home directory anywhere you want. You can use your own initials or anything else you want. If you are following UNIX custom, put it at c:\home\<*login-name*>. If you want to stick to the Windows NT custom, put it at $WINDIR\Profiles\<*your login*>. I recommend you put in on the C:\ drive. If you add a new hard drive or CD-ROM drive to Windows 95/98, your drive letters are at the mercy of the system BIOS, and C: is the least likely to be moved, so it is the least likely to be disrupted by adding a new hard drive. (Windows NT users can use the Disk Administrator to reassign drive letters.)

If you are on a multiuser system, make the home directory private to the individual user.

bin

bin is short for *binary*, and is UNIX's traditional name for directories that contain executables. Use bin for your own executables, such as programs you have on your computer for your own use. Put that under your home directory, wherever it is. If you follow UNIX custom, it will be at c:\home\<*login-name*>\bin. You'll put it into your path in a minute.

Emacs also has a bin directory, for its executable files. But you'll put that where everyone who uses your computer can get at it.

GNU

I use the GNU directory as a handy place for Free Software Foundation software (of which I use a lot). So I put all my FSF software under C:\GNU. You can call it anything you want, of course. Some programs have problems dealing with spaces in filenames, so you should not bow to Redmond and use c:/program files/gnu.

> Normally, Windows (and UNIX) treats spaces as delimiters, so spaces indicate to Windows the end of one command-line argument and the beginning of the next. To help avoid problems with spaces in filenames, always specify arguments to command lines (such as in short cuts, associations, and batch files) by quoting them. For example, later I will show you how to install gnuclientw. When you create associations to gnuclientw, put the command-line argument in quotes:
>
> ```
> gnuclientw "%1"
> ```
>
> This encloses in quotes the filename that the association passes to gnu-clientw, and ensures that the association properly handles paths with spaces in them.
>
> To see how this works, try the following on the command line:
>
> ```
> dir c:\program files
> dir "c:\program files"
> ```

Installing to Hard Disk from the CD-ROM

Now is the time to insert the CD-ROM into the CD-ROM drive and install Windows NT Emacs. It runs its own setup program on Windows, so all you have to do is follow the installation program. If you are running Windows 95 or Windows 98, you will have to reboot to complete the installation.

Congratulations! you should now have a working NT Emacs! Go to the GNU Emacs entry in the Start menu, and click the Emacs entry in it. In a few seconds (depending on how fast your computer is) you should have Emacs running on your desktop.

You now have a minimal installation of NT Emacs (if "minimal installation of Emacs" is not an oxymoron). There are a number of things you can do to improve your installation, and I'll cover those next.

Postinstallation Bug Fixes

NT Emacs has a problem with font locking. Font locking is the Emacs mode that displays programs in color, making them easier to read. Put the following into your .emacs file to work around the font locking bug:

```
;; Begin work-around for Emacs 20.3 bug in lazy-lock. See the FAQ under
;; upgrading from 19.34.6 to 20.3.1. When doesn't work on 19.34.6
(if (>= emacs-major-version 20)
(when (and (= emacs-major-version 20) (= emacs-minor-version 3))
       (let ((emacs-minor-version 2))
  (require 'lazy-lock))))
;; End work-around for Emacs 20.3 bug in lazy-lock
```

Postinstallation Add-ons

Emacs on UNIX and other operating systems depends on a number of external programs to do some of its work. For example, you can compile programs from within Emacs, but that requires a shell program such as cmd.exe (Windows NT's command-line shell). Win32 operating systems don't come with many of these programs, so you have to get them elsewhere and install them yourself. I'll look at ispell for spelling, gnuclient for filename associations, and VisEmacs for working with Microsoft Visual C++ and Microsoft Visual Studio.

None of these add-ons is required for Emacs to run. They are conveniences for some people and necessities for others. These add-ons bring NT Emacs up to the level of usefulness that UNIX Emacs users already enjoy.

ispell for Spelling

If you are interested in Emacs only for working with source code, and imagine you aren't interested in spell-checking, think again. Many users judge a program by its user interface, and how well your text messages are spelled is part of how they will judge your program. One thing Emacs lets you do is block out a text message in your source code and spell-check it.

ispell is on the CD-ROM that accompanies this book. Run the CD-ROM and install ispell from it.

gnuclient for Associations

In the Win32 world, it is possible to associate a file extension (the last three or four characters of a filename, separated from the rest of the filename by a period or dot [.]) with a particular application. You can click a filename, and Windows launches the associated application and loads that file into it. Often *.txt is associated with Notepad or WordPad. *.html is associated with a Web browser such as Lynx or Netscape.

In a directory window (such as the one you get when you click My Computer), select the View pull-down menu and the Options entry. Click the tab File Types. You can select a file type, and edit its association there. You *could* associate a file type with runemacs.exe directly if you wanted to, but that has a major problem: Each time you select a file, Windows will launch a new instance of Emacs to edit it. Emacs is a bit of a memory hog; you don't want to do that. Instead, get gnuclient.

gnuclient is a package of four programs: gnuserv, gnuclient, gnuclientw, and gnudoit. The one in which you are most interested is gnuclientw. It lets you send filenames to Emacs and have Emacs open them for editing them.

Getting gnuclient

gnuclient is on the CD-ROM that accompanies this book. If you installed NT Emacs from the CD-ROM or are running it live, gnuclient is already installed on your computer.

Using gnuclient

Put the following into your .emacs file to start the gnuserv server:

```
;; start gnuserv on Windows
(if (or (eq window-system 'w32) (eq window-system 'win32)) ;
➡Windows NT/95
    (progn
      (require 'gnuserv)
      (setq server-done-function 'bury-buffer
      gnuserv-frame (car (frame-list)))
      (gnuserv-start)
      ;;; open buffer in existing frame instead of creating new one...
      (setq gnuserv-frame (selected-frame))
      (message "gnuserv started.")))
```

To associate file types with Emacs, go back to the File Types window and edit a suitable association, say for batch files. The file type to edit is MS-DOS Batch File. Highlight that file type, and click Edit. Under Actions, select Edit, and then click the Edit button. Either use browse to locate gnuclientw.exe or type the full path to it. Include the extension, or Windows will reject the association. When you insert the command-line parameter, remember to put it in quotes:

```
gnuclientw "%1"
```

If you are unable to edit the existing Edit action, create a new one, Edit with Emacs, and go from there.

One of the most powerful things you can do is provide a link to gnuclientw in your SendTo folder. This lets you right-click a file and send it to Emacs to open, whether you have associated it with Emacs or not.

Open the SendTo folder on your computer. On NT, there is a SendTo folder for each profile. On Windows 95/98, there is one under the c:\windows directory. There, create a shortcut pointing to gnuclientw.exe, with the parameter in quotes.

```
Insert Illo: emacs.prop.gif
```

VisEmacs for Visual C++

You can find VisEmacs on the CD-ROM. If you are using a non-Intel processor, you should be able to compile from the extracted source. If you are accustomed to working with the Microsoft Visual products, you should have no problem following Christopher Payne's installation instructions in the file ReadMe.txt.

There are further notes in the FAQ on integrating Visual C++ and NT Emacs. They are unfortunately slightly out of date, as they were written for Emacs 19.34.1 on Windows 95, using Visual C++ 4.0 Standard Edition. Emacs is now up to 20.3.1, and Visual C++ up to Version 6.

Setting Up for Printing

For most people setting the printer for NT Emacs is simple. You leave it alone and Emacs prints to the default printer.

If that doesn't work, you have some experimenting to do. You have to set the name of the printer. You can use `customize` (see Hour 10, "The Emacs Help System and Configuration System") or put a Lisp expression in your `.emacs`, such as the following:

```
(setq printer-name "LPT1:")
```

Put this or something like it into your `.emacs` file. Although `PRN` is the preferred default printer for Windows (it always points to your default printer), sometimes you are better off selecting a specific printer such as `LPT1`.

You can also set your printer to a network shared printer:

```
(setq printer-name "//server/deskjet")
```

To test printing, select a small region of a buffer, and pull down the Tools menu with your mouse. Under Print select Print Region.

If you can't get printing working any other way, make your printer sharable, and print to its share name. It's ugly but it gets you there.

PostScript Printing

PostScript printing is very nice under Emacs. Emacs provides a banner in the top inch of the first page, which makes it easy to identify printouts. Also, if font-lock mode is active in the buffer you print, PostScript printing picks up the colors. Black-and-white printers print grayscale for the colors. Color printers print your file in full color.

To set up PostScript printing, set the variable `ps-printer-name`. This snippet of elisp code sets Emacs's printer to be the printer `deskjet` on the server named `server`:

```
(setq ps-printer-name "//server/deskjet")
```

If you don't have a PostScript printer, you can also send PostScript printing to a shared printer. Maybe someone else on the network has one.

2

Not all Windows NT servers are true Windows NT servers. If you operate in a mixed Windows and UNIX environment, you should look into Samba as a way to share files and printers on UNIX machines with Windows computers. See http://samba.anu.edu.au/pub/samba/ for more information.

Ghostscript

If you don't have access to a PostScript printer, you can fake it. Ghostscript is a free program that takes a PostScript file as input and prints it on your printer. It is available under the Aladdin Free Public License, which is similar to the General Public License under which Emacs is distributed. Check out http://www.cs.wisc.edu/~ghost/. Unfortunately, due to licensing restrictions, Sams was unable to include it on the CD-ROM that accompanies this book.

If you use Ghostscript, you can adjust Emacs's variables to run Ghostscript directly. Use something such as the following in your .emacs file:

```
(setq ps-printer-name t)
(setq ps-lpr-command "gswin32c")
(setq ps-lpr-switches '("-q" "-dNOPAUSE" "-"))
```

Customizing Emacs

Emacs is probably the most customized program in the known universe. There are all sorts of things that you can do, and some of them will be covered in other hours. Here, I'll look at customizing Emacs to look more like a Windows application, and customizing Windows to look more like UNIX.

Emacs on Windows finds itself bridging two worlds, that of UNIX and that of Windows. I'll describe how to make Emacs look more like a typical Windows application, and how to make Windows look a bit more like UNIX.

Windows

If you are accustomed to Windows and its predecessors, you are accustomed to applications working in certain ways. IBM and Microsoft, back when they were talking to each other, set out certain standards for the ways applications would treat certain keystrokes. For example, the Home key should move the cursor to the left end of the line. This standard is called Common User Access (CUA).

Emacs doesn't do that. It has its own standards. If you are accustomed to the way most applications work on Windows, that can be frustrating. Fortunately, there is a way to deal with that. Two, in fact.

delsel

delsel is short for delete-select. It lets you mark a region, as you would for normal killing. But you can simply replace the region from the clipboard or by typing, without having to delete it first. For example, you can type the word foo and block it out using the normal Emacs selection method. Then, to replace foo with bar, type the b. That replaces the word foo. Type ar, and you're finished.

To activate it, press M-x (delete-selection-mode).

pc-select

pc-select lets you use the Windows standard keystrokes to select text and mark it. For example, with this mode enabled, you can mark a region by moving point and holding the Shift key down. To activate it, press M-x (pc-selection-mode).

Check the FAQ at http://www.cs.washington.edu/homes/voelker/ntemacs.html from time to time. New tricks show up there.

UNIX

There are also people who are accustomed to UNIX and find themselves dragged, kicking and screaming, to Windows, and pine for the good old days on UNIX. Well, I have some relief for them.

Microsoft has some tools that will let you make your Windows system more like X. Check out http://www.microsoft.com/windows/downloads/contents/wutoys/w95pwrtoyset. Note that these are unsupported freebies.

One bit of customizing you probably won't have to do is to set Emacs to use a three-button mouse. It should do so automatically. If not, check the FAQ.

There are a number of ports of UNIX shells available for Win32. Some are included on the accompanying CD-ROM. Check the Windows NT Emacs FAQ for details. Setting up Emacs to run the shell of your choice is a matter of setting some variables. I recommend the Cygnus GNU tools port, which is included on the CD-ROM, only in part because it is licensed under the General Public License. It includes Bash, which is probably the UNIX shell most used by NT Emacs users.

> Note that setting Emacs to use a shell other than command.com or cmd.exe affects interactive compiles from Emacs (M-x; compile), so you might not want to use another shell if you use Microsoft Visual Studio or any of the Microsoft Visual products.

Check the FAQ at `http://www.cs.washington.edu/homes/voelker/ntemacs.html` occasionally.

Things NT Emacs Does Not Do Well

Windows NT is not UNIX, and there are some things it simply does not do according to the UNIX philosophy. When Emacs runs up against those things, it has problems. Often there is a workaround, and the following sections cover a few of them.

Files with Streams

Windows NT has a concept called *named streams*. This allows a program to treat one file as several logical files within the one file. NT Emacs does not support named streams in any way. In fact, if you change a text file with one or more named streams, the named streams will be destroyed.

ange-FTP

Emacs has a neat facility called ange-FTP. This lets you edit a file on a remote computer via the FTP protocol. If you can read the file and write to it via FTP, you can edit it with Emacs, and Emacs will hide most of the FTP stuff for you. Versions of NT Emacs prior to 20.3.1 had problems using Windows's native FTP client. 20.3.1 works with the Windows client, so that might be a good reason to upgrade from a prior version.

One problem you will have with ange-FTP is that ange-FTP's filename code does not understand MS-DOS drive letters such as `C:`. So files on a Windows computer might not be accessible to Emacs even though the FTP server has permission to make the file available.

One workaround is to make the file available as a network share. You can then access the file through the share name. After you have typed in the UNC name of the share (`\\server\files\`, for example), tab completion works as it does with local files.

command.com

One thing users of Windows 95/98 should beware: `command.com` (the standard Windows 95/98 command-line shell) does not support multitasking or multiple shell buffers under Emacs. `command.com` does not respond well to `C-c` commands, which is what Emacs uses to shut down shells that it runs. The result might be zombie copies of `command.com` that make it impossible to shut down Windows gracefully.

There are two solutions. The most UNIX-like and most effective is to install the Cygnus Bash port. BASH is a shell found on UNIX. It is the standard shell for Linux, for example. The Cygnus port of Bash is primarily intended for Windows NT, and some users have reported problems with it on Windows 95. It is probably the UNIX shell most used by NT Emacs users.

If you use command.com, note that the end-of-line handling code in Emacs version 20.3.1 prevents command.com from being used as the interactive shell on Win95 out of the box. To use command.com as your shell, place the following in your startup file:

```
(setq process-coding-system-alist
      '(("cmdproxy" . (raw-text-dos . raw-text-dos))))
```

Also, make sure you have msdos-shell-fix.el and w32-shellex.el both installed in your site-lisp directory. They make command.com more bearable on Windows 95/98. If you installed Emacs from the CD-ROM, you already have them installed. To make them effective, add the following to your .emacs file:

```
(if (memq window-system '(win32 w32))     ; Windows NT/95
    (progn

      ;; add w32-shellex.
      (require 'w32-shellex)

      ;; NT Emacs on W95 has a problem leaving command.com as a
      ;; orphan process when Emacs is shut down. This fixes that
      ;; problem, It appears to be harmless on NT.

      (add-hook 'comint-exec-hook
        (function (lambda () (require 'msdos-shell-fix))))

      ))
```

How to Tell Which Computer You Are On

Many Emacs users use multiple computers, often with different operating systems. They use Emacs on all of them in order to provide a consistent interface (as well as to get an excellent editor). It is nice to use one .emacs on all your computers. You usually know which computer you are working on (although with X on UNIX, it isn't always easy). But Emacs has to be told which computer it is on so that it can select attributes and variables specific to each computer.

Which Operating System?

There is a routine on the CD-ROM in the file what-env.el you can use to tell which environment you are running on. It sets a variable, what-env (short for *what environment?*). If you installed Emacs from the CD-ROM, it is in your site-lisp directory. To use it, put the following line into your .emacs file:

```
(load "what-env")
```

With what-env in place, if you want to know your environment, you can test for the contents of what-env. For example, on Windows 95, if Emacs displays the time in the mode line, the screen saver never kicks in. This code sets up the time display. However, by first testing what-env for Windows 95, you avoid running the time display on Windows 95. You can use this skeleton to customize your .emacs file for different computers.

```
; Don't display the time on W95. I have problems w/ this interfering
; with my screen saver/monitor power control SW on w95. NT 4 seems to
; be OK. You need this to enable the appointment notification.

(if (not (string-equal what-env "Windows_95"))
    (progn (setq display-time-24hr-format t)
           (setq display-time-day-and-date t)
           (display-time)
           (message "Time display running!"))))
```

Which Version of Emacs?

You also might need to examine which version of Emacs you are running. You saw one example of this already with the font-lock fix earlier in this hour:

```
(when (and (= emacs-major-version 20) (= emacs-minor-version 3))
      (let ((emacs-minor-version 2))
        (require 'lazy-lock)))
```

This code looks at the Emacs major and minor version numbers. Only on 20.3 will it execute the next two lines. Another reason to know the version is that a lot of Windows variables are win32-x under Version 19, and w32-x for version 20 and up. You can test for each version, or you can test for one or the other. The following phrase of elisp evaluates to t on Windows regardless of the version of Emacs.

```
(or (eq window-system 'w32) (eq window-system 'win32))
```

The following line of code evaluates to w32, win32, or nil, as appropriate:

```
(memq window-system '(win32 w32))
```

Which Computer Name?

The computer name is often the only way to tell which of several identical machines you are running on. The following phrase tells you whether Emacs is running on Windows 95 and on the computer named LAPTOP:

```
(if (and (string-equal what-env "Windows_95") ; do this if on the
➥laptop & running w95
         (string-equal system-name "LAPTOP"))
         blah, blah, blah...
         )
```

Summary

In this hour, you have installed NT Emacs on Windows NT or Windows 95/98. You have decided whether to use a live filesystem on the CD-ROM or install to your hard drive, and installed accordingly. You should now be able to launch Emacs by clicking on its Start menu icon. You should also have some associations with file types, so that you can launch Emacs by clicking on an associated file.

You have also learned a little (there is more to come) about customizing Emacs and how to customize Emacs differently for different platforms.

You have also learned something very important: where to go to get more information and get help from your fellow NT Emacs users.

Q&A

Q Where is the first place to go for help on Windows NT Emacs?

A The help system, which you access with C-h. Hour 10 explains more about the help system.

Q Where is the second place to go for information on NT Emacs?

A Go to the FAQ, at http://www.cs.washington.edu/homes/voelker/ntemacs.html.

Q If you don't get an answer there, where do you go?

A The NT Emacs list. To subscribe, see the FAQ.

Exercises

1. If you haven't already done so, make an association for HTML files with Emacs. You will see that there is already an association with a Web browser, which is handy for viewing the HTML file. Can you create another association that lets you edit with Emacs instead of viewing it?

2. From the command line, find a suitable text file (say, c:\autoexec.bat). Use gnu-client and gnuclientw to have Emacs open the file. What is the difference between them? (To close out the file when you are finished, C-x k kills the buffer without saving changes. C-x c exits.)

3. To see what gnudoit does, go to a command line and type one of the following:

```
gnudoit (beep)
```

```
gnudoit (message \"Hi there!\")
```

What results did you get? (Check the minibuffer after the second experiment.)

Hour 3

Getting Started with Emacs

Before you can learn everything worth knowing about Emacs, it is necessary to learn a few concepts about Emacs. This is necessary for two reasons:

- Emacs is very different from word processors or even other editors. If you do not realize this, you will find Emacs hard to understand and hard to learn. It isn't; it is simply different (and much more powerful).

- When you have learned the basic concepts, it is much easier to understand the different parts of Emacs. (Think of a car: It is very hard to tell someone how the engine works if that person doesn't realize that a car can move by itself!)

Do not skip this hour (not even if you are a little familiar with Emacs), because it contains much information required by the other hours. If you skip it, you'll find the other hours difficult or even impossible. Keep up—after all, this is a very short hour.

First you will start by looking at what you see when you start Emacs and what you find in the menus. Later, I'll introduce you to the vocabulary used when talking about Emacs.

Layout of the Screen

When you start Emacs, you see a window, which looks like either Figure 3.1 or Figure 3.2, depending on whether you are using GNU Emacs or XEmacs.

If you are using Emacs version 19, this window might be a bit different from the one you would see in version 20.

GNU Emacs on Windows looks very much like the UNIX screen illustration in Figure 3.1.

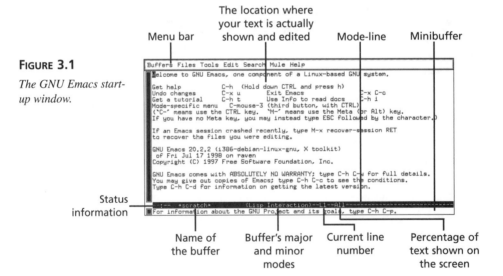

FIGURE 3.1

The GNU Emacs start-up window.

The menu bar, located at the top of the window, is where many of the functions in Emacs are located. This is a perfect location to start when you want to investigate Emacs on your own. Many functions available from the menu bar are also available on the keyboard. In these cases the keybinding is shown in the menu bar. This should make it easier for you to get used to using the keyboard whenever possible.

Minibuffer Mode-line

The location
where your text
is actually shown
and edited

Menu bar

FIGURE 3.2

*The XEmacs startup
window.*

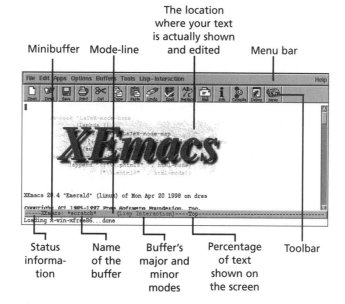

Status
informa-
tion

Name
of the
buffer

Buffer's
major and
minor
modes

Percentage
of text
shown on
the screen

Toolbar

3

Below the XEmacs menu bar is a toolbar.

Next is the actual location where you edit your files and, believe me, I'll talk about this a
lot more. Beside it is a scrollbar, with which you can scroll through the text. In XEmacs
and in GNU Emacs in Windows, this scrollbar looks like one you might know from any
application. In GNU Emacs in UNIX, however, the scrollbar is a bit different. If you
press on it with the first mouse button (most often the left one on your mouse), the text
scrolls one window down. Pressing on it with the third mouse button (likely to be the
right one on your mouse) scrolls the window one page up. Finally, pressing the second
mouse button (likely to be the middle one) scrolls the file to this location. That is, if you
press 25% from the top of the scrollbar, Emacs scrolls 25% down in the text. This is, in
fact, how the scrollbar works in XTerm too.

If your mouse has only two buttons and you are using Linux, there is still
hope! Your X setup can be configured so that pressing both mouse buttons
at the same time makes Emacs think that the (missing) middle mouse button
was pressed.

The second-to-last line (the one in inverse video) is called the mode-line. This line is a
status line, which contain different kinds of information about the status of Emacs.

Different kinds of information are located in this line, but it always contains at least the following:

- Status information— This tells you the state of your file with two characters. (In GNU Emacs, these are the two characters after the colon.) It includes certain combinations. — indicates that the content which Emacs shows is equal to the content of the file on disk, and that you are allowed to edit it. ** indicates that the file has changed in Emacs and has not been synchronized with the version on disk (that is, it has not been saved to disk). %% indicates that the file is not editable (that is, the file is write-protected on disk). Finally, %* indicates that the file is write-protected on disk, but you nevertheless have managed to edit it. (You need to take special actions to be allowed to edit a file in Emacs that is write-protected on disk!)

- The name of the buffer— The word *buffer* is the name for the entity you are editing. (In most cases, a buffer corresponds to a file, but this is not always true.) This will be discussed shortly (see "Buffers, Windows, and Frames"). The name of the buffer in the screen dumps is *scratch*.

- The major and minor modes enabled— Major and minor modes are discussed shortly.

- Line number— In GNU Emacs the line number is by default shown in the mode-line, but it isn't in XEmacs.

- Percentage of text shown— Finally information is given about which part of the text is shown. This might be All to indicate that you see all the text, Top to indicate that you are viewing the top of the text, Bot to indicate that you are looking at the bottom of the text, or, say, 27% to indicate that the first line onscreen is 27% from the top.

The last line of the screen is the minibuffer. This is the area where Emacs asks questions such as Buffer modified; kill anyway? (Yes or no); likewise, Emacs might show information to you in this area. The minibuffer is discussed later in this hour.

Menus

As you saw in Figure 3.1 and 3.2, Emacs has menus at the top of the screen with lots of functions available. The content of the menus differs from GNU Emacs to XEmacs.

It would not make much sense to tell you about all the functions in the menus at this point, because I've yet to describe many of the available functions. I will, however, shortly describe what you can find in the different menu items. The menus are not in every case called by the same name, so the following list begins with the GNU Emacs menu name, and then introduces XEmacs name:

- Buffers— This contains a list of all the buffers available. Selecting one from the list changes your view to this buffer (Your current buffer isn't removed, it is hidden. You can later get back to it by selecting it from this list). In Hour 6, "Editing Several Files at Once," multiple buffers will be described in detail.

- Files, File— This entry contains functions for opening, saving, and killing files and for splitting windows (that is, showing two or more files in the Emacs window). In XEmacs it also contains functions for printing.

- Edit and Search, Edit— The Edit menu in XEmacs contains almost the same information as the Edit and Search menus in GNU Emacs. The menus contain Cut, Paste, Undo, and Spell-check. The XEmacs Edit menu contains search functions, whereas this is located in the Search menu of GNU Emacs. In XEmacs, functions for recording and playing macros are also located in the Edit menu.

- Tools, Tools and Apps— The Tools menu in GNU Emacs is split into two menus in XEmacs, namely Tools and Apps. The menus contain an entrance to auxiliary functions. Examples of these are functions for searching for text in multiple files located on the disk (the UNIX command grep), functions for reading and sending mail and news, functions for compiling and debugging programs, and functions for finding the difference between files.

- Help— This menu contains functions for searching for extra help on Emacs and other programs. This includes the info pages, a man page browser, searching through built-in functions, and a FAQ (frequently asked questions) file.

- Options— XEmacs contains a menu entry called Options from which much information can be configured. A few configuration options are available in GNU Emacs from a Help submenu called Options.

- Mule— In version 20 of Emacs multicharacter language support has been added. This is of interest only if you need to write in Japanese, Chinese, or Russian. In the menu entry Mule, information for this is available.

Some of the menu items are grayed out to indicate that the item is not available at the moment. An example of this might be the Copy entry which would copy text to the clipboard. This entry would be grayed out when no text is marked.

| To find out what a given menu entry does, try pressing C-h k (describe-key) and select the menu entry. |

Menus When Not Using X Window

If you, for some reason, are using Emacs on a character-based terminal instead of X Window, the menus are still available. This time, however, you can't access them with the mouse. Instead you must press the escape key, release it, and press the backtick key (`).

> If you want to try this out, you can start GNU Emacs with the option -nw.

> Please note that menus are not available when running XEmacs on a terminal display.

In Figure 3.3, you can see Emacs when M-` has been pressed. To navigate the menus, press the letter of the menu item (for example, E to enter the Edit menu). Unfortunately, it's impossible to back up in the menus. If you change your mind, simply press the escape key three times. (This is a universal oops-what-have-I-done key, which tells Emacs to abort what you've told it to start.)

FIGURE 3.3

The non–X Window version of GNU Emacs.

The Minibuffer

The very last line of the Emacs window is called the minibuffer. It is used by Emacs to ask you questions about files to open, buffers to change to, permission to kill buffers and much more. Furthermore it will be used to give you information about various things, such as which files have been saved, the progress of fontifications, and when automatic backup is done.

Seeing Old Messages from the Minibuffer

The messages shown in the minibuffer are also copied to a special buffer. This is very valuable knowledge if several messages come after each other and you don't finish reading the first one before the next is shown (overwriting the first one).

Seeing the Content of the Message Buffer

Follow these steps to get to the message buffer and to get back to your current buffer:

1. Press C-x (that is, press the Control key, hold it down while you press x, and release the Control key) and press b.

2. Emacs will now ask for a buffer to switch to in the minibuffer:
   - For GNU Emacs, type *Messages*.
   - For XEmacs, type *Message-Log* (note the initial space).

   Press Return.

3. The message buffer now be appears, and you can browse through it with the cursor keys. When you are finished, press C-x b.

4. Again Emacs asks for a buffer to switch to. By default, it suggests the latest buffer you visited, so you can simply press Return.

This might seem terribly cumbersome, but when you get used to Emacs, you will see that it is simple to change to the *Messages* buffer, just as you can change to any other buffer. In GNU Emacs and in XEmacs version 20, you can press the Tab key when you have typed part of the name to ask Emacs to complete it for you. This, unfortunately, doesn't work in XEmacs version 19.

Interaction with the Minibuffer

There are several different kinds of questions that Emacs might ask you in the minibuffer. The simplest kind are questions where you are allowed to answer only yes or no. There are in fact two kinds of yes/no questions:

- Those where Emacs wants you to press either y or n
- Those where Emacs forces you to answer *yes* or *no* followed by Return

The latter type are for questions that have a large influence on your situation. An example of this is Buffer modified; kill anyway? (yes or no). The other kind of question is for situations where the wrong action might be irritating but not fatal. An example of this is Quit spell checking? (y or n). If you give Emacs an invalid answer, it tells you the available choices you have and asks you again.

In other situations, Emacs asks you for a filename, a buffer name, or one of its functions. (You will see numerous examples of the latter in which you press M-x and subsequently type a function name.) In these situations, you can press the Tab key to ask Emacs to complete as much as possible of what you already typed. Thus when you open files, it is not necessary to type the whole path for the file, but only what is necessary to make it unique, as the following task shows.

Using Filename Completion when Opening Files

The following steps show how you can let Emacs do typing for you when you want to open a file:

1. Press C-x C-f. Emacs asks you for a file to open. (In Emacs terminology, this is called *finding a file*.) Emacs inserts the working directory of the buffer you are currently editing (see Figure 3.4).

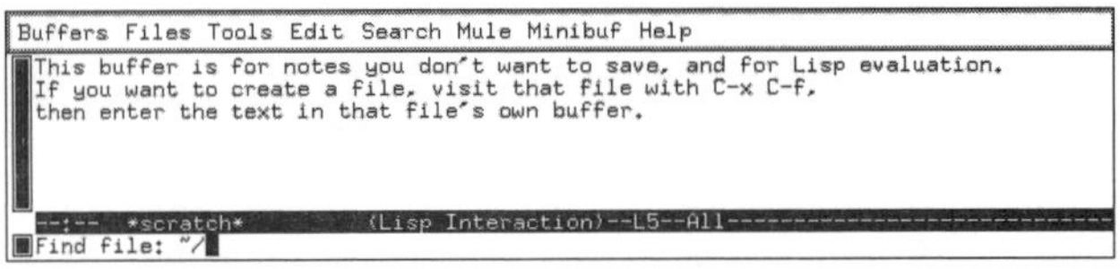

FIGURE 3.4

Emacs asks for a filename and suggests your current directory. (In this case this is my home directory.)

```
Buffers Files Tools Edit Search Mule Minibuf Help
This buffer is for notes you don't want to save, and for Lisp evaluation.
If you want to create a file, visit that file with C-x C-f,
then enter the text in that file's own buffer.




--:--  *scratch*        (Lisp Interaction)--L5--All-------------------------
Find file: ~/
```

2. Now type /et (see Figure 3.5).

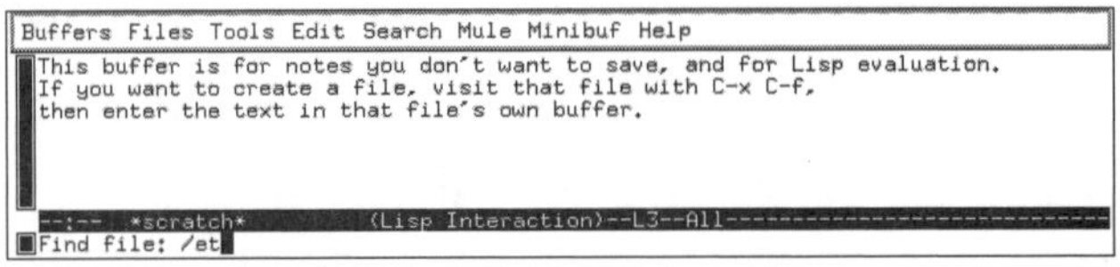

FIGURE 3.5

Typing /et and the Tab key makes Emacs complete the directory name for you.

```
Buffers Files Tools Edit Search Mule Minibuf Help
This buffer is for notes you don't want to save, and for Lisp evaluation.
If you want to create a file, visit that file with C-x C-f,
then enter the text in that file's own buffer.




--:--  *scratch*        (Lisp Interaction)--L3--All-------------------------
Find file: /et
```

3. Press the Tab key and watch how Emacs completes the filename for you to /etc/ (see Figure 3.6).

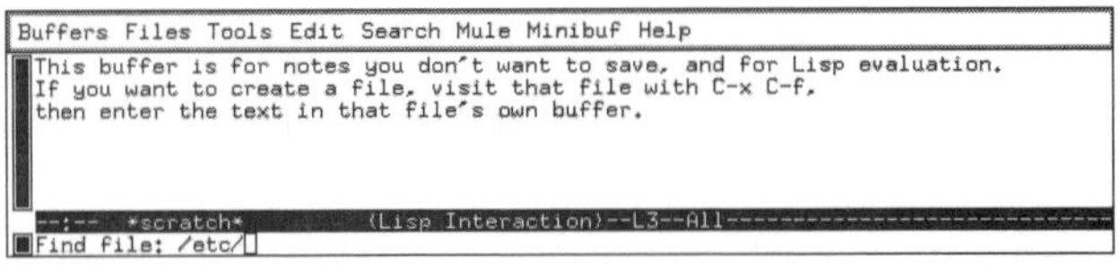

FIGURE 3.6

Emacs fills in c/ in the word /etc/.

```
Buffers Files Tools Edit Search Mule Minibuf Help
This buffer is for notes you don't want to save, and for Lisp evaluation.
If you want to create a file, visit that file with C-x C-f,
then enter the text in that file's own buffer.




--:--  *scratch*        (Lisp Interaction)--L3--All-------------------------
Find file: /etc/
```

4. Now you can continue typing. Type the letter p and press the Tab key again (see Figure 3.7).

Pressing the Tab key when Emacs can't add any unambiguous characters makes it show you a list of possible completions.

```
Buffers Files Tools Edit Search Mule Minibuf Help
Click mouse-2 on a completion to select it.
In this buffer, type RET to select the completion near point.

Possible completions are:
pam.conf                        pam.d/
papersize                       passwd
passwd-                         passwd.dpkg-dist
--:--  *Completions*    (Completion List)--L1--Top----------------
Find file: /etc/p
```

5. Because there are several possible completions for `/etc/p`, Emacs asks you to type a bit more. It does, however, list the possible completions. You can now continue this way until you have typed the whole filename. When you have finished that, press Enter and Emacs opens the file for you to edit.

Using Emacs's filename completion can save you much time. Think of how much you would have to type to open a file such as `/usr/share/emacs/20.2/lisp/progmodes/`
▲ `perl-mode.el` if you didn't have completions.

Buffers, Windows, and Frames

It is important in Emacs to distinguish between the file read into Emacs (but still located on disk) and the content that you edit in the Emacs window. The reason for this is twofold:

- It is clearer that a given operation edits only the content within Emacs, not the content located in the file.
- Sometimes Emacs shows text to you that in fact isn't a file at all. Examples of this are output from different programs (such as `grep`, `find`, or `diff`) and customization options.

Therefore a special word, *buffer*, has been appropriated to describe the entity containing the text which you edit in Emacs.

A buffer, therefore, contains the text you look at or edit. A buffer might either be a copy of the text from a file, or text that Emacs has generated by other means. When a file is loaded into a buffer in Emacs, this buffer is, of course, also written to this file when you save it later.

By default, buffers that do not correspond to files on disk contain stars around their names.

In Emacs it is possible to edit several buffers at a time (you do of course edit only one at any given time, but it's possible to shift between several *active* buffers). You can also show several buffers at a time in one X11 window. Each of these buffers is said to be shown in a *window*. Furthermore it is possible to make Emacs show its content in several X11 windows. Each of these windows is called a *frame*. This can be seen in Figure 3.8.

FIGURE 3.8

Buffers, windows, and frames.

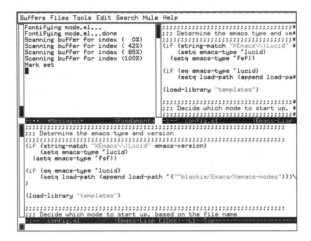

In Figure 3.8, one frame is shown. This frame displays three windows. Two of the frames in these three windows are the same buffer, whereas the third buffer does not correspond to a file.

 Be warned of possible confusion here! One X11 or Microsoft Windows window is called a *frame* not a *window*. A frame can show several windows, each showing a buffer.

Point, Mark, and Region

The location in a buffer where text is inserted when you type is called the *point*. The point is located between two characters and is indicated by highlighting the subsequent character in inverse video. In Figure 3.9, point is located between the two *f*s in *buffer*. Note how the second *f* is in inverse video. If the window does not have focus, point will be shown only as a border around the character.

FIGURE 3.9

The point.

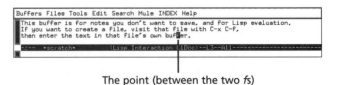

The point (between the two *f*s)

Hey, stop here! What was it the point was? From now on the point will be referred to as *point*, not the insertion cursor, the cursor, or anything else— simply *point*. So please be sure that you are familiar with this name.

To cut or copy something from a window, you need to mark the text which you want to cut or copy. This marked part is called a *region*. A region has two ends, one at the location of point, the other at a location called the *mark*. Thus, without using the mouse, you mark a region by going to one of its boundaries, setting the mark at this location and then go to the other end (point will then be there). (Using the mouse to mark the region works a bit differently.) The mark is set by pressing either C-SPC or C-@ (set-mark-command). In Figure 3.10, you can see the point, the mark, and the region (you can, in fact, see the mark only because you can see the boundary of the region).

FIGURE 3.10

Point, mark, and region.

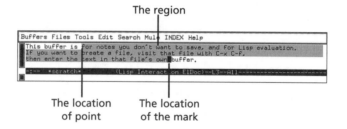

Please note that point is a characteristic for a window, whereas the mark is a characteristic for the buffer. This means that you can't have two different regions for one buffer shown in two different windows, because they share the mark, which is one end of the region. (See Hour 15, "Getting an Overview of a File," for a workaround for this.)

There will always be exactly one point and one mark in a buffer, thus there will always be a region. (Technically, this is not 100% true; there is in fact a whole set of marks, but that is beyond the scope of this book.) If the region should always be highlighted, as can be seen in Figure 3.10, some part of the buffer would be in inverse video. There are two ways to avoid this:

- Never highlight the region.
- Highlight the region only when it is active.

The region is active when the mark has been set, and no commands other than movements have been invoked.

The drawback of the first solution is that you can never see the region (you can, however, ask Emacs to show you the mark). The drawback of the second solution is that you have to activate the region when you need to use it.

You can exchange the location of point and mark by pressing C-x C-x (exchange-point-and-mark). As a side effect, this activates the region. This might, therefore, be a solution to the drawbacks in the preceding methods. If the region is never shown, you can exchange the location of mark and point to see where point is and, in method two, you can use this command to activate the region.

GNU Emacs chose the first method as the default, whereas XEmacs chose the second one. One thing is for sure: Regardless of which of the two methods you prefer, it is irritating that there is a difference between GNU Emacs and XEmacs. Therefore you should decide which of these methods you like the best and insert one of the lines shown in the following sections into your .emacs file. (If you use both GNU Emacs and XEmacs, you should remember to insert a test around the appropriate lines to ensure that they are executing only in the appropriate Emacs. See Hour 1, "Introducing Emacs," for a discussion of this.)

Highlighted Regions in GNU Emacs

To obtain a region that is highlighted in GNU Emacs when it is active, insert the following lines into your .emacs file:

```
(transient-mark-mode)
```

Always Active Regions in XEmacs

To obtain the GNU Emacs default for regions in XEmacs (that is, that regions are never highlighted but always active) insert the following into your .emacs file:

```
(setq zmacs-regions nil)
```

Modes

When you edit an HTML file, your way of working will be much different from the way you work when you write a C program. One could, in fact, develop two different editors, one for writing C programs and one for writing HTML documents. These two editors would present much duplicate work, because they'd have many similar functions. An alternative is to write one editor that can be customized in two different ways, one for writing HTML documents and one for writing C programs. This editor would have the advantage that you would be familiar with it; for example, you would have to learn only one way for searching. You might think that there exists only one way to do these things, but you are wrong. Look at some of your favorite applications and think about it.

The Emacs way of doing this is to offer major and minor editing modes for different files and programs. For example, one major mode exists for editing HTML files, and another for editing C programs. There are many different editing modes, such as cc-mode (for C and C++ programs), emacs-lisp-mode (for Emacs Lisp), and latex-mode (for LaTeX documents).

Major Modes

Exactly one major mode is enabled at a time for a given buffer. That is, the major mode is local for each buffer, and every buffer is always in a given major mode. The major mode might contain different configurations. Most of them include the following:

- Specialized keybindings— Many major modes redefine the meanings of the Tab and Return keys, but other keys can also be redefined. To get a list of keybindings for the major mode, press C-h m (describe-mode) when it is enabled.

- Specialized functions— These are often available with C-c as a prefix (that is, type C-c and another key to get to the function). To see which bindings exists for the C-c prefix, press C-c C-h.

- Adding functions to menus— Some major modes create a menu entry for the major mode functions.

- Configuration of variables— Many different variables can be configured by the major mode. Examples of these include

    Comment characters—These are used by functions that comment out a region, for example.

    Outline regular expression—This is used by the outline library, which makes it possible to get an outline of the buffer.

    Fontification descriptions—This is a set of variables that describe how a buffer can be colorized to make it a bit more readable.

To enable a major mode, simply press M-x and type its name. You can specify which major mode should be loaded when a file is read, depending on the name of the file. This is done by configuring the variable auto-mode-alist (See Hour 22, "Learning Lisp Basics," for a description of this.)

To disable one major mode, you have to enable another one. If no major mode seems appropriate then you can enable the major mode called fundamental-mode, which is a major mode without any specialization.

Minor Modes

Emacs has taken the customization grouping one step farther and developed a concept called minor modes. A minor mode is a set of customization options or functions that makes Emacs behave in a certain way. Any number of minor modes can be enabled at a time (this includes zero). Some minor modes are local to buffers, while others affect all of Emacs. The following list contains a few examples of some of the minor modes in Emacs:

- font-lock-mode (local for a buffer)

  This mode enables fontifications of special constructs. Examples of this are hyperlinks in HTML files or keywords in C files. See Hour 12, "Visible Editing Utilities," for a description of this minor mode.

- outline-minor-mode (local for a buffer)

  This mode adds functions to show an outline of a buffer that is hiding lines which are not header lines. See Hour 15 for a description of this minor mode.

- auto-fill-mode (local for a buffer)

  This mode makes Emacs break your lines at a given column. See Hour 12 for a description of this mode.

- overwrite-mode (local for a buffer)

  In overwrite mode, typed-in characters replace existing text on a one-for-one basis, rather than push it to the right. (Override mode can be toggled using the Insert key.)

- flyspell-mode (local for a buffer)

  This mode enables on-the-fly spell checking. See Hour 11, "Editing Utilities," for a description of this mode.

- mouse-avoidance-mode (affect all buffers)

  When this mode is enabled, the mouse cursor moves if it gets too close to point. Try it out; it's quite funny and can be useful to some people.

- resize-minibuffer-mode (affect all buffers)

  When this mode is enabled, the minibuffer automatically resizes if the text shown in it fills more than one line.

- icomplete-mode (affect all buffers)

  When this mode is enabled and you press M-x, available completions are listed as you type.

To enable or disable a minor mode, simply press M-x and type its name. Minor modes can also be turned on together with a major mode (that is, whenever the given major mode is loaded, the minor mode is loaded too). To learn how to do that, please refer to Hour 24, "Installing Emacs Add-Ons."

Layout of the Keyboard

You have already seen that both the Control key and the Meta key are used in Emacs (C-x b to go to another buffer and M-x to type commands in the minibuffer). There seems to be a general plan about where what is located. It is very useful to be aware of this plan; therefore, here it comes:

- All letters, numbers, and symbols on the keyboard insert the label given on the key, if pressed without Control or Meta.

- All functions that are used very often are available with either the Control or Meta key pressed down. (For example, Go to End of Line is bound to C-e, Undo is bound to C-_, and Paste is bound to C-y.)

- If the Control prefix is bound to a function that works on characters for a given key, the Meta prefix works on words (if this gives any meaning for the given function). Likewise if the Control prefix works on lines, the Meta prefix works on sentences. Examples of this include C-t, which transposes two characters, whereas M-t transposes two words. C-e moves point to the end of the line, whereas M-e moves point to the end of the sentence.

- Functions that are used less often are bound with the prefix C-x. Examples of this include C-x C-c, which exits Emacs, and C-x 2, which splits the window in two, with a buffer in each one.

- Functions that are specific to a given mode are prefixed with C-c.

- Functions that aren't often used or which should not be bound on the keyboard are not bound at all, but are accessible by pressing M-x and typing the name of the function.

- The prefix C-x 4 is reserved to functions that operate on another window. Examples include opening a file in an other window, which is bound to C-x 4 C-f (find-file-other-window). Likewise, C-x 5 is the prefix for functions that operate on another frame. C-x 5 C-f (find-file-other-frame) opens a file in another frame. Note how these two functions have the same keybinding as C-x C-f (find-file) with the exception of the letter 4 or 5 inserted in the middle. (This is not a coincidence!)

Summary

You learned your way around the menus, but be warned that using the mouse too much might not be good for you; you should try to learn as many keybindings as possible. This also enables you to work more fluently and quickly.

Please review the section "Buffers, Windows, and Frames" whenever you have doubts about what is what in the subsequent hours.

You also learned the concept of major modes and minor modes. Before you know it, you will want all your other applications to work this way too.

Q&A

Q I don't need the menus; is there any way I can get rid of them?

A Are you sure you do not need them?! Okay, if you really want to get rid of them, the procedures are different in GNU Emacs and XEmacs.

In GNU Emacs, try `M-x menu-bar-mode`. (The same command enables them once again.) If you want to remove them at startup, insert the following line into your `.emacs` file:

```
(menu-bar-mode nil)
```

If you want to get rid of them only when you are using Emacs on a non–X terminal, insert the following into your `.emacs` file:

```
(if (equal window-system nil)
    (menu-bar-mode nil))
```

You might be interested in doing that to save screen space on a terminal with a very limited number of lines.

For XEmacs, insert the following line into your `.emacs` file:

```
(set-specifier menubar-visible-p nil)
```

Q Is it possible to get rid of the toolbar in XEmacs?

A Yes. Insert the following line into your `.emacs` file:

```
(set-specifier default-toolbar-visible-p nil)
```

Q It often says "Find file:" in the minibuffer. Why?

A The reason for this is that you have pressed `C-x C-f` (find-file) to open a file, but before you finished that job, you pressed the mouse button in a buffer. This enables you to edit the content of the buffer (while still waiting for you to tell it the name of the file to open). To make it go away, press the mouse button in the minibuffer and press `C-g`.

Exercises

1. Without looking back, please explain what *point* and *mark* are. Why do you need them?

2. What is the difference between a file and a buffer? What about between a window and a frame?

3. What is the key combination for getting to the menu bars when using Emacs in a non-X and non-Windows setup?

4. What is the difference between a major mode and a minor mode?

5. How many major modes can be active at a time in a given buffer? How many minor modes?

6. Are you allowed to have different major modes for different buffers?

7. What is a major mode connected to? The buffer, the window, or the frame? What is the minor mode connected to?

3

HOUR 4

Basic Editing

Now it's finally time to get started learning the basic editing skills of Emacs. When you finish this hour, you will have learned enough to use Emacs as effectively as you might use any simple editor.

In this hour, you'll learn how to insert and delete text, move around in Emacs, cut and paste, and load and save files. Although it is a bit beyond the scope of this book, this hour also tells you about several functions that are very useful when you need to read in a new file.

Inserting and Deleting Text

Inserting and deleting text in Emacs is as simple as typing on a typewriter. You simply type the text. If you wonder why I'm telling you this, you're obviously not a vi user (vi is an alternative editor in UNIX). In vi you must be in a special insertion mode to insert text, which is not the case in Emacs.

If you see the text *C-h (Type ? for further options)*—in the minibuffer when you press the backspace key, your backspace key is misconfigured. This is beyond the scope of this book, but consult section 7.0, "Emacs Backspace Binding Problem," at the following URL: `ftp://cs.uta.fi/pub/ssjaaa/ema-keys.html` or look at items 112 and 113 in the Emacs FAQ (available on this book's CD-ROM).

In Emacs there are several different ways to delete text. The simplest way is to press the Backspace or the Delete key. In most newer Emacs installations running on X or in Windows, Backspace deletes the previous character, whereas Delete erases the following character. If neither of them delete the following character, you can press C-d (delete-char) instead, which does it. In Figure 4.1 you can see which key deletes what.

FIGURE 4.1

The Delete and Backspace keys.

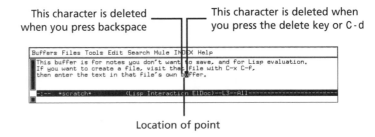

There are several other ways to delete text in the buffers. This will be described later in this hour.

Automatic Line Breaking when Typing

When you reach the end of the line, Emacs does not break the line for you; instead it indicates that the line continues onto the next one and lets the text continue there. The indication is located in the last column of the text with a backslash in GNU Emacs and a newline arrow in XEmacs (see Figures 4.2 and 4.3).

 Although you might not see any difference to you between breaking the line and continuing on the next, there most certainly is. Try to break the line yourself (by pressing the return key) and then make the window wider. You should notice that the broken line does not combine with the one at the location where you broke it. This isn't, however, the case when newline arrows or backslashes appear. In that case, if you let Emacs break the line for you and then make the window wider, the line wrap indicator vanishes and the two lines combine together.

FIGURE 4.2

Indication of continued lines in GNU Emacs.

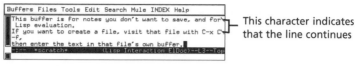

This character indicates that the line continues

FIGURE 4.3

Indication of continued lines in XEmacs.

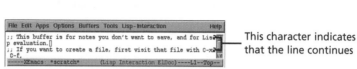

This character indicates that the line continues

After all I've told you about Emacs so far, it shouldn't surprise you that you can configure Emacs to do automatic line breaking when you reach a given column. This is described in detail in Hour 12, "Using Visible Means," but until then, it might help you a lot to know that you enable this by pressing M-x and typing `auto-fill-mode` (this is a minor mode).

Moving Around in the Buffer

In Emacs there are many ways of moving around. This might make a new user a bit insecure (to be honest, it scared me!), especially if you read the Emacs reference manual, available from the info pages, or the online tutorial; these sources tell you the whole truth in one go and tell you about keybindings, which can be used from any kind of keyboard.

Don't panic! Moving around in Emacs today with a modern keyboard is as simple as it is in any other program. Simply use the arrow keys to move around. Furthermore, you can jump one page at a time with the page-up and page-down keys.

If you get in a situation where the cursor keys don't work, alternative keybindings are available for the movement functions. These are

- Forward one character—C-f (forward-char).
- Backward one character—C-b (backward-char).
- Go to the previous line—C-p (previous-line).
- Go to the next line—C-n (next-line).
- Scroll forward one page—C-v (scroll-up). This is equal to the key Page Down.
- Scroll backward one page—M-v (scroll-down).

4

Add a Blank Line at the End of the Buffer

The most basic example of Emacs configuration is the following. What should be done when you ask Emacs to take you to the next line and you already are located at the last line of the buffer? There are two possible and equally good answers to this question:

- Insert a blank line, and go to this line.
- Ring the bell to indicate that this is not possible.

Which solution is the better depends solely on your preferences, taste, state of mind, and so on. Therefore this can be configured in Emacs.

To select the setup where a newline is inserted, add the following into your .emacs file:

```
(setq next-line-add-newlines t)
```

To select the setup where the bell rings, insert the following into your .emacs file:

```
(setq next-line-add-newlines nil)
```

I'm telling you this now because GNU Emacs and XEmacs have different defaults for this option.

Moving by Word, Line, Sentence, or Paragraph

Emacs has many functions for moving around. You do not need to learn every one of them right away, because the important point is that you know they exist. You can take one at a time, as you find that you need it.

Two functions exist for moving to the beginning or the end of the line. These are bound to C-a (beginning-of-line) and C-e (end-of-line). These are not very mnemonic, but don't let that scare you. When you have used Emacs a few days, these bindings will be located in your fingertips.

You can also move forward and backward by words. This is faster than moving by characters and, fortunately, it is very easy to remember its keybindings—C-right or Ctrl+right arrow (forward-word) and C-left or Ctrl+left arrow (backward-word). A word is defined as a number of letters or numbers.

Functions also exist that move by sentences, paragraphs, and pages. The definitions of these three items are tricky, but fortunately they are much like what you might expect. There is one thing to note: For a sentence to end in the middle of the line, two spaces need to follow it. Pages are separated by Ctrl+L (to insert a page break, press C-q C-l). The functions are M-e (forward-sentence), M-a (backward-sentence), M-} (forward-paragraph), M-{ (backward-paragraph), C-x] (forward-page), and C-x [(backward-page).

To learn more about these functions and what exactly describes an end of a sentence, paragraph, or page, press C-h f (describe-function) and type the name of the function. You might however want to wait until you have read Hour 9, "Regular Expressions," because the delimiters are described by regular expressions.

In Figure 4.4, you can see where each of the functions listed previously will take you.

 Text within several figures throughout this book is excerpted from *The Hitchhiker's Guide to the Galaxy* by Douglas Adams.

C-a (beginning-of-line) ─ ─ M-a (backward-sentence) and M-{ (backward-paragraph)

The location of point ─ ─ C-right (forward-word)

FIGURE 4.4

Movement functions.

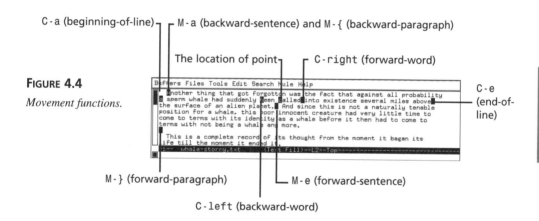

C-e (end-of-line)

4

M-} (forward-paragraph) ─ ─ M-e (forward-sentence)

C-left (backward-word)

 There are also two functions for going to the matching starting or ending brace called forward-sexp and backward-sexp.

These functions are most useful when programming. It might be a good idea to bind these two functions to Meta-left arrow and Meta-right arrow, which is done by inserting the following Lisp code into your .emacs file:

```
(global-set-key [(meta left)] 'backward-sexp)
(global-set-key [(meta right)] 'forward-sexp)
```

Note that this is done by default in XEmacs.

Enhanced Page Up and Page Down Scrolling

When you scroll one page backward and then one page forward again, point does not always end up in the same position. This seems to be a bug in Emacs. Fortunately, a library exists, called *pager*, that offers an alternative implementation of this feature. It is located on this book's CD and an installation description is given in Appendix A, "Installing Functions and Packages from the CD."

This library contains another very useful feature, namely the capability to scroll one line at a time without changing the position of point in the window. That is, if point is located in the middle of the window, it will be located in the middle of the window after you have scrolled. It will, of course, be located on a different line! This can be seen in Figures 4.5 and 4.6.

FIGURE 4.5

Initial state before scrolling.

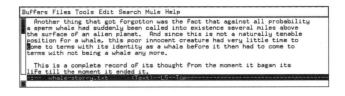

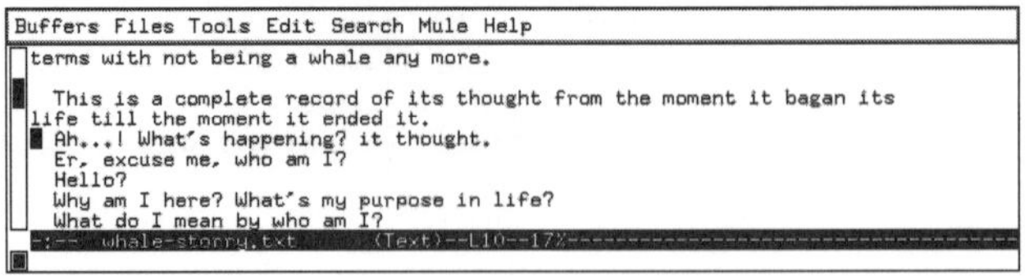

FIGURE 4.6

Here five lines have been scrolled since Figure 4.5.

Figure 4.5 is the initial state, and in Figure 4.6, the window has been scrolled five lines (with the command pager-row-down). Note how point was located in the middle of the window before and after the scroll command.

The previous commands can be very useful if point is located in the middle of the screen and you want it to be there, but you want to see the line below the last line shown in the window.

Moving to a Line Specified by a Number

It is sometimes useful to be able to go to a line by giving its number. This can be done using the command goto-line, which is bound to M-g in XEmacs, and unbound to keys in GNU Emacs. If you want it on M-g in GNU Emacs, insert the following line into your .emacs file:

```
(global-set-key [(meta g)] 'goto-line)
```

Recentering the Window

If your window has been garbled or you want to place point in the center of the window, press C-1 (recenter). This redraws the window and places point in the middle of the window without changing its position in the buffer. (That is, it locates point in front of the same word and on the same line, but this line is shown in a different location in the window.)

Cut, Copy, and Paste

A capability that makes a computer better than an ordinary typewriter is cut-and-paste, which is the capability to move text around in your documents, copy text into several places, and so on.

To mark a region you want to cut or copy, you can use either the mouse or the keyboard.

Marking Text for Cut-and-Paste Using the Mouse

▼ To Do

This task shows you how to mark a region using the mouse and copy this region to the clipboard (called kill-ring in Emacs). Follow these steps:

1. Place the mouse over the start of the text you want to mark.
2. Click the left mouse button and, while you keep the mouse button down, drag to the location where the selection should end.
3. Release the mouse button.
4. If you want to copy the text to the clipboard (that is, don't delete it from the buffer), select the Edit menu, and chose Copy. If, on the other hand, you want to cut the text to the clipboard (that is, delete it from the buffer), go to the Edit menu and select Cut.

▲ If you need to copy the text, it is not necessary in GNU Emacs to select the copy entry from the menu.

Marking Text for Cut-and-Paste Using the Keyboard

▼ To Do

This task shows you how to mark a region using the keyboard and copy this region to the clipboard (called kill-ring in Emacs).

1. Place point at the start of the text you want to select.
2. Press Ctrl+Spacebar. Below the buffer, the text *Mark set* should appear.

4

▼   3. Go to the location where you want the selection to end.

   4. If you want to copy the text to the clipboard, press M-w (kill-ring-save); otherwise
      press C-w (kill-region) to cut the text to the clipboard.

▲ It is often useful to mark the region using the mouse and then cut or copy using the keyboard. That is, use steps 1–3 from the previous task and step 4 from this task.

Although it might seem difficult to remember the keybindings, you should try to do so.
They make your interaction with Emacs much faster, for example, if you do not need to
use the mouse when you use cut-and-paste.

You can paste using either the mouse or the keyboard. To paste using the mouse simply
press the middle mouse button at the location where you want to insert the text. To paste
using the keyboard, place point at the location where you want the text to be inserted and
press C-y (yank).

Emacs saves not only the latest selection made but several of them. This makes it possible to paste an old selection into the buffer. To paste an old selection, press C-y (yank),
which pastes the latest selection made into the buffer. Next, press M-y (yank-pop), which
replaces the inserted text with the second-to-last selection. Subsequent M-y's replace the
text with even older selections.

Pasting the Second-to-Last Selection into the Buffer

The following steps show you how to paste an earlier selection into the buffer as
described previously.

▼   1. Before I created Figure 4.7 I cut the text *One*, *Two*, and *Three* in that order (that is,
      Three is the latest selection, *Two* is the previous, and *One* is the first). The initial
      content of the buffer is shown in Figure 4.7.

FIGURE 4.7

*Layout before C-y was
pressed the first time.*

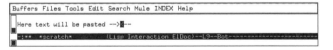

   2. Now press C-y (yank). This inserts the latest selection (see Figure 4.8).

FIGURE 4.8

*Now C-y is pressed.
The latest kill is
pasted in.*

▼

▼ 3. Press M-y once to replace the pasted text with the second-to-last selection (see Figure 4.9).

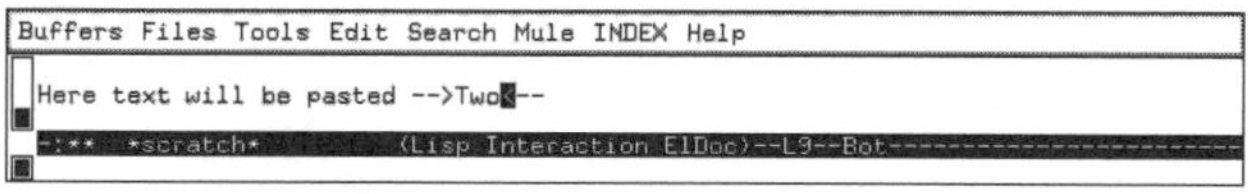

FIGURE 4.9

After C-y, M-y is pressed, pasting in the second-to-last kill.

```
Buffers Files Tools Edit Search Mule INDEX Help
Here text will be pasted -->Two--
-:**  *scratch*      (Lisp Interaction ElDoc)--L9--Bot----------
```

4. Pressing M-y once again replaces the pasted text again, this time with the third-to-last selection (see Figure 4.10).

FIGURE 4.10

Finally, pressing M-y once again paste the third-to-last to kill.

```
Buffers Files Tools Edit Search Mule INDEX Help
Here text will be pasted -->One--
-:**  *scratch*      (Lisp Interaction ElDoc)--L9--Bot----------
```

▲ If you press any other key between C-y and any of the M-y's then you are stuck with the given selection. That is, you won't be able to press M-y to get to older selections.

If you are using GNU Emacs you might also find the older selections in the menu bar. They are located in the Edit menu, under the submenu Select and Paste. Please note that this is not available in XEmacs.

Other Copying Commands

Apart from the command bound to C-w (kill-region), other commands delete text from the buffer and copy it to the clipboard. The most useful of these is C-k (kill-line), which removes from point to the end of the line and inserts it on the clipboard. You can press it several times to remove several lines and append them to the text on the clipboard. That is, when you paste the text, all the lines are pasted as one entity.

Remember from earlier in the hour that C-d deletes the next character. Likewise the Delete key deletes the previous character. Two other very useful commands cut text— M-d (kill-word) deletes the next word and M-DEL (backward-kill-word) kills the previous word. Both these commands cut text to the clipboard.

An other way to insert some text into your document is to simply insert a whole file. You can do that by pressing C-x i (insert-file).

4

> GNU Emacs interacts with the Windows Clipboard similarly. The top item in the kill-ring is inserted into the Clipboard, ready for you to paste into another application.
>
> If you go to another application and copy some text into the Clipboard, you can copy it into GNU Emacs with C-y. Your previous Emacs kill is still in the kill-ring, and you can still get at it with M-y. Data entered into the Clipboard from other applications affect the GNU Emacs kill-ring only if you paste from the Clipboard into Emacs.

Editing a File

The simplest way to edit a file in Emacs is to start Emacs with this filename as an argument. When you have Emacs running, you can load a file by pressing C-x C-f (find-file). This asks you for a filename, as can be seen in Figure 4.11.

FIGURE 4.11

Type C-x C-f (find-file) to open a file.

This is the path of the current buffer

Emacs suggests the current buffers path to you to start with. The reason for this is that most of the time you open files located in the same directory as the one you are currently editing. If the file you are searching for is in another directory, you can edit the suggested path. An alternative is to type the new path (see Figure 4.12).

FIGURE 4.12

Double slashes in pathnames.

The directory Emacs suggests——⌐ ⌐Two backslashes ignore all text up to this point, and start from the root directory

A double slash (//) means ignore everything up to this point and interpret the rest of the line as a path from the root of the filesystem. Likewise /~/ means forget all up to this point and interpret the rest of the line as a directory rooted in your home directory. (/usr/local/~/Emacs is thus equal to .emacs.) This is very handy if you want to open a file in another place on your hard drive (for example, your home directory). Simply type the path as if Emacs hasn't suggested anything.

If the file you name doesn't exist on the hard drive, it is interpreted as a request for a new file. Thus creating a new file is equal to opening a nonexistent file. When you have opened a nonexistent file, Emacs reminds you that this is a new file by displaying a message in the minibuffer (see Figure 4.13).

FIGURE 4.13

Opening a nonexistent file is equal to creating a new one.

The following are two reasons you might open a nonexistent file:

- You intend to edit a new file.
- You typed the wrong name (that is, it was another file you wanted to edit).

In the latter case, you can kill the buffer created for the new file with the command C-x k (kill-buffer) and then try once again to open a file. A better alternative, though, is to press C-x C-v (find-alternate-file), which does both things in one go.

> In Emacs, loading a file or opening a file is called *finding* a file. This is for historical reasons. Thus the command that loads in a file is called *find-file* and not *load-file*.

Saving Buffers to a File

To save a buffer, simply press C-x C-s (save-buffer). This saves the content of the buffer to the file from which it was originally loaded. If the buffer does not correspond to a loaded file—which is the case if you write text in the initial buffer that you see when Emacs starts—Emacs asks for a filename for the buffer.

You might sometimes get in a situation where you read in text from one file and need to write it to another file. Pressing C-x C-s does not do it, because it saves your buffer to the file it was read from without asking for a name. Instead you can press C-x C-w (write-file), which asks for a filename and saves the buffer to that file. You can also use this method if you have edited a buffer that you haven't read in from a file (for example, the *scratch* buffer, which you are presented with when you start Emacs).

> When you have written the content of your buffers to a new file, all subsequent saves will be to this file too!

Exiting Emacs After Editing

When you are finished editing, you can exit Emacs by pressing C-x C-c (save-buffers-kill-emacs). If any of your buffers contain unsaved information, Emacs asks you whether you want to save them first.

> If it's hard for you to remember the commands in this section, it might help you to know that both are available from the Files menu in GNU Emacs and from the File menu in XEmacs.
>
> Even though these keybindings can be difficult—and tough to remember—don't interpret this as an indication that Emacs is hard to use. Realize that you won't use these commands as much you do others (such as cutting and pasting); therefore, these commands don't need to be as accessible as the others.

Miscellaneous File Commands

In this section you will learn how to edit a file on a remote machine and how to edit a compressed file. If you are in a hurry, you can skip this section, but please make sure that you get back here later, because it contains very useful information.

Files on Remote Machines

Emacs enables you to edit files on a remote host. This is almost transparent to you with two exceptions:

- You have to use a bit of special syntax to tell Emacs the location of the file.
- You need to have a connection to the remote host, when you load or save the files.

To load a file from another host, you must tell it two things:

- The name of the host on which the file is located
- Your username on this host

Emacs then uses FTP to connect to this host and download the file for you to edit.

To use this feature, you must be able to FTP to the remote host.

To ask Emacs to load a file on another host, simply use the commands that you already know for opening files on your local host. You've already learned about C-x C-f (find-file) and C-x C-v (find-alternate-file). As the name of the file, you need to specify your username on the remote host and its name. Use the following syntax:

/user@host:filename

That is a slash, your username, the symbol @, the hostname, a colon, and the filename on the local system.

For example, to load the file /etc/passwd as the user root on the host linux.homenet, type /root@linux.homenet:/etc/passwd.

If your username on the remote machine is the same as the one on your current machine, you can leave out the username@ part. An example would be to edit the file .tcshrc in your home directory on the host linux.homenet. This is done with the filename /linux.homenet:~/.tcshrc

Note how I used the tilde (~) in the preceding. The tilde refers to your home directory on the remote host.

If you are using a UNIX machine, this is a convenient way of editing a file as root on your local machine. As the username, type root and, as the name of host, type localhost, which refers to the machine on which you are located. This saves you from logging in as root and starting a new Emacs session, which would likely have a setup other than you are used to.

Be warned, however, that some systems don't enable you to FTP into the machine as the superuser.

When Emacs is connected to the remote host it asks you in the minibuffer for the password on the remote host.

Compressed Files and Archives

Emacs has the capability to edit compressed files and archives; that is, files ending in .gz, .Z, .tar, .zip, .arc, .lzh, and .zoo. This makes it possible to avoid uncompressing files or extracting archives when you are low on disk space, for example, or when you do not want to clutter up your hard drive with the content of an archive.

4

Compressed Files

The library named jka-compr adds capability to Emacs, which makes it capable of transparently reading and writing files compressed by `gzip` or `compress`. *Transparent* means you never notice that the file is, in fact, compressed.

For Emacs to recognize that the file is compressed, the file must end in `.gz`, `.Z` or `.tgz`. The last suffix is for files archived with tar and compressed with gzip.

When you load a compressed file, Emacs simply decompresses it for you before it shows it to you. When you later save the file, it compresses it before writing it to the hard drive. Totally transparent to you! To enable this feature, add the following to your `.emacs` file:

```
(require 'jka-compr)
(jka-compr-install)
```

If you are not using XEmacs, the second line is unnecessary.

Archives

When you load an archive, Emacs shows you a list of the files in the archive. Tar archives are handled by the library called tar-mode, whereas Zip, Arc, Lzf, and Zoo archives are handled by the library called arc-mode. This means that the interfaces for these two sets of archives are a bit different, as can be seen in Figures 4.14 and 4.15.

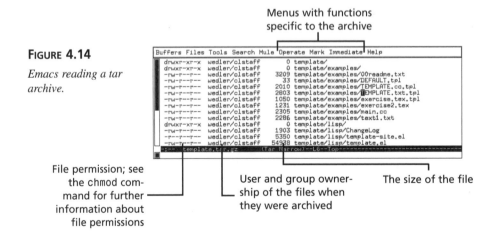

FIGURE 4.14

Emacs reading a tar archive.

Menus with functions specific to the archive

File permission; see the chmod command for further information about file permissions

User and group ownership of the files when they were archived

The size of the file

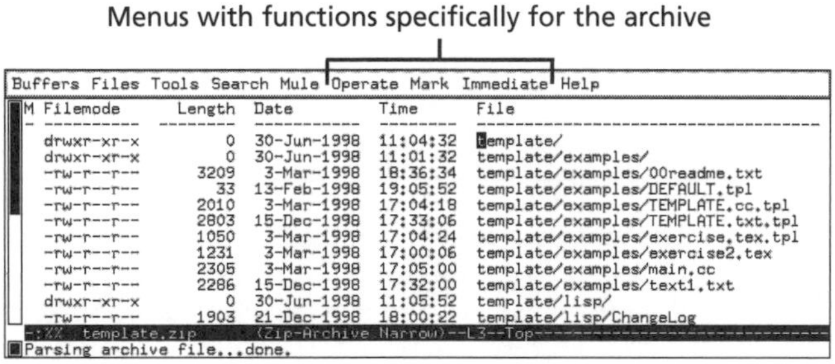

Menus with functions specifically for the archive

FIGURE 4.15

Emacs reading a Zip archive.

```
Buffers Files Tools Search Mule Operate Mark Immediate Help
M Filemode     Length  Date        Time     File
  --------     ------  ----        ----     ----
  drwxr-xr-x        0  30-Jun-1998  11:04:32  template/
  drwxr-xr-x        0  30-Jun-1998  11:01:32  template/examples/
  -rw-r--r--     3209  3-Mar-1998   18:36:34  template/examples/00readme.txt
  -rw-r--r--       33  13-Feb-1998  19:05:52  template/examples/DEFAULT.tpl
  -rw-r--r--     2010  3-Mar-1998   17:04:18  template/examples/TEMPLATE.cc.tpl
  -rw-r--r--     2803  15-Dec-1998  17:33:06  template/examples/TEMPLATE.txt.tpl
  -rw-r--r--     1050  3-Mar-1998   17:04:24  template/examples/exercise.tex.tpl
  -rw-r--r--     1231  3-Mar-1998   17:00:06  template/examples/exercise2.tex
  -rw-r--r--     2305  3-Mar-1998   17:05:00  template/examples/main.cc
  -rw-r--r--     2286  15-Dec-1998  17:32:00  template/examples/text1.txt
  drwxr-xr-x        0  30-Jun-1998  11:05:52  template/lisp/
  -rw-r--r--     1903  21-Dec-1998  18:00:22  template/lisp/ChangeLog
-:%%  template.zip        (Zip-Archive Narrow)--L3--Top----------------
Parsing archive file...done.
```

If you press Enter when point is located on a file, the file is loaded into a buffer, where you can edit it. When you save it, the archive is automatically updated.

This is only half true for tar files. To make it update the tar files, you need to save the buffer that contains the archive (that is, the tar file). In Hour 6, "Editing Several Files at Once," you will learn how to get to this buffer.

In the menus are different functions for manipulating the files of the archive: copying files to or from the archive, renaming files in the archive, changing their permissions, and so on.

Document Templates

One of the main philosophies of Emacs is that you should spend your time being a genius instead of doing trivial monotonous tasks! If you remember this when you use Emacs, you'll find that you spend time on things that Emacs can do for you with a single keystroke or even no keystrokes!

An example of this is creating a new file. When you create a new file, you most often spend the first few minutes inserting the same text that you inserted the last time you created a similar file, for example, the last time you created an HTML document.

The solution to this problem is to make Emacs insert a template. This template is different depending on whether you write C programs, HTML documents, or even a letter to Grandma. Furthermore, the template might differ between one set of HTML files to another. The HTML files of your personal Web page might be quite different from those you make for your company. Likewise templates for one programming project can be quite different from those of another.

4

On the CD is a library called `template`. The installation is described in Appendix A. When this library is enabled, Emacs inserts templates for you. You must, of course, define the templates first.

 This library is powerful and configurable but, for simple document templates, you will never use all its power. When you finish with this book and want to learn more, I strongly suggest that you take a look at the top of the Lisp file (discussed in Hour 1, "Introducing Emacs").

Finding the Template File

When a new file is created, Emacs searches for a template with a name based on the file's extension. That is, if you create a file with the name `test.html`, Emacs searches for a template file called `TEMPLATE.html.tpl`. Likewise if you create a new file called `letter.txt`, Emacs searches for the template file `TEMPLATE.txt.tpl`.

When searching for a template, Emacs first looks in the directory in which the new file is to be located. If Emacs doesn't find the file there, it looks in the subdirectory of this one with the name `Templates`. If Emacs still doesn't find the file, Emacs continues searching in the parent directory and a subdirectory of this called `Templates`. Emacs continues searching for the file in this way until Emacs gets to the root of your home directory. If Emacs still hasn't found the file at that point, Emacs searches for the file in a directory that you might have defined as a template directory.

An example might clarify the matter. Imagine that you are creating the file `~/work/Emacs-project/note.txt` and all your standard templates are located in the directory `~/lib/templates`. Emacs searches for the following files in this order. The first it finds it uses as the template:

1. `~/work/Emacs-project/TEMPLATE.txt.tpl`

2. `~/work/Emacs-project/Templates/TEMPLATE.txt.tpl`

3. `~/work/TEMPLATE.txt.tpl`

4. `~/work/Templates/TEMPLATE.txt.tpl`

5. `~/TEMPLATE.txt.tpl`

6. `~/Templates/TEMPLATE.txt.tpl`

7. `~/lib/templates/TEMPLATE.txt.tpl`

You might think that it is strange behavior searching so desperately for a template; however, it's important for the following reasons:

- By searching in both the current directory and the Template subdirectory, you have the opportunity to hide the templates in a subdirectory if you don't want them to lie around with all your other files. On the other hand, you are not forced to do so!

- By searching trough the path, you might find specific templates in subdirectories and generic templates in top-level directories. As an example, you might have a directory called Letters that contains all your letters. In this directory, you might have a generic template, which inserts something like *Dear...* and the current date. In a subdirectory to the Letter directory you might have a directory with letters to your girl- or boyfriend. This template might include text such as *Yours forever*, and so on.

- By looking in the standard template directory at the end, you can have some templates that are general for all files ending in .txt (letters, configuration descriptions, and other kinds of text files) located in one place.

> If you use Windows, you know that you seldom edit files located in your home directory (not as often as you would if you used UNIX). You might need to tell Emacs to search for templates farther down in the directory structure than in your home directory. To do this, insert the following line into your .emacs file:
>
> ```
> (setq template-home-directory "/")
> ```

The Content of a Template

The templates can contain ordinary text combined with stand-ins. These stand-ins either are replaced with other text or mark positions in the buffer at the time a new file is created based on this template. The stand-ins are in the form (>>>*letter*<<<). Examples include >>>P<<<, which sets the point of the newly created document at this location in the buffer, and >>>A<<<, which inserts your email address.

The simplest kind of templates are those that simply insert text combined with one of the predefined stand-ins. The predefined stand-ins can be seen in Table 4.1.

TABLE 4.1   ALL THE CODES THAT REQUIRE NO USER DEFINITION

Code	Example	Description
Files and Directories		
(>>>DIR<<<)	~/Letters/	Directory part of the filename
(>>>FILE<<<)	Gretchen.txt	The filename without the directory
(>>>RILE_RAW<<<)	Gretchen	The filename without the extension
(>>>EILE_EXT<<<)	txt	The extension of the filename (without the dot)
Time and Date		
(>>>DATE<<<)	07 Jan 1999 20:17:29	The date and time
(>>>ISO_DATE<<<)	1999-01-07	The ISO 8601 date
System Information		
(>>>AUTHOR<<<)	blackie@ifad.dk	The full email address
(>>>LOGIN_NAME<<<)	blackie	The login name
(>>>HOST_ADDR<<<)	ifad.dk	The hostname
(>>>USER_NAME<<<)	Jesper Pedersen	The user's real name
Locations		
(>>>POINT<<<)		This sets the point; only one point can be set, of course
(>>>MARK<<<)		This sets the mark; again, only one mark can be set
(>>>1<<<) ... (>>>9<<<)		These are ten possible locations that you can get to later. To get to any of these locations, press c-x r j (jump-to-register) and the number given previously.

A sample template might be the following:

```
                              Odense (I<<<)
Dear (>P<<<)


Our record number: (>1<<<)

Cheers (>U<<<)
```

In Figure 4.16, you can see a new file created with this template.

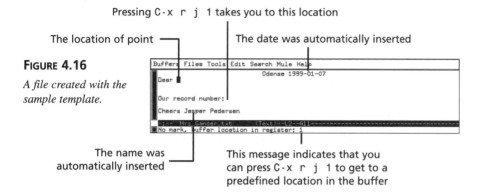

Pressing C-x r j 1 takes you to this location

The location of point ──────┐   ┌─── The date was automatically inserted

FIGURE 4.16

A file created with the sample template.

The name was ─────────────┘   This message indicates that you
automatically inserted   can press C-x r j 1 to get to a
                                        predefined location in the buffer

Inserting the Result of Asking a Question

In your template, you can also insert text that is the result of asking a question. Thus in the previous example, you might want to be prompted for the name to be inserted after the word *Dear*. (It is very important to you that you do not forget this name.)

Questions like this can be inserted in the template, as you can see in the following template:

```
                        Odense (>>>I<<<)
Dear (>>>name<<<)
(>>>P<<<)


Our record number: (>>>number<<<)

Cheers (>>>U<<<)

>TEMPLATE-DEFINITION-SECTION<<
("name" "What is the name of the customer? ")
("number" "What is the record number? ")
```

To make Emacs ask you questions, you need to insert a line that indicates that the definitions section starts. Text after this line is for defining the questions, so be very careful not to insert text that does not have the syntax you see in the preceding template.

Each question is associated to a word (the question *What is the name of the customer?* is associated with the word *name*). This word is used as the stand-in for the text (that is, the text (>>>name<<<) after the word Dear).

When you open a new file, Emacs now asks you these questions, as you can see in
Figure 4.17, and your answers are inserted at the appropriate locations in the buffer, as
you can see in Figure 4.18.

FIGURE 4.17

Emacs asks for information within the template.

FIGURE 4.18

The answer is inserted in the text.

Summary

You have now learned the basics of using Emacs. If you feel that Emacs is difficult to
use, due to the different functions for doing one thing (such as moving around), please
stick to the simple functions and when you get used to these, learn the other functions.

In this hour, you saw some powerful things, such as reading compressed files. See how
many other editors are capable of doing this! If you are totally new to Emacs, please read
these sections without trying to remember everything. They provide a sense of what
Emacs can do. Later, when you need to use these features, you can return and read this
hour more carefully.

Q&A

Q **Why is c-a used to go the beginning of the line and not c-b?**

A c-b moves the cursor one position to the left or, in other words, backward. Emacs
was developed long before the cursor became common. Therefore a keybinding
was necessary. Unfortunately the word *backward* has the same initial letter as
beginning of line.

Q **Why are the commands for deleting text called kill-*something*, rather than delete-*something* (for example, kill-region)?**

A In Emacs, the deleting commands are grouped in two categories: One (kill-ring) copies the deleted text to the clipboard, whereas the other removes the text. The commands that copy the text to the clipboard are called kill-*something,* whereas the others are called delete-*something*.

Q **Why isn't jka-compr enabled by default? Is there something about it that might make Emacs more unstable?**

A No; jka-compr isn't enabled by default only because it needs to define functions to be enabled at Emacs's start-up time, which takes time. The discussion about why this is necessary is too technical to include here but, believe me, if you have one extra second each time you start Emacs and you often edit compressed files, you should really load it in your .emacs file.

Exercises

1. Find a book and insert some text from it.

2. Try this both with and without auto-fill-mode enabled. Can you see the difference?

3. Now move to the beginning or end of the line, word, and so on.

4. Copy some text around in the buffer.

5. Kill several pieces of text and paste the second-to-last one into your text again.

6. Pack a directory with whatever archive you are used to (zip or tar, for example) and read the compressed file with Emacs.

7. Develop templates for the type of files you normally edit.

4

Hour 5

Recovering from Errors

Emacs has several different facilities that help you avoid a disaster. These include

- Undo commands, which let you get back to the state of your document before your most-recent edits.
- Automatic backup, which makes a backup copy of your files when you start to edit them
- Autosave, which saves your buffer to a temporary file within a given interval. This should, you can hope, lessen the catastrophe if you forget to save the content of your buffer when leaving Emacs or in case either Emacs or your computer crashes.

Undo and Redo

When you edit you sometimes get into a situation where you are unhappy about the latest changes. There might be several reasons for this:

- You might regret the edits you have done.

- You might, by accident, execute a macro or press a key that makes unexpected changes to your buffer.

Fortunately Emacs contains a very powerful Undo mechanism, which makes it possible for you to discard these changes. Unlike many other applications, Emacs keeps several steps of Undo available, not just one. To undo a command press C-_, or Control-underscore (undo). This undoes the latest command. If you press it once again, it undoes one step further back. You can continue this way until you get back to the beginning of the buffer or until you have hit the limit of the Undo commands (which is in the order of 20,000 character insertions). Any command other than the Undo command breaks the Undo chain.

If you use Emacs over a modem line or in another situation where C-_ doesn't work, use C-x u instead. This is, however, two key sequences, which means that it is very slow to use when undoing several steps. (That is, you have to press C-x u C-x u C-x u... instead of pressing C-_ several times.)

Not all commands add Undo information to the buffer, only those which actually change the buffer. Thus movement commands can not be undone, nor can the outline commands described in Hour 14, "Finding Differences Between Files."

Rather than having a Redo mechanism (that is, by default) the Undo commands of Emacs can themselves be undone. This might be very confusing to newcomers to Emacs but, if you get it right, it is in fact very simple: "Undo commands of Emacs are commands that later can be undone themselves."

An Undo Example

This task shows you an example of how the Undo commands work.

1. Insert the numbers *1*, *2*, *3*, and *4* on separate lines, as shown in Figure 5.1. This is necessary because Emacs otherwise interprets the four numbers as one entity, causing them to be removed in one step by the Undo mechanism.

FIGURE 5.1

Initial layout before you start your Undo journey.

2. Now press Undo twice. This removes the *4* first, and *3* next, as shown in Figure 5.2.

FIGURE 5.2

Press Undo twice to remove 4 and then 3.

3. Now insert the number *5*, as shown in Figure 5.3.

FIGURE 5.3

Insert 5. This breaks the Undo sequence and puts you in insert mode again (technically, there is no such thing as insert mode, but it might help think about it that way).

4. Now press Undo once. You can see, as shown in Figure 5.4, that 5 is once again removed. When you inserted 5, the Undo sequence was broken, and you now start to undo again.

FIGURE 5.4

Pressing Undo removes the latest text inserted, which is 5.

5. Continue pressing the Undo command. The first time *3* is inserted, the next time *4* is inserted, as shown in Figure 5.5. These are the numerals which were removed by the previous Undo commands.

5

FIGURE 5.5

Pressing Undo twice now inserts 3 and then 4.

6. If you continue pressing Undo, you see that first *4* is removed, then *3* is removed, then *2* is removed, and finally *1* is removed. Pressing Undo once more rings the bell, because you now are back at the initial state of the buffer. (This is, of course, true only if you did no editing in the buffer before you started this task.)

If you find this behavior strange, please think about what you would expect from the Undo mechanism. Should it reel back your changes as if you were recording them on video and reeling back the VCR? Okay, then please look through these steps again; you will, in fact, see that this is exactly what is happening! It includes you reeling back during your first Undo session.

If you accidentally press a key, and Emacs does some fancy thing and you simply must know what is, try pressing C-h l (view-lossage). This splits your window in two and shows you what keys you have pressed. To make your buffer take up all Emacs's space again, press C-x 1 (delete-other-windows).

The Redo Library

Having only the Undo command is a drawback if you need to get back to a state you had some time ago. An example might be that you make changes and, five minutes later, you find that this is a bad idea after all. Emacs contains enough Undo information to get back to the state before you started your changes. The problem, however, is to find the exact location if you made changes before you started the current editing (that is, you didn't load the file into Emacs and started editing on the change you now regret, but you had already made some changes).

If you undo only a few commands and break the Undo sequence (for example, by inserting a space), you can't Undo anything else past that because you have to undo your Undo before you can undo the real typing. Think about it!

Okay, what you really want is a Redo mechanism which simply reverses an Undo when you are undoing so you can reel forth and back around the point where the changes started, and thus find the exact point.

This feature is available in the library called Redo. It is included in XEmacs but not in GNU Emacs.

If you are using GNU Emacs, you can copy the library from the CD that comes with book to your Lisp directory.

To install it, simply add the following into your .emacs file:

```
(require 'redo)
```

This makes the command redo available, but you should also bind it to a key. You might, for example, want to bind Undo to F5 and Redo to Shift+F5, which can be done by inserting the following lines into your .emacs file:

```
(global-set-key [(f5)] 'undo)
(global-set-key [(shift f5)] 'redo)
```

> Adding this library does not alter the way ordinary Undo works; it simply causes Emacs to start a bit more slowly.

Reverting to the File on Disk

If you regret everything you have done since you last saved your file, you can ask Emacs to reload it from disk for you by pressing M-x and typing revert-buffer. Be careful; this deletes the changes you made to the buffer forever!

> This might also be used if your file changed on disk since you loaded it or saved it the last time. A log file might be an example of this.

5

Automatic Backup

When you load an existing file into Emacs, it makes a backup of it for you the first time it saves this file, in case you later find that you need the original version.

> Please note that it does not make a backup each time you save the buffer, but only when you save it the first time after you read it into Emacs.

There are two different ways Emacs can do these backups:

- Single backup—In this mode only one backup is kept of the file. When you edit the file for the second time in Emacs, the first backup is overwritten. The filename used for the backup is the original filename with a tilde (~) appended to the end of the file. (This is the default.)

- Numbered backup—In this mode, each new backup is numbered consecutively; thus, you might have several backups of the same file. The filename used for the backups is the original with `.~42~` appended (for the 42nd backup of the file).

There are a number of variables that configure this feature. First of all, you can disable backup entirely. Please think carefully before you do this! To disable backup, insert the following line into your `.emacs` file:

```
(setq make-backup-files nil)
```

If you would like Emacs to do a single backup (and it doesn't already), you must insert the following lines into your `.emacs` file:

```
 (setq make-backup-files t)
(setq version-control 'never)
```

Finally, if you want Emacs to make numbered backups, you must insert the following lines into your `.emacs` file:

```
(setq make-backup-files t)
(setq version-control t)
```

Configuring Numbered Backups

To avoid filling up your disk with backup files, Emacs only keeps a certain number of numbered backups. This number can be configured with two variables:

- kept-old-versions—This number of old versions is always kept. Thus if this variable is set to 3 then the first three numbered backups are never deleted. For example, `file.~1~`, file.~2~, `file.~3~`. As I see it, there are only two meaningful values to this variable, 0 and 1. 0 means do not keep a backup of the file from before you edit it the first time, and 1 means do. Having a value of 3, say, makes the two first edits more significant than the rest of them. I don't know why. The default value for this variable is 2.

- kept-new-versions—This number of backup files is kept, excluding the initial backups described by the variable. Thus if this variable is 2, and you are about to make backup number 20, all backup files except number 19 (that is `file.~19~`) and number 20 (that is `file.~20~`) are deleted (except, of course, the initial backup file described by the variable). The larger you set this variable, the more versions of files are stored on the disk and the more secure you are that you can find edits discarded by later versions of the file. This variable's default value is 2.

As an example, the following lines make Emacs keep the original file before you start to edit it and the five latest versions of it:

```
(setq kept-old-versions 1)
(setq kept-new-versions 5)
```

It should, of course, be inserted into your .emacs file along with the lines that enable numbered backups.

When old numbered backup files are about to be deleted, Emacs asks you for permission to do so. In the long run, this is very annoying, so when you have gained confidence in Emacs and its deletion of old backup files, you might want to insert the following into your .emacs file, which makes it silently delete the old backup files:

```
(setq delete-old-versions t)
```

Keeping All the Backup Files in One Directory

Backup files are normally written next to the files that they are a backup of. This has the advantage that they are easy to find, but it also has the disadvantage that they tend to clobber your hard disk. An alternative is to keep all your backup files in one directory.

 To do this, you need the library called backup-dir. It is part of XEmacs, but GNU Emacs users need to copy it from the CD to their Lisp directory.

The library contains many different configurations. It is beyond the scope for this book to discuss all of them. (See the header of the Lisp file for the others.) One way to use it, however, is to make Emacs do all autosaving in one directory. To do this, insert lines similar to the following into your .emacs file:

```
(require 'backup-dir)
(setq bkup-backup-directory-info
      '((t "/home/blackie/.backups" ok-create full-path)))
```

You should of course replace /home/blackie/.backups with the directory in which you want your backup files to be located.

To use this library in GNU Emacs version 19, you need to install the customize library or the cust-stub library. See Appendix A, "Installing Functions and Packages from the CD," for instructions for installing these.

5

Recovering from a Crash

In the previous section, you saw that Emacs makes a backup of your files when it writes a new version of them the first time. This enables you to revert to an old version in case you decide to discard the changes made. This does not, however, save you if you edit a document for several hours without saving once in awhile, and Emacs or your system crashes, or you leave your window manager without asking Emacs to save.

I strongly suggest that you save your files often, which would make the amount of data lost in this case smaller. But fortunately Emacs helps you here too. Emacs saves your files once in a while: normally, every 300 keystrokes or when you have been inactive for 30 seconds.

> Please note that only buffers that have been loaded from a file or written to a file are saved. Thus you should always start writing a new file by opening it with C-x C-f (find-file). An alternative that you should not use is to write in the *scratch* buffer, and then write this to a file with C-x C-w (write-file).

When writing the backup files, Emacs uses a special filename, namely the original name with a hash mark, or pound symbol, (#) in front and in back of it. Thus the file index.html will be autosaved to the file #index.html#. It does not save to the original filename for a couple of reasons:

- If Emacs or your computer crashes while Emacs is writing the backup file, or if there is no more space left on your hard drive, all will be lost, and all you have to hope for is the backup file made when you first saved the file (which might have been several days ago).
- If you are editing a live file (one that can be read when you are editing it, such as the password file) then the consistency of the file might be lost. (If there is an error in the password file, people cannot log in to the system!)

When Emacs does autosaving, it might freeze for a few seconds (depending of the size of the file), but you can still type; it shows up a bit later on your screen. To indicate to you that it is autosaving, it shows the text Auto-saving... in the minibuffer.

When you save the buffer, Emacs removes the autosave file; thus when you exit Emacs with all your buffers saved, there should be no autosave files left on the hard drive.

Recovering an Autosave File

When you load a file with an autosave file into Emacs, it tells you this and suggests that you recover this file, as you can see in Figure 5.6.

FIGURE 5.6

Emacs suggests recovering from the autosave file.

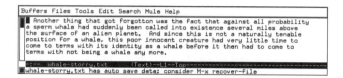

Recovering from an Autosave File

Follow these steps to recover from an autosave file:

1. Press M-x and type `recover-file`. Emacs now asks you for the filename to recover (that is, the name without the # characters), as shown in Figure 5.7.

FIGURE 5.7

Emacs asks for the file to recover.

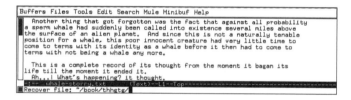

2. Type the name and press Enter, as shown in Figure 5.8. Remember you can press the Tab key here to complete the filename.

FIGURE 5.8

Type the name to recover—without the # characters!

5

3. As shown in Figure 5.9, Emacs shows you the size and the date of the original file and the autosave file to make sure that you know what you are doing. To confirm that you are sane and ready to recover the file, type **yes**.

Figure 5.9

Emacs asks you a final time whether you want to recover from the autosave file.

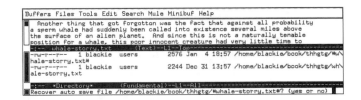

If you start editing the file when Emacs has told you about the autosave file, you will be out of luck if you plan to recover from it. A new one will be written when you have typed 300 characters or have been idle for 30 seconds (whichever comes first!)

If it was an accident that you started writing, hurry up and hit the Undo key, which will cancel this and let you do your recovering.

▲ This procedure is no different from copying the autosave file to the original file, and then starting Emacs with this file. But I hope you find it a bit easier.

Recovering Sessions

If you had several files loaded and changed at the time Emacs crashed, you might have several autosave files to recover. Emacs makes this a bit easier for you by creating a list of all these files in a file within your home directory. This file is called `.saves-`*pid*`-`*hostname*, where *pid* is the process identifier of your Emacs (*pid* is a number; if you don't know what it is, don't bother), and *hostname* is the name of the machine running the Emacs. Rather than invoking `recover-file` you can use the function `recover-session`.

Recover Autosave Files

Follow these steps to use recover-session to recover multiple autosave files in one go:

1. Press M-x and type **recover-session**. Emacs now shows you a list of all the session files, sorted by date, as shown in Figure 5.10.

FIGURE 5.10

Buffer with earlier sessions.

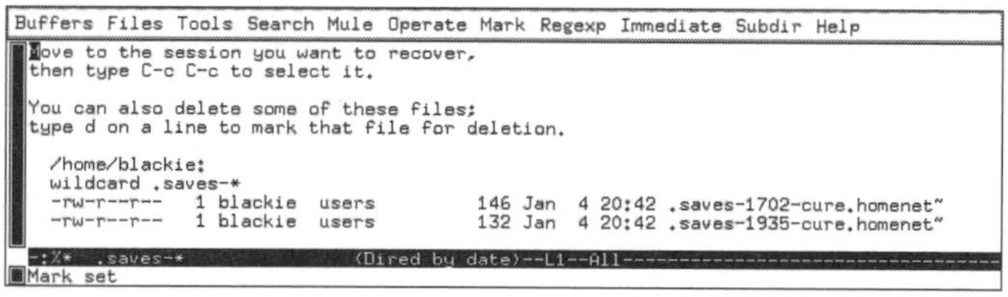

2. In this buffer, you can press Enter on top of a session to see which files it contains, as shown in Figure 5.11.

FIGURE 5.11

The contents of a session file.

3. To get back to the session buffer, simply kill the buffer with the information about the session. You do this by pressing C-x k (kill-buffer) and pressing the Enter key.

4. Now you should be back with the session list, as shown in Figure 5.12. Press C-c C-c on top of the session you want to recover.

FIGURE 5.12

Emacs asks you whether you want to recover the .emacs file.

5. Emacs now asks you whether it should recover the first file of the session. You have the following choices:

y   Press **y** to answer Yes, recover this file.

n   Press **n** to answer No, skip this file and continue with the other files.

!   Press the exclamation mark to make Emacs recover all the files of the session without asking you for each of them.

q   Press **q** to ask Emacs to quit recovering files.

.   Press the period to ask Emacs to recover this file but skip recovering the others.

5

▼   Finally, if you forget what the different bindings mean, press C-h to ask Emacs for
        a description of them.

        After you give Emacs permission to recover a file from the session, it asks you
        again to make sure you know what you are doing (see Figure 5.13).

FIGURE 5.13

*Emacs asks a final
time whether you want
to recover a file.*

```
 Buffers Files Tools Edit Search Mule Minibuf Help
   -rw-r--r--    1 blackie  users        44 Jan  4 20:51 .saves-1936-cure.homenet"
   -rw-r--r--    1 blackie  users       146 Jan  4 20:51 .saves-1702-cure.homenet"
   -rw-r--r--    1 blackie  users       132 Jan  4 20:42 .saves-1935-cure.homenet"

 -:%*  .saves-*          (Dired by date)--L11--Bot-----------------------------------
   -rw-r--r--    1 blackie  users       808 Jan  4 20:51 /home/blackie/#.emacs#
   -rw-r--r--    1 blackie  users       787 Dec 29 19:37 /home/blackie/.emacs


 -:--  *Directory*       (Fundamental)--L1--All------------------------------------
 ■Recover auto save file /home/blackie/#.emacs#? (yes or no) ■
```

        When you have answered all of Emacs's questions, the files are read into buffers and are
▲   ready to edit, so please do not forget to save them!

> If you find that this is not the Seventh Wonder and you are actually quite
> annoyed with having the session files located in your home directory, you
> can disable the creation of these by inserting the following into your .emacs
> file:
>
> (setq auto-save-list-file-prefix nil)
>
> Although you have disabled this, you can still recover the files by using
> recover-file on each one of them.

Summary

You have now learned three different ways to recover from errors, each of which can
help you avoid banging your head against a wall because you have lost the last 10 minutes, 10 hours, or even 10 days of work. But please do not let this make you think that it
is not necessary to back up your files anymore!

Q&A

Q Should I use a single backup or numbered backups?

**A That is a strictly personal matter, but unless your hard drive space is very limited, I
   suggest that you use numbered backups, because this gives you more security.**

Q **I have backup files lying all around my hard drive, which is very old. How should I clean them up?**

A First of all, keeping all your backup files in one directory can help you a lot. If you are using UNIX, you might consider using `crontab` to remove backup files older than a given number of days with a command such as the following:

```
"find -name \*~ -mtime +10 ¦ xargs rm"
```

Please read the manual pages for `crontab`, `find`, and `xargs` before you actually do anything. (If you forget the tiny little tilde character in the preceding command, all your files older than ten days will be removed, so watch out!)

Q **What is the difference between autosave and backup files?**

A Autosave files are files written in short intervals to help you recover if Emacs or your computer crashes. Backup files on the other hand are written the first time Emacs saves to the files to help you recover if your changes were irreversible and fatal.

Exercises

1. Play around with the Undo mechanism until you are familiar with it.

2. Try the example from the text with the Redo package.

3. Edit a file and make sure that it does autosave, kill Emacs without saving the file, and start Emacs on the given file.

4. Try exercise 3 with several files, and use recover-session instead.

5

Hour 6

Editing Several Files at Once

Up to now, you have seen how you can use Emacs to edit files, but only one at a time. You might, however, often want to edit several files at a time. For example, consider this situation. You are editing your current project which contain several C files. While you edit them, you need to see a definition in another file. Suddenly your boss comes in and demands that you write a given letter at once. (You had promised him that you'd have it in two weeks.) While you edit the letter, the telephone rings. It is your girlfriend, who wants you to add a few items to your shopping list (which you, of course, have on your computer).

Do you get my drift? The letter for your boss and the shopping list can, of course, be edited by a separate Emacs, which you start for only this purpose. But it is not realistic that you would start a separate Emacs for each file in your programming project.

Fortunately, Emacs supports editing in multiple buffers at the same time.

Working with Multiple Buffers

When you open a new file with C-x C-f (find-file) a new buffer is created with the content of the file and the buffer is shown to you in the current window. The old buffer is not destroyed by this action; it is merely hidden. You have many ways to get back to the other buffer. The most basic is to press C-x b (switch-to-buffer). Emacs then asks you for the name for the buffer to switch to. (In many cases this is the same name as the file; later you will see other cases.)

Switching Buffers

This task shows you the most basic way to get to another buffer.

1. Press C-x b (switch-to-buffer). Emacs asks you for the name of the buffer to switch to (see Figure 6.1). As the default it suggests the buffer that you last visited (that is, the buffer before your current one). If you want to switch to this buffer, simply press Enter.

FIGURE 6.1

Emacs asks for a buffer name to switch to.

```
Buffers Files Tools Edit Search Mule Minibuf Help
;(setq debug-on-error t)
(setq setup-location ~HOME)
(setq load-path (cons "/home/erik/pgnus-0.52/lisp/" load-path))

;(if (eq setup-location 'IFAD)
;    (load-file ""blackie/Emacs/ifad.elc"))
(setq load-path (cons "/home/blackie/Emacs" (cons "/home/blackie/Emacs/Modes" lo\
ad-path)))
(load-library ""blackie/Emacs/config.el")
(load-library ""blackie/Emacs/functions.el")
--:--  .emacs          (Emacs-Lisp)--L1--Top-------------------
Switch to buffer: (default customize.el)
```

2. Now you can start to type the name of the buffer that you want to switch to. To make Emacs complete as much of the name as possible for you, press the Tab key. If it can't unambiguously fill in any letters for you, it lists the possible completions, as you can see in Figure 6.2.

FIGURE 6.2

When no letters can be added unambiguously when pressing the Tab key, Emacs lists the possible completions.

```
Buffers Files Tools Edit Search Mule Minibuf Help
;(setq debug-on-error t)
(setq setup-location ~HOME)
(setq load-path (cons "/home/erik/pgnus-0.52/lisp/" load-path))

--:--  .emacs          (Emacs-Lisp)--L1--Top-------------------
Click mouse-2 on a completion to select it.
In this buffer, type RET to select the completion near point.

Possible completions are:
config.el                           customize.el
--:--  *Completions*     (Completion List)--L1--All-----------
Switch to buffer: (default customize.el) c
```

3. When you have finished typing the name, press Enter to tell Emacs to open this file for you.

If you type the name of a nonexistent buffer, Emacs creates a new empty buffer. This buffer is not associated with any file, and thus no auto-saving is done! In most cases, you should kill this buffer right away and switch to the one you intended to move to in the first place.

Note that this is the only way you can create a new buffer without inserting any default content. This might be handy in times when you need to test an editing function.

When you finish with a buffer, you can kill it by pressing C-x k (kill-buffer). Emacs asks you for the name of the buffer you want to kill, in the same way it asks for a name when you switch buffers. If the buffer has a file loaded into it, Emacs forgets all about the file, too. If the file has changed since it was last saved to disk, Emacs suggests that you save it before you kill it, as you can see in Figure 6.3.

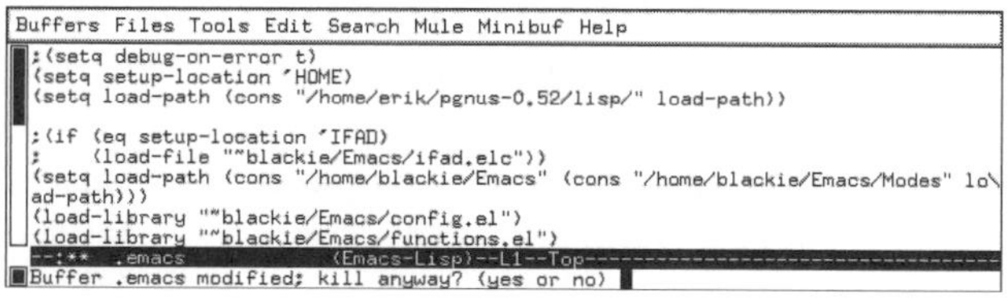

FIGURE 6.3

Emacs asks you whether you really want to kill the buffer without saving it.

```
Buffers Files Tools Edit Search Mule Minibuf Help
;(setq debug-on-error t)
(setq setup-location 'HOME)
(setq load-path (cons "/home/erik/pgnus-0.52/lisp/" load-path))

;(if (eq setup-location 'IFAD)
;    (load-file ""blackie/Emacs/ifad.elc"))
(setq load-path (cons "/home/blackie/Emacs" (cons "/home/blackie/Emacs/Modes" lo\
ad-path)))
(load-library ""blackie/Emacs/config.el")
(load-library ""blackie/Emacs/functions.el")
--:** .emacs          (Emacs-Lisp)--L1--Top------------------------------------
Buffer .emacs modified; kill anyway? (yes or no)
```

Note that this is one of the answers where you must type yes or no (that is, spelled out) and subsequently press the Enter key. This is to avoid accidentally killing a buffer that has been modified.

Managing Buffers

Emacs has a special interface for managing buffers. This interface itself is simply a special buffer with special keybindings. You'll see these buffers a lot!

To get to this buffer, press C-x C-b (list-buffers). This splits your current window in two, as you can see in Figure 6.4.

6

The buffer-managing buffer does not have focus. Press C-x o (other-window) to switch to this window

FIGURE 6.4

The interface for managing buffers.

Indicates that this is the active buffer (that is, the one from which this buffer was activated)

Indicates that the buffer is read-only

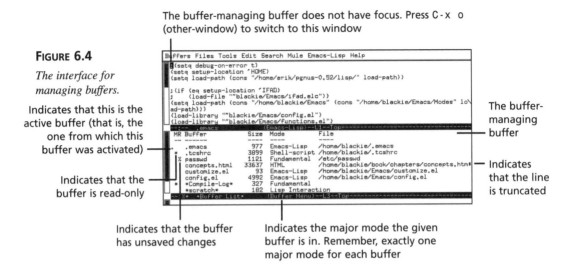

The buffer-managing buffer

Indicates that the line is truncated

Indicates that the buffer has unsaved changes

Indicates the major mode the given buffer is in. Remember, exactly one major mode for each buffer

From this buffer you can select, delete, and save files and much more. Each of the functions are bound to a single key. You are not allowed to insert text into this buffer, therefore it's okay to use the letter f for something else, for example. When pressing a key, the operation operates on the line in which point is located. The most important bindings in this buffer include

- 1—Pressing 1 makes the buffer on the current line the only visible one in the given frame.
- o or C-o—By pressing the letter o or C-o, the buffer is selected in another window. The difference between the two is that o moves the cursor to the other window, whereas C-o doesn't.

In both cases the buffer menu is still visible. In Figure 6.5, C-o has been pressed.

FIGURE 6.5

C-o has been pressed, which loaded the file .tcshrc into the other window. Focus is still in the buffer list window.

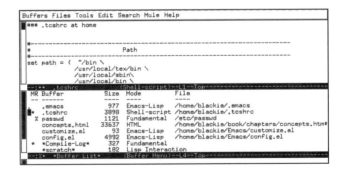

- d, C-d, and x—Pressing d marks the buffer on the current line for deletion, and moves down to the next line. Likewise C-d marks for deletion but moves to the previous line. The buffer is not deleted right away. To do the actual deletion, you must press x (for execute). The reason for this two-stage deletion is that you can execute a macro, for example, that marks the buffers. When the macro has been executed, you can verify the list before you waste the buffers. If any of the buffers are modified, you are asked whether you want to save them before you delete them.

- s—Pressing s marks the given buffer for saving. Again, the buffer is not saved right away, but only marked.

In the first column the letter D indicates that the given buffer is marked for deletion, whereas the letter S in the second column indicates that it has been marked for saving (see Figure 6.6).

FIGURE 6.6

Indication of marked buffers.

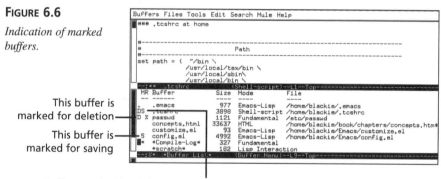

This buffer is marked for deletion

This buffer is marked for saving

Buffers marked both for deletion and saving are saved before they are deleted, which means that Emacs will not ask whether you want to delete a modified buffer

Buffer Names

When a buffer is loaded from a file it gets the same name as the file's name excluding the directory path. This makes it easy to find a given buffer, if you know which file it contains. This is most definitely the most intuitive name for the buffer. There is one exception, namely if a buffer exists with the same name. This is possible if two files with the same name from different directories are loaded into Emacs. In this case a number is appended to the end of the filename. Thus if Emacs already contains a buffer with the name index.html, and you load another file with this name into Emacs, the second buffer is called index.html<2>. The third buffer is called index.hmtl<3>, and so on. The files that the buffers were loaded from are, of course, not renamed.

6

If you have two buffers in Emacs called index.html and index.html<2>, the second is not renamed to index.html when the first is killed. That is, when a buffer has been named, it will not be renamed.

Besides the buffers which you create, Emacs also creates and manages some itself. Up to now, you have seen a few of these, namely the message buffer, containing old messages from the minibuffer, and the buffer menu buffer described in the previous section. To make it easier for you to distinguish these buffers from those you create yourself, the names for these buffers have a star at the beginning and the end. Examples of these buffer names include *Messages*, *Buffer List*, and *Help*.

The Buffer Menu

In Hour 3, "Getting Started with Emacs," you saw that the buffer list was available from the Buffers entry in the menu bar. In Figures 6.7 and 6.8 you can see what it looks like.

FIGURE 6.7

The Buffers *menu entry from GNU Emacs.*

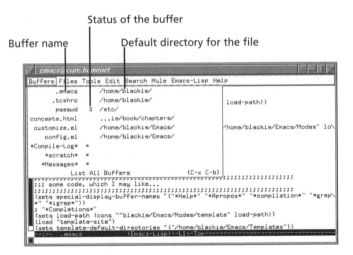

FIGURE 6.8

The buffer menu in XEmacs.

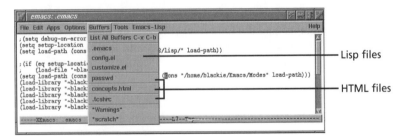

There is a bit of difference between GNU Emacs and XEmacs at this point. The main difference is that the files are sorted by category in XEmacs (that is, HTML files in one group and Lisp files in another), which is not the case in GNU Emacs.

> Using the msb library, GNU Emacs can be enhanced to have categorized entries in the Buffers submenu. It is, however, beyond the scope of this book to describe this library, because it requires some knowledge of Lisp programming.

Traveling Through the Buffers

If you want to go to a buffer, and you can't remember its name very well, there are hints in the following two subsections. Both tell you about a different package that makes it simple to get to a buffer using the keyboard. If, on the other hand, you think that pressing C-x b and using the Tab key to find the correct buffer is enough for you, you can skip the rest of this section. But please come back here when you have begun to use Emacs in such a way that you often have more than 15–20 buffers alive at the same time. (No, that is not unusual at all!)

When you press C-x b Emacs suggests the name of the previous buffer you visited. This is especially useful if you switch between two buffers. Initially you open the first buffer and then the next one, but from then on you can simply press C-x b RET to go to the other one (given, of course, that you do not switch to another buffer in between).

This approach, however, does not work if you edit three files that you have to frequently switch between. An alternative is to use the library yic-buffer, which lets you travel through the list of buffers without naming any files. Simply think of all the buffers as keys in a key ring. With the functions from yic-buffer you have the capability to go to the next or previous buffer in this ring.

 To install this library, copy the file yic-buffer.el from the CD to your Lisp directory, and insert the following into your .emacs file:

```
(load-library "yic-buffer")
```

By default this library binds C-x C-p to *go to the previous buffer*, whereas C-x C-n is bound to *go to the next buffer*. Thus with these two functions you can cycle through all the buffers. Why C-x C-p? Well, C-p goes to the previous line. (You saw that in Hour 2, "Using Emacs in Microsoft Windows," where I mentioned that arrow-up was enough in most cases.) Therefore it was logical for the author to bind it to C-x C-p. If you would

6

rather bind it to Ctrl-Page-Up and Ctrl-Page-Down, insert the following into your .emacs file:

```
(global-set-key [(control prior)] 'bury-buffer)
(global-set-key [(control next)] 'yic-next-buffer)
```

As a shortcut, it also binds C-x C-o to the functionality of pressing C-x o RET (described previously) and C-x C-k to the functionality of pressing C-x k RET (that is, kill the current buffer without asking—it of course still asks whether it is modified).

Naming a Buffer in an Easier Way

When switching buffers with C-x b, you can press the Tab key to make Emacs fill in as much as possible unambiguously. If no additional characters can be filled in unambiguously, Emacs shows you the possible completions in a buffer. In some cases, you might either find it annoying that this extra buffer suddenly is shown, or find it irritating that the completions aren't shown all the time. If this is the case, you should most definitely try the library called iswitchb.

> This library is part of the standard installation of both GNU Emacs and XEmacs but only in version 20. That is, this does not work in version 19.

To load it, insert the following lines into your .emacs file:

```
(require 'iswitchb)
(iswitchb-default-keybindings)
```

When it is loaded, the key sequence C-x b is bound to the function iswitchb-buffer. Therefore when you press C-x b, Emacs shows you a list of possible completions as you can see in Figure 6.9.

At first, all possible completions are shown, because you have not typed anything yet. When you type something, the list is immediately updated with the limited set of buffer names that match the text you have typed (see Figure 6.10). Please note that a buffer name matches if it contains the text as a substring. Thus if you type fig, the buffer name config.el matches, because it contains fig as a substring.

FIGURE 6.9

Switching buffers using the iswitchb *library.*

The text between these braces is a list of possible completions

FIGURE 6.10

Switching buffers using the iswitchb *library.*

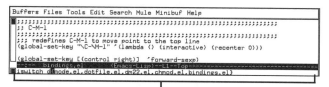

Locations of a match for the text d

 In previous figures, the minibuffer is two lines high. To resize the minibuffer, I enabled resize-minibuffer-mode, which comes with Emacs. See the next section for a description of this.

If you press the Enter key when there still is more than one element left to complete, Emacs switches to the buffer listed in the front of the list.

Pressing C-s rotates the list one element to the left. That is, the second element becomes the first one, the third becomes the second, and the first wraps over to become the last one. Likewise C-r rotates the list one element to the right. This can be seen in Figure 6.11, where C-s has been pressed.

FIGURE 6.11

All elements rotated one element to the left, compared to Figure 6.10.

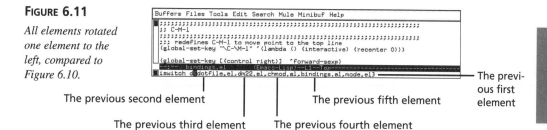

The previous second element

The previous third element

The previous fourth element

The previous fifth element

The previous first element

6

Saving the Buffer List

When you leave work or school, or anywhere you use Emacs, you might need to turn off the computer (or you might do this to save energy). Turning off the computer does, of course, also mean shutting down Emacs. If you are working on a set of files (for example, a lot of C files in a project or the HTML documents for your home page), it might be desirable to be able to make a dump of Emacs. This dump should contain enough information to make Emacs configure itself to the state it had before you exited it, so you later may get back to it and continue your work. The library called desktop does in fact do this.

This library makes Emacs save the list of buffers and some information about these buffers to a file. Each directory can contain one such file (its name is .emacs.desktop). When Emacs is started it checks whether such a file is located in the startup directory and, if this is the case, the state is read from this file.

To make it work, insert the following lines into your .emacs file:

```
(load "desktop")
(desktop-load-default)
(desktop-read)
```

When a desktop has been loaded, it is saved to the same file on exit, but the first time you need to tell it to save. To do this, press M-x and type desktop-save.

The window layout for the buffer is not saved to a file.

Working with Windows and Frames

Often when you work with multiple buffers, you might find it handy to have several buffers on the screen at the same time. Examples of this include

- When you write a program and you use a function in one file that is defined in another one. In this case, it is handy to have both files on the screen, so you can see which arguments the function takes when looking at its use.

- When you copy text from one buffer to another. It is very handy to have both buffers on the screen at the same time.

- When you answer a letter from a colleague. It might be handy to have both the buffer in which you write your answer available at the same time as another file (for example, the .emacs file in which you have a configuration your colleague asks about).

Before I continue discussing various ways to use windows and frames, refresh your memory about what a window is and what a frame is:

- A frame is another name for a top level window—that is, one with *iconify buttons, resize buttons* and so on. A frame can be divided into several subareas, each of these are called *a window.*

- Each frame always contains at least one window, a mode-line, and the minibuffer (the minibuffer is *not* regarded as a window in the rest of this hour, although technically it can be).

Basic Window Movement: Creation and Deletion

Pressing C-x 2 (split-window-vertically) splits the current window in two with one above the other. Pressing C-x 3 (split-window-horizontally) likewise splits the window in two, but with one window next to the other. This can be seen in Figure 6.12 and 6.13.

FIGURE 6.12

Splitting the window in two with C-x 2 *(split-window-vertically).*

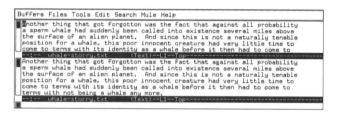

Indicates that the line is truncated

FIGURE 6.13

Splitting the window in two with C-x 3 *(split-window-horizontally).*

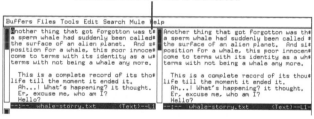

Each of the windows can further be split in two with any of the preceding commands. Two commands exist for removing a window: namely C-x 1 (delete-other-windows), which deletes all windows but the active one, and C-x 0 (delete-window), which deletes the active window.

In GNU Emacs it is also possible to use the mouse to create and delete windows. Pressing the second mouse button on the mode-line of a window deletes all the other windows of that frame, which is also what C-x 1 does. Likewise, pressing the third mouse button on the mode-line deletes the given window, which is equal to C-x 0.

6

Finally, pressing Ctrl and the second mouse button on either the mode-line or the scroll-bar splits the window at that point. (If your mouse has only two buttons, simply press both mouse buttons to obtain the functionality of the second one.)

In XEmacs you get a menu with the preceding functions if you press the third mouse button on the mode-line, as you can see in Figure 6.14.

FIGURE 6.14

Windows commands in XEmacs.

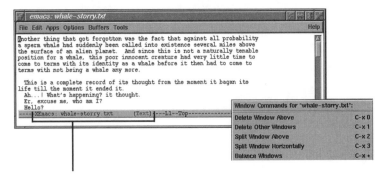

This part of the mode-line brings up other
menus, so it should be outside this range.

You can get from one window to another by pressing C-x o (other-window). In cases where you have several windows (as in Figure 6.15), C-x o moves forward, as if it were a page of a book that you were reading. If you want to go in the opposite direction, you need to give a negative prefix of one to C-x o . Press C— 1 C-x o (that is, Ctrl-minus 1, Ctrl-x o).

FIGURE 6.15

Moving from one window to another using C-x o.

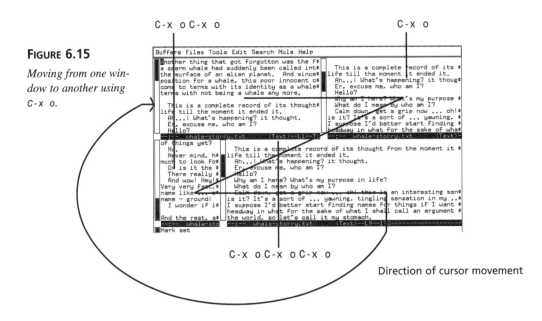

> In sams-lib.el a function exists called sams-other-window-backwards, which does the same as C-x o with a negative prefix argument. Thus if you want to use Ctrl-+ and Ctrl-[ms] on the numeric keypad to move forward or backward, insert the following to your .emacs file:
>
> (global-set-key [(control kp-add)] 'other-window)
>
> (global-set-key [(control kp-subtract)] sams-other-window-backwards)

Resizing Windows

The windows can be resized vertically using the mouse, by dragging the mode-line with the first mouse button. Unfortunately it is not equally easy to resize the windows horizontally, because dragging the scrollbar scrolls the window. (It is not possible to define one function for dragging horizontally, and another for dragging vertically.) To resize horizontally you must press C-x { (shrink-window-horizontally) and C-x } (enlarge-window-horizontally). If you use these functions once in a while I suggest that you add them to your keyboard quick reference card, as the bindings are hard to remember and, even worse, hard to type many times after each other.

When resizing the windows, and when creating them, there is a lower limit for how small a window can get. The lower limit is controlled by the variables window-min-width, which is 10 by default, and window-min-height, which is 4 by default.

Truncated Lines

When splitting a window into two windows side by side, any lines longer than the width of the window are truncated (refer to Figure 6.13).

> The idea behind this is that when you split windows in two side by side, you often want to compare two files. By truncating the lines, the text shown on line 10 in both windows is the content of line 10 of the files. Otherwise the content of the tenth line of the screen might be some other line due to a wrapped line previous to this one.

6

In sams-lib.el a function called sams-toggle-truncate exists, which toggles between truncation and nontruncation for a single buffer.

When truncation is enabled you can scroll the buffer horizontally by pressing C-x > (scroll-right) and C-x < (scroll-left). In XEmacs horizontal scrollbars are added when necessary.

> If you are short on screen height it might be desirable to not have the horizontal scrollbars in XEmacs. To disable them, insert the following line into your `.emacs` file:
>
> ```
> (set-specifier scrollbar-height 0)
> ```

The Minibuffer

The minibuffer is a special window. It cannot be deleted, but you can resize it as you can other windows (refer to Figure 6.9). Its minimum height is 1. It is seldom useful to have it fill more onscreen space than necessary, so what you really need is to have it resize itself dynamically to use enough space to show all its content at any given time. To make it do that, insert the following code in your `.emacs` file:

```
(resize-minibuffer-mode)
```

Basic Frame Movement: Creation and Deletion

New frames are created either by any of the commands described in the next subsection or by pressing `C-x 5 2` (make-frame-command). A frame is deleted again with `C-x 5 0` (delete-frame).

Using the command `make-frame-on-display`, a frame can be created on another display. This makes it possible for two persons to work on the same buffer at the same time, each sitting at their computer. This function is not bound to any keys, but is accessible from the menus. It is located in the File(s) submenu, and is called Make New Display in GNU Emacs and Frame on Other Display in XEmacs.

> In Windows, `make-frame-on-display` is only an alias for `make-frame-command`, and does not make a frame on an X server.

Pressing `C-x 5 o` (other-frame) gives another frame the focus, in the same way that `C-x o` (other-window) gives another window focus. Iconified frames will, however, never get focus this way.

In the same way that you can give `C-x o` a negative numeric prefix to move in the *other* direction, so you can with frames. In `sams-lib.el` the function `sams-other-frame-backwards` exists, which works like `C-x 5 o` with a negative numeric argument. Thus you can bind Meta-+ and Meta-- on the numeric keypad to move between frames by inserting the following into your `.emacs` file:

```
(global-set-key [(meta kp-subtract)] 'sams-other-frame-backwards)
(global-set-key [(meta kp-add)] 'other-frame)
```

> Earlier I suggested that you bind Ctrl-+ and Ctrl-[ms] to switch between windows, so Meta-+ and Meta-[ms] is an obvious choice for switching between frames. Remember Meta works on larger entities than control does, whenever possible. (See Hour 3.)

Extra Window and Frame Commands

Some additional commands exist with the keybinding prefixes `C-x 4` and `C-x 5`. Those with prefix `C-x 4` operate on *another window* in the same frame as your current buffer, whereas those with prefix `C-x 5` operates on *another frame*. The bindings resemble those for `C-x`; `C-x b` switches buffers in the current window, whereas `C-x 4 b` switches buffers in another window, and `C-x 5 b` switches buffers in another frame, for example. To see a complete list of these commands, press `C-x 4 C-h` and `C-x 5 C-h`, respectively.

Dedicated Frames

It is possible in Emacs to make frames which are dedicated to a single buffer; that is, only this buffer is allowed in the frame and, when the buffer is killed, the frame is killed too. This can be very useful if you want to ensure that a file stays visible in a frame all the time

Two functions exist in the `sams-lib.el` that make it possible to create such dedicated frames:

- `sams-find-file-dedicated-frame`, which asks for a filename, loads this file into a buffer, and shows this buffer in a dedicated frame.
- `sams-switch-buffer-dedicated-frame`, which asks for a buffer name and loads this buffer into a dedicated frame.

Emacs can also place buffers in dedicated frames itself. This can be useful for the buffer containing help or info files. To tell Emacs which buffers it must create dedicated frames for, insert something such as the following into your `.emacs` file.

```
(setq special-display-buffer-names '("*Help*" "*Apropos*"
                                     "*compilation*" "*grep*" "*igrep*"))
```

6

Be very careful with the syntax of the preceding! If you have patience, you will learn an easier way to configure variables in Hour 10, "The Emacs Help System and Configuration System."

Summary

In this hour, you learned about multiple buffers, windows, and frames. Before you know it, you'll have all your C projects loaded into Emacs at the same time, and you'll move from buffer to buffer, and have things organized in a more beautiful way than you ever had. Your boss will be thrilled. But be warned, having twice as many windows on your screen doesn't mean that you'll get twice as much work done.

Q&A

Q Isn't it overkill to have such a comprehensive interface for managing buffers?

A No, in fact this interface is similar to other interfaces in Emacs with about the same functionality. In the directory browser, you manage files in the same way as you manage buffers here.

Q Once in a while, I load the wrong file into Emacs. This seems like a thing I might do often. Is there another way I can throw this file away and load another?

A Yes, you can press C-x C-v (find-alternate-file). Otherwise, this would be a good candidate for a macro. You will learn about macros in Hour 13, "Macros."

Q Why do I have frames where I'm not allowed to change to another buffer?

A The frame is probably a dedicated frame. That is the concept of dedicated frames: They do not allow you to change to another buffer and, in this way, hide the dedicated one.

Q I like the `make-frame-on-display` command, but when one of the users of the buffer activates the mark, the region is highlighted in both frames. Is there a way around this?

A Yes. In Hour 15, "Getting an Overview of a File," you will learn how to make indirect buffers, which solves this problem.

Exercises

1. Load several buffers and travel between them using

   a. The functions from `iswitchb`

   b. The buffer menu

   c. The functions from yic-buffer

   Which do you like the best? Is there one that makes the other unnecessary?

2. Is it possible to destroy the window containing the minibuffer?

3. Think about good uses for dedicated windows and find a good location to bind the functions sams-find-file-dedicated-frame and sams-switch-buffer-dedicated-frame.

6

PART II
Searching

Hour

HOUR 7

Searching for Text in a Buffer

After you learn the basics of editing in Emacs, you will be ready to continue to the next topic of editing files. That is, locating the text that you want to change. Although this might seem like an issue that you can cover in three minutes, it isn't! This issue includes many different search situations, such as the following:

- Searching for text in the current buffer
- Listing lines that match a particular pattern
- Searching for text in several files
- Replacing some text with other text
- Keeping a list of locations in different files

This subject is split over three hours. This hour describes various ways to do search-related tasks in one buffer. Hour 8, "Searching for Text in Multiple Files," describes how to do search-related tasks in several files. Finally Hour 9, "Regular Expressions," describes searches that include regular expressions instead of ordinary text.

Incremental Search

Two of the searching functions in Emacs are bound to C-s (isearch-forward) and C-r (isearch-backward). These functions search forward and backward in the text, respectively. Before I discuss them, you should try them out. Yes, now—go on and try them and come back later; I'll discuss them afterward. When searching with C-s and C-r, Emacs starts searching for the text as soon as you start typing. This helps you speed up your work, because you seldom need to type the whole word or phrase that you are searching for.

▼ To Do — Searching for Words in Text

This task will show you an example of an incremental search, in which the word alarmingly is searched for. The steps are shown together with an Emacs window that shows the search progress. The important thing to notice is the location of the point. To begin, follow these steps:

1. Press C-s (isearch-forward) to start searching. This prompts you with the text I-search: in the minibuffer (see Figure 7.1). Had you chosen to search backward, the prompt would be I-search backward:.

FIGURE 7.1

Press C-s or C-r to start your search.

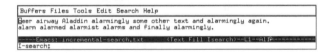

2. Press the letter a. Emacs will immediately position the point at the first location in the buffer, where the substring a is (see Figure 7.2).

FIGURE 7.2

Pressing a makes Emacs proceed to the first location with an a.

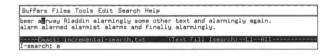

3. Press the letter l (that is, the lowercase letter *L*). Because the letter after a at its current position isn't the letter l, Emacs continues its search, and this time it moves the point to the letter l in *Aladdin* (see Figure 7.3).

FIGURE 7.3

Typing the letter 1 makes Emacs search forward in the text for this, because the next letter at the previous location wasn't an l.

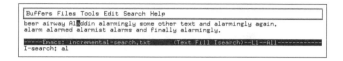

 4. Press the letter a again. This time Emacs doesn't need to start searching again, because its current match can be extended with the letter *a* (see Figure 7.4).

FIGURE 7.4

The current location also matches ala, *so Emacs doesn't need to continue searching through the document.*

5. Press the letter r, and Emacs will continue searching until it finds the substring *alar*. Now you have found the first occurrence of the word *alarmingly* (see Figure 7.5).

FIGURE 7.5

The word alarmingly *has now been found.*

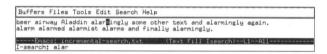

6. Press C-s to continue searching for the text *alar*. This will bring you to the next occurrence of *alarmingly* (see Figure 7.6).

FIGURE 7.6

Pressing C-s will make Emacs proceed to the next match of the string alar.

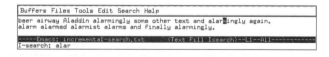

7. You might press C-s a few times until you get to the third occurrence of *alarmingly*; but an alternative is to press C-w, which will append the rest of the word to the search string, and then press C-s with this modified search string. Try pressing

 C-w (see Figure 7.7).

FIGURE 7.7

Typing C-w *will make Emacs append the rest of the current word to the search string.*

```
Buffers Files Tools Edit Search Help
beer airway Aladdin alarmingly some other text and alarmingly█again.
alarm alarmed alarmist alarms and finally alarmingly.
----Emacs: incremental-search.txt      (Text Fill Isearch)--L1--All-----------
I-search: alarmingly
```

 8. Finally, press C-s, which brings you to the third occurrence of the word *alarmingly* (see Figure 7.8).

FIGURE 7.8

Pressing C-s *will now continue the search, this time for the word* alarmingly.

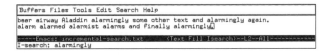

```
Buffers Files Tools Edit Search Help
beer airway Aladdin alarmingly some other text and alarmingly again.
alarm alarmed alarmist alarms and finally alarmingly▊
----Emacs: incremental-search.txt      (Text Fill Isearch)--L2--All-----------
I-search: alarmingly
```

9. Now that you have found the location at which you want to edit, press the Enter key to exit the incremental search.

Although these steps might seem difficult and cumbersome, they aren't. Quickly review what you did: You started to type the word you were searching for. When you came to a location where you could see that you needed to type many letters before the search would continue to a new word, you pressed C-s. When you got to the word you searched for, you pressed C-w and continued the search with C-s. After you have these keybind-ings in your fingers, you'll be amazed how quickly you can find the right location.

Incremental searches are not limited to word boundaries. Your search string might match in the middle of a word. For example, if you search for the, Emacs will also match *aesthetic*, because it contains the letters *the* in it.

Exiting a Search

It might seem obvious, but the purpose of searching for something is to find it; when you have found it, you want the point to be at that location so you can continue editing from there. To do so, press the Enter key when you have found the correct location. An alter-native is to press one of the keys that do not have special meaning within the search (you'll learn about this shortly). Thus you can press M-b (backward-word) to exit search and go to the beginning of the word in which you found a match.

> The previous paragraph is only accurate only if you (or your system administrator) haven't set the variable search-exit-option to nil. If you find that Emacs says that M-b isn't valid when you press it while searching, search-exit-option is set to nil.
>
> To disable it, insert the following into your .emacs file:
>
> (setq search-exit-option t)
>
> Hitting Enter will then be your only way to exit the search.

If, on the other hand, you do not find what you are searching for, you might want to get back to the location where you started your search. To do that you must press C-g either once or twice. If you type characters that aren't found, you need to press C-g twice; otherwise, it is enough to press it once. In a situation where you press extra characters that aren't found, the first C-g will remove these characters from the search string, and the second C-g will exit your searching.

Using an Old Search String

If you search for a string once, you're likely to search for it again. For that reason, Emacs has the capability to recall old search strings. The most valuable of these features is the capability to do the previous search once again.

If you press C-s or C-r as the first letter of your search string, Emacs will search again for the string that you searched for the previous time you searched. (C-s will search forward and C-r will search backward.) If you searched for the string beer in your previous search, and you press C-s C-s, you will search for the word beer once again, forward from your current location in the buffer.

You can also search backward in the history of search commands (just like you can search backward for previously opened files when you press C-x C-f [find-file]). To do this, press either C-s or C-r to search through your search history, and then press M-p to search backward in the history of search strings. If you get too far back, you can press M-n to search forward once again. When you find the string that you want to use, you can modify it if it is not the exact string you want to search for. When you are happy about the string, you can start the search by pressing the Enter key.

If you have marked some text and you want to append this to your search string, you can press M-y. This also means that if you have some marked text that you want to search for, you simply press C-s M-y.

7

Please note that the keybinding for pasting the text onto the search string is M-y and not C-y. C-y does normally mean *paste*, but not when searching. When searching, C-y means append to the search string all the text from the point to the end of the line.

When the Search Fails

When you search forward in the buffer and Emacs gets to the end of the buffer without finding a match for your search string, it beeps and displays Failing I-search. At this point, you can press C-s to make Emacs continue searching from the beginning of the buffer. In case you should forget it, Emacs indicates that this has happened by changing its prompt from I-search to Wrapped I-search. If you continue searching, Emacs will at some point pass your original starting point. To indicate this, its prompt changes to Overwrapped I-search.

The same applies when you search backward in the buffer—with the natural difference that the point where searching becomes wrapped is at the beginning of the buffer instead of the end.

Cases in Search Operations

When searching for some text in Emacs, case matters only if you have included case in your search string. Thus if you search for the text foo (all lowercase), Emacs will find every text string that matches foo regardless of its case. Emacs will find *FOO*, *Foo*, and *fOo*. If, on the other hand, your search string includes letters in uppercase, only words that match the case will be found.

As everything else in Emacs, its behavior can be changed. If you want Emacs to always match using case (such as, Foo should not be matched by foo), insert the following line into your .emacs file:

(setq-default case-fold-search nil)

Searching for a String from the Window Manager's Clipboard

An ordinary nonincremental nonword search mechanism is available by pressing C-s and the Enter key. You will very seldom use this way of searching, because you will find incremental search a very convenient way of searching. There is one situation, however, where this is useful. Namely if you have marked some text in another application that you want to search for in Emacs. Because this text is not available in your kill-ring, it cannot be appended to the search string by pressing M-y when searching. In these situations you should press C-s to start your searching, press the Enter key to enter ordinary text search, paste the text into the search string using the mouse, and press Enter again to start the search.

> GNU Emacs on Windows will bring the contents of the Clipboard into the minibuffer with C-y. The Clipboard is the top of the kill-ring.

Highlighting the Matches

It is very useful if your match is highlighted when searching, instead of the point being located next to the match. An example of such highlighting is shown in Figure 7.9.

FIGURE 7.9

Highlighting the matches when searching.

To enable highlighting when searching, insert the following line in your .emacs file:

```
(setq search-highlight t)
```

To highlight matches when using search-and-replace (search-and-replace is described in the next section), insert the following line in your .emacs file:

```
(setq query-replace-highlight t)
```

Marking and Searching in XEmacs

If point is located at the beginning of a text piece that you want to mark for cut-and-paste, you can set the mark at the location as usual by pressing C-SPC (set-mark-command). After that you can search forward to find the end of the region, and use the desired cut-and-paste function.

If you use XEmacs, there is one point to be aware of. Namely that XEmacs deactivates the mark when starting to search. This means that the region is not active after searching, and thus cannot be used for cut-and-paste. The mark, however, still exists, so you can reactivate the region by pressing C-x C-x (exchange-point-and-mark) and afterward do the cut-and-paste operation.

7

Searching for Words

If you are looking at a formatted version of your document (that is, a document formatted with HTML or LaTeX), you will not know where the line breaks are in your input file. This makes an ordinary incremental search inappropriate, because searching for two words with a space in between might not match the occurrences you are looking for, because the occurrences might be split with a line break instead of a space in your file. For that purpose Emacs has a nonincremental search mode called word search, which interprets a space in the search string as either a space, a tabulator, or a newline. Furthermore, it forces the search string to match whole words, that is the text the will only match the word *the*, not *there* or *then*.

To search using word search, you must press C-s RET C-w for searching forward and C-r RET C-w to search backward. These bindings exist only for historical reasons, and if you use them often, it might be a very good idea to bind them to, for example, C-S-s and C-S-r (that is, Control-Shift and the letter s or r, which are unbound per default in Emacs). The functions invoked are called word-search-forward and word-search-backward.

The main drawback of using word search is that it is nonincremental. If you are willing to resign from matching at word boundaries, you can use regular-incremental-search to obtain the capability to interpret line breaks as ordinary spaces in incremental search. To do this, you must insert the following line into your .emacs file:

```
(setq search-whitespace-regexp "[ \t\r\n]+")
```

Instead of using C-s (isearch-forward) and C-r (isearch-backward), you must now use M-C-s (isearch-forward-regexp) and M-C-r (isearch-backward-regexp) instead. These functions are regular expression searches; therefore, characters such as ., ?, [,], and * have special meanings and you must not use them in your search string. (If you really need to, you must prefix them with a backslash—for example, \?).

For more information on regular expression searches, see Hour 9.

Search and Replace

Most editors have the capability to replace one string with another throughout a whole document. Emacs also has this feature, but it has another which is much more user-friendly. The difference between the ordinary search-and-replace mechanism and Emacs's query-replace is that each time it finds a match, it asks you what you want to do with it. Your choices include the following:

- Replace this occurrence.

- Skip this occurrence and continue to replace unconditionally throughout the rest of the document (this is much like the ordinary search-and-replace).

- Pause the replacement process, so you can fix another error which you have just spotted, and continue when this has been fixed.

Replacing One String With Another

This task will show you how query-replace works, with text from the previous search example.

1. Press M-% to start query-replace. Emacs will ask for the string to replace in the minibuffer. Type alarm and press Enter (see Figure 7.10).

FIGURE 7.10

Press M-% to start query-replace. Emacs tells you in the minibuffer that it wants the string to search for.

2. Emacs now wants to know what this string should be replaced with. Type warn and press Enter (see Figure 7.11).

FIGURE 7.11

When you have told it the string to search for, Emacs asks for the string to replace these matches with.

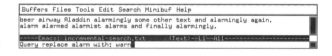

3. Now Emacs searches for the string alarm and, when it finds the string, asks you what to do with it (see Figure 7.12).

FIGURE 7.12

Emacs asks, at each occurrence, for confirmation to replace.

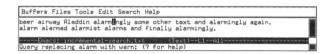

7

▼   4. If you have enabled highlighting of query-replace as suggested before, the string
matched will be highlighted as shown in Figure 7.13.

FIGURE **7.13**

This is what it looks
like if you have
enabled highlighting of
query-replace.

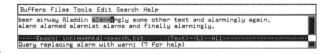

5. You can now press y to replace the string (*y* for *yes*) or n to skip this string and
continue until the next one (*n* for *no*). Press y (see Figure 7.14).

FIGURE **7.14**

When you press y
Emacs replaces the
text, proceeds to the
next occurrence, and
asks for confirmation.

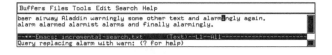

6. Emacs will continue until the next match. If you are certain that your replacement
is okay, you can press ! (the exclamation mark) to replace all occurrences in the
rest of the document (see Figure 7.15).

FIGURE **7.15**

When you are finished
replacing the text,
Emacs informs you on
the number of
replacements.

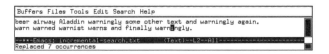

If you want to do an unconditional search-and-replace, the easiest way is to do a query-
▲   replace and, when it asks for confirmation on the first occurrence, press !.

It is important to be aware that the search-and-replace operation works
only from your current location in the buffer to the end of the buffer. Thus
if you want to do search-and-replace on the whole buffer, you must go to
the beginning of the buffer.

In the minibuffer M-p and M-n let you visit earlier strings used for search-and-replace.

Options when Replacing

For each occurrence of the search string, Emacs offers to do one of several actions. Previously, you saw two of them: Replace this occurrence and replace the rest of the occurrences.

The following choices exist:

- Space or y—This replaces the current match and continues to the next one.

- Delete or n—This skips the current match and continues to the next one. In other words, it doesn't replace the current match.

- Enter or q—This terminates the query-replace operation and, therefore, doesn't replace any more matches. The matches already replaced will remain replaced.

- !—This replaces the remaining occurrences in the rest of the buffer without asking for permission.

- , (the comma character)—This replaces the current match but doesn't continue to the next one. That way, you can get the match replaced and see whether Emacs does it correctly. To continue on to the next match, press y. If you dislike the replacement, you can either abort the query-replace and undo, or use recursive editing to fix it. (Recursive editing is described in the following section)

- c-g—This aborts the search-and-replace operation.

- ^ (the caret character)—This moves the cursor back to the previous replacement. (You can go back as many steps as you want.) To continue your replacement press y. If you want to correct the previous replacement, you must use recursive editing).

- c-l—This centers the line with the match in the middle of the window. This enables you to see the text around the match.

- c-r—This enters recursive editing, which is described in the following section.

Recursive Editing

When you use query-replace in your buffer, you might find that there is an error of some kind in the surrounding text of the word being replaced. You can do several things about that.

7

You can try to remember the location and go back to it, when you are finished with your search-and-replace. Unfortunately, this method works only if you have a superb brain like Einstein; otherwise, you will forget the location when you are finished with your search-and-replace. An alternative is to write the location down. This is better than the first solution, but if your document is large, you might end up with many such notes on your paper, and when you get back to the location, you will find that you have forgotten what the problem was.

The ultimate solution is to fix the problem immediately and continue your search-and-replace afterward.

Totally aborting your search-and-replace operation is not a good idea, because this means that you might have to tell Emacs to skip several replacements when you start search-and-replace again. What you really need is to tell Emacs to pause the search-and-replace operation, fix the problem, and ask Emacs to continue after you finish.

Fortunately, Emacs offers exactly that capability. It is called *recursive editing*.

To enter recursive editing from your search-and-replace operation, press C-r. When you finish that, you can work with Emacs as you normally do. (You can, in fact, start another search-and-replace operation while the first is pausing; watch out if you do, because things might get messy).

When you enter recursive editing, the modeline includes a pair of square brackets around the parentheses to indicate that you are in recursive editing.

To exit recursive editing and continue with your search-and-replace press C-M-c.

> If you change the buffer while editing recursively, remember to get back to the one in which the search-and-replace operation was started.

> If you find at some point that you have forgotten to finish a recursive edit, and you do not want to go back to your original operation, you can press C-] (abort-recursive-edit), which will exit the recursive editing without continuing the original task.
>
> It might be easier to remember this key binding if you notice that the key is the same as the indication in the mode line (that is, the ending square bracket).

It might be a good idea to mark your book at this point so you can return to it later and refresh your knowledge of recursive editing. I have seen people forget about it all too often and instead use the solution of writing down the location to return to for editing when the operation is finished.

It might also be a good idea to insert the keybinding for exiting recursive editing into your database of tips.

Cases in Search-and-Replace Operations

Search-and-replace operations are made up of two parts. First Emacs searches for a match. Next it replaces the match. The use of cases in search operations is described in a previous section.

If the replacement string contains cases, no case conversion is done. Case conversion is also not done if the variable case-fold-search is set to nil, as described in the section "Cases in Search Operations." When the text string is in lowercase, Emacs tries to preserve case when replacing. Emacs can preserve case in three different situations:

- When the match is in all lowercase, Emacs will insert the replacement in all lowercase. Thus foo will be replaced with bar.

- When the match is in all uppercase, Emacs will insert the replacement in all upper case. Thus FOO will be replaced with BAR.

- When the match is in mixed case, the case of the first letter in the replacement is preserved and the rest of the letters are made lowercase. Thus Foo, FoO, and FOo are all replaced by Bar; likewise, f0O, foO, and fOo are all replaced by bar.

Listing Lines that Match a Pattern

Sometimes it is easier to find some text, if you can get a list of all lines in the buffer that contain the text you are searching for, instead of having to travel to each and every match with an incremental search. Emacs has a function, which is not bound to any key, called occur. To use it, press M-x and type occur and the text which you are searching for. When you finish that, each match is listed in a buffer called *OCCUR*, with one match at every line. If you give this function a numerical prefix (that is, by pressing C-3 before the function) then that many lines of context are shown. In Figure 7.16, an example of the output from occur can be seen.

7

FIGURE 7.16

*Sample output from
C-2 M-x occur RET
<h3> RET.*

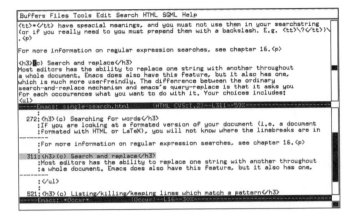

The text you insert in the minibuffer is interpreted as a regular expression. For simple search strings, this doesn't affect you, but you should be careful when you use symbols such as *, ., and so on.

The screen is split in two—in the upper part your original buffer is shown, and in the lower part, the special occur buffer is shown. If you press Enter or the middle mouse button over one of these matches, Emacs will proceed to this location in your original buffer.

On the CD-ROM included with this book, a library called sams-lib.el exists in the directory usr/share/emacs-lisp/sams. This lets you edit the matches in the occur buffer (which, with this library, is called *ALL*). To go to a match in the original buffer, press C-c C-c. To use this library, insert the following line in your .emacs file:

Killing Lines that Match or Do Not Match a Pattern

In sams-lib.el, there exist two functions for keeping and killing lines that fulfill a regular expression. These functions are called sams-keep-lines and sams-kill-lines, respectively.

The functions work from point to the end of the buffer, so if you want to kill or keep lines that match a regular expression in the whole buffer, you need to go to the beginning of the buffer before you invoke the function.

The functions are, in fact, based on built-in Emacs functions that do the actual deleting of lines, but without a security belt.

When you invoke the functions, they first count the number of lines that match your query and ask whether you are certain that you want to delete this many lines in your buffer. This ensures that you do not delete hundreds of lines by accident without noticing. If you confirm to delete them, the actual deletion takes place.

In a situation where your buffer was originally unmodified, Emacs offers to mark it as unmodified after the deletion (that is, without actually saving to disk) and makes it read-only. This makes it possible to delete thousands of lines in a buffer and view it without the risk of you saving it by habit and, thus, losing all the lines.

Summary

You have now learned enough ways to search for text in one buffer for much of your future work. You have also learned how to replace one text string with another in one file. In Hour 9, you will learn an even more advanced mechanism called regular expression searches. In that hour, you will, of course, also learn what regular expressions are all about. As you might have noticed, several of the commands seen in this hour do, in fact, support regular expressions; therefore, after you read Hour 9, it might be a good idea to return here and review what you have learned.

Sometimes, however, it is not enough to have the capability to search for text in one buffer. You might, for example, want to find a definition of a function that might be in one of several files, or you might want to find a document where you wrote about a given topic. Hour 8 teaches you many of the ways you can search for text spread over several files.

Q&A

Q What is the difference between word search and incremental search?

A In incremental search, you start your search right away. This is not the case in word search; in word search, the matches are limited to the word boundaries.

Q What command do you use to start query-replace when replacing one string with another?

A Press M-%.

Exercises

1. Search for the text ar in the text from the examples, and count the number of times it matches.

2. Search once again for the text ar, but this time use word search. Why doesn't it match any text?

3. Search for the text som using word search. Why doesn't it match the word some?

4. Read in your .emacs file and find all the locations where you set a variable. (This is the text starting in setq.)

5. List all the locations where you set variables using occur.

6. Type all the different combinations of the word *foo* (that is, *foo*, *Foo*, *fOo*, and so on). Then search for *foo* and investigate how the cases matter.

HOUR 8

Searching for Text in Multiple Files

It is often necessary to search for text in several buffers. Examples of this include

- Searching for a definition of a function when programming.
- Searching for a tag for a given reference when writing LaTeX documents.
- Searching for the location where you wrote that Linux was interesting.

Searching can be split in two categories:

- In the first category, you have a set of files in which you might search for things several times. This might include the C files of the program you are working on right now, the LaTeX files of your upcoming book, and so on.
- In the other category, you have a set of files in which it is likely that you won't be searching for awhile—or at least it is very likely that the set will have changed before you search in it again. This can include the standard C `include` files, all the files in your home directory and below, and so on.

If this split-up seems unclear to you, read on. When you have read the next two sections, you will know exactly which tool to use in a given situation. Later in this hour, you will study two different mechanisms for making bookmarks in files—bookmarks make it easy to return to specific locations. The difference between the methods is that in the first one, the bookmarks are saved between Emacs sessions, whereas in the other, they are not.

Searching for a Definition in a Set of Files

When searching for text in several files, you have two choices:

- You can spend time initially to index the files, which will speed up later searching.
- You can skip the initial indexing. Every search will then be slower than if you had indexed the files.

This section describes the method where the files are indexed.

Creating a TAGS File

The indexing method used by Emacs is to divide the text into two categories—*definitions* and *ordinary text*.

Definitions are indexed and written to a file called the *TAGS file* (its name is TAGS), whereas ordinary text is not indexed. The meaning of *definitions* depends on the files involved. In programming languages such as C, Java, and Perl, *definition* means the definition of functions, global variables, and, eventually, #define TAGS. In LaTeX files, *definition* means the definition of things such as \chapter, \section, and \label.

Searching for a definition is very fast, but searching for a nondefinition is no faster than an ordinary search without an index, because of the index. It has one advantage still, which is that the set of files must only be determined once, namely at the time when the index is created.

To create an index, you must use the command etags, which comes with Emacs. If your file has a format and an extension that are known by etags, the following command should work for you:

```
etags files
```

Thus to create an index for all the C files in a directory, simply write etags *.c at your command prompt.

The etags program is usually included in the Emacs installation directory under BIN, but in the UNIX world SysArdm routinely moves binaries to /usr/local/bin.

Whenever you change some of the definitions, you should rerun `etags` if you want subsequent TAGS searches to know about the change.

8

In Table 8.1, you can see the file formats that `etags` recognizes. If you have a file in a known format but with the wrong extension, you can use the `-l` option. For example, if you give your prolog files the extension `.pro` instead of `.prolog`, you can index them with the command `etags -l prolog *.pro`.

TABLE 8.1 FILE FORMATS KNOWN BY etags PROGRAM

File Format	Extensions
asm	`.a, .asm, .def, .inc, .ins, .s, .sa, .src`
C	`.c, .h*, .cs, .hs`
C++	`.C, .H, .c++, .cc, .cpp, .cxx, .h++, .hh, .hpp, .hxx, .M, .pdb`
COBOL	`.COB, .cob`
erlang	`.erl, .hrl`
FORTRAN	`.F, .f, .f90, .for`
Java	`.java`
LISP	`.cl, .clisp, .el, .l, .lisp, .lsp, .ml`
Pascal	`.p, .pas`
Perl	`.pl, .pm`
PostScript	`.ps`
proc	`.pc, .m, .lm`
Prolog	`.prolog`
Python	`.py`
Scheme	`.SCM, .SM, .oak, .sch, .scheme, .scm, .sm, .ss, .t`
TeX	`.TeX, .bib, .clo, .cls, .ltx, .sty, .tex`
yacc	`.y, .ym`

If, on the other hand, you have files in a format that is unknown to `etags`, you can still use it, but you have to supply a regular expression, which tells it what should be regarded as definitions. If you come upon this situation you should consult the manual page for `etags`. Or consult the info pages for Emacs and search for TAGS. Two examples are given here.

To index files written for TCL, use the following command:

```
etags -l none --regex='/proc[ \t]+\([^ \t]+\)/\1/' files
```

To index files written for HTML, use the following command:

```
etags -l none --regex='/.*/\1/' --regex='/.*\([^<]+\)/\1/' files
```

Searching Using TAGS

As mentioned in the previous section, Emacs has two commands for searching using TAGS files:

- One for searching for definitions
- One for an ordinary search over several files

> To be completely honest, the search is, in fact, a regular expression search. As mentioned before, however, with ordinary search strings (that is, strings without characters such as *, ?, [,], and \), this fact will not affect you.

Searching for Definitions

When you program, you often need to find a function definition for the function at point. This task teaches you how to do that using the TAGS facilities. Follow these steps:

Create a TAGS file for the files of the given program, as described in the previous section. Place point at the function name for which you would like to see the definition and press M-. (find-tag) (see Figure 8.1).

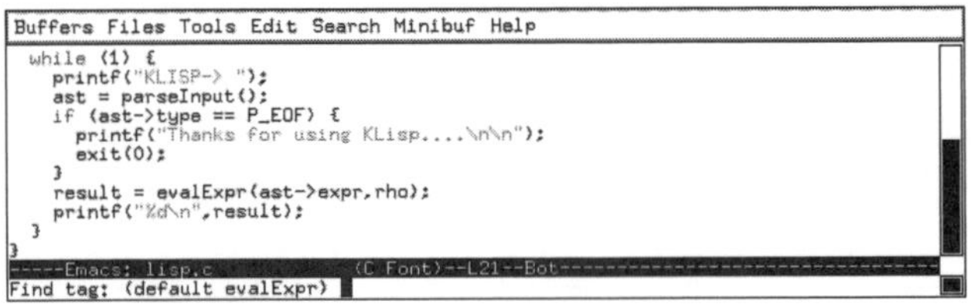

FIGURE 8.1

Press M-. to search for a definition. Emacs will ask for the name of the definition and suggest the word located at point as the default.

```
Buffers Files Tools Edit Search Minibuf Help
  while (1) {
    printf("KLISP-> ");
    ast = parseInput();
    if (ast->type == P_EOF) {
      printf("Thanks for using KLisp....\n\n");
      exit(0);
    }
    result = evalExpr(ast->expr,rho);
    printf("%d\n",result);
  }
}
-----Emacs: lisp.c          (C Font)--L21--Bot------------------
Find tag: (default evalExpr)
```

2. Emacs will now suggest the function at which point is located. If this is the function you are searching for, simply press Enter. Otherwise, type the name of the function and press Enter.

In this buffer you can use M-p and M-n to travel through the list of names you have searched for earlier.

3. If this is the first time in this Emacs session that you use a command related to the TAGS mechanism, Emacs will ask you for a TAGS file, which defaults to a file named TAGS in the same directory from which you asked for a TAGS search (see Figure 8.2).

FIGURE 8.2

Emacs asks for a file with the TAGS definitions. As the default, it suggests the file named TAGS *in the buffer's current working directory.*

```
Buffers Files Tools Edit Search Minibuf Help
 while (1) {
   printf("KLISP-> ");
   ast = parseInput();
   if (ast->type == P_EOF) {
     printf("Thanks for using KLisp...\n\n");
     exit(0);
   }
   result = evalExpr(ast->expr,rho);
   printf("%d\n",result);
 }
}
-----Emacs: lisp.c          (C Font)--L21--Bot------------------
Visit tags table: (default TAGS) "/KLisp/
```

If a TAGS file exists in the same directory as your current file, XEmacs does not ask for a file; instead, it uses the current TAGS file. If this isn't the file you intend to use, you can change it using the command visit-tags-table.

You can, if you want, attach M-x in front of accessible Emacs commands (such as the one in the preceding Caution) that are not bound to keys.

When you tell Emacs which TAGS file to use, it searches for the definition, opens the file that contains the definition in your current window, and jumps to the line with the definition (see Figure 8.3).

FIGURE 8.3

When you tell Emacs which definition to jump to, it replaces your current buffer with this buffer. That is, it loads the new buffer into your current window.

```
Buffers Files Tools Edit Search INDEX C Help
#include "lisp.h"

/*****************************************************/
/*                  Expression                      */
/*****************************************************/
int evalExpr(expr *expr, Map *rho) {
  enum AST_TYPES type = expr->type;
  char *key;

  switch (type) {
  case P_VALUE:
-----Emacs: eval.c          (C Font)--L6--Top-------------------
```

8

▼ Searching for definitions using TAGS files is useful when you are programming and you want to see either the definition of a subfunction or exactly which arguments the function takes. After you find the location, you might want to return to the location where you came from. For that purpose the bookmarks described in the section, "Managing Bookmarks," are very useful.

As mentioned previously, M-. (find-tag) replaces the buffer in the current window with the buffer containing the definition. Two other commands exist that open the file with the definition in another window or another frame. These commands are C-x 4 . (find-tag-other-window) and C-x 5 . (find-tag-other-frame). Note the bindings contain three keys: C-x, either 4 or 5, and finally a period (.).

If you press C-u M-. instead of M-., Emacs searches for another definition that matches your previous search. This can be useful when you are searching for a function that can
▲ be defined in several classes (such as in C++ or Java).

Searching for Nondefinitions

If you are searching for text that is not a definition (for example, the use of a function), you can use the command tags-search, which is not bound to any keys by default. (That might be a good candidate for your function keys, right?) This starts a search through all the files defined in the TAGS file. The search starts from your current location in the given file. When Emacs has found an occurrence, it lets you do whatever editing you want to do at this point. Later (or eventually at once), you can continue your search by pressing M-, (tags-loop-continue)—that is, Meta + comma.

Listing and Completing Definitions

If you have the name of a definition on the tip of your tongue but can't find it, the function tags-apropos might help you. It asks for a regular expression and lists all names of definitions that match this regular expression. If, on the other hand, you are perfectly aware of the name but it is long and might even contain some capitalization, you can use the command complete-tag, which by default is not bound to any keys. Some major modes can, however, bind this to M-TAB. This command searches the TAGS table for a definition of the word located before point and searches for a completion of it using the definitions in the TAGS table.

Search-and-Replace Using TAGS

The main thing that makes the TAGS feature worth learning is its capability to do search-and-replace over several files (without having to start it in each file). The function M-x, tags-query-replace, is the one that does search-and-replace in several files. It is not bound to any key by default in Emacs's standard setup, so it might be a good idea to bind it to a function key. It works much like the ordinary query-replace function described in Hour 7, "Searching for Text in a Buffer." The only difference is that it does search-and-replace in all the files mentioned in the TAGS file. For each match you have the same options as for ordinary search. For more information, see the section "Options when Replacing" in Hour 7.

You should be aware of three things when searching and replacing using TAGS:

- The function of the ^ key (go back to previous replacements) is limited to the current file. That means that if you replace a number of matches in file A, and advance to file B, you cannot go back to matches in file A. Don't panic—this is not a big issue, because you can always change the buffer, and undo with C-_ (that's Control + underscore).

- The function of the ! key (replace the rest of the matches) is limited only to the current buffer. That means that pressing ! will not replace unconditionally in the rest of the buffers, but only in the rest of the current buffer.

- If you abort a tags-query-replace operation, you can continue it from your current position by pressing M-, (tags-loop-continue). This is very useful if you, for example, have a file that you want to skip during tags-query-replace.

Search-and-replace using TAGS has nothing to do with the definitions in the files, thus you can use it to do search-and-replace in any file that Emacs can read!

You can't use tags-replace if your files are in version control, such as RCS or CVS. Etags doesn't know how to check out files before replacing. If you don't know what version control is, or what RCS, CSSC, or CVS are, don't bother.

Using grep from Within Emacs

If you are used to UNIX, you will most certainly know the two commands called grep and find. grep lists the lines of a file that contain certain text, whereas find lists files that match a pattern. Together, these two commands can search for a given string in all files in a directory structure. Emacs has a command called grep (that is, M-x grep) which interfaces to the grep command. Now that you know about it, forget it please! I told you about it, in case you ever find yourself without igrep and really need to use grep instead. igrep has a much more user-friendly interface than grep. Furthermore, it combines find and grep, which makes it possible to search for files in a directory hierarchy. In the igrep library is a set of different functions:

- fgrep—This grep command searches for fixed string matches (that is, no regular expressions).

- igrep—This is the usual grep command, which searches using regular expressions.

- agrep—This is an approximative grep, that is an ordinary string grep that allows a few errors. For example, it would match *aproximative* when searching for *approximative*.

agrep is not included in the usual grep packages, so it might not be installed at all at your system. It is, however, available from the WWW at http://glimpse.cs.arizona.edu/.

To tell agrep how many errors are allowed, press C-u before pressing M-x agrep. This makes Emacs ask for options to agrep. Here, you must type -2 to tell it to accept two errors, for example.

Each of the three functions described previously searches for text in files in one directory. There also exist three functions called fgrep-find, igrep-find, and agrep-find, which work the same as those without the extension -find, but they work recursively in a whole directory structure—that is, files in the current directory and all its subdirectories.

Igrep.el by Kevin Rodgers is part of the XEmacs distribution but not part of the GNU Emacs distribution, so if you use GNU Emacs, you should copy igrep to your lisp directory. (If you use both GNU Emacs and XEmacs you should still copy it to your lisp directory. There is no trouble in using this one instead of the one shipped with XEmacs.) In Appendix A, "Installing Functions and Packages from the CD," there is a description on what you should do to install igrep (including what to put in your .emacs file).

If you are using Windows 95 or 98, you will have to install one of the UNIX tool kits available for Windows, such as the Cygwin tools. There are copies on the CD-ROM. Again, see Appendix A.

Windows NT supports regular expressions somewhat in its program `findstr`, but most UNIX `grep`s are more powerful. `findstr` will do in a pinch if you put the following into your `.emacs` file:

```
(setq grep-command "findstr /n")
```

If you use Bash as your shell, insert the following into your `.emacs`:

```
(setq w32-quote-process-args ?\")
```

But then you won't need to substitute `findstr` for `grep`.

However, neither operating system has a substitute for `find`.

Searching for a Definition in Standard C `include` Files Using `fgrep`

This task will demonstrate the `igrep.el` package by showing how you can search through all the standard C `include` files on your system for a given function. Follow these steps:

1. First you have to locate yourself in the base directory for your `include` files. (If you want to try this example and do not have `include` files installed, you might try it with your home directory and a search string that you want to search for in your files.) To go to this directory, press `C-x C-f` (find-file) and type the name of the directory. This loads the content of the directory into a special buffer. The mode for this buffer is called dired-mode (for *directory editor*) and is described in detail in Hour 16, "Interfacing with the System" (see Figure 8.4).

FIGURE 8.4

In Emacs you can open a directory as easily as you can open a file. This is discussed in detail in Hour 16.

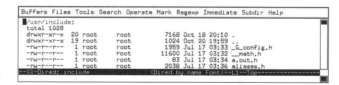

If you already are in the directory in which you want to search, you can skip this step.

▼   2. Now press M-x (fgrep-find). Emacs will ask you for an expression to search for. This is simply the search string when you use `fgrep` (see Figure 8.5).

FIGURE 8.5

Emacs asks for the text to search for.

```
Buffers Files Tools Edit Search Minibuf Help
/usr/include:
total 1028
drwxr-xr-x  20 root     root      7168 Oct 18 20:10 .
drwxr-xr-x  19 root     root      1024 Oct 20 19:59 ..
-rw-r--r--   1 root     root      1959 Jul 17 03:33 _G_config.h
-rw-r--r--   1 root     root     11600 Jul 17 03:32 __math.h
-rw-r--r--   1 root     root        83 Jul 17 03:34 a.out.h
-rw-r--r--   1 root     root      2038 Jul 17 03:36 aliases.h
--%%-Dired: include          (Dired by name)--L1--Top--------
[find] Fgrep   Expression: memmove
```

3. Finally Emacs wants to know which files to search for the string in. By default it suggests *, which means all files. This is simply a pattern, known from the shell. So here you can tell it to search only in files ending in .h by typing *.h (see Figure 8.6).

FIGURE 8.6

Emacs asks for a pattern describing the files in which it should search.

```
Buffers Files Tools Edit Search Minibuf Help
/usr/include:
total 1028
drwxr-xr-x  20 root     root      7168 Oct 18 20:10 .
drwxr-xr-x  19 root     root      1024 Oct 20 19:59 ..
-rw-r--r--   1 root     root      1959 Jul 17 03:33 _G_config.h
-rw-r--r--   1 root     root     11600 Jul 17 03:32 __math.h
-rw-r--r--   1 root     root        83 Jul 17 03:34 a.out.h
-rw-r--r--   1 root     root      2038 Jul 17 03:36 aliases.h
--%%-Dired: include          (Dired by name Font)--L1--Top----
[find] grep   File(s) (default *): *.h
```

Now Emacs searches recursively for matches, splits the window in two, and, in the lower part, displays the matches, one line for each match (see Figure 8.7).

▼

FIGURE 8.7

When Emacs has found some matches, it splits the window and shows the matches in one of the panes.

The buffer showing the matches   The original buffer

The command used to find the match

The first match

The filename for the match

The line with the match   The content of the matched line

▼ The first three lines are simply the command used to find the matches. The actual matches start on the third line, which tells you which file the match is located in and which line it is located on and shows you the line.

I have resized the window for your eyes only. Emacs doesn't resize itself.

4. Now you can open the files with the matches and go to the line with the match, either by clicking the middle mouse button on the match or by moving point to the match and pressing Enter (see Figure 8.8).

FIGURE 8.8

Pressing Enter on one of the matches makes Emacs show this match in the other window and jump to the given line.

```
Buffers Files Tools Edit Search INDEX C Help
#define memcpy(t, f, n) \
(__builtin_constant_p(n) ? \
 __constant_memcpy((t),(f),(n)) : \
 __memcpy((t),(f),(n)))

#define __HAVE_ARCH_MEMMOVE
extern inline void * memmove(void * dest,const void * src, size_t n)
{
if (dest<src)
__asm__ __volatile__(
            "cld\n\t"
            "rep\n\t"
--%%-Emacs: string.h<2>          (C)--L452--72%-------------
./asm/string.h:452:extern inline void * memmove(void * dest,const void * src, si\
ze_t n)
./linux/string.h:32:extern void * memmove(void *,const void *,__kernel_size_t);
./g++/std/straits.h:129:     { return (char_type*) memmove (s1, s2, n); }
./g++/stl_algobase.h:147:  memmove(result, first, sizeof(T) * (last - first));
./g++/stl_algobase.h:184:  memmove(result, first, last - first);
./g++/stl_algobase.h:190:  memmove(result, first, sizeof(wchar_t) * (last - firs\
t));
./g++/stl_algobase.h:219:  memmove(result - N, first, sizeof(T) * N);
./g++/stl_uninitialized.h:78:  memmove(result, first, last - first);
./g++/stl_uninitialized.h:84:  memmove(result, first, sizeof(wchar_t) * (last - \
first));
./string.h:41:extern __ptr_t memmove __P ((__ptr_t __dest, __const __ptr_t __src\
./string.h:186:/* Copy N bytes of SRC to DEST (like memmove, but args reversed).\
-----Emacs: *igrep*          (igrep:exit [0])--L4--21%-------------
```

If you have the feeling of déjà vu now, it might simply be because the interface that igrep uses is the same interface used by occur, which is described in Hour 7. In fact, ▲ this interface is used a lot of places in Emacs.

If you press M-u once before you press M-x fgrep, Emacs will ask you for options to give to fgrep. You can consult the manual page for fgrep for information about these options. There are two useful options, namely -i, which makes the searches not case sensitive, and -# (where # should be replaced with a number), which tells grep to display a number of context lines.

Unfortunately, the options to agrep are not compatible with the options to, for example, fgrep. This means that -# does not tell how many lines of context to use but instead how many errors to accept. It does in fact seem that agrep doesn't support context lines.

In Figure 8.9, you can see an example of the output where two context lines are displayed.

FIGURE 8.9

Output from igrep, *where two lines of context are shown.*

Lines before the match

The line with the match

Lines after the match

Separator to indicate the beginning of the next match

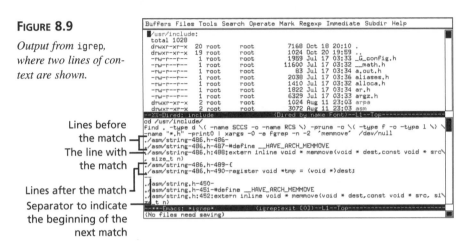

Keeping Points in Buffers for Several Sessions (Bookmarks)

You might have several locations you are looking at often in your computer!

Examples of these might include

- The end of your .emacs file
- The info page on Emacs
- The directory with your current project (using the dired-mode described in Hour 16)
- The /etc/passwd files (edited as root from your current login)
- The ftp directory with GNU software

To help you easily access these locations, Emacs has a bookmarks feature that is similar to bookmarks in World Wide Web browsers. The two basic commands used with bookmarks are setting a bookmark that is bound to C-x r m (bookmark-set) and jumping to a bookmark which is bound to C-x r b (bookmark-jump). You might think that these bookmark commands aren't very useful when they are bound to such difficult-to-remember keys, but they are, and I strongly suggest that you bind these commands to functions keys.

Setting the bookmark is simple: Go to the location where you want to set the bookmark and press C-x r m (bookmark-set). Emacs will then ask you for a name for the bookmark. This name is for your use when you later want to return to the bookmark. Besides recording the filename of the bookmark, Emacs also records its location in the file. This recording includes text before and after the bookmark, which makes Emacs capable of finding the location even though the buffer might have changed. When you want to jump to a bookmark, press C-x r b (bookmark-jump). Emacs then, in the minibuffer, asks you for the name of the bookmark you want to jump to. In the minibuffer you can use the tabulator key to complete the bookmark name.

> If you have many bookmarks, you might be interested in organizing these in a menu structure. This is, unfortunately, not possible, but you can use the fact that completion is available when naming the bookmark to jump to. Thus you might name your bookmark book/Chapter 1/search to indicate a menu structure consisting of book at the outer level, Chapter 1 as a subentry to book, and search as a subentry to Chapter 1.

Managing Bookmarks

In addition to creating and jumping to bookmarks, you might also want to rename, list, annotate, and delete bookmarks. All these actions can be handled in a special buffer, which contains a list of all the bookmarks. To get to this list press M-x (list-bookmarks). This will bring up a buffer similar to the one shown in Figure 8.10.

FIGURE 8.10

The list of bookmarks is obtained by pressing M-x *(list-bookmarks).*

```
 Buffers Files Tools Edit Search Help
% Bookmark
- --------
■ Interactive Codes        /usr/info/elisp
  chapters                 ~/bog/chapters/
  gnu emacs - 19           /usr/info/emacs-19/emacs
  gnu emacs - 20           /usr/info/emacs-20/emacs
  lisp-dir                 /usr/share/emacs/19.34/lisp/
  passwd                   /root@localhost:/etc/passwd
  root                     /root@localhost:/
  xemacs - 19              /usr/info/xemacs-19.16/xemacs.info
  xemacs - 20              /usr/info/xemacs-20.4/xemacs.info
--%*-Emacs: *Bookmark List*    (Bookmark Menu)--L3--All------------------
```

This is not an ordinary buffer for editing but a buffer for managing your bookmarks; thus, the bookmark managing functions are bound to single keys. This is like the buffer for managing the list of buffers described in Hour 6, "Editing Several Files at Once." If you press ?, the window splits in two and in one of the windows, the available commands are listed. There are many commands regarding jumping to bookmarks.

By pressing the number 1, you jump to the bookmark on the current line. To delete some bookmarks, move to each of the lines describing the bookmarks and press d (for *delete*). A capital *D* will show in the left-most column indicating that the bookmarks have been marked for deletion. To actually delete the marked bookmarks, press x (for *execute*). If you change your mind before you have pressed x, you can unmark the bookmark by pressing u (for *undelete*). To rename a bookmark, press r on the line with the bookmark (for *rename*). Emacs will ask, in the minibuffer, for the new name of the bookmark. By pressing M-p you can access the original name for the bookmark.

Saving Bookmarks

Bookmarks are, by default, saved to the file $HOME/.emacs.bmk. The default name can, of course, be changed. (See the info pages on Emacs for a description on how to do this, if you really need to.) This should however not be necessary. The bookmarks are saved to the file when Emacs exits. This might not be good enough for you if you have the habit of exiting your window manager without exiting Emacs first. To make Emacs save your bookmarks to a file every time you change, delete, or add a bookmark, insert the following line into your .emacs file:

```
(setq bookmark-save-flag 1)
```

You should really do that, because this spares you a lot of trouble. Saving the bookmarks takes no time unless you have hundreds of them.

Keeping Points in Buffers for the Current Session

When you use TAGS to jump to definitions, you might often want to go back to the location where you came from. You can use bookmarks to locate the place you came from, but bookmarks are not made for this job, so they are very cumbersome to use for this. An alternative solution exists in sams-lib .

sams-lib offers two functions: sams-cm-save-point to make or delete a mark to get back to, and sams-cm-rotate to jump to the next mark. You might have several marks set around in several buffers, which you can jump to using these functions. When you invoke the function sams-cm-save-point, you insert a new mark in the ring of marks unless you are located on one of the marks; in that case, you will instead remove the mark from the ring of marks.

When you invoke the function sams-cm-rotate, Emacs jumps to the most recent mark that's been set or visited. If you invoke the function once more, Emacs will jump to the previously set mark, and so on.

The set of marks is called a ring, because Emacs jumps to the most recently set mark if you invoke sams-cm-rotate when you are at the oldest mark. To get a feel for how this jumping works, create a buffer with four lines, set a mark on each line, and then invoke the function M-x sams-cm-rotate several times to see how it jumps around.

Although the word *marks* is used several times in the preceding paragraph, these marks have nothing to do whatsoever with the mark that is used to describe the region.

8

Summary

Now you have learned to search through several buffers at once using different tools, each one perfect for its specific task: Tags searching makes it easy to jump from match to match, whereas `igrep.el` makes it easy to get an overview of matches in several buffers. Furthermore, TAGS searches make it easy to jump to the definition of a function, for example.

In this hour, you have also learned two different mechanisms for setting marks in buffers, which you can return to later. One mechanism is for multisessions; the other isn't. In one of the methods you must name your marks, although this is unnecessary in the other.

Q&A

Q The TAGS facility is only for programmers, not for people who use Emacs to write letters, HTML documents, or LaTeX files, right?

A *Wrong!* The TAGS facility is indeed very useful for programmers, but it is also a general search tool for multiple files. With `grep` you can get a list of all occurrences of specific text, but the TAGS facility is the optimal tool to jump from occurrence to occurrence. Furthermore, you need the TAGS facility to do search-and-replace in several files in one go. The alternative is to open the files one at a time, and to perform ordinary search-and-replace in each of them.

Q I still don't see what the difference between TAGS and `igrep` is; could you please make that clear to me?

A `igrep` shows you the lines that match in a separate buffer, whereas TAGS let you travel from match to match. TAGS offers search-and-replace, whereas `igrep` doesn't. When you use TAGS, you need to create a TAGS file that you don't need when using `igrep`.

Q When I use one of the grep commands, Emacs complains about not being able to find the grep command.

A You might not have the command installed. If you are using UNIX, you can find the grep package at ftp://SunSITE.doc.ic.ac.uk/gnu/. If you are using Windows, please refer the Windows Note in the section about grep. Another reason might be that you do not have the grep command in your search path. A common mistake is that you start Emacs from your window manager and that its search path is not set up correctly.

Q Can I set bookmarks in every kind of buffer?

A No. You can set bookmarks only in buffers that visit files. (Info files are included, because they are in fact just visiting files—in a smart way.) You can't set them in buffers that are generated by some command. As a rule of thumb, buffers that start and end with a star cannot have bookmarks set in them.

Exercises

1. Make a TAGS file for one of your directories with HTML documents, C, C++, or Java files and

    a. Jump around in it using M-.—that is, search for definitions in it.

    b. When jumping from *use* to *definition*, you might want to set marks using the commands from sam-lib.el so you can get back to the *use* when you are finished reading the *definition*. Try it!

    c. When you have made a backup of your files, try to replace all the occurrences of some text in all the files using tags-query-replace.

2. Go to the top of your home directory and search through all your files (recursively) for specific text (for example, Emacs).

3. Create a bookmark at the end of your .emacs file, so you can get to this location fast.

HOUR 9

Regular Expressions

In the shell (also know as the commands prompt) you often use *wildcards* (also known as *patterns*). Wildcards are a way of specifying several files in an easy way. Examples of this include

- *—Lists all files. You can, for example, execute the command `rm *` to erase all your files. (No, don't try it!)
- *.el—Lists all files ending in .el.
- file{A,B,C}—Matches fileA, fileB, and fileC.

Patterns have some limitations, which made the people behind Emacs choose to use the more-powerful regular expressions. These limitations are not that important in the shell, but they are when you search for text in a buffer, for example. Things which you can't do with patterns but you can do with regular expressions include

- Searching for the phrase *this word*, where the space in between the two words can be a number of ordinary spaces, tabs, or newlines.
- Searching for the word *search* somewhere on the line, but not the word *research*.
- Matching text for later reference.

Regular Expression Crash Course

In Hours 7, "Searching for Text in a Buffer," and 8, "Searching for Text in Multiple Files," you already saw examples where Emacs wants a regular expression and, believe me, you will see numerous examples in the hours to come. In most cases, however, you only need a very limited subset of the power of regular expressions. Therefore Table 9.1 lists some expressions written both as patterns and as regular expressions. This should give you enough information to read the hours to come.

TABLE 9.1   CONVERSION FROM PATTERNS TO REGULAR EXPRESSION

Pattern	Regular Expression	Comments
file42	file42	This pattern does not contain any of the special characters listed in this table.
file.txt	file\.txt	The dot is one of the special characters; therefore, it must be prefixed with a backslash.
*.txt	.*\.txt	The star represents a number of characters in the pattern. It is replaced with .* in regular expressions. The dot that separates the star and txt is always special for regular expressions, so it must be prefixed with a backslash.
file?.txt	file.\.txt	A question mark represents a single character in the pattern. It is translated to a dot.
file0[1-6].txt	file0[1-6]\.txt	The pattern represents the text file01.txt, file02.txt...file06.txt.
file{AB,CDE,F}	file\(AB|CDE|F\)	This pattern represents the text fileAB, fileCDE, or fileF.

In regular expressions, the following characters are special: $, ^, ., *, +, ?, [,], and \. To include any of these (without their special meanings) in a regular expression, prepend them with a backslash. Thus, to insert the text abc\tdef? as an ordinary string in a regular expression, use the text abc\\tdef\?.

All the regular expression operators are listed in Table 9.2. You will learn more about these operators throughout this hour. So keep reading.

TABLE 9.2   REGULAR EXPRESSION SYMBOLS

Symbol	Meaning
Repeaters	
*	Repeats the previous regular expression any number of times (including zero times).
+	Repeats the previous regular expression any number of times (at least one time).
?	The previous regular expression matches zero or one time.
Grouping / Character Groups	
\(...\)	Groups the text for later reference or to overcome precedence problems.
[...]	Matches any of the characters within the group. (But only one character; if you need to match a number, combine this with *, +, or ?.)
[^...]	Matches any character not in this group.
Positions	
^	Matches the beginning of the line or string.
$	Matches the end of line or string.
\<	Matches the beginning of a word.
\>	Matches the end of a word.
Special Characters	
.	Matches any character.
\w	Matches any character from a word (in most cases, equal to [0-9 a-z A-Z]).
\W	Matches any character not from a word ([^0-9 a-z A-Z]).

If you are eager to learn how to use Emacs in your work right away, go ahead and skip the rest of this hour. However, make sure to come back before you finish the book so you know how to use expressions.

Regular Expressions—Basics

In the previous section you learned enough about regular expressions to use them as simple patterns. This should be enough in most cases. However at some point you will get into a situation where you need more power. For this sake, here comes the whole story about regular expressions and what you can do with them.

Regular expressions describe characteristics which must be fulfilled when you, for example, search for a string. If this sounds abstract for you, please think about how you would search for words containing exactly eight letters. You would not write down all possible combinations of eight letters and search for them one at a time, would you? I guess not; you would most certainly do something a bit smarter. What you would do is this: *Search for words that have the characteristic that they have eight letters*.

Likewise if you knew that, somewhere in your text, you have a word starting in *the*, you would not do an ordinary search for *the*, because this would match all kind of words that contain the substring *the*, such as *aesthetic*, *farther*, and *smoothed*. No, you would search for words having the characteristic that they start with the letters *the*.

There are a number of characters that have special meanings in regular expressions. These include $, ^, ., *, +, ?, [,], and \. If you want to use one of these characters without its special meaning, you have to prefix it with a backslash. When you prefix a special character with a backslash, you are said to *escape* it. The simplest regular expression is one without any of these special characters (or with the given characters escaped). Therefore the following strings are not special regular expressions (that is, they have no other meaning than text):

`Yes it works!`	This matches the string "Yes it works!" No special characters are in this string.
`Don't Leave`	Again, no special characters.
`100\$\+200\$=\?`	This matches the string `100$+200$=?`. All the special characters ($, +, and ?) have been escaped.
`Enough\.`	This matches the string `Enough.`. The dot, which has a special regular expression meaning, has been escaped.
`\\\$`	This matches the text `\$`. First, the backslash has been escaped. Next, the dollar sign has been escaped, which result in a backslash and a dollar sign.

Repeating Elements

Regular expressions are built using a number of special characters that add special meaning to the string. The first element of these characters is the asterisk (*). This one is not new to you if you know it from the shell, but be warned it is not entirely like the asterisk from the shell.

The asterisk must be used with another regular expression and means repeat the other regular expression a number of times (even zero times). The string a is a regular expression that matches a single a. The regular expression a* matches, therefore, the empty string, the string a, the string aa, the string aaa, and so on.

> The asterisk used in patterns means any characters, whereas the asterisk used in regular expressions means repeat the previous regular expression a number of times. The regular expression .* has the same meaning as a single asterisk in patterns.

Two other special characters exist that are similar to the asterisk:

- +—The plus sign means repeat the previous regular expression a number of times, but at least one time. Thus it is equivalent to the asterisk with the exception that it doesn't match the empty string. Therefor a+ matches a, aa, aaa, and so on, but *not* the empty string.

- ?—The question mark means match the previous regular expression zero or one time. Therefore a? matches the empty string and the string a.

Combining Regular Expressions

Until now, the regular expressions you have seen have been very dull. The reason for this is that you still haven't learned how to combine two regular expressions.

If you have two regular expressions A and B, the concatenated regular expression *AB* means that a given text should match first A then B. If you, for example, have a regular expression a*, this regular expression matches a number of a's, and likewise b* matches a number of b's. Therefore a*b* would match every string which starts with any number of a's, and ends in any number of b's, with nothing in between: ab, aaa, bbb, aabbbbbb, and so on.

You can likewise build a regular expression that matches either A or B, namely the expression A\¦B (that is the regular expression A concatenated with a backslash, and a pipe symbol concatenated with the regular expression B). The regular expression a*\¦b* matches therefore a number of a's or a number of b's but not mixed: a, b, aa, bb, and so on.

You might now very well ask, How do I create a regular expression that matches a number of a's and b's mixed together, as in the example baaabbaabb? The regular expression a\¦b matches an a or a b. Does a\¦b* match a number of a's mixed with b's, then? If you think so, please let me know what a regular expression, which matches one a or a number of b's look like. (You will most likely suggest the same regular expression, namely a\¦b*.)

If you are a computer geek you should immediately recognize the preceding problem as a matter of precedence. If on the other hand you are not a computer geek, I can tell you that the preceding problem is equivalent to the problem of telling whether the mathematical expression 3 + 4 * 5 gives the result 23 or 35 (The result is 23!). In mathematics the rule is that you must evaluate * before you evaluate +. Thus a subresult in the expression preceding is 3 + 20 (and not 7 * 5). If you are bad at remembering which one is evaluated first, you can always use parentheses to indicate your intention. Thus 3 + 4 * 5 is equal to 3 + (4 * 5). Likewise in regular expressions, you can use parentheses to indicate which group a given operator works on. Grouping in regular expressions is done by surrounding the group with \(and \).

> To avoid using too many backslashes and having too many special symbols, grouping using parentheses in regular expressions is done using \(...\) instead of (...) as in math. Had this not been the case, then you would have the parentheses as special symbols too.

The regular expression \(a\¦b\)*, therefore, means a number of elements that can be matched by the regular expression a\¦b.

It is beyond the scope of this book to tell you the whole truth about the rules for when it is necessary to use parentheses and when it is not. A general rule of thumb that you can use is that *, +, and ? need their arguments enclosed in parentheses unless the argument is a single letter. Thus it is not necessary to use parentheses in a*, but if you need to match a number of abc's—that is, abc, abcabc, abcabcabc, and so on—you need parentheses, as in the regular expression \(abc\)+. If it said abc+, it would mean an a, a b, and one or more c's.

Hey! Now you have in fact learned a lot about regular expressions! Before I continue, Figures 9.1 and 9.2 show you a few regular expressions together with explanations, so you can get a feel for it.

FIGURE 9.1

A regular expression that can be used to match section headings in LaTeX.

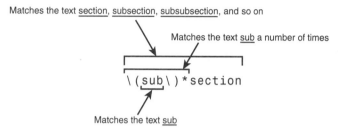

Matches the text <u>section</u>, <u>subsection</u>, <u>subsubsection</u>, and so on

Matches the text <u>sub</u> a number of times

`\(sub\)*section`

Matches the text <u>sub</u>

FIGURE 9.2

A regular expression that can be used to match letters sent to or from a .com email address.

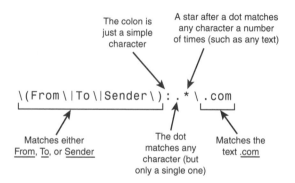

The colon is just a simple character

A star after a dot matches any character a number of times (such as any text)

`\(From\|To\|Sender\):.*\.com`

Matches either <u>From</u>, <u>To</u>, or <u>Sender</u>

The dot matches any character (but only a single one)

Matches the text <u>.com</u>

All in all, the regular expression in Figure 9.2 matches any text starting with `From:`, `To:`, or `Sender:`, and ending in `.com`, with any text in between.

> You will later learn how you can use part of a match in replacement text. The text you would use could, for example, be the text matched by .* in Figure 9.2.

Character Groups

There is one final construct you have to learn before you know every possible way of constructing text for matches. That is the characters group.

If you know the `[...]` construct from the shell, you are lucky, because that is exactly the same! If you don't, keep on reading.

Character groups is a way of defining a group of possible characters. The simplest character group is one where you list a number of characters. An example of this is `[abcde]`. This group matches any of the characters a, b, c, d, or e.

This does not add more power to regular expressions because you simply could have written this as \(a\¦b\¦c\¦d\¦e\). It is, however, more convenient.

Within character groups, you can also define a range of characters, such as [0-9], that match a single digit. Multiple ranges can be specified and mixed with single letters such as [a-zA-Z_], which matches any letter or an underscore.

Character groups can be negated; that is, you can specify a range that it might not match. To do this, include a caret as the first character after the opening bracket. An example of this is [^a-zA-Z_], which matches any character that is neither a letter nor an underscore.

To use a caret in the group as a character to match, put it somewhere that is not the first position. To include a dash in the list, put it before the closing bracket. Finally, to include an ending square bracket, put it next to the opening one, such as []A-Z], which matches either a closing bracket or a capitalized letter.

The regular expression in Figure 9.3 matches an assignment (or at least part of one) in Pascal. The focus here is that variables in Pascal can include any letter including underscores and numbers, with the exception that a letter must be the first character of the word.

FIGURE 9.3

A regular expression that matches assignments in Pascal.

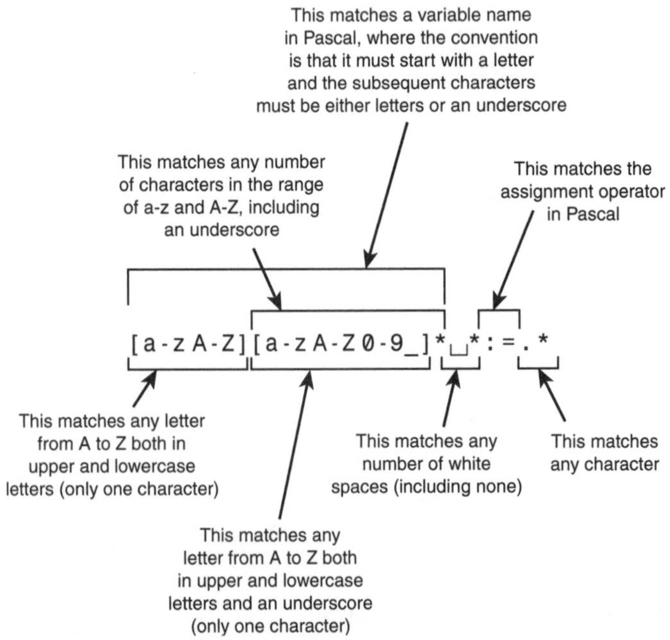

This matches a variable name in Pascal, where the convention is that it must start with a letter and the subsequent characters must be either letters or an underscore

This matches any number of characters in the range of a-z and A-Z, including an underscore

This matches the assignment operator in Pascal

```
[a-zA-Z][a-zA-Z0-9_]*␣*:=.*
```

This matches any letter from A to Z both in upper and lowercase letters (only one character)

This matches any number of white spaces (including none)

This matches any character

This matches any letter from A to Z both in upper and lowercase letters and an underscore (only one character)

Matching Positions

So far the regular expressions have been concerned with matching text, but you are also often interested in specifying an anchor for this text one way or another. The anchors include

- Anchoring to the word boundary.
- Anchoring to the beginning or end of the line or string matched.

Some functions that use regular expressions match the regular expression on a string, whereas others match regular expression on part of a buffer. Matching a header field from an email letter can be an example of the first kind, whereas regular-expression search is an example of the second kind.

The characters ^ and $ anchor the rest of the regular expression, respectively, to the beginning or the end of the string being matched or, in case the operation works on a buffer, to line-start or line-end.

Thus the regular expression ^a*$ matches a string only if the string contains only a's. If it is used in regular-expression-search, it matches only lines that contain only a's (or, of course, the empty line).

There also are two other regular expressions that match a location, namely \< and \>, that matches, respectively, the beginning of a word or the end of a word. A letter of a word is, in this context, defined as the regular expression [a-zA-Z0-9] or, in other words, ordinary letters from the alphabet and a digit.

The regular expression \<search matches any word that starts with *search*, such as search, searching, and searches. The regular expression search\> matches any words that end in *search*, such as search and research.

> The difference between ^ and \< is that ^ forces the match to start at the beginning of the line, whereas \< forces the match to start at the beginning of a word. The same is true for $ and >.

Finally there are two expressions that match, respectively, a single word character or a single nonword character. These are \w for word characters and \W for nonword characters. These regular expressions are equal to [a-zA-Z0-9] and [^a-zA-Z0-9], respectively.

Regular Expression in Your `.emacs` File

Regular expressions can also be used to configure options. An example is the variable auto-mode-alist, which describes which major mode to load depending on the filename. The filename is described using a regular expression. These configurations are often located in your `.emacs` file.

If you insert a regular expression into your `.emacs` file, or if you configure one using the customize library described in Hour 10, "The Emacs Help System and Configuration System," you need to escape all the backslashes. If you, for example, want to use the regular expression `^\.emacs$` to uniquely describe the file `.emacs`, the regular expression that you must use in the `.emacs` file is `^\\.emacs$`.

 An alternative to literally inserting the regular expression into your `.emacs` file is to use the `sregex.el` library located on the CD. This library lets you write your regular expression in a more readable, but cumbersome, way.

Regular Expression Searches

You have now learned everything about matching text with regular expressions, so now look at how the regular expression search mechanisms in Emacs actually work.

There are two functions for regular expression searches in Emacs. An incremental one and an nonincremental one. The incremental one is bound to `C-s-s` (isearch-forward-regexp), and the nonincremental one is bound to `C-s-s RET`.

There is nothing special about these two functions except that they use regular expression in the search string. There is, however, one feature in incremental regular expression searches that you must be aware of. When you search incrementally, Emacs moves forward to a location that matches your search. (This is known behavior from ordinary incremental searches). In regular expression incremental searches Emacs can, however, suddenly move back, if there is an earlier location in the buffer which matches the text.

Moving Backward in a Regular Expression Incremental Search

This task shows you how a regular expression incremental search can match some text that is prior to the current match. Follow these steps:

1. Go to the beginning of the buffer and press `M-C-s` (isearch-forward-regexp). This starts a regular expression incremental search. Now type `text`. This makes Emacs move forward to the first match of this word (see Figure 9.4).

2. Now continue the regular expression by typing `\|`. This makes Emacs move back to the beginning of the search, because it concludes that whatever you type after the `\|` might match text from the beginning (see Figure 9.5).

▼

FIGURE 9.4

Searching for text makes Emacs move to this location.

Search started here

3. Finally type ot. Emacs moves to the first word, which matches the regular expression text\¦ot (see Figure 9.6). This point is in fact prior to the match text, which it moved to before you typed the alternative character in the regular expression.

▲

FIGURE 9.5

Appending \¦ to the regular expression text makes Emacs move backward, because anything can be appended to the string that can match from the beginning of the search.

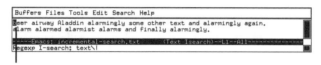

Search started here

FIGURE 9.6

Typing ot makes Emacs search forward for the first occurrences of text or ot. This happens to be before the first location Emacs found in Figure 9.4.

Search started here   The first match of the text text\¦ot.

If you press C-s while you are typing text for the regular expression search, Emacs moves to the next location that matches the regular expression typed so far, which is similar to its behavior in ordinary incremental searches. This has the side effect, however, that the point where you type C-s is marked as the start of the search. This affects the matches found if you later press \¦ (that is, insert an alternative).

An Alternative to Word Search

Hour 7 describes how you can search for words only, making Emacs ignore special symbols such as commas, exclamation marks, and so on. This function also has the feature that it treats any number of spaces, tab spaces, and line breaks as one white space. This had the advantage of enabling you to search for marked-up text that you have a copy of on paper. (That is, you might not know where line breaks are located in the binary version of your document.)

Unfortunately, this solution also has the drawback that it is not incremental. You can search incrementally with a regular expression search if you simply insert \< and \> around the word you are searching for and \W in between.

Yet another alternative is to set the variable search-whitespace-regexp to a regular expression that matches what you would expect to be white space.

This can be obtained by inserting the following into your .emacs file.

```
(setq search-whitespace-regexp "[ \t\r\n]+")
```

With the preceding in your .emacs file you can obtain an incremental search which sees any number of white spaces, tab spaces, and line breaks as a simple white space. Thus you can use C-S-s (isearch-forward-regexp) as an ordinary search, with two exceptions: You need to escape the special regular expression symbols, and you do not need to care about how the space which you see in between the words is actually represented in your text.

 If you get so fond of using regular expression search that you use it more often than ordinary search, you can make it more accessible by shifting the meaning of C-s and C-S-s and, likewise, for C-r and C-S-r. Do this by inserting the following into your .emacs file:

```
;;; shift the meaning of C-s and C-M-s
(global-set-key [(control s)] 'isearch-forward-regexp)
(global-set-key [(control meta s)] 'isearch-forward)
(global-set-key [(control r)] 'isearch-backward-regexp)
(global-set-key [(control meta r)] 'isearch-backward)
```

Regular Expression Search-and-Replace

The function query-replace-regexp is the regular expression equivalent to query-replace described in Hour 7. The difference is that you can use regular expressions in the search string, and you can refer to some part of the text matched in the search string.

To match text for reference in the replacement string, you must group the given text with \(...\). To use the content of a given match, simply count the number of opening braces, and use that number after a backslash. For example, you can use \1, \2, \3, and so on. You do not need to use all such references, as some of them simply might be for handling precedence.

Match Text in a Regular Expression Search String

This task shows you how to match text in the regular expression search string, which you can use in the replacement string. Follow these steps:

1. Press M-x, type query-replace-regexp, and press Enter.

2. Emacs asks for a regular expression to search for.
   Type ^Dear *\(Mr\|Miss\)\. *\(.*\)$. This, for example, matches the string Dear Mr. Jesper Peterson. Press Enter.

3. Emacs now asks for replacement text. Type Hi \2, long time no see. Finally press Enter to search the query replace operation.

▲ Note that in the preceding, the first set of parentheses only served to group the alternative and therefore is not referenced in the replacement text.

9

Summary

You have now learned about regular expressions and different ways to use them. You can be certain that you will forget all this within two or three months if you do not start using them right away. Each time you search for something, or need to replace text, ask yourself, Can I use regular expressions here? It might slow down your work a bit in the beginning, but when you get a feel of it, you will see that regular expressions can make your work safer and faster. As an example, you will not by accident replace authentic with auwhentic when you replace then with when. Replacing several words with others (for example, f1 with file_f1, f2 with file_f2, and so on) can be done with one query-replace-regexp. This makes it much easier to check each replacement in cases where there are many matches that should not be replaced.

Q&A

Q How do I develop a regular expression that is a negation of another? (For example, a regular expression that matches all nonheader lines in HTML?)

A Unfortunately you can't do that in a simple way. This is a limitation of regular expressions.

Q I have developed this huge regular expression for Search-and-Replace, but back references from 10 and up don't work (\10, \11, and so on). Am I doing something wrong?

A Unfortunately, you are allowed to have back reference only from one to nine (that is, \1, \2, ..., \9).

Q Is it possible to develop a regular expression that matches `printf(...)`?

A Yes, that's easy, as long as you can be sure that there is no ending parenthesis within the argument to `printf`. If, on the other hand, there can be parentheses in between the parentheses, it is not possible with regular expressions. See Hour 12, "Using Visible Means," for an alternative way to do this.

Exercises

1. Develop a regular expression that matches lines more than 70 characters long.

2. Develop a regular expression to search for headers in HTML and LaTeX. (In HTML header lines start with `<h1>`, `<h2>`, ...`<h6>`. In LaTeX the following headers exist: `\chapter`, `\section`, `\subsection`, `\subsubsection`, and so on).

3. Show how to do search-and-replace from *<name>* `:=` *<value>* to `set(`*<name>*`,`*<value>*`)`. where *<name>* can be any valid name in Pascal as described earlier in this hour, and *<value>* is any text on the rest of the line.

PART III
Emacs Tools

Hour

HOUR 10

The Emacs Help System and Configuration System

The reference manual to Emacs says the following:

"Emacs is the extensible, customizable, self-documenting display editor."

In this hour you will see why they call it *customizable* and *self-documenting*. *Extensible* refers to the fact that users can develop Lisp libraries themselves to drastically change the behavior of Emacs.

I'll start by looking at the different ways you can get information about Emacs and continue by describing one of the new features in Emacs version 20—namely its customizable library, which makes it easy to customize Emacs in several minor ways.

General Help Facilities in Emacs

Several help functions describe and explain almost every part of Emacs. Emacs can answer the following questions:

- What does a given key do?
- At which key is a given function located?
- What does a given function do?

The following questions might arise in the following situations:

- I would like to bind C-x C-k to the function yic-kill-current-buffer. What is currently on that key?
- In the XEmacs Optimize menu is a submenu called Frame Appearance, which has a function called Frame-local font menu. What does it do?!
- You explained that the function edit-kbd-macro is bound to the key C-x C-k, but it seems that my system administrator has bound another function to that key. Can you tell me whether the function edit-kbd-macro is bound to some other key?
- In the help pages I found a function called end-of-buffer-other-window. What exactly does it do?

The key to answering each of these questions is C-h, which is the general prefix for all the help commands. If you press C-h twice in GNU Emacs or three times in XEmacs, a buffer appears with all the help commands. In Figure 10.1, you can see the help buffer from GNU Emacs, and, in Figure 10.2, you can see the one from XEmacs.

FIGURE 10.1

The help buffer from GNU Emacs.

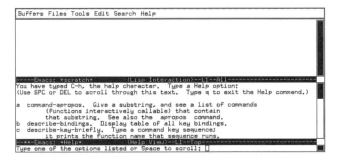

From the help buffer you can click the letter in the left column to execute the function described in the right column. These functions can also be accessed without getting into this menu; simply press C-h and the key from the left column.

FIGURE 10.2

The help buffer from XEmacs.

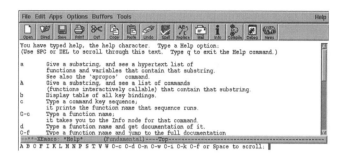

The following sections describe the most useful of these functions. You can read about the rest of them in the help buffer.

What Is Bound to This Key?

If you want to bind something to a key, it might be a very good idea to examine what is already bound to the key. You can do that by pressing C-h k (describe-key). This splits the window in two, and, in one window, the key's function will be named and described. If you are searching only for the name of the function that the key executes, you can press C-h c (describe-key-briefly), which lists its name in the minibuffer and, therefore, does not split any windows. Another use for describe-key is to see what a menu item does. Simply press C-h k (describe-key) and select the item from the menu bar.

In a few cases, however, this doesn't work in Emacs, for reasons too technical to include here.

If you want to know all key bindings active at the moment, press C-h b.

Is There a Function that Does This?

Emacs has hundreds of functions that do almost anything. So if you have a reasonable need, there is a great chance that a function exists that does what you need. Another possibility is that one of the functions might be configured to fulfill your need.

There are two kinds of functions:

- Those that are intended to be used right from Emacs
- Those that are intended to be used when programming Lisp

Invoke the first kind by pressing the keys they are bound to, if any, or by pressing M-x, and then typing the name. The latter are not accessible from the keyboard. (Actually, they are, but you haven't learned it yet. See Hour 22, "Learning Lisp Basics," for a description on how to use these.)

In Emacs is a function called apropos-command, bound to C-h a in GNU Emacs and C-h A in XEmacs. With this command you can search for other commands and user-definable variables. In XEmacs, however, you will seldom use this command, because a much smarter one exists that will be described shortly. To search for commands only, press C-h a for GNU Emacs and C-h A in XEmacs. If you instead want to search for both commands and variables, you must press C-u C-h a in GNU Emacs and C-u C-h A in XEmacs. Emacs then queries you for a name in the minibuffer and lists all commands (and eventually variables) that match this name. An example of the output can be seen in Figure 10.3.

FIGURE 10.3

The output from apropos-command (used in GNU Emacs).

```
 Buffers Files Tools Edit Search Help
█If you move the mouse over text that changes color,
 you can click mouse-2 to get more information.
 In this buffer, type RET to get full documentation.

append-next-kill           M-C-w
   Command: Cause following command, if it kills, to append to previous kill.
backward-kill-paragraph    Type M-x backward-kill-paragraph RET
   Command: Kill back to start of paragraph.
backward-kill-sentence     C-x DEL
   Command: Kill back from point to start of sentence.
backward-kill-sexp         C-M-delete, C-M-backspace
   Command: Kill the sexp (balanced expression) preceding the cursor.
backward-kill-word         M-DEL, C-delete
   Command: Kill characters backward until encountering the end of a word.
clipboard-kill-region      Type M-x clipboard-kill-region RET
   Command: Kill the region, and save it in the X clipboard.
clipboard-kill-ring-save   Type M-x clipboard-kill-ring-save RET
   Command: Copy region to kill ring, and save in the X clipboard.
comint-kill-input          Type M-x comint-kill-input RET
----Emacs: *Apropos*       (Apropos)--L1--Top-----------------------
```

In this buffer, you can see all the functions that match the word *kill*. If you click the middle mouse button on one command, you get the full documentation for the function.

> When you invoke this function, your window is split in two. I've maximized the window shown in Figure 10.3, so that you can see as many help descriptions as possible.

XEmacs has (in my opinion) a much smarter function, called hyper-apropos, bound to the key C-h a. The differences between the ordinary apropos command and this one are that the output is much more compact and the variables and functions are kept in separate. The output from this command can be seen in Figure 10.4.

FIGURE 10.4

Output from hyper-apropos (used in XEmacs).

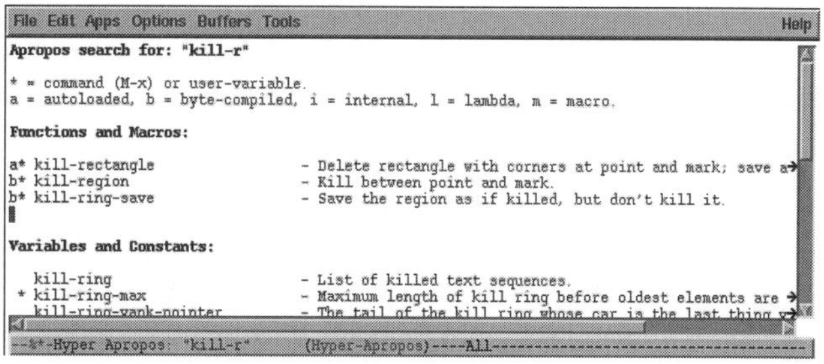

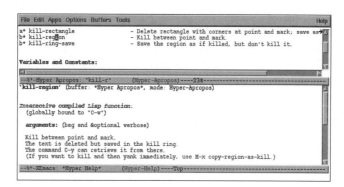

Each match takes up only one line, and the description is lined up, which makes it much easier to read. If an asterisk is located in front of a match, this means that the match is either a user command or a user variable, which means that it is meant for you. Nonuser functions and variables are for use only if you program Lisp. Don't let the other symbols in front of each match bother you (that is, *a*, *b*, *i*, *l*, and *m*). You will learn in Hour 22 what they are about.

If you click the middle mouse button over a match, the window splits in two and a detailed description for the command is shown. An example of this can be seen in Figure 10.5.

FIGURE 10.5

The description of a command using hyper-apropos.

If you have found a variable that seems to do what you want, it's time to set it. If you are using Emacs version 19, I've bad news for you: You'll first learn how to set variables in Hour 22. If, on the other hand, you are using Emacs version 20, be patient a bit more; I'll tell you how to configure variables in the final section of this hour.

Is This Function Bound to Any Keys?

Everywhere in this book where a function is described, I provide its default key binding and its name. The default key binding is listed to make it easier for you to use what is described. Fortunately, or perhaps unfortunately (depending on your point of view), your system administrator can change the bindings by default; or you might have loaded a package that changes it (which you haven't told me about). Therefore, the bindings might not be as described. When you find that the key listed isn't executing the described function, it's time to see whether the function might have been moved to another key. To do this, simply press C-h w (where-is) and type the name of the function that you are searching for. Emacs then tells you on which key this function is located, if any. If you use GNU Emacs, this description includes information about whether the function is in any of the menus.

To make XEmacs also tell you about functions located in the menu, insert the following into your .emacs file:

```
(global-set-key [(control h) (w)] 'sams-where-is)
```

This line alters the behavior of GNU Emacs.

> You might often want to know if a given keybinding is available elsewhere (for example, in the menus). For this purpose, sams-list-all-bindings exists. When you invoke this function, it asks for a keypress and shows you all the places where the function that's bound to this key is bound elsewhere.
>
> You can bind this function to C-h C-c with the following command:
>
> ```
> (global-set-key [(control h) (control c)]
>                 'sams-list-all-bindings)
> ```

What Does This Function or Variable Do?

Given a function name or variable name, you might want to find out what it is doing. You can do this in one of two ways, depending on the level of accuracy you want for the information.

The low-level way is to press C-h f (describe-function); this asks you for a function name and shows the description in a buffer for itself.

The high-level way is to press C-h C-f. This is the function Info-goto-emacs-command-node in GNU Emacs and Info-elisp-ref in XEmacs. This looks up the function in the info pages and, if it exists, it takes you to the location where it is described. The info pages are described in detail in the next section.

Getting Extra Help Using the Info System

Long before the World Wide Web was invented, the info system was invented. It is a hyperlinked information system, intended to replace ordinary manual pages. It works much like the Web, with the important difference that the document can be read sequentially like a book.

If you press C-h i (info), you are taken to a whole new world of information. If you use a new Linux distribution, you can find info pages for most of the programs on your machine. Otherwise you can at least find information about Emacs. In Figure 10.6 shows one of the info pages.

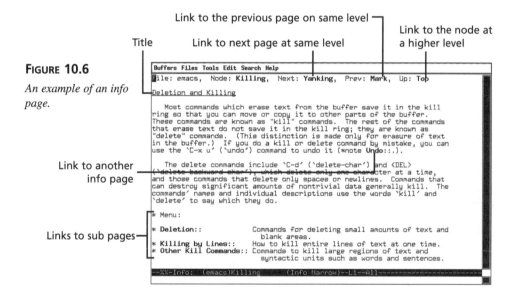

FIGURE 10.6

An example of an info page.

Each info page is built up from the following parts:

- The topmost line contains special information about how this info page relates to the rest of the pages in the given document. The Next and Prev fields link, respectively, to the next and the previous page on the same level as this page. To illustrate this, think of a book. If this node is a section, Next and Prev point to the next and the previous sections of the book. If it is a subsection, they point to the next and the previous subsection. The Up field links to the node at a higher level. In the book example, this would be the chapter node for a section.

Not all info pages contain all these links; this depends solely on whether the link is meaningful or not. A link to the previous page has, of course, no meaning at the first page of a document.

- The second line of the page is the title. This info page describes "Deletion and Killing."
- Then comes the actual text of the node. In the text there might be links to other pages of the document. An example of this is the link to the node on Undo. All such references contain the text *(*note* before the link and *::.)* after the link. (Remember, this was invented long before the Web and must work with terminals that do not support highlighting or underlines).
- At the bottom of the page, there are links to subpages on the given topic. Again, from the book example, these would be links to all subsections of the given section. In this part, the lines start with *.

Traveling the Info Pages

To get around in a single info page, use the arrow keys. Following links is done by either clicking the middle mouse button over them or moving point to the location and pressing Enter.

The info browser has a Back function similar to Web browsers. Press l to get back to the info page that you visited before this one.

Unfortunately, the info browser has no Forward function. In addition to using the links at the top, you can access the previous and next pages at the same level by pressing p and n and the up link by pressing u. Furthermore, the topmost info page (the one you arrive at when you enter the info system for the first time) is available by pressing d.

Searching the Info Pages

The ordinary search mechanism described in Hour 7, "Searching for Text in a Buffer," is still available in the info pages but, as always, applies only to the current buffer. Furthermore, there's a command for searching in a document, which is bound to s. When you press s Emacs asks you for a search string. To continue the search, press s again and, when Emacs asks you what you want to search for, simply press Enter; this makes Emacs continue the current search. You can also press , (comma) to continue the search, but that is one more key binding to remember.

> The search command works only with documents, not with the whole hierarchy of info pages.

Customizing Emacs's Features

The most important feature in Emacs 20 (seen from the point of view of a newcomer to Emacs) is the customization utility. Customization support makes it a hundred times easier to configure Emacs.

Customization in Emacs is done using a variant of the Lisp programming language, called *elisp*. Thus, to configure Emacs to beep instead of inserting a blank line when you click arrow down (next-line) on the last line of a buffer, you must insert the following line into your .emacs file:

10

```
(setq next-line-add-newlines nil)
```

There are many chances for a person unfamiliar with programming languages or unfamiliar with elisp to make a mistake when inserting the preceding code line. Such a mistake would cause the line to have no effect and, in most situations, the lines following it would also have no effect. An alternative for customizing the preceding code line is to offer the user (that's you) a semi-graphical user interface. This is exactly what the customize library does. In Figures 10.7 and 10.8 you can see the customization of the preceding variable using the customize library in XEmacs and in GNU Emacs.

FIGURE 10.7

Customization of next-line-add-newlines using the customize library in XEmacs.

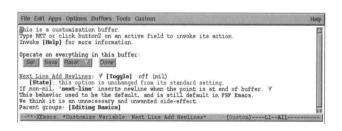

FIGURE 10.8

Customization of next-line-add-newlines using the customize library in GNU Emacs.

As discussed in the Introduction to this book, XEmacs is more graphically oriented than GNU Emacs, which you can easily see in Figures 10.7 and 10.8.
The rest of this hour uses figures from XEmacs, because they are much easier
to interpret when you're only seeing them. You should have no problem if
you use the GNU Emacs customize interface instead, because the command
buttons highlight when the cursor moves over them, which indicates that
they are, in fact, buttons.

Customization using the customize library is done by using graphical elements such as
check boxes (or something that resembles check buttons), text entries, pull-down menus,
and so on. Each element is discussed in detail in the next section. The customize library
contains about 2,500 options split over approximately 400 pages.

Figure 10.9 shows a customization buffer.

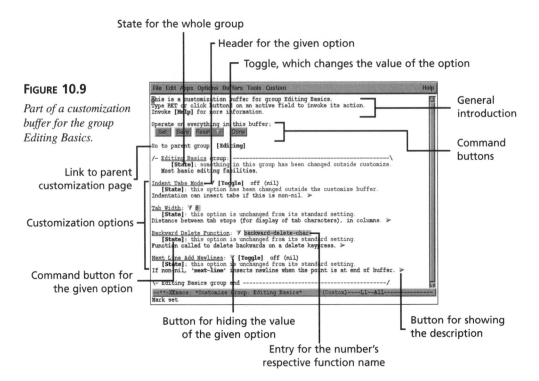

FIGURE 10.9

*Part of a customization
buffer for the group
Editing Basics.*

> The group shown in Figure 10.9 is very large, so I had to remove some of the options to include all details of the customization page. In general, the options that you see on your customization pages might be different from mine, especially if you use GNU Emacs.

This buffer shows four options. Two of them are two-stated values, that is they might be either on or off. The other two are entries where the user can type a value. Each option part contains a header, which makes it easy to distinguish them from each other.

Apart from the header, the option section contains the following items:

- A value field and a value description. This is the part with the toggle command button or the entry field. This is the actual configuration.
- The state button and state description. See the following section.
- A description of the option. If the description fills more than one line, the sequential lines are truncated. To show these lines, click the arrow at the end of the line. Likewise, the value part can be truncated. To do so, click the arrow next to the option title. (See the arrows in Figure 10.9.)

Set/Save/Reset/Done

When you have configured what you want on a given page, it's time to set the variables, which makes Emacs behave as the options say. To do this, click either the Set button or the Save button at the top of the page. *Set* means set the variables for the current Emacs session, but do not save to the `.emacs` file, whereas *Save* means set the variable and save to the `.emacs` file. To leave the page, click the Done button.

> When you click the Done button, the configuration page will be removed. No warnings are given if you have not saved the option on the given page.

> By default Emacs writes the customization to your `~/.emacs` file. If you are trying to keep it well organized, this is not desirable. To tell Emacs to save to another file, insert the following lines into your `.emacs` file:
>
> ```
> ### Tell customize to save to ~/Emacs/customize.el TI
> ➥(setq custom-file "~/Emacs/customize.el")
> ### Load the customizations.
> (load-file "~/Emacs/customize.el")
> ```

If you change your mind or want to get back to the state before you invoked customize, click the Reset button, which shows a pop-up menu with the following items:

- Reset to current—This resets to the current settings of the page. This is equivalent to closing the page and reopening it.
- Reset to saved—This resets to the values that are in the .emacs file. This is equivalent to closing Emacs and restarting it (if no other pages are unsaved).
- Reset to standard settings—This sets the settings as they are, if no configuration of Emacs has been done. This is equivalent to removing your .emacs file and restarting Emacs.

If you have edited only one option, but you are not certain whether the other options are changed and you do not care to check, you can select the Set/Save/Reset functions from the State menu for the given option, instead of selecting the buttons from the top of the buffer. This will then affect only the current option.

Before you save a given option to the .emacs file, you might want to test it a bit first. You can do that by setting the option (that is, do not save it) and, when you have tested it, you can press M-x and type customize-customized. Emacs will then create a customization page for you, with the unsaved options.

The customize library offers customization of 2,400 options! The customization options have been split in almost 500 groups of options. Each group can contain subgroups or customization options.

Customization Widgets

The customization library contains only a few different widgets, which it does the actual customization with. These widgets and their meanings are described in the following sections.

The Toggle Button

The Toggle button, shown in Figure 10.10, has already been discussed in the previous section. It is used to select between two values, often on or off.

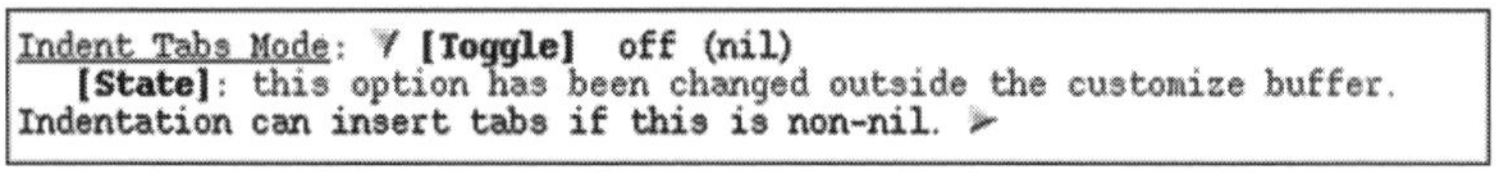

FIGURE 10.10

The Toggle button shown onscreen.

```
Indent Tabs Mode: ⍢ [Toggle]  off (nil)
        [State]: this option has been changed outside the customize buffer.
Indentation can insert tabs if this is non-nil. ➤
```

The Entry Widget

You have also already seen the Entry widget, in which you can insert text (see Figure 10.11). To use it, place the point in it, and press Enter. Then you are queried for the value in the minibuffer. Here you also have completion, for command names and variable, in case the entry requires one.

FIGURE 10.11

The Entry widget shown onscreen.

```
Tab Width: ▼ 8
     [State]: this option is unchanged from its standard setting.
Distance between tab stops (for display of tab characters), in columns. ▶
```

The Value Menu

The value menu is used when there is a small limited set of values available for the given option (see Figure 10.12). When you click the widget, a pull-down menu appears with the possible values.

FIGURE 10.12

The Value menu widget shown onscreen.

```
Require Final Newline: ▼ [Value Menu] Add
     [State]: this option has been changed outside the customize buffer.
Value of t says silently ensure a file ends in a newline when it is saved. ▶
```

The Multi Widget

The Multi widget is used when you are required to list a number of strings. The example shown in Figure 10.13 lists a number of modes for which Brace mode is enabled. To add an element, click the INS button on the line where you want a new entry. To delete an element, click the DEL button.

The Multi widget can in fact also be used with some of the other widgets, not only the entry widget. This is, however, seldom seen.

FIGURE 10.13

The Multi widget shown onscreen.

```
Brace Modes: ▼
[INS] [DEL] Mode: c++-mode
[INS] [DEL] Mode: c-mode
[INS] [DEL] Mode: java-mode
[[INS] [DEL] Mode: tcl-mode
[INS]
     [State]: you have edited the value as text, but you have not set the option.
List of language major modes which define things with brace delimiters.
```

The Face Widget

Faces in Emacs refers to a combination of font, color, and typeface attributes (that is underlining, italics, and bold). Figure 10.14 shows the configuration of Face. The column of check buttons is used to indicate whether the line they are in front of is to be regarded. Thus the widget in Figure 10.14 defines only the foreground color and the background color. The other values are taken from the default.

FIGURE 10.14

The Face widget shown onscreen.

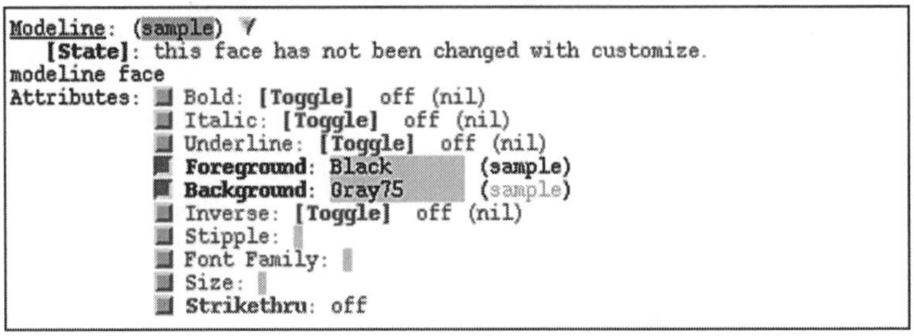

```
Modeline: (sample) Y
   [State]: this face has not been changed with customize.
modeline face
Attributes: ▨ Bold: [Toggle]  off (nil)
            ▨ Italic: [Toggle]  off (nil)
            ▨ Underline: [Toggle]  off (nil)
            ▉ Foreground: Black        (sample)
            ▉ Background: Gray75        (sample)
            ▨ Inverse: [Toggle]  off (nil)
            ▨ Stipple: ▊
            ▨ Font Family: ▊
            ▨ Size: ▊
            ▨ Strikethru: off
```

In the State menu, you can select an element called Show All Display Spec. If you do that, you can specify the face for the given option based on the characteristics of the display used. For example, is the display black-and-white or color? The Multi widget is used here to give you the opportunity to describe several display types. As indicated previously, the left column of check buttons indicates which elements to use. Thus, in Figure 10.15, the display is a grayscale X, but nothing is said about the background brightness.

FIGURE 10.15

The Face widget, including display characteristics.

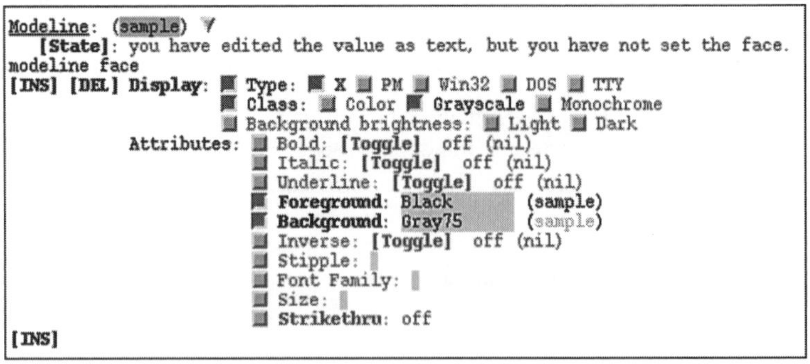

```
Modeline: (sample) Y
   [State]: you have edited the value as text, but you have not set the face.
modeline face
[INS] [DEL] Display: ▉ Type: ▉ X ▨ PM ▨ Win32 ▨ DOS ▨ TTY
                     ▉ Class: ▨ Color ▉ Grayscale ▨ Monochrome
                     ▨ Background brightness: ▨ Light ▨ Dark
            Attributes: ▨ Bold: [Toggle]  off (nil)
                        ▨ Italic: [Toggle]  off (nil)
                        ▨ Underline: [Toggle]  off (nil)
                        ▉ Foreground: Black        (sample)
                        ▉ Background: Gray75        (sample)
                        ▨ Inverse: [Toggle]  off (nil)
                        ▨ Stipple: ▊
                        ▨ Font Family: ▊
                        ▨ Size: ▊
                        ▨ Strikethru: off
[INS]
```

Customization Commands

Emacs offers a set of different entries to customize. All these are located in the menu bar, so there is no need to remember them unless you use them often. In GNU Emacs the commands are located as a submenu to the Help menu. In XEmacs, there is an item on the menu bar called Custom.

The entries to customize are as follows:

- If you know exactly which variable you want to customize, you can use the function customize-option (or customize-variable, which means the same thing—you might find one name easier to remember than the other).
- If it is a face you want to configure, you can use the command customize-face.
- If you do not know the exact name of the variable or face, use the command customize-apropos, which finds all options, faces, and groups that match the pattern you're searching for. This is similar to command-apropos described in the beginning of this hour.
- If you know the name of a group that you want to configure, you can proceed directly to this group with the command customize-group.
- If you want to browse through the different options available, use the command customize or customize-browse. The difference between the two is that customize opens the topmost group for customization with an interface like what you've seen so far in this hour, whereas customize-browse opens a window that resembles a directory browser. The latter can be seen in Figure 10.16.

10

Indicate configuration of face

FIGURE 10.16

Buffer used for customize-browse.

Configuration option ⎯

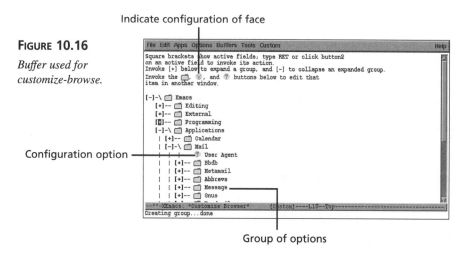

Group of options

Summary

Although you didn't learn any new editing tools as you have in previous hours, you still gained very powerful knowledge about Emacs. You learned how to search for new commands, read additional information in the info pages, and customize all the different variables that make Emacs the most powerful editor available. (I haven't even covered Lisp programming yet!) It's now time to browse through some of the almost 400 pages of configuration options that customize offers. I'll bet you that if you're already a little familiar with Emacs, you'll find answers to a lot of questions you have had for some time, such as, "Why doesn't Emacs do it this way?"

Q&A

Q Has the hyper-apropos library been ported to GNU Emacs?

A No. But when I'm finished with this book, I'll work on it. Check the home page for a possible solution.

Q I use Emacs 19. Is there no chance that I can use the customize library?

A Nope, the customize library isn't well supported in Emacs 19. Older versions exist for Emacs 19, but they do not work with newer versions of the package.

Q Why doesn't Emacs use Web pages for information instead of those info pages?

A The info system is tightly bounded to Emacs and is very fast at startup compared to most Web browsers. Furthermore the info pages are easier to search than Web pages are (that is, search over several pages). Therefore, GNU has decided to keep using the info system. Don't be afraid, though, you will quickly learn to use info. If, however, you prefer to read the pages through your Web browser, you can use the info2html converter, which can convert your info pages to HTML pages (http://www.che.utexas.edu/info2www/info2www). Furthermore, the Emacs reference manual and the Lisp manual are located on the CD-ROM as HTML.

Q When I've configured an option using the customize library, is there a way I can see which variable and which value to use (for example, for use in Emacs 19)?

A Yes, you can transfer the variable to Emacs 19 (given that the variable exists in Emacs 19) or to another part of your Emacs file (for example, a part specific to XEmacs). The code inserted by customization looks like the following:

```
(custom-set-variables
 '(next-line-add-newlines t))
```

To set this option elsewhere, you must insert the following:

```
(setq next-line-add-newlines t)
```

When you have done this, you must not customize the variable from customize anymore, because this inserts a new item such as the preceding code line in your .emacs file.

Exercises

1. Find out what is bound to the key C-a and find the documentation for it—both the short one and the info pages.

2. Find the info pages on bookmarks, described in Hour 8, "Searching for Text in Multiple Files." Is there an Emacs command that locates point on a specific line? If yes, is it bound to a key?

3. Find the customization page for customize and see whether there is anything that you want to change.

4. C-k erases the text to the end of the line but does not remove the line break itself. Try to change this so Emacs will remove the line break too.

10

HOUR 11

Editing Utilities

Imagine writing a document on a typewriter. When you finish, you ask someone to check the document for you and, when she is finished, you have to type everything once again to reflect the spelling corrections made. Well that was the reality for most people fewer than 10 years ago! Think about it! Today, however, we have spelling checkers, which help us track down spelling errors and, with minimal effort, correct them.

Some of the errors are not real spelling errors but, rather, a problem with your fingers being incapable of typing as fast as your brain thinks. You might, for example, type *yuo* when you intend to type *you*. These errors are more appropriately fixed by means other than a spelling checker. This will be discussed later in this section.

Using a Spelling Checker

Emacs interfaces to the spelling checker program, called ispell, and you can use it to spell-check a single word, a region, or a whole buffer. Furthermore, a library called `flyspell` exists, which makes it possible to get on-the-fly spell-checking; that is, whenever you type a word, it is spell-checked and, if it contains errors, the word is highlighted and you are offered a menu of suggestions.

Three basic spelling commands exist—ispell-word (bound to M-$), ispell-region, and ispell-buffer. The latter two are not bound to any keys by default. For each word that you request a spell-check on, Emacs looks it up in a dictionary. Every time it's incapable of finding a given word in the dictionary, it searches for near matches and asks you for help. This can be seen in Figure 11.1, where the word *forgotton* is misspelled.

FIGURE 11.1

Spell-checking of a buffer using ispell-buffer.

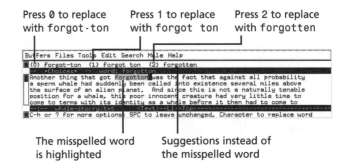

Press 0 to replace with forgot-ton

Press 1 to replace with forgot ton

Press 2 to replace with forgotten

The misspelled word is highlighted

Suggestions instead of the misspelled word

If you should be so lucky that the word you intend to write is one of the suggestions, simply type the number (or, in general, the symbol) next to it, and Emacs continues to the next misspelling.

This is, however, not always the case. The following alternatives exist:

- The word is so greatly misspelled that Emacs is incapable of finding it.
- The word is a technical term, a foreign-language word, or maybe slang which Emacs does not know about.
- The word simply isn't in Emacs's dictionary. This is an important point. Not every dictionary that comes with ispell is complete, so be warned: A word might be spelled correctly, although Emacs says it can't find it.

Replacing a Misspelled Word

When Emacs finds a word that is not in its dictionary it searches for an alternative. Sometimes it fails because the word is too greatly misspelled (such as *requcnice* for *recognize*). In these cases either it finds no alternatives at all for you, or none of the alternatives it presents is correct.

In these cases you have to tell it which word is the correct one. To do this, press r (for *r*eplace). Emacs asks you for a word to replace the misspelling with, as can be seen in Figure 11.2. It types the word to edit, so you do not need to retype it all to fix the error.

FIGURE 11.2

Pressing r when spell-checking lets you type the correct word yourself.

Emacs's suggestion is not what you intended.

Misspelled word. Should have been *against*

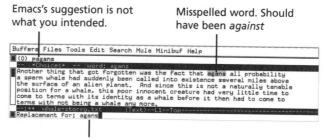

Emacs fills in the misspelled word so you do not need to retype it, but only need to edit it.

When you have typed the correct word (or what you at least think is the correct word), Emacs spell-checks it, to ensure that you do not replace a wrong word with another wrong word.

If the misspelling comes from an assumption that the word should be spelled that way, you might, in fact, misspell it several places in the document. In this case it is useful (and most often time saving) to replace the misspelled word throughout the whole document once and for all. To do this, press R (for *R*eplace). Emacs then asks you for the word to replace with and, when you have told it the word, it does a query-replace throughout the rest of the region or buffer (depending on whether you started ispell-region or ispell-buffer).

At the beginning it might be a bit confusing to you that Emacs invokes query-replace when you are spell-checking but, when you get used to it, you will enjoy the fact that replacing a word when spell-checking is similar to any other kind of replacing. Think about the alternatives! Emacs might instead have offered a button that said "replace all occurrences" and, when you pressed it, all occurrences would be replaced unconditionally. Having this interface would make you ask: "Why can't I have the capability to do query-replace when spell-checking, so I might avoid replacing occurrences that I do not want to replace?" Aha! This is, in fact, what you have now!

In the cases where the word is very misspelled, you might, in fact, be unable to spell it correctly, even when you get a second try. (I find it hard to spell *miscellaneous*.) In these cases you can ask Emacs to look into the dictionary once again, and this time show you all the words that match a given pattern (That is, the star from patterns is available). Thus in my example, I would ask it to look for words matching *miscel*. To ask Emacs do this, press l (for *l*ist) This can be seen in Figures 11.3 and 11.4.

11

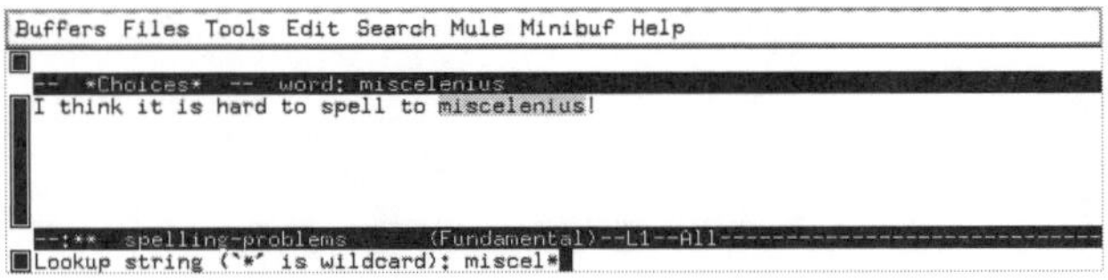

FIGURE 11.3

When pressing 1 during spell-checking, you can ask Emacs to search for a given pattern in the dictionary. Please note that Emacs wasn't able to help me with this word during normal spell-checking.

FIGURE 11.4

This is the list Emacs shows me, when I ask for miscel*.

Fixing an Error While Spell-Checking

When you are spell-checking you might find that there is an error of some kind in the surrounding text of the word being checked. There are several things you can do about that. Hey! Stop! Haven't we been through this before? Yes, we have! Recursive editing was discussed in Hour 7, "Searching for Text in a Buffer." When you spell-check, it is also possible to do recursive editing. To enter recursive editing, press C-r. If you have forgotten what recursive editing is all about, I strongly suggest that you review Hour 7.

Accepting a Word

There are, of course, also situations where Emacs is incapable of finding a given word in its dictionary, even though the word is perfectly spelled. In these cases, you have to tell Emacs that the word is okay. You can do this in several ways:

- You can tell Emacs that this word is okay, and ask it to continue on to the next word. If this word is found once again in another place, Emacs complains once again. This is most useful in situations where you are not entirely certain that the word is spelled correctly, but you do not care to take the time to double-check it. To ask Emacs to continue this way, press the Spacebar.

- You can tell Emacs that the word is okay, and ask it to continue spell-checking. If it later finds this word, it ignores it as if it were spelled correctly. This applies only to the current Emacs session. Next time you start Emacs and spell-check the document it complains about the word again. This solution is bound to a (for *a*ccept).

- If you really believe that this word is spelled correctly, but you recognize it as, for example, being a technical expression, which is likely to be used only in the given buffer, tell Emacs to record this word as correct for this buffer for all future Emacs sessions. Do this by pressing A. The actual recording is done by inserting a section in the button of your document containing the word. This section is inserted in a way that makes it look like a comment. (Thus, in C, it is inserted within /* ... */), given, of course, comments exist in the file's major mode. In Figure 11.5 you can see an example of this.

FIGURE 11.5

ispell dictionary local to a given buffer.

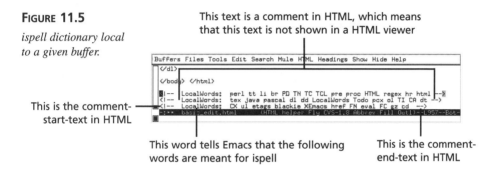

This text is a comment in HTML, which means that this text is not shown in a HTML viewer

This is the comment-start-text in HTML

This word tells Emacs that the following words are meant for ispell

This is the comment-end-text in HTML

11

To insert a word in the dictionary in the given buffer, press A (for *Accept*)

- Finally you can tell Emacs to insert the word into your personal dictionary. This means that every subsequent spell-checking operation will think that the given word is okay. Your personal dictionary is located in your home directory under the name .ispell_*dictionary-name*, where *dictionary-name* is the name of the dictionary used (see the section "Changing the Spelling Language"). Press i (for *i*nsert) to insert the word in your local dictionary).

If you find it hard to remember these keys you can always press ? to get a list of the available commands when spell-checking. Furthermore, please note that in the cases where a command is bound to both a lowercase letter and a capital one, the capital one does the most. For example, r replaces the word one time, whereas R replaces the word throughout the rest of the spell region.

On-the-Fly Spell-Checking

An alternative to spell-checking the whole buffer in one go is to do on-the-fly spell-checking; that is, when you finish typing a word, it is spell-checked and, if it is not in the dictionary, the word is highlighted to indicate to you that you need to change this word. The highlighting is active until you correct the word. This can be seen in Figure 11.6.

FIGURE 11.6

On-the-fly spell-checking.

As soon as the exclamation mark was pressed, Emacs recognized that the word was finished, spell-checked it, and highlighted it

Misspelled words

```
Buffers Files Tools Edit Search Mule Help
I think it is hard to spel to miscelenius!

--:** spelling-problems    (Fundamental Fly)--L1--All---------------
```

Fly indicates that flyspell-mode is enabled (that is, the mode that offers on-the-fly spell-checking)

GNU Emacs on Windows won't highlight the text, but will beep at you if it detects a misspelling.

To correct the word, you can either edit it or press the second mouse button on top of the word. Pressing the second mouse button brings up a menu with suggestions, such as with ispell (in fact, it is ispell that is invoked behind the scenes). This can be seen in Figure 11.7.

FIGURE 11.7

Window shown when spell-checking using flyspell-mode.

If you select this item, the word is saved to your personal dictionary.

If you select this item, the word is accepted throughout this session as long as your current Emacs is running.

The spell-checked word and the dictionary used.

Suggested replacements for the misspelled words.

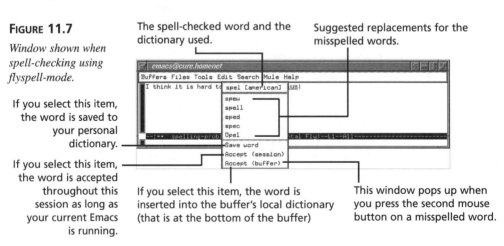

```
emacs@cure.homenet
Buffers Files Tools Edit Search Mule Help
I think it is hard to spel [american] us!
                          spew
                          spell
                          sped
                          spec
                          Opel
--:** spelling-prob            tal Fly)--L1--All--------------
                          Save word
                          Accept (session)
                          Accept (buffer)
```

If you select this item, the word is inserted into the buffer's local dictionary (that is at the bottom of the buffer)

This window pops up when you press the second mouse button on a misspelled word.

As mentioned previously, the mode that gives on-the-fly spell-checking facilities to Emacs is called flyspell-mode. This mode comes as the default with XEmacs 20, but not with GNU Emacs 20. For GNU Emacs, you have to install it in your Lisp directory from the CD. The version of ispell.el that comes with XEmacs contains a bug, which causes flyspell.el not to work unless you replace it. See Appendix A, "Installing Functions and Packages from the CD," for a description of this.

 Unless you never write documents that need to be spelled correctly or you never make a spelling error, it's a good idea to have the spelling commands bound to keys. I suggest using the function keys. You might find the following layout useful: F10—Spell word, S-F10—Spell region, C-F10—Spell buffer, and M-F10—toggle fly-spell mode.

Using the Dictionary to Search for a Word

When you are writing, you might find that there is a word that you do not know how to spell. In such a case you might try to spell it, ask ispell to spell-check it for you, and hope that the word is close enough to the real word. If it isn't, ask ispell to search for a word, given a pattern as described in "Replacing a Misspelled Word" earlier this hour. Fortunately there is an easier way: Ask ispell to complete a given word. This is identical to the method described in "Replacing a Misspelled Word," with the exception that you do not need to spell-check the word first. This function is available using the function ispell-complete-word. This function is bound to C-Tab in text mode, and might be bound to this in other modes, but many modes use this key for another purpose. It might, therefore, be a good idea to add this to a function key.

Changing the Spelling Language

Several different dictionaries exist for the ispell package, including German, French, British, and Danish. To change a dictionary, you must invoke the command ispell-change-dictionary. An alternative is to select the dictionary from the menu bar under the Edit, Spell menu.

 The list of dictionaries listed in the menu bar does not reflect which dictionaries are installed on your system! Several additional dictionaries can be downloaded for the ispell program. If the command ispell-word results in a message similar to Can't open /usr/lib/ispell/british.hash, it means that you do not have this dictionary installed.

11

A given file almost always needs only one dictionary; therefore, it is desirable to specify which language a given file should be spell-checked with. This can be done by inserting the following at the end of the file:

```
/* Local Variables: */
/* ispell-dictionary: "british" */
/* End: */
```

british must be replaced with the dictionary that you want to use. /* and */ should be replaced with the comment characters for the given file. For a further description of this method, please refer to the section "Configuring Options for a Single File" in Hour 22, "Learning Lisp Basics."

Automatically Replacing One String with Another

Some errors are better fixed using means other than spell-checking, such as correcting words that you habitually spell incorrectly. I, for example, often write *teh* when I intend to write *the*. Likewise, I often write *writting* instead of *writing*. A spelling checker could easily tell me about these errors, but given that I make them often, it is a waste of time and an irritation to fix them over and over again.

> Remember, Emacs helps you to be creative and avoid doing trivial tasks over and over again!

The alternative is to set Emacs up to replace one word with another whenever it is typed. Thus, when I type *teh* and press any nonalphanumeric symbol (for example, a period or a comma), Emacs replaces this with *the* without asking me. It replaces the word only if it is a standalone word. Thus, *Teheran* isn't replaced with *Theeran*.

This feature was designed to expand abbreviations into full words.

> It should go without saying that you should be very careful when defining abbreviations. Defining *the* as an abbreviation for *the hundred elephants* is definitely not a good idea, because you would get the text *the hundred elephants* whenever you type *the*.

To enable this feature press M-x and type abbrev-mode, which turns it on for the given buffer. If you always want it enabled, you must add it to a hook function. See the section "Controlling Options" in Hour 24, "Installing Emacs Add-Ons."

There are two sets of abbreviations: those local to a given major mode and those for all modes. To add an abbreviation for your current major mode, press C-x a i l (inverse-add-mode-abbrev). To add one for all modes, press C-x a i g (inverse-add-global-abbrev). When typing one of the two, the abbreviation must be located before point. Emacs then asks what this abbreviation should expand to. This can be seen in the following To Do section.

Creating an Abbreviation

This task shows you how to assign the abbreviation *tdg* to *The Dotfile Generator*. Follow these steps:

1. Load abbrev-mode if it isn't loaded already (it is loaded if the text Abbrev is in the mode-line). To load it, press M-x and type abbrev-mode.
2. Type tdg (this is the word that expands to *The Dotfile Generator*).
3. Press C-x a i g (inverse-add-global-abbrev).
4. Emacs now asks you what word the abbreviation should expand to. Type The Dotfile Generator.

The abbreviation has now been defined as a global abbreviation, which means that it works in any mode. Try typing tdg and a space, and you can see how Emacs replaces this with *The Dotfile Generator* and the space.

If you, for one reason or another, need to type a word that is an abbreviation, type the word and press C-q and the word delimiter. Thus if you define *tdg* to be an abbreviation, to insert *tdg* and a space in the text, type tdg, press C-q, and finally press the spacebar (or any other word delimiter).

Editing Abbreviations

If you press M-x and type edit-abbrevs, a buffer appears in which you can edit the abbreviations (see Figure 11.8).

FIGURE **11.8**

The buffer in which you can edit your abbreviations.

This column describes how many times the given abbreviation has been used

This column defines the text that the given abbreviation expands to

The following abbreviations are for html-helper-mode

This column defines the abbreviations

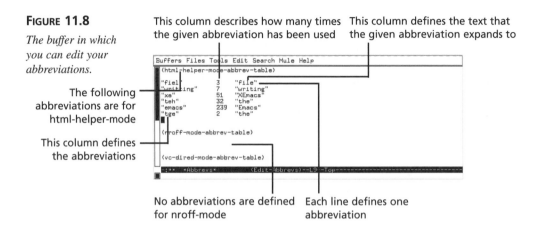

No abbreviations are defined for nroff-mode

Each line defines one abbreviation

In this buffer you can add, delete, or edit the abbreviation. When you finish, press C-x C-s and kill the buffer.

Loading or Saving an Abbreviation to a File

If you want the abbreviation to exist from one session to the next, you must insert the following line into your .emacs file:

```
(read-abbrev-file)
```

When this line is in the .emacs file, abbreviations are loaded during startup of Emacs; when Emacs exits they are written. If you want the abbreviations to be saved as soon as they are defined, insert the following into your .emacs file:

```
(sams-write-abbrev-at-once)
```

Completing Text from Another Part of the Buffer

Sometimes you type a word over and over again in a document. In the previous section, you saw how to define an abbreviation which might expand to difficult-to-type text. There are, however, situations where you do not want to define an abbreviation for a word, due to the fact that it'll take you some time to define it, and you might not know how many times you have to type this word. You might even be in a situation where you know that you have typed the word before, but you are not sure that you will type it again.

In these situation, you want Emacs to complete the word from a word earlier in the document. For this purpose dynamic abbreviations exist. Simply type part of the word and press M-/ (dabbrev-expand). Emacs then searches all your buffers for a word to complete to.

A much more powerful function called hippie-expand exists. This function expands almost anything. This includes Lisp function names, filenames from the hard disk, and text from the buffer. To use it, bind it to a key. To bind hippie-expand to meta-space, insert the following into your .emacs file :

```
(global-set-key "\M- " 'hippie-expand)
```

Now type part of a word, a filename, or a Lisp function-name, and press meta-space. If you are not happy about what it finds for you, ask it to continue its search for a completion by pressing meta-space one more time.

This function is not included in XEmacs 19.

11

hippie-expand tries several different possibilities to find a piece of text that matches your need. Which expansions these are and the order in which they are tried can be seen in Table 11.1.

TABLE 11.1 EXPANSION FUNCTIONS IN HIPPIE-EXPAND

Number Tried	Name	Description
2	try-complete-file-name	This function completes to a filename. If several completions are possible, it selects the first one. If you are not happy about that, simply press Meta-space once more.
1	try-complete-file-name-partially	This function completes the filename as much as is possible, unambiguously (such as filename completion works in the minibuffer). When this function is used, the previous one must come after it in the list of try-functions.
3	try-expand-all-abbrevs	This function searches through all the abbreviations (described in the previous section) in all modes for a completion.
5	try-expand-line	Searches the buffer for an entire line that begins exactly as the current line.

continues

TABLE 11.1 CONTINUED

Number Tried	Name	Description
	try-expand-line-all-buffers	Like try-expand-line but searches in all buffers (except the current). Thus if you want to search for a line-match first from this buffer and later from other buffers, you must first insert try-expand-line in the list, and next this one.
4	try-expand-list	Tries to expand the text back to the nearest open delimiter, to a whole list from the buffer. This might be convenient when programming.
	try-expand-list-all-buffers	Like try-expand-list but searches in all buffers (except the current).
6	try-expand-dabbrev	Works exactly as dabbrev-expand.
7	try-expand-dabbrev-all-buffers	Like dabbrev-expand but searches all Emacs buffers (except the current) for matching words.
	try-expand-dabbrev-visible	Searches the currently visible parts of all windows. This function can be put before try-expand-dabbrev-all-buffers to first try the expansions you can see.
8	try-expand-dabbrev-from-kill	Searches the kill ring (that is text earlier deleted with one of the kill functions) for a suitable completion of the word.
	try-expand-whole-kill	Like the previous function, but inserts the whole content of the delete cell matched. This can be seen as an alternative to pressing C-y (yank) and then M-y (yank-pop) a number of times to get to the right item.
10	try-complete-lisp-symbol	Completes to a Lisp function name or variable name. The difference between this one and the next is the same as the difference between try-complete-file-name and try-complete-file-name-partially.
9	try-complete-lisp-symbol-partially	See previous item.

The expansions are implemented as Lisp functions so that a user can add an extra one in case he or she needs another expansion. This is the reason for the description of this as try-functions.

The order in which expansions are tried can be customized by setting the variable `hippie-expand-try-functions-list`. Simply insert the following into your `.emacs` file. Order the functions the way you like, with new ones added or some removed:

```
(setq hippie-expand-try-functions-list
  '(try-complete-file-name-partially
    try-complete-file-name
    try-expand-all-abbrevs
    try-expand-list
    try-expand-line
    try-expand-dabbrev
    try-expand-dabbrev-all-buffers
    try-expand-dabbrev-from-kill
    try-complete-lisp-symbol-partially
    try-complete-lisp-symbol))
```

Transposing and Changing Case

Earlier in this section, I told you about my problem with writing *teh* when I intended to write *the*. In fact, a general problem that many people have is that they type keys in the wrong order. The people behind Emacs recognized this problem and made a solution that is accessible through one keystroke—C-t (transpose-chars). To be entirely accurate, you need two keystrokes, because you need to move point to the location between the two characters. In sams-lib an additional function exists called sams-transpose-prev-char that transposes the previous character and the one before it. This makes the problem solvable with one keypress. You can, for example, bind this function to Ctrl-Shift-t, which is done with the following:

```
(global-set-key [(control T)] 'sams-transpose-prev-char)
```

There are also commands for transposing words, lines, sentences, and paragraphs. Although transposing words is useful for keeping your mental state as described above, the second two are not, as you need to think anyway when you decide to transpose two lines or sentences. The commands are M-t (transpose-words), C-x C-t (transpose-lines), transpose-sentences, and transpose-paragraphs.

Changing Case

Three functions exist that make it easy for you to change the case of a word—M-l (downcase-word), which lowercases the word; M-u (upcase-word), which uppercases the word; and M-c (capitalize-word), which sets the first character in uppercase, and the rest in lowercase.

It is important to note that the three functions work from point until the end of the word. Thus if point is before *r* in *word*, and you press M-u then it is translated to *woRD*. As a side effect, point is moved to the end of the word. Thus if you have a sequence of words that you want to uppercase, simply press M-u a number of times. An alternative is simply to mark all the words as a region, and then press M-u.

Summary

You have now learned how to spell-check your documents, both in once-and-for-all mode and on-the-fly. I strongly suggest that you try on-the-fly spell-checking for a few days. I use it all the time now, and it has given me the bonus that I actually have learned to spell new words.

Talking about abbreviations, you have also learned how you can avoid spelling out long words that you write over and over again, and how to make Emacs fix those little, but very irritating, typographical errors, such as *teh*.

Finally, you learned a few functions for transposing text and changing case. In Hour 13, "Macros," you will find that these functions are especially useful in macros.

Q&A

Q **When I want to replace a word throughout an entire document (during spell-checking), is there a way to select one of the words from a list of suggestions, rather than having to type it myself?**

A Yes and no. There is no nice way to do it but, because the minibuffer is a buffer and the window with the suggestions is a buffer, you can switch to this window with C-x o (other-window), and cut-and-paste from it to the minibuffer.

Q **Should I insert the line (sams-write-abbrev-at-once) into my .emacs file as you suggest? If it's that smart, why isn't it the default?**

A The reason that this is not the default is due to taste. Some people might like it, whereas others might not. If you add it, abbreviations are saved as soon as they are defined. If you do not add it, abbreviations are saved only when you exit Emacs. This means that if you forget to exit Emacs before you shut down your computer, they are never written! This is not the whole truth, actually. They are also saved when you press C-x s (save-some-buffers), but the problem is still there.

Q I have a project where I have some specialized abbreviations. Is there any way I can make these abbreviations local to a single directory?

A Unfortunately, abbreviations are not developed with that in mind, so there is no clean way to do that. There is a hack, though. Insert something such as the following at the end of the file for which these abbreviations are to be defined:

```
; Local Variables:
; abbrev-file-name: "~/Project/.abbrevs"
; eval: (read-abbrev-file abbrev-file-name)
; End:
```

This makes Emacs read the abbreviations from this file. When you later save abbreviations, they are saved to this file, too. Be aware, however, that you will not have access to your global abbreviations from the standard abbreviations file.

Q I have defined some abbreviations, but, nevertheless, nothing happens! Why is that?

A You have most likely forgotten to turn on abbrev-mode. (You have forgotten if the word Abbrev is not part of your mode-line). Simply press M-x and type abbrev-mode.

Exercises

11

1. Find a document you have written without using a spelling checker, and spell-check it. If you never make any mistakes, you can skip this exercise! If you can't find any documents with spelling errors, create some errors and then spell-check the document.

2. Try doing a spell-check in which you ask Emacs to query-replace some text. Is there a way with which you can turn this into an unconditional replace instead of a query-replace?

3. Try doing a spell-check, in which you pause it using recursive-edit and continue afterward.

4. Write a document using on-the-fly spell-checking, and estimate how much extra time you use or spare, compared to doing the spell-check in one go afterward.

5. Define abbreviations for the words *miscellaneous*, *abbreviation*, *accessibility*, and the phrase *Emacs is my best friend*. Which of these could be made easily using dynamic abbreviations?

HOUR 12

Visible Editing Utilities

There are several ways to use visible means in Emacs. This includes changing the font, blinking the screen instead of ringing the bell, highlighting matching parentheses, and displaying part of a text in a special font or color to indicate syntax. All of these are described in this hour.

Changing the Font in Emacs

If the font or the font size in your Emacs is too small, too big, or simply too ugly for you or your monitor, this can make your interaction with Emacs harder. Fortunately it is quite easy for you to change these things. Unfortunately, this is done differently in UNIX and in Windows and differently in GNU Emacs and in XEmacs.

There are two ways to change the font:

- Just for the current session
- For all future sessions

Changing the Font for the Current Session in GNU Emacs in UNIX

To change the font for the current session in GNU Emacs, simply press Shift and the first mouse button. This brings up a menu with fonts as can be seen in Figure 12.1.

FIGURE 12.1

Choosing a font in GNU Emacs under UNIX.

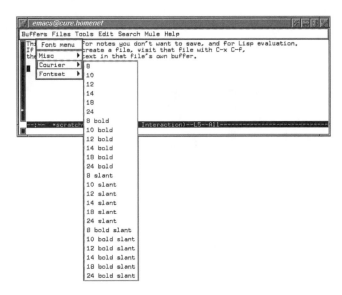

This list of fonts is very limited, because the fonts are hard-coded into Emacs and must, therefore, be valid in every Emacs (that is, the lowest common denominator).

To get a list which is valid for your current X setup, you should copy the library called xf.el from the CD-ROM to your load path, and insert the following lines into your .emacs file:

```
(load "xf")
(xf-load-fonts)
```

The header of xf.el offers instructions on how to cache the font list that this function extracts. This limits the time taken by this library at startup. I don't, however, think this matters that much nowadays when computers are much more powerful than they were in 1994, when this library was developed. Furthermore, it has the drawback that the list is limited to one X setup (that is, one computer).

Changing the Font for the Current Session in XEmacs in UNIX

To choose a different font in XEmacs, you must select the Options menu. In this menu, you will find three items related to the font:

- Font—here you choose the font family
- Size—here you choose the size of the font
- Weight—here you choose font properties

I believe you will seldom have to edit any of these options. In Figure 12.2, you can see the XEmacs font selection.

FIGURE 12.2

Choosing a font in XEmacs.

Changing the Font for the Current Session in GNU Emacs in Windows

Font selection in GNU Emacs under Windows is much like font selection in GNU Emacs under UNIX, with the exception that a Windows-like font window appears from which you can choose a monotype (fixed-width) font (see Figure 12.3).

FIGURE 12.3

Choosing a font in GNU Emacs under Windows.

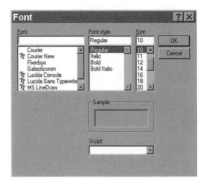

Changing the Font Once and for All Under UNIX

In UNIX applications, defaults are configured in the file called $HOME/.Xdefaults or something similar (it depends on your UNIX system). This file contains a database of user preferences for the programs running in X Window. For a description of this file see the manual page for the program called xrdb.

Inserting the following line into this file changes the font in Emacs:

```
Emacs*font:8x13
```

> Emacs must be written with a capital *E* for this to work in XEmacs.

Setting the Default Font Under UNIX

This task shows you how to set the default font under UNIX to the font currently selected.

1. Depending on your Emacs, choose one of the previously described methods to set the font of your Emacs. For this method you must have already changed the font in this Emacs session (this seems to be a bug in Emacs).

2. Open the $HOME/.Xdefaults file, and go to an appropriate location in it. If you do not know which location is appropriate, go to the end of the file.

3. Press M-x and type sams-insert-font-setup. This inserts two lines similar to the following:
   ```
   Emacs.font:-Adobe-Courier-Medium-R-Normal—18-180-75-75-M-110-
   ➡ISO8859-1
   Emacs.geometry:113x38+0+0
   ```

▼ The first line sets your default font to the one you have loaded right now, whereas the second sets the default size of your Emacs to the size of your current frame. If you do not want the default size set, just remove the line.

4. Save the buffer. (Gee, that was a surprise, huh?)

5. If you want to test it out at once, go to a shell, type xrdb -merge $HOME/.Xdefaults, and start Emacs.

> If you change the name Emacs in the two lines to something else, say *book*, you can start Emacs with a -name option, which makes Emacs read these options instead of the default you might have specified elsewhere. Thus if you start Emacs as
>
> Emacs -name book
>
> the options specified with book.font and book.geometry are read instead of those specified with Emacs.font and Emacs.geometry.

▲

Changing the Font Once and for All Under Windows

First, enter the following code into a buffer for evaluation. If you want to keep it permanently, add it to your .emacs file.

```
(if (eq window-system 'w32)          ; emacs 20 & up
    (defun insert-x-style-font()
      "Insert a string in the X format which describes a font the
user can select from the Windows font selector."
      (interactive)
      (insert (prin1-to-string (w32-select-font)))))
```

Before you can use this function, you must evaluate it. Put the cursor after the last parenthesis, and type C-x C-e.

To use the function, put the cursor where you would like to place the name of the font you select, and call this function by name: insert-x-style-font. Create an empty buffer named foo with C-x b foo RET. Now execute M-x insert-x-style-font. The function inserts an X-style string description into the buffer, surrounded with quotes.

Any variable that the UNIX user can set with the Xdefaults file is one that the NT Emacs user can set in the Registry. Create a file in your home directory, called emacs.reg. You can call it what you want, but the .reg extension is associated with the registry, and you'll learn how to use that in a minute. In the file, enter the following:

```
REGEDIT4

[HKEY_LOCAL_MACHINE\SOFTWARE\GNU\Emacs]
"EMACS.FONT"=
```

12

With the cursor still after the equals sign, execute `M-x insert-x-style-font`. You will see the font string show up in the buffer, like so:

```
REGEDIT4

[HKEY_LOCAL_MACHINE\SOFTWARE\GNU\Emacs]
"EMACS.FONT"="-*-Courier New-normal-r-*-*-16-120-*-*-c-*-*-ansi-"
```

This produces 12-point Courier New in your Emacs. To make it effective, close Emacs down entirely. Then execute `emacs.reg`, either from an MS-DOS window or by clicking it. After clicking OK in the dialog box, start Emacs up again. You should have 12-point Courier New in your Emacs frame.

As you read further in this hour, add variables to your `emacs.reg` file or edit existing ones, and execute it again. You will have to shut Emacs down and restart it to see your changes.

One thing you can't do to the Registry with a `.reg` file is delete a key. For that you have to use `regedit.exe` to delete the unwanted key. Alternatively, set the key to the default value in your `emacs.reg`.

Changing the Foreground and Background Color in UNIX

Besides changing the font and size of X resources you can also change the background and foreground colors, also known as the color of the background and the color of the text. To make the text white on a black background, insert the following into your `.Xdefaults` file:

```
Emacs*Background: black
Emacs*Foreground: white
```

To obtain black text on a white background (which is the default in GNU Emacs, but not in XEmacs) insert the following instead:

```
Emacs*Background: white
Emacs*Foreground: black
```

Finally if you want something that your boss will describe as bizarre, try

```
Emacs*Background: blue
Emacs*Foreground: yellow
```

Changing the colors of the foreground and background will not affect the colors used in font-lock mode (described in the next section). This is unfortunate because the colors will have the inverse meaning, when the background and foreground are transposed. For example, in normal color setup (black on white) light yellow is not a color seen easily, while dark blue is. On the other hand in inverse setup (white on black) light yellow is very easily seen, while dark blue is not. Thus you should only use white on black if you know what you do!

Parentheses Matching

When you write programs, parentheses of different kinds often comes in pairs. In the rest of this section *parentheses* refers to all the different kinds of parentheses: <>, [], (), and {}. When writing a closing parenthesis, it is useful to be able to see which parenthesis is actually *closed*. Likewise, when reading the code later, it is very useful to see which parentheses actually match.

The following is three examples where parentheses come in pairs. The first is from Lisp, the second from C, and the third from TCL:

- `(setq d (- (* b b) (* 4 (* a c))))`
- `printf("the variable d has the value %d", sqr(b) - (4*a*c))`
- `set d [expr [sqr $b]-4*$a*$c]`

These three examples are merely trivial examples where only a few parentheses are needed. Look at `sams-lib.el`; you will see lots of parentheses.

There are two different situations where parentheses can be highlighted:

- When inserting a closing parenthesis
- When point is positioned at either a closing parenthesis or an opening parenthesis

In most cases you will not see the difference between the two, because the parenthesis will be matched by method two, just after it was inserted and shown by method one. If you dislike blinking parentheses when traveling over them, you can, however, disable this feature, and still have them highlighted when writing the closing parentheses.

Showing Parentheses when Moving over Them

There are two methods of showing parentheses in common between GNU Emacs and XEmacs, namely "Showing the matching parenthesis" and "showing all the text in

12

between". In addition XEmacs has a third method, where the matching parenthesis blinks (that is, it blinks as long as point is located at its match).

In Figures 12.4 and 12.5, you can see the two different styles of showing the matching parenthesis.

FIGURE **12.4**

Showing matching parenthesis.

The matching parenthesis

FIGURE **12.5**

Showing a region between parentheses.

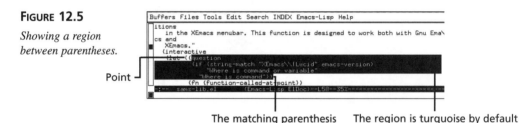

The matching parenthesis   The region is turquoise by default

The following five code listings show how to obtain a parentheses-showing method mentioned previously.

Showing matching parentheses in GNU Emacs:

```
(setq show-paren-mode t)
(setq show-paren-style 'parenthesis)
```

Showing region between parentheses in GNU Emacs:

```
(setq show-paren-mode t)
(setq show-paren-style 'expression)
```

Showing matching parentheses in XEmacs:

```
(paren-set-mode 'paren)
```

Showing region between parentheses in XEmacs:

```
(paren-set-mode 'sexp)
```

Blinking matching parentheses in XEmacs:

```
(paren-set-mode 'blink-paren)
```

If the matching parenthesis should be outside the visible part of the window, you can always jump to it using the following functions: `forward-sexp` or `backward-sexp`.

Besides showing the matching parentheses, Emacs also indicates to you when you have matched a couple of parentheses incorrectly. For example, if you close a brace with a parenthesis. This indication is done by using a different face (a different color and style). The face used can be customized using the customization library. In GNU Emacs, this is all included in the group called show-paren. In XEmacs, on the other hand, this must be customized separately from the other options concerning parentheses matching. This is done by pressing `M-x` and typing `customize-face` pressing `return`, and typing `paren-match` or `paren-mismatch`. The other options concerning parentheses showing is customized in the group called `paren-matching`.

Showing Parentheses when Writing the Closing Parenthesis

If you do not want the parentheses to be matched when traversing them, you can get a limited edition of parentheses highlighting, namely showing the opening parenthesis when typing the closing one. This is done by inserting the following line into your `.emacs` file:

```
(setq blink-matching-paren t)
```

Even though you have parentheses showing as described previously, you might want to enable this feature anyway, because it has the effect that the text around the opening parenthesis is shown in the minibuffer when writing the closing parenthesis and the opening one is outside the visible part of the buffer, as can be seen in Figure 12.6.

12

FIGURE 12.6

The opening parenthesis is outside the visible part of the buffer when closing it.

The parenthesis that is actually matched

Beginning of the text after the matching parenthesis (see Figure 12.5)

Using a Visible Bell

When an error occurs in Emacs, the audio bell rings to draw your attention. This is to keep you from typing for half an hour before finding that no text is actually inserted. If, however, you look at your screen when typing (rather than on your keyboard), you might find the audio bell annoying and want Emacs to simply blink when an error occur. This is obtained by inserting the following line into your .emacs file:

```
(setq visible-bell t)
```

 To see how the visible bell works, add the previous line and press C-g a few times.

Highlighting Syntax Using Fonts and Colors

Today's monitors have the capability to show text in different colors, fonts, and shapes. Why not use this to make the text more readable?

 The font, the color, and the shape are, together, referred to as the *face*.

Using the face to help show the meaning of the text is what font-lock mode does. Using information built in to the major mode with which you edit a given text, font-lock mode knows enough about your text to show keywords in one face, comments in another, text literals in a third, and so on. An example of this can be seen in Figure 12.7. To make is easy for you to see it in a black-and-white printed book, I configured, for this figure, font-lock mode to show text literals in italic, keywords in bold, and comments in inverse video. In the default setup for font-lock-mode different colors would be used instead.

The colors used in GNU Emacs 20 can be configured by customizing the group called font-lock-highlighting-faces; in GNU Emacs 19 and in XEmacs, you have to stick with the default fonts chosen, because configuring in these setups is much more difficult than using customize.

FIGURE 12.7

Font-lock mode works with information built in to your major modes.

Keywords

Font-lock mode tells you about its work in the minibuffer

A text literal   A comment

Starting Font-lock Mode

If you want font-lock mode enabled for all the major modes that know about font-lock and you are using GNU Emacs, simply insert the following line into your .emacs file:

```
(global-font-lock-mode)
```

If, on the other hand, you do not want it loaded for all modes or you use XEmacs, you have to explicitly enable it for each major mode, using a construct like the following:

```
(add-hook 'c-mode-hook 'turn-on-font-lock)
```

c-mode should be replaced with the major mode that you want to start font-lock mode for by default. Thus, if you want font-lock mode to be started by default in html-helper-mode, c-mode, and emacs-lisp-mode, insert the following into your .emacs file:

```
(add-hook 'html-helper-mode-hook 'turn-on-font-lock)
(add-hook 'c-mode-hook 'turn-on-font-lock)
(add-hook 'emacs-lisp-mode-hook 'turn-on-font-lock)
```

12

> This method is described in detail in Hour 24, "Installing Emacs Add-Ons." It does require that the given major mode define a hook called major-mode-hook, but this should always be the case.
>
> Font-lock mode can be turned on or off explicitly by pressing M-x and typing font-lock-mode.

Asking for Refontification

To make your buffer look nice, font-lock mode must do some pretty hard work. In most situations you will hardly notice, but if you have a very slow computer or a very large file, this might be a problem for you. To make everyone happy, font-lock mode offers different levels of fontification. What is fontified at a given level depends on the major mode. To find the truth, you have to either look in the Lisp file or try it out. By default, font-lock mode works in full-fontification-mode, but using the variable `font-lock-maximum-decoration` you can change this. To set font-lock mode to a low fontification level, insert the following into your `.emacs` file:

```
(setq font-lock-maximum-decoration 1)
```

> A more advanced method for getting cheap font-lock can be obtained using the minor modes called fast-lock-mode and lazy-lock-mode. Use `C-h f` (describe-function) for a discussion of what they do.

Even with fast computers, font-lock mode can be slow given, for example, a file with the size of 100MB. Thus font-lock mode can be configured to not do fontifications when a new file is opened with a size above a given value. This value is configured using the variable `font-lock-maximum-size`. Its default value is 256KB, which should be enough in most situations.

If you, however, sometimes read a file into Emacs that's larger than this size, you can either set the value higher or force Emacs to fontify your buffer, using the function `font-lock-fontify-buffer`.

The fontification can sometimes be done wrong due to the fact that font-lock mode tries to be as lazy as possible (that is, whenever you insert a character, it does not fontify your whole buffer). In these situations, press `M-g M-g` (font-lock-fontify-block), which should fix it. In situations where this also fails, use the function `font-lock-fontify-buffer`.

Filling

When writing ordinary text you often want Emacs to break the lines for you when a word goes beyond a given column. The text should not be broken in the middle of the word, but instead in between two words. In Hour 4, "Basic Editing," you already saw that auto-fill-mode could do that for you. What you might have discovered, however, is that when you break a line, Emacs does not automatically align the text for you. This is a feature, *not* a bug! Emacs does nothing you haven't asked it to do. To make Emacs fill a paragraph, press `M-q` (fill-paragraph).

A paragraph is defined using the variable paragraph-start, which is a regular expression defining the start of a paragraph and therefore also the end. In many major modes a paragraph is simply defined to start after a blank line, but in other major modes this might be more complex so a section heading might, for example, start a paragraph too.

If you do not want to fill a whole paragraph, you can instead use the function called fill-region. Unfortunately this is not bound to any key by default, so you might want to add this function to M-q (when a region is active), which you do by inserting the following into your .emacs file:

```
(global-set-key [(meta q)] 'sams-fill)
```

M-q then works as always when the region is inactive, but when the region is active, M-q instead invokes fill-region rather than fill-paragraph.

This works only if you use transient-mark-mode. The reason that it does not work when you are not using transient-mark mode is that the region always is active then.

Filling Parameters

Two extra parameters exist for configuring filling, namely the column at which the lines should break, and the prefix added to the beginning of every line.

There exist two different ways you can set the column where lines are broken:

- Press Escape, type the number, and press C-x f (set-fill-column).
- Go to the column where you want lines to break and press C-u C-x f.

Setting the column where lines are broken affects line breaking, both when inserting ordinary text (with auto-fill-mode enabled) and when invoking one of the fill commands.

When the lines are broken, Emacs can insert some initial text. This might, for example, be the comment character for the given major mode. To tell Emacs what this prefix should be, go to the end of it, and press C-x . (set-fill-prefix; control-x-period). This can be seen in Figure 12.8.

12

FIGURE 12.8

Setting the fill prefix.

The point ─┘

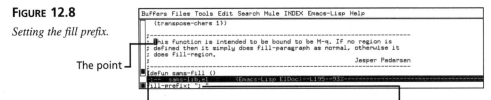

```
Buffers Files Tools Edit Search Mule INDEX Emacs-Lisp Help
  (transpose-chars 1))
;-----------------------------------------------------------------
; This function is intended to be bound to be M-q. If no region is
; defined then it simply does fill-paragraph as normal, otherwise it
; does fill-region.
;                                                    Jesper Pedersen
;-----------------------------------------------------------------
(defun sams-fill ()
;-- sams-lib.el        (Emacs-Lisp ElDoc)--L195--93%-------------
Fill-prefix: "; "
```

These two characters are now the fill prefix   This message indicate what the fill prefix is

Adaptive Filling

In many situations, it isn't necessary to explicitly set the fill prefix, because Emacs has a feature called *adaptive filling*. Using adaptive filling, Emacs itself tries to guess which fill prefix you want.

Adaptive filling is one of the new features in Emacs 20, so this section does not apply to Emacs 19 users.

The rules for guessing the prefix depend on the major mode, and they are kind of complex. The following can be taken as a rule of thumb (although it's not the whole truth):

- If the line starts with the comment string for the major mode, the comment string is used as a fill prefix when breaking the line.
- If the line starts with punctuation characters, the subsequent lines are filled with white spaces of the length of the punctuation characters.

For the whole truth on adaptive filling, refer to the section "Adaptive Filling" in the reference manual available from the info pages.

If you dislike adaptive filling, you can disable it by inserting the following text into your .emacs file:

```
(setq adaptive-fill-mode nil)
```

Getting Double Height Windows

Sometimes you might be interested in seeing many lines of text on your screen at the same time, just to get a good overview. You can do this by making the font very small, but then you can't read it, can you?

Another solution is to show the text in two windows side by side, with each window showing a different part of the text. To avoid having to scroll both windows separately, you can use the minor mode called follow-mode. In Figure 12.9, you can see a buffer that spans two windows, starting at the top of the first and continuing to the next.

FIGURE 12.9

To use follow-mode on a given buffer, simply start it and split the window, showing the buffer horizontally by pressing C-x 3 (split-window-horizontally). Below the window on the left is a virtual window.

The buffer now continues from the left window to the right window. This is totally transparent to you (except for the fact that your buffer now shows twice as many lines with half the width). When you move point one line down at the bottom of the left window, it appears at the top of the right window. Likewise, scrolling is done simultaneously in both windows.

If you really need lots of screen height, you can split one of the windows horizontally a second time, which gives you three windows side by side, showing the buffer in the height of three windows, as can be seen in Figure 12.10.

FIGURE 12.10

Showing a buffer in three windows using follow-mode.

Rectangular Commands

In Hour 4, you saw how to cut and paste characters from one location in the buffer to another point (a region). In certain situations, you are not interested in cutting and pasting from one point or character to another, but rather using rectangles. An example of this can be seen in Figure 12.11, where you want to remove the initial characters of each line. These lines are from the file pager.el, where the given lines are inserted into the .emacs file. They have, however, the Lisp comment characters in front of them, which you need to remove.

Figure 12.11

Example of a rectangle.

The rectangle —
to be removed

The location where mark must be set to remove this rectangle,
given that point is positioned as can be seen in the figure

To remove this rectangle, place point at one end of the rectangle, and the mark at the other end (as can be seen in Figure 12.11), and press C-x r k (kill-rectangle). This is easy to remember, in fact: C-x is the prefix for most complex commands, r for *rectangle*, and k for *kill*.

Besides killing a rectangle you can also paste it back in another location. This is done by pressing C-x r y (yank-rectangle). The upper-left corner of the rectangle is anchored at the place where point was located when C-x r y was invoked and space is made for the rectangle in all affected lines. Although this is a silly example, it can be seen in Figure 12.12 where the rectangle killed in Figure 12.11 was just pasted in.

Figure 12.12

A rectangle is pasted in using C-x r y (yank-rectangle).

The location of —
point before pasting

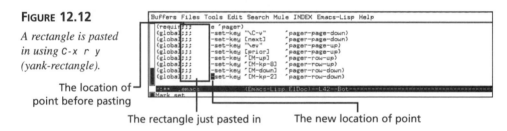

The rectangle just pasted in   The new location of point

Finally, it is possible to insert a text string at the left side of each line that the rectangle spans. This is done by pressing C-x r t (string-rectangle), when a rectangle has been defined. Emacs asks for the text to insert in the minibuffer; when you type it and press Enter, the text is inserted.

Summary

You have now learned different ways for changing the font in Emacs. You will not do that often, but it can be useful to get a font that fits your monitor and eyes perfectly.

When you get used to parentheses matching and font-lock mode, you will find that these are invaluable tools that make it easier for you to get an overview and get find the right context very fast. If you haven't already played with using different faces for font-lock mode, it might be a good idea to try it out now.

Filling is a tool that you won't even notice in your daily work, unless it is disabled. Adaptive filling is a feature that in itself is worth changing to Emacs 20 for!

Q&A

Q Why is parentheses matching different in GNU Emacs and XEmacs?

A Well, they're two different programs and parentheses matching is one of the things that was modified after the time XEmacs branched off of GNU Emacs. This is one of those little things that you have to live with.

Q Is there no simple way to make font-lock mode start by default for every mode in XEmacs?

A Well, there is a hack. Insert the following into your `.emacs` file:

```
(add-hook 'find-file-hooks 'turn-on-font-lock)
```

This, however, works only when you load a file into Emacs, not when creating a new buffer. But in 95% of the cases you will only just read in a new file.

Q How do I start auto-fill mode for every buffer in text-mode?

A Using the same method you used to start font-lock mode:

```
(add-hook 'text-mode-hooks 'auto-fill-mode)
```

Q I've found some editing commands with a `C-x 6` prefix—for example, `C-x 6 2` (2C-two-columns)—with names that indicate that they are for two columns. How do they related to follow-mode?

A They have nothing to do with follow-mode. The commands are for splitting a buffer at some horizontal point and then editing it in two separate buffers, one for the left side, and another for the right side. To be honest, I haven't found many applications for it, but who knows, that might be something with special interest for you.

12

Exercises

1. Change the font of your Emacs to 18 points and make it permanent.

2. If you use UNIX, make the 18-point font a permanent one that you can get by starting Emacs with `-name` test.

3. NT Emacs users should try various fonts and sizes. Try setting the font to bold, italic, and both. If you like a setting, make it permanent.

4. Try the different methods for parentheses matching. If you are using GNU Emacs, try to change the face used.

5. Enable font-lock mode for the major modes you often use, and find out whether you can see any differences between the various levels of fontifications.

Hour 13

Macros

The most wonderful thing about Emacs is its capability to do the trivial part of your work for you. Sometimes having Emacs do your work takes more time than solving the original task, but you have still learned two things:

- You have learned a bit more about Emacs.
- Monotonous work often tends to be error prone because you inattentively do it over and over again. This is avoided by letting Emacs do it for you.

Emacs has two ways to do your work for you. The complex way is by programming the solution in Lisp; the other and easier way is to develop a macro. Programming Lisp is beyond the scope of this book, but fortunately macros can do the job in many situations. (You will, however, learn a little about Lisp in Hour 22, "Learning Lisp Basics.")

I guess it's time to tell you what a macro is, right? A macro is a recorded sequence of keystrokes that you can execute over and over again. If you doubt that this should do all your monotonous work for you, please think about all the actions that you do very often. The following are examples where a macro might help you typing:

- Making the first character of each paragraph uppercase. (You can press M-c (capitalize-word) to capitalize the word in front of point).

- Renumbering all sections of a document due to the fact that a section is inserted in the middle.

- Replacing every occurrences of printf(...) with write {...}. (No, you cannot use search-and-replace, because this would miss the replacement of the end parenthesis with the end brace.)

> If you ever catch yourself in a situation in which you type the same word over and over again and the result is that the keyboard makes a weak sound (it sounds like *tik taak tik tik*), it might be worth it to create a macro!

There are two kinds of macros:

- Those that do a task repeatedly over several lines—for example, capitalizing every paragraph.

- Those that do a complicated action for you (such as inserting some text and repositioning point to the middle of this text). These macros are not intended to be repeated several times after each other but rather to be executed once in awhile when you need the keystrokes of the macro executed.

In the first kind of macro, you often want to get the macro executed a certain number of times or within a specific region of text. This is described in detail in the section "Repeating Macros". In the second kind of macro, you often want to build a macro that interacts with you to insert some text, for example to fill out a form. This is described in the section "Recording a Macro for Filling Out a Simple Text-Based Database." You might sometimes want to save a macro for later Emacs sessions. This is described in the section "Saving a Macro for Later Sessions."

> In the Emacs documentation, macros are referred to by the name *keyboard macros*. The reason for this is that macros in Lisp have nothing to do with the macros discussed in this hour.

Writing a Simple Macro

Define a macro by telling Emacs to record the keystrokes to come, doing what your macro should do, and finally telling Emacs that you are finished defining the macro.

Recording and Executing Macros

To let Emacs type for you, you can record a sequence of keys that it can retype at your command. Follow these steps:

1. Press C-x ((start-kbd-macro) to tell Emacs to start recording your macro.

2. Do whatever you want Emacs to do for you later. This can include typing text, moving point, changing buffers, and executing commands. Press C-x) (end-kbd-macro) to tell Emacs to stop recording the macro.

3. To execute the macro just recorded type C-x e (call-last-kbd-macro).

If some commands during the recording of the macro ring the bell (that is, an error occurs), the macro is automatically aborted. To manually abort the recording of a macro, simply press C-g (keyboard-quit).

Capitalize the First Character of Each Section

This task shows you how to capitalize the first character of each paragraph by using a macro. Follow these steps:

1. Go to the beginning of the first section you want to capitalize. Press C-x ((start-kbd-macro). This starts recording the macro. Note that the text *Def* is shown in your modeline to indicate that you are recording a macro.

2. Press M-c (capitalize-word). This capitalizes the first word in the paragraph.

3. Press M-} (forward-paragraph). This takes you to the beginning of the next paragraph.

4. Press C-x) (end-kbd-macro). This stops recording the macro. Now you can press C-x e (call-last-kbd-macro) several times to capitalize several paragraphs.

13

For a macro such as the preceding to work successfully, it needs to finish in a position that can be used as a starting point to be repeated again. In the preceding example, the starting point is the beginning of a paragraph. When the macro has been executed, it places point at the start of the next paragraph.

> Only one macro can be current at a time. To execute the current macro, press C-x e. To have several macros available at one time, you need to give each one a name. When they have names, they are available by pressing M-x. This is described in the section "Saving a Macro for Later Sessions."

Repeating Macros

Some of the macros are developed to be executed several times after each other, such as the one in the previous section. Sometimes you know exactly how many times you want the macro to be executed, and other times you have a region in which you want your macro to execute. Unfortunately, there are some times where you know neither of these things. You might, for example, know that you have exactly ten subsequent paragraphs, and you want these ten paragraphs to be capitalized.

An example of a macro which could be executed several times within a region is given in the previous section, where you developed a macro to capitalize paragraphs. Using this macro, you can capitalize every paragraph in a region. In other words, you can execute the macro until it finishes one execution with the point outside the region.

> If you want to execute a macro several times in succession but you cannot determine a region or a number of times, you have to press C-x e (call-last-kbd-macro) several times. This might be irritating, because this is two keystrokes and difficult to do fast. A solution to this problem would be to bind the command call-last-kbd-macro to one of the function keys or a modified function key (for example, S-F1).

To execute a macro a number of times, you must give it a numeric prefix. Do this by pressing the Control key down, and, while holding it, typing the number. Thus to execute the previous defined macro 10 times, press and hold the Control key, type 10, release the Control key, and press C-x e. To be completely accurate, this is, of course, equivalent to pressing C-1 C-0 C-x e.

Repeating a Macro over a Region

The following are two approaches to repeating a macro over a region:

- Execute the macro once for every line in the region. In each iteration, point is located at the start of the line to be processed.

- At the beginning of the execution, point is located in the beginning of the region, and the macro is executed repeatedly, until one execution of the macro ends outside the region.

The first approach has the advantage that you do not need to worry about getting point to the correct location for the next iteration, but it has the drawback that you cannot create a macro, such as the one preceding, that capitalizes paragraphs throughout the region.

 The first approach is available through the function apply-macro-to-region-lines, which comes with Emacs as standard. The other is available through the function sams-apply-macro-on-region, which is located on the CD as part of `sams-lib.el`. See Appendix A, "Installing Functions and Packages from the CD" for a description on how to install this library.

In the rest of this section, the second approach is described, because it is the most powerful one.

There are a few rules that must be followed when you record a macro that should be executed repeatedly with the command sams-apply-macro-on-region (some of them also apply when you record a macro for execution several times using a numeric prefix):

- Remember that the macro is executed first with point located at the beginning of the region.

- The macro must advance down the buffer. The reason for this is that the macro continues until you move past the end of the region. If you move upward in the buffer or if you do not move at all, the function will never terminate.

- The macro must reposition point so that it is located at a similar position at the end of the execution compared to where it started. When you reposition, do not use relative commands. That is, if you want to go to the end of the line, do not use the arrow key (forward-char), because this depends on how long the line is; instead, use `C-e` (end-of-line).

The macro which you defined in the previous section does, in fact, fulfill the preceding requirement. To uppercase paragraphs in a region, place the region in such a way that it starts at the first character of the first paragraph (this is important, because the macro starts by uppercasing the word at point) and press `M-x` (sams-apply-macro-on-region).

After you get used to this command, you will use it over and over again, so it's good advice to bind this command to a key.

13

Saving a Macro for Later Sessions

Only the most-recently-defined macro is available by pressing C-x e (call-last-kbd-macro). If you want to have several macros defined at a time, you need to give them names and, instead of pressing C-x e to execute them, you must press M-x and the name that you gave to the macro.

Naming a Macro

To get several macros available at a time or to save a macro to a file, you need to give it a name. Follow these steps to name a macro:

1. Record the macro as described previously in the To Do section "Recording and Executing Macros." Press M-x (name-last-kbd-macro), press Return, and type a name for the macro.

> It's wise to prefix the name of the macro with your initials to avoid overriding an existing function that is defined in Emacs. If you want to name a macro that does some special opening of files, you could name it jkp-openfile (given that your initials are jkp).

2. When you have named the macro, you can access it by pressing M-x and its name. Until you define a new macro, it's still available by pressing C-x e (call-last-kbd-macro).

If you do not save your macro to your startup file, the macro will be forgotten the next time you start Emacs. This is fine for many macros, but if you have developed a macro that you think is your best piece of work ever, and you believe that this macro will save you lots of time in the future, it might be a good idea to save it for later sessions.

Saving a Macro to Your Startup File

This To Do task teaches you how to save a named macro to your startup file (that is, your .emacs file or a file specific for macros). Follow these steps:

1. Define and name your macro as described in the previous To Do task.

2. Switch to the file in which you want to save your macro.

3. Press M-x (insert-kbd-macro). Press Return and type the name of your macro.

   If you save a macro in your .emacs file or another file read by your .emacs file, your macro will be available in all your Emacs sessions in the future. If you use the macro often, it might be wise to bind it to a key.

> If you have developed a set of macros that you want to use on only a given file (or a limited set of files), you can save these macros to a separate file and insert the following lines at the end of the files that use these macros:
>
> ```
> % Local Variables:
> % eval: (load-file "macros.el")
> % End:
> ```
>
> The percent sign might be replaced with any text (for example the comment symbol in C files) and macros.el should be replaced by the name of the file in which you saved your macros. This is described in detail in Hour 24, "Installing Emacs Add-Ons."

Making Macros that Ask for Permission to Continue

Sometimes when you create a macro to do the same thing over and over again hundreds of times, you might be afraid that your macro will accidentally change text that should not have been changed. As an example, think of the macro that replaces `printf(...)` with `write {...}`. This macro can search forward for the next occurrences of `printf`, replace it with `write`, and do some more stuff to replace the parentheses with curly braces. This macro might fail to do what you want it to do because you also have occurrences of `sprintf` that you don't want to be replaced. The solution to your problem is to pause the macro just before it does the replacement. To do this, press `C-x q` (kbd-macro-query).

Replacing `printf(...)` with `write {...}` the Secure Way

This task creates a macro that replaces `printf(...)` with `write {...}`. The macro pauses just before the replacement takes place, so the user can validate whether the replacement should take place.

13

> It wouldn't be necessary to use a macro, were it not for the ending parenthesis that must be replaced with a brace. Regular expression replacement wouldn't do it either, because braces might exist within the parentheses that should be replaced.

▼ Follow these steps:

1. Press C-x ((start-kbd-macro) to record the macro. Press C-s (isearch-forward) and type printf(. This searches forward for the next occurrence of printf(.

2. Press C-x q (kbd-macro-query) to make the macro stop for validation at this point.

3. Press the left arrow key to place the point before the parenthesis.

4. Press C-@ (set-mark-command) to set the mark (this makes it possible to get back to this point where you replace the ending parenthesis).

5. Press M-x (forward-sexp). This brings you to the ending parenthesis, replacing the parenthesis with a brace.

6. Press C-x C-x (exchange-point-and-mark), which sets the point at the location where the mark is (that is, before the opening parenthesis), replacing it with a brace.

7. Press C-x) (end-kbd-macro) to stop recording the macro.

> Note that this macro does not fulfill the requirement for macros that should be executed with sams-apply-macro-on-region. This is not a problem if all occurrences should be replaced. But it is a problem if only some of them should be replaced, because the macro will continue beyond the limit of the region and do one more replacement before it stops.

▲

In Figure 13.1, you can see how Emacs asks you for permission to continue the macro. You have the following choices:

- Y or Spacebar—This tells Emacs that the macro can continue.

- N or Delete—This tells Emacs that you do not want the macro to continue for this iteration, but if you have invoked, for example, sams-apply-macro-on-region, it can continue to execute the macro.

- Q or Enter (or Return)—This is like N, but the difference is that sams-apply-macro-on-region will not continue either. In other words, if you want the macro to repeatedly execute throughout a region (or a number of times, given with prefix argument), this will be terminated and the macro will not be executed at all anymore.

- C-l (that is, Control and a lowercase L)—Pressing C-l recenters the page, so you can see the context of the location.

- C-r—This enters recursive editing. This is just like recursive editing in search-and-replace (see Hour 7, "Searching for Text in a Buffer").

Emacs suggests the keys Y, N, and Enter, whereas XEmacs suggests the keys Space, Delete, and Q. Don't let that confuse you, because all six key bindings work in both GNU Emacs and XEmacs. Adapt to the ones that your version of Emacs suggests.

FIGURE 13.1

Emacs asks for permission to continue executing the macro.

Another (or an extra) check is to create a copy of the file before you let your macro do its work. Afterwards you can then use `ediff` to validate that only the intended changes were made.

Further Interaction with the Macro

Sometimes you might want to alternate repeatedly between letting a macro do some work and writing something yourself. You could implement this by creating macros that do all the macro actions, calling them one at a time, and typing in between. But, of course, Emacs has a method that is much smarter.

In Hour 7, you saw how you could pause a search-and-replace action to edit an error you have found. This was called *recursive-edit*. The same mechanism is available during macro execution.

When you record your macro, press C-u C-x q (kbd-macro-query with a C-u prefix). When your macro is executed later, the macro enters recursive editing at this point. In other words, it lets you do some editing before it continues. To tell it to continue, you must press M-C-c (exit-recursive-edit).

There is one minor thing that is important to understand here, which is that the macro recording itself is paused when you press C-u C-x q. To continue recording the macro, press C-M-c.

13

Recording a Macro for Filling Out a Simple Text-Based Database

Follow these steps to learn how pausing macros can help you fill out an entry in a simple database with fields called Name, Street, and so on:

1. Press C-x ((start-kbd-macro) to record the macro.

2. Type Name:, which should be the first entry in the database.

3. Press C-u C-x q (kbd-macro-query) to make the macro pause. What you type now will not be part of the macro, so you can fill out the first entry in your database. Type a name.

4. Press M-C-c (exit-recursive-edit) to continue recording the macro.

5. Type Street:, which is the second entry in your simple database.

6. Press C-u C-x q again to enter recursive edit.

7. Again, the following text is not part of the macro, so here you fill out the location of the person that you are inserting. Press M-C-c (exit-recursive-edit) to continue recording the macro.

   Continue this way until you have all the fields for your database.

8. Press C-x) (end-kbd-macro) to stop recording your macro.

> Emacs does not enable you to exit the macro during recursive edit and, thus, abort recording the macro. You have to leave recursive edit before you can abort recording the macro.

In Figure 13.2, you can see an example of the database macro that you have defined.

FIGURE 13.2

Execution of the macro recorded.

Squared brackets indicate recursive editing

Please note the square brackets around (Text) in the figure. This indicates that the macro is waiting for you to let it continue. (Technically, it does mean that you are editing recursively, but that is the same in this case.)

If you want to abort the macro when you are in recursive-edit, you can press C-] (abort-recursive-edit). This also applies if you find that you forgot to finish a macro and, therefore, are in recursive editing.

It might be easier to remember this keybinding if you notice that the key is the same as the indication in the mode line (that is, the end square bracket).

Editing a Macro

After you have recorded a macro, you might find that it is erroneous or that it would be nice if it went a bit farther. Starting at the later requirement, this is easy: Press C-u C-x (—start-kbd-macro with a C-u prefix—instead of C-x (to start recording the macro.

To edit a macro, you must press C-x C-k (edit-kbd-macro). This asks you which macro to edit in the minibuffer. You have the following possibilities:

- C-x e—This edits the most-recently defined macro; that is, the one that is available by pressing C-x e.

- M-x—This enables you to edit a macro that you have named (as described in task "Naming a Macro"). When you press M-x, Emacs asks you for the name of the macro in the minibuffer.

- C-h l—This lets you use the latest 100 keystrokes as the macro. When you save your editing, it is saved as the macro available through C-x e.

The key sequence C-h l comes from the command with the given binding (view-lossage). This command enables you to see the last 100 keystrokes, so you can see what you did. Now that you have learned to use edit-kbd-macro, you might find this interface more useful than the one from C-h l.

This key sequence, unfortunately, doesn't work if you have redefined C-h l to a command other than view-lossage, which is in fact what the package ehelp does.

13

- Keys—This tells you that you can press a key sequence that is bound to a macro. It is the macro to which these keys are bound that is edited.

When you have selected the macro to edit, the buffer shown in Figure 13.3 appears.

This information tells you how to quit this buffer

FIGURE 13.3

Editing the macro.

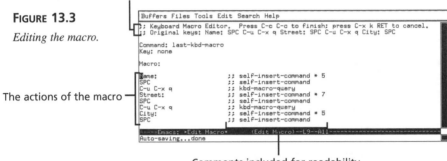

The actions of the macro

Comments included for readability

In the first two lines, you see how to exit this buffer again and what the content of the macro was when you entered this buffer (in case you suddenly are in doubt whether your changes are correct). As it says, you can press either C-c C-c to save your changes to the macro you edit or C-x k to discard them. Both actions delete the buffer and restore the original one.

The following two lines tell you which macro you're editing and which key it is bound to, if any.

Finally comes the content of the macro. In the left column is the content of the macro, and in the right column is the Lisp function that the keys execute. If you do not understand a word of what the right column says, don't bother. Don't delete the two semicolons without deleting the rest of the line. It should be simple to read what it says. Ordinary inserted characters are shown the way they were inserted. Examples of this include Name:, Street:, and City:. Another alternative would be text that describes special keys. This includes SPC for a space, RET for the return key, DEL for the delete button, and <left> for the left-arrow key. Finally a keypress can be shown (such as C-u C-x q in the example).

You can edit this buffer as you would any other buffer. The only difference is that when you press C-c C-c, the content of the buffer will be used to define a macro.

When you edit this buffer, you can press C-c C-q to insert a keypress into your macro. If you want to move point one character to the left, you should press C-c C-q and then the left-arrow key. Ordinary text is inserted verbatim, thus if you want to change the word

Name to *First Name*, insert the word *First* at the line before *Name*, followed by a line-break and the text **SPC**.

> You should be aware that using the Spacebar does not insert a space. Instead you should type **SPC**.

Summary

You have now learned to create macros; so start using them! In the beginning it might take more time to create the macros than they will save you, but remember the following:

- It is more fun to create a macro than to do trivial work.
- With the macros, you can make fewer mistakes.
- In the long run, you will save lots of time.
- The more macros you make, the better you will be to recognize the need for a macro.

Table 13.1 lists the functions that were described in this hour.

TABLE 13.1 FUNCTIONS CONCERNING MACROS

Default Keybindings	Function Name	Description
C-x (	start-kbd-macro	Start recording a macro. If you give it a numeric prefix (C-u), you instead continue the previous macro recorded.
C-x)	end-kbd-macro	Stop recording a macro.
C-x e	call-last-kbd-macro	Execute the macro recently defined.
M-x	name-last-kbd-macro	Give a name to the most recent defined macro.
M-x	sams-apply-macro-on-region	Run a macro on a region until point is outside the region after an iteration.
C-x q	(kbd-macro-query)	Make the macro ask the user for permission to continue. Given a numeric prefix (C-u), the macro instead enters recursive editing, which lets you type some text before the macro continues.

continues

13

TABLE 13.1   CONTINUED

Default Keybindings	Function Name	Description
C-x k	edit-kbd-macro	This asks you for a keyboard macro to edit and places you in a buffer with the macro in a readable form.
M-C-c	exit-recursive-edit	When the macro pauses for your editing (that is, in recursive-edit) pressing M-C-c continues the macro.

Q&A

Q Tell me honestly: Do you often use macros yourself? Can you give me an estimate on how much time it saves you?

A Yes, I use macros several times every hour I'm in front of my computer. Most of the macros do very simple things that save me only 5–10 keystrokes, but I also create macros that can take up to half-an-hour to develop. The latter macros are those that edit large parts of files and must, therefore, be tested more intensely than those that do simple editing on the line.

How much time I save by using macros depends on the kind of work I'm doing. If I'm writing text, I use macros less frequently, and thus save less time. (The writing job is not monotonous enough to make macros very useful). If I, on the other hand, am maintaining documents (C files, HTML documents, or simple text files), the macros can save 10–50% of my time compared to if I didn't have macros.

Exercises

1. Develop a macro that you can use to copy paragraphs containing the word *Emacs* to another buffer. You might need the commands M-a (backward-sentence) to get to the beginning of a sentence and M-e (forward-sentence) to get to the end of a sentence.

2. Hour 7 describes the bookmark feature and the command bookmark-jump. Unfortunately, no function called bookmark-jump-other-window exists, which would jump to a bookmark in another window. Develop a macro that splits your current window in two and jumps to the bookmark in one of the windows.

3. Develop a macro that uses TAGS to search for a definition of the word before point and copy it to the next line of your current buffer. (This can be useful when you don't remember the number or types of arguments to a function when you program.)

4. On the CD is a file called `counter.el`. This library lets you insert a series of numbers that are very useful in macros. Find this library and develop a macro that creates 10 numbered section headers (for example, Hour 1, Hour 2...Hour 10).

13

Hour 14

Finding Differences Between Files

Using the UNIX program diff, you can find the differences between two files that are almost identical. The two files might be

- The original file before a change and the changed file.
- A file edited by two different persons (for example, two different persons who work together on a project).
- A file located on two different machines and edited on both machines. An example of this might be your `.emacs` file that you might have a copy of both at home and at work.

In the last two examples, both files have a common ancestor, namely the file before it was modified. When this is the case, the program diff3 might make it easier for you to create one file, which is the original file plus the modifications made.

The output from the command-line version of diff is hard to interpret, unless the changes are few or you are really cool at looking at these outputs.

Fortunately, Emacs contains an interface to diff, called Ediff, that makes it much easier. Besides making it easier to look at the output from one diff, Emacs also offers functions for merging the files and applying patches. Applying patches is beyond the scope of this book, but if you apply patches often, I urge you to take a look at the info pages for Ediff. Emacs also has the capability to find the differences between the files of two directories. This is especially useful if you have a set of files that you work on in two different places (such as your Lisp files located at work and at home).

Windows doesn't include diff, so you have to install a copy. There is a diff program included with the Cygwin tools on the CD-ROM. Other UNIX tool sets might also include diff, but you should test them to make sure that Emacs understands the output from another version of diff.

Regardless of the version of diff you use, you might have to customize the variable diff-command so that Emacs can execute it. (See Hour 10, "The Emacs Help System and Configuration System," for a description of how to customize variables.)

Diffing Two Files with Ediff

A number of functions in the Ediff library lets you diff two items.

- ediff-buffers—This asks for the name of two buffers and diffs them.
- ediff-files—This asks for the name of two files, loads them into Emacs, and diffs them.
- ediff-windows-linewise, ediff-windows-wordwise—These ask you to point at two windows and then diff the content of these windows. The -linewise function is faster than the -wordwise, but on the other hand, the -wordwise function generally does a better job, especially with small regions. -linewise compares buffers line-by-line, while -wordwise compares them word-by-word.
- ediff-regions-linewise, ediff-regions-wordwise—These ask for the names of two buffers and then diff the region of these. Note that you can have only one region in each buffer, therefore it is not possible to create two regions in the same file for diffing. However, in Hour 15, "Getting an Overview of a File," a method for diffing two parts of the same buffer is shown (technically it is not the same buffer, but it seems so to the user).

Don't let it scare you that there are so many different functions for diffing two files; after all, they are easy to remember, because they are all called ediff-*what-you-want-to-diff*.

In Figure 14.1, an Ediff session is shown. Emacs has found four differences between the two files. The current difference is number one and is highlighted, which makes it easier to find. The differences reported by the diff program can span more text than is actually the difference, therefore Emacs highlights the part which is actually different. Thus in the upper buffer, the line that is the current difference is green, except for the word redo, which is dark blue, to indicate that this is the actual difference. Likewise the line in the buffer below is yellow, except the word undefined, which is light blue.

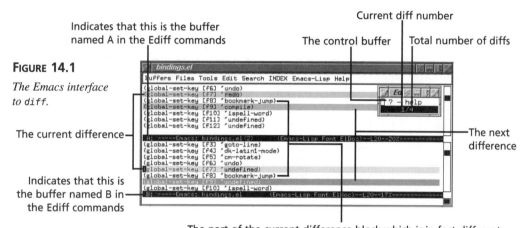

FIGURE 14.1

The Emacs interface to diff.

Indicates that this is the buffer named A in the Ediff commands

Current diff number

The control buffer | Total number of diffs

The current difference—

—The next difference

Indicates that this is the buffer named B in the Ediff commands

The part of the current difference block which is in fact different

Figure 14.1 includes the window managers border, which you can see at the top of the window. This is merely to show you that the control buffer is located in its own frame.

This might be the right time to tell you, before you get too excited, Ediff really does require a color monitor. It is capable of showing the difference with a black-and-white monitor, but the output is much harder to interpret.

If you make the window with the control buffer the active one, you can invoke the command that controls the Ediff session.

14

If you press ? in the control buffer, the buffer expands to show the available keybindings in it. This can be seen in Figure 14.2

FIGURE 14.2

The control buffer expanded to show available commands.

```
■   Move around      |    Toggle features    |      Manipulate
====================|=======================|==========================
p,DEL -previous diff |   | -vert/horiz split  | a/b -copy A/B's region to B/A
n,SPC -next diff     |   h -hilighting        | rx -restore buf X's old diff
    j -jump to diff  |   @ -auto-refinement   |  * -refine current region
   gx -goto X's point|                        |  ! -update diff regions
  C-l -recenter      |  ## -ignore whitespace |
  v/V -scroll up/dn  | #f/#h -focus/hide regions| wx -save buf X
  </> -scroll lt/rt  |   X -read-only in buf X | wd -save diff output
    ~ -swap variants |   m -wide display      |
====================|=======================|==========================
    R -show registry |   = -compare regions   |  M   -show session group
    D -diff output   |   E -browse Ediff manual|  G   -send bug report
    i -status info   |   ? -help off          |  z/q -suspend/quit
--------------------|-----------------------|--------------------------
For help on a specific command:  Click Button 2 over it; or
                                 Put the cursor over it and type RET.
-- *Ediff Control Panel*   At start of 4 diffs           Quick Help
```

Moving Around

There are several ways with which you can move from diff to diff. The most basic one is by pressing n or p in the control buffer. These move, respectively, to the next or previous diff.

> In the following text it is understood that all the commands are invoked in the control buffer. The two buffers showing the difference are modifiable as always, thus if you press a key such as n in this buffer, it is simply inserted into the buffer.

If you know the number of a difference, you can jump directly to this diff by pressing the number and the letter j. Thus pressing 4j in the control buffer takes you to difference number four.

> It is also possible to take the content of the diff region from one buffer and insert it in the other. Furthermore, it is possible to ask Emacs to recalculate the difference. This means that the number of a difference region might change, because a previous region might not be different anymore and therefore the number of diffs might have decreased by one.

When you browse one of the difference buffers, you might find a location of special interest. You can synchronize both buffers to the same location by locating the point in the difference region and, in the control buffer, pressing ga or gb depending on whether the buffer where you placed the point is buffer A or buffer B. (The name of the buffer is indicated in the mode line.)

The buffers with the differences are editable like always; therefore, you can also scroll them up and down to see other parts of the buffers without having to advance to another difference. Sometimes you might want to scroll both buffers simultaneously. To do that press v to scroll downward in the buffer, and V to scroll upward. Likewise if the lines are truncated, you can scroll both buffers horizontally at the same time by pressing either < or >.

To quit one of the Ediff commands press q (*q* for *q*uit).

Refinement

Ediff uses the diff program to calculate the differences. The region that is marked as different, but actually isn't different, is the output from diff. Emacs can optionally do extra refinements of the difference, but this costs extra computer power. If you have a slow computer (or it is hard at work), this might not be desirable. By pressing @ in the control buffer, you can turn off this extra refinement; pressing @ again turns it back on.

To avoid spending a lot of time refining huge regions, Emacs contains a variable called `ediff-auto-refine-limit`, which is a number saying how many characters at most a region must contain for automatic refinement to take place (see Hour 10, "The Emacs Help System and Configuration System," for a description of how to customize variables).

> This option doesn't seem to work in the version of Ediff that is shipped with GNU Emacs version 19. You must have GNU Emacs version 20.

When automatic refinement has been disabled or was not done due to a huge region, you can press * to force Emacs to do the refinement.

You might run into situations when a large chunk of text has been edited and then moved to a different place. In such cases, these two chunks of text are unlikely to belong to the same difference region, so the refinement feature of Ediff will not be able to tell you what exactly differs inside these chunks. In these situations you can mark the text that should be almost identical in both buffers and press = (the equals sign). This starts a new Ediff session for the subpart of the buffers.

> This feature doesn't work in the version of Ediff that is shipped with GNU Emacs version 19. You must use GNU Emacs version 20.

14

You might often want to skip the diffs that contain only differences in the number of white spaces. To do this, press ## (two hash marks). Emacs then simply skips these regions.

Copying from Buffer to Buffer

Though Ediff has special functions for merging two buffers into one, it is often easier to use Ediff and copy the resulting files into one of the files. This can be done by pressing either a or b. a copies the diff from buffer A to buffer B, while b copies the text the other way.

If you later find that it was wrong to overwrite a given region, you can restore it again by pressing either ra or rb, for restore region in buffer A or in buffer B.

When you have copied a region from one buffer to the other, you might want to recalculate the difference between the two buffers. This can be done by pressing ! (the exclamation point).

Diffing Two Files with a Common Ancestor

When diffing two files that are the same file edited in two different places (for example, by two different persons working on the same project) you can get into a situation where file A contains text that isn't in file B. In these situations, there are two possibilities:

- The text might have been added to file A
- The text might have been deleted from file B

To find which of the two possibilities is the correct one, you need to look in the original file. If the text is in the original, it must have been deleted from file B; otherwise it must have been added to file A.

To ease the work in situations such as this, Emacs has two functions called ediff-buffers3 and ediff-files3. These functions take three files and shows their differences. The order of the files doesn't matter, as long as the files include the original file and its two variants. Figure 14.3 shows the Emacs window when ediff-buffer3 is used.

All the commands for moving around and copying between buffers that were described in the previous section still apply, with the exception that instead of typing a for copying text from buffer A to buffer B, you must now type ab to copy text from buffer A to buffer B. Likewise there are commands to copy text in other directions, for example, cb to copy text from buffer C to buffer B.

FIGURE 14.3

The Emacs interface to
diff-buffers3.

Indicates that buffer A
is equal to buffer B

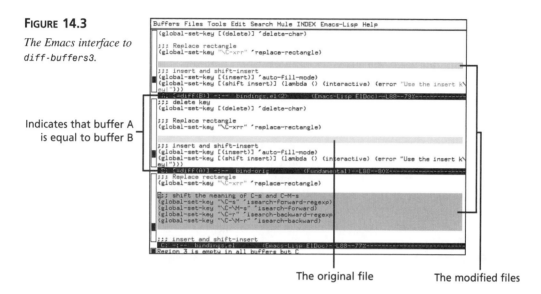

The original file   The modified files

Ediff Session

When you get used to Ediff, you will find yourself trying to figure out what the difference is between several pairs of files. In these cases you might want to have several Ediff sessions running at the same time. Emacs supports this. By pressing z in the control buffer you suspend the Ediff session. You can then start a new Ediff session. To get to an another Ediff session, press R in the control buffer or press M-x and type eregistry. This brings you to a buffer called *Ediff Registry*. This buffer contain a list of all the Ediff sessions currently running. It can be seen in Figure 14.4.

FIGURE 14.4

The Ediff registry,
used to select an Ediff
session.

An Ediff session with
the files config.el<2>
and config.el

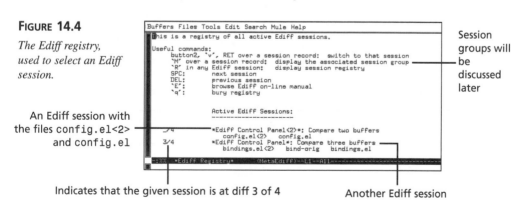

Session
groups will
be
discussed
later

Indicates that the given session is at diff 3 of 4   Another Ediff session

14

To jump to a given Ediff session, simply press the second mouse button or the Enter key over it.

Merging Files

In case you have two files that you want to merge, but none of the files are allowed to be overwritten, you should use one of the functions `ediff-merge-files`, `ediff-merge-buffers`, `ediff-merge-files-with-ancestor`, or `ediff-merge-buffers-with-ancestor`. The first two ask for two files or buffers to merge, while the later two ask for two functions or buffers to merge and a common ancestor.

> Please be aware that the functions called `emerge-files` and `emerge-buffers` do similar jobs to the Ediff equivalents, but are much older and more primitive. When you have Ediff, you will never want to use these functions.

With a common ancestor Emacs can decide which part is the modified one, when a diff exists between the two buffers. Both parts can be modified.

Merging Without an Ancestor

In Figure 14.5 you can see the Emacs interface to `ediff-merge-buffers`.

The current diff

FIGURE 14.5

*The Emacs interface to
ediff-merge-buffers.*

The combined match

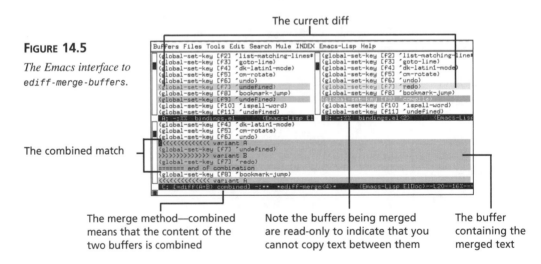

The merge method—combined
means that the content of the
two buffers is combined

Note the buffers being merged
are read-only to indicate that you
cannot copy text between them

The buffer
containing the
merged text

There are several different ways Emacs can merge the files for you initially. That is the default action taken to insert some text in the merge buffer before asking you what to do. It might as default expect that the content of buffer A is the text to be used. Likewise it might use the text from buffer B. Finally it might merge the text as can be seen in Figure 14.5. The default action can be specified by pressing & (the ampersand).

If you do not agree with the default action that Emacs has taken, you can press a to use the content of buffer A, b to use the content of buffer B, or + to insert the content of the two buffers merged (like in Figure 14.5). If you want to undo one of these commands for the given diff, press r. (Just like with the Ediff commands.)

When text has been inserted in merged form, you can edit the merge buffer to be like you want it to.

Merging with an Ancestor

Merging using a common ancestor is much like merging without. There are a few differences, however. First, Emacs now has a chance to guess which buffer contains the modification. This means that in the cases where one of the buffers is equal to the ancestor, Emacs simply uses the content of the other buffers as the difference. Emacs can, in fact, be told to do these *trivial* merges itself; press $ to do so. Emacs then skips the diffs where one of the buffers is equal to its ancestor.

Using Ediff with Directories of Files

If you have been a good boy or girl and done what I've told you, you will have a directory with all your Lisp configuration. Furthermore if you use Emacs both at home and at work, you will have this directory located on two different machines. You have already learned that you can use Ediff to keep files synchronized, but because you have a whole directory of files to keep synchronized, you need bit extra to ease your work.

Emacs has four functions that let you work on directories of files: `ediff-directories`, `ediff-directories3`, `ediff-merge-directories`, and `ediff-merge-directories3`. The functions that end in 3 are functions that work with a directory of ancestors. All functions work by creating a buffer such as the one in Figure 14.6, from which you can start individual Ediff or ediff-merge sessions.

14

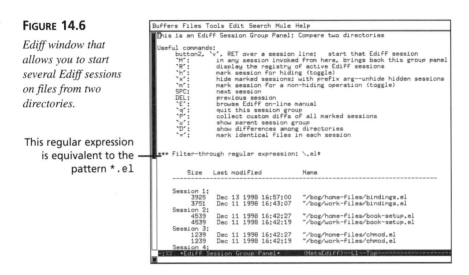

FIGURE 14.6

Ediff window that allows you to start several Ediff sessions on files from two directories.

This regular expression is equivalent to the pattern *.el

When you invoke one of the functions listed earlier, Emacs asks you for a regular expression that the filename must match to get in the list.

Pressing the second mouse button or the Enter key over one of the sessions starts an Ediff or ediff-merge with the files listed for the given session. When you quit the given session, Emacs returns to this buffer. You can also return to it by pressing M, as listed in the help text in the top of the buffer.

If the directories contain many files, you might want to remove some of the sessions from the session group. This can be done with a regular expression as described earlier, but this method has one drawback: It is hard to develop a regular expression that excludes some files. For example, it would be hard to write a regular expression that excludes all files ending in .elc. An other solution is to press h (h for hide) when point is located on top of a session that you do not want to see. This marks the given session for hiding. When you have selected some buffers for hiding, you can press x (x for execute), which does the actual hiding.

If the session contains two subdirectories rather than two files, Emacs brings up a session group for the files of the two subdirectories.

By pressing = in this buffer you tell Emacs to flag all sessions that have files that are not different. This can help you when you are trying to merge two directories coming from different machines. Unfortunately the mark that Emacs put on these files cannot be used to hide the files with x. Fortunately, you have learned about macros in Hour 13, "Macros," so you are capable of developing a macro that can hide all files flagged as different. (See the exercise at the end of the hour.)

If you select at startup a regular expression that lists only files ending in .el, for example, you will not get subdirectories listed. Therefore it is often easier—if you want all files or subdirectories of the given directory listed in the session group, and you want to hide the files that you do want to look at—to use a macro. This macro can search for these files, mark them for hiding, and finally hide them.

Only files located in both directories are shown in the session group buffer, so press D to see which files are not in both directories.

Hey, did you get that? This is important if you use Ediff to merge a set of files from one machine with a set of files on another machine, take the result with you to the first machine, and overwrite the original files. This way you have a new way of unintentionally deleting files!

Sessions that have been invoked are flagged with a minus sign in the first column.

Ediff and Version Control Systems

The Ediff library offers the functions `ediff-revision` and `ediff-merge-revisions`, which do the same thing as `ediff-files` and `ediff-merge-files`, except that one or two of the files that they need for Emacs to do its job can come from the version control system. Revision control in Emacs is covered in Hour 19, "Programming Utilities."

This is a convenient way to see what you have changed before you check in the files in the revision control system. Now you can actually write meaningful check-in messages.

Summary

Now that you have been introduced to the concepts of Ediff, you might find that you never want to use the command-line versions of diff or patch anymore. Furthermore you might find that you can work with several people on a project, each having a copy of the file, and then use Ediff to merge each member's work together. (If you do this much, you should, however, consider using the program package called CVS.)

14

If you find that you frequently use Ediff, you should read the documentation which comes with Ediff. It is available through the info pages.

Q&A

Q   Why isn't the current difference in both buffer A and buffer B highlighted with the same color?

A   To be honest, I don't know. But a guess is that the people who made Ediff were so happy about colors that they simply *had* to use different colors. Fortunately, you have learned to use customize, and Ediff's colors are customizable, so please change them at your will.

Q   How can Ediff help me patch files?

A   It will let you step through the patches one by one, as if you have asked Emacs to diff the original file, and the patched file.

Q   I use GNU Emacs version 19, and I really need to increase the value of the variable `ediff-auto-refine-limit`. Unfortunately you say that this doesn't work in GNU Emacs version 19. Is there something I can do?

A   Yes. On the CD-ROM accompanying this book is a newer version of Ediff (version 2.67). You can replace the one that came with Emacs with this one. For this to work, however, you also need to install the customize library. Maybe you should consider whether this is the time to install Emacs 20.

Exercises

1. Develop a macro that hides all files that are different in the session group buffer.

2. Ediff is a powerful tool. So you should really try it on some of your files now, and try to understand the quick help available in the control buffer, so you can refer to this later instead of having to find this book and look it up.

3. Windows 95 users know that program installations can modify `autoexec.bat` and `config.sys`, littering `C:\` with old copies of those two files. Now you have a tool that lets you see exactly what changes were made. Look at some of your old `autoexec.*` files and diff them against your `autoexec.bat`.

HOUR 15

Getting an Overview of a File

In this hour you will learn several different methods with which you can focus on part of your document:

- First you'll see how to make Emacs act as if you have only part of your document. This is especially useful if you need to do a search-and-replace on only part of a file, for example.

- Next you'll see two different ways to get an outline of your buffer. You might, for example, show only titles in a document.

Focusing on Only Part of a Buffer

Emacs has a very useful feature that enables you to narrow your view of a buffer to only part of it. Narrowing to only part of a buffer makes the part appear as if it were the whole buffer, both to you and to many of the functions that operate on a buffer, such as search-and-replace. In other words, it is nearly equivalent to copying the part to another buffer and working on it there.

When you save a buffer that is narrowed, text that is invisible to you will still be saved. Likewise the invisible text will still be backed up.

In Figure 15.1 you can see a buffer that is being narrowed. If you look carefully at the mode-line, you'll see that Emacs acts as if this were all the buffer. For example, it shows the text All to indicate that you're looking at all the buffer (even though the buffer, in its entirety, is several hundred lines long).

FIGURE 15.1

A narrowed buffer.

Indicates that the buffer is narrowed

Emacs acts as if it were showing all the buffer

To narrow to part of a buffer, mark a region and press C-x n n (narrow-to-region). To show the whole buffer again, press C-x n w (widen).

Well that is it! That is the whole truth about narrowing. Simple, but very useful. Unfortunately it is so simple that most people have a tendency to overlook its power, so here comes an example that I hope will make you remember its power.

When you are writing a large report, you might have two conflicting interests:

- You might want all of the report (or at least the chapter) in one file, so that it is easy for you to search for text in it and to get an overview (using, for example, outline mode described in the next section).

- You might want each section (or even each subsection) to be located in a file for itself, so that it is easy to focus on the current part, and easy to search backward in the current section, without getting too far back in case your search doesn't match anything in the current section.

Narrowing can help you fulfill both wishes. Place the whole chapter in one file, and then narrow to a given section when you work on it. This way searching applies only to the given section, and you can still work with the whole chapter in one file for larger searches.

Getting an Outline of Your Document

When you are writing a large document, you might at some point want to get an overview, or outline, of your document. You can obtain such an overview by asking Emacs to show you only the heading lines of your document. Emacs must, of course, be told what a headline looks like. Fortunately, this is quite simple, and many major modes contain definitions for it (for example, sgml mode, cc mode, and AucTeX. (see Hours 17, "Editing LaTeX and HTML Files," and 18, "Editing C, C++, and Java Files," for a description of these).

In Figure 15.2, you can see an example of a buffer where only an outline is shown. This buffer contains an HTML document. In HTML heading lines are of the form <h1>...</h1>, where the number one can be exchanged with any number from one to six.

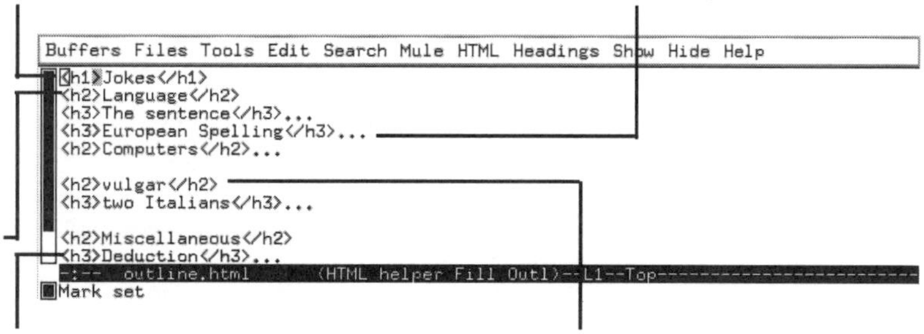

Level 1 headline (equal to chapters of a book)   Ellipses indicate that the body has been hidden

FIGURE 15.2

An example of a buffer where only an outline is shown.

Level 2 headline (equal to sections of a book)

```
Buffers Files Tools Edit Search Mule HTML Headings Show Hide Help
<h1>Jokes</h1>
<h2>Language</h2>
<h3>The sentence</h3>...
<h3>European Spelling</h3>...
<h2>Computers</h2>...

<h2>vulgar</h2>
<h3>two Italians</h3>...

<h2>Miscellaneous</h2>
<h3>Deduction</h3>...
--:--  outline.html      (HTML helper Fill Outl)--L1--Top----------------------
Mark set
```

Level 3 headline (equal to subsections of a book)   No ellipsis indicates that there are no hidden lines between the level 2 header and the first level 3 header.

It is important to understand that this HTML document contains hundreds of lines of text, with text below each headline, but the text is hidden, to give an overview of the document.

> If you remove the ellipses that indicate that there is hidden text, you will, in fact, remove all the hidden text!

Accessing the Outline Functions

A major mode and a minor mode exist that offer the outline functionality. Only one major mode can be active at a time, so the outline major mode is of interest only in special buffers where you do not need another major mode. When you edit text, you will most likely have a favorite major mode for this type of text, and you will therefore use the minor mode. All the outline functions in the major mode are bound to the key prefix C-c, whereas they are bound to C-c @ in the minor mode.

The horrible minor mode prefix is in fact the only reason for an outline major mode. Fortunately the key prefix for the outline functions are customizable. Personally I think that the outline functions are so useful that I want them bound to more accessible keys. To bind them all to a different prefix, set the variable outline-minor-mode-prefix to a keybinding. An example might be to bind them to C-o. This prefix is easy to remember, and, because all the outline functions are bound to keys prefixed with C, it is also easy to type.

Unfortunately C-o is already bound to the function open-line. This function might, however, be bound to M-o instead then. You can do this by inserting the following code into your .emacs file:

```
(setq outline-minor-mode-prefix [(control o)])
(global-set-key [(meta o)] 'open-line)
```

To start either the major mode or the minor mode, press M-x and type outline-mode (the major mode) or outline-minor-mode (the minor mode).

To learn how to start either the major or the minor mode when a file is loaded, refer to Hour 24, "Installing Emacs Add-Ons."

Hiding/Showing Text

Several functions exist for hiding/showing part of the text. All the functions for showing text are located under the menu entry Show, whereas the functions for hiding text are located in the menu Hide.

A structured document can conceptually be seen as a tree. On a tree, a branch can have several subbranches, each of which can also have several subbranches. Likewise a document can have several headings, each of which can have several subheadings and so on. On a branch of a tree other branches and leaves can be located. Likewise, in a document, a chapter can have several sections in it and several lines of ordinary text. (The lines of text are named body-lines when talking about them in the context of the outline functions.) The parallel between a tree and a document can be seen in Figure 15.3.

FIGURE 15.3

A document is conceptually like a tree.

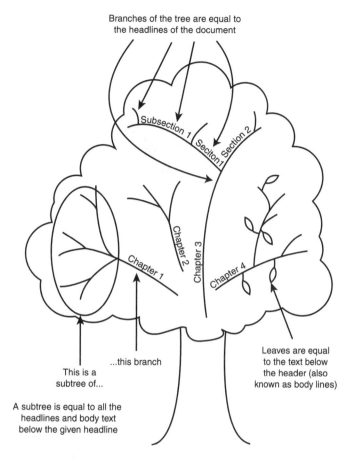

Branches of the tree are equal to the headlines of the document

Subsection 1 | Seciton 1 | Section 2

Chapter 1 | Chapter 2 | Chapter 3 | Chapter 4

Leaves are equal to the text below the header (also known as body lines)

...this branch

This is a subtree of...

A subtree is equal to all the headlines and body text below the given headline

The hiding and showing functions come in two classes: those that work on the whole document, and those that work only on the subtree in which point is located. All available functions are shown in Table 15.1. The functions that hide text do not show any text, although the description might sound like that. Likewise functions for showing text do not hide any text. In the table the key prefix for the minor mode is shown; please remember that the key prefix for major mode is C-c.

TABLE 15.1 AVAILABLE OUTLINE COMMANDS

Name and Binding	Description
Hide—Whole Document	
sublevels (C-c @ C-q)	This collapses the whole tree, showing only the topmost heading lines. Given a numeric prefix, this command shows deeply nested sublevels. M-3 C-c @ C-q thus shows the top most heading lines and two more levels of heading lines.
body (C-c @ C-t)	This hides all the body lines of the document—that is, showing only the heading lines. This is a very convenient way to get an overview of the whole document.
other (C-c @ C-o)	This hides everything except the body lines in which point is located and the branches above it. The body lines of the branches above the line with point are also hidden. Note this does not seem to work in GNU Emacs 20.
Hide—Subtree	
entry (C-c @ C-c)	This hides the body lines of the given headline, but not its sub-branches.
leaves (C-c @ C-l)	This hides all the body lines of the subtree rooted in the given headline, but not the branches. This is equivalent to hide body described previously, but only for the given subtree.
subtree (C-c @ C-d)	This hides all body lines and branches in the subtree located at the given headline.
Show—Whole Document	
all (C-c @ C-a)	This shows the whole tree. That is, it unfolds anything hidden by any of the outline functions.
Show—Subtree	
entry (C-c @ C-e)	This shows the body lines of the given headline. That is, neither the branches nor any of their content.
children (C-c @ C-i)	This shows the immediate branches of this headline. Section heading lines will be shown for a chapter, but subsections, sub-subsections, and body lines are not shown.
branches (C-c @ C-k)	This shows all branches in the subtree for the given headline.
subtree (C-c @ C-s)	This shows the whole subtree for the given headline. That is, all heading lines and body lines below the given headline.

Don't get frustrated by all these functions. You will seldom use more than a few of them.

15

Jumping to Heading Lines

Besides offering the capability to hide some text, the outline mode also offers functions for jumping to the heading lines. All the jumping functions are available under the menu entry Headings. Table 15.2 shows all the commands for jumping between heading lines.

TABLE 15.2 COMMANDS FOR JUMPING BETWEEN HEADERS

Name and Binding	Description
Up (C-c @ C-u)	This command jumps up one level of heading lines. If you, for example, are located in a section, this brings you to the headline of the chapter in which this section is located.
Next (C-c @ C-n)	This brings you to the next headline (not regarding its depth, only that it is a headline).
Previous (C-c @ C-p)	This brings you to the previous headline (regardless of depth).
Next same level (C-c @ C-f)	This brings you to the next headline of the same level. If you, for example, are located in the body text of a section, this brings you to the next section, not regarding that your current section can have several subsections.
Previous same level (C-c @ C-b)	This brings you to the previous headline of the same level (see previous item).

XEmacs Glyphs

In XEmacs, small figures (called *glyphs*) are added next to the heading lines in outline-major mode, as can be seen in Figure 15.4.

Click this glyph to show the body of this headline

FIGURE 15.4

Glyphs support in XEmacs.

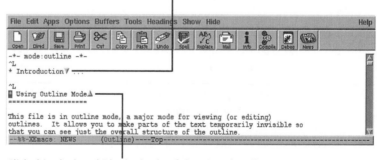

Click this glyph to hide the body of the given headline

If you want this enabled whenever you use one of the outline modes, insert the following line into your .emacs file:

```
(add-hook 'outline-minor-mode 'outl-mouse-minor-mode)
```

You should, however, be aware that this is not supported in GNU Emacs so, if you share your .emacs file between GNU Emacs and XEmacs, you should put a test around the line, to ensure that it is activated only in XEmacs, as described in Hour 1, "Introduction to Emacs."

Clicking the down glyphs shows the children of the headline (that is, the branches, but not the body text or the branches' body text). Clicking it once more then shows the body text of the headline, but not the body lines of the branches. Likewise, clicking the up glyphs hides the body lines on the first click. The second click hides the branches.

Before you continue reading, it might be a good idea to try the outline functions. To do that, press C-h n (view-emacs-news), which brings you to a buffer containing Emacs news since last release. This buffer is automatically in outline-major mode.

In this buffer, the topmost heading lines (that is, the chapters) are represented with one star. Heading lines below this are marked with two stars, and so on.

Please be aware that the keybindings listed previously are for outline minor mode. In outline major mode you must not use the @ in the key sequences.

Configuring Outline

I hope you have now learned everything that is worth knowing about using the outline mode. Many major modes support outline mode; that is, they contain information for outline mode about the text they are supposed to be used with. You can, for example, use outline mode on an HTML document if you use sgml mode major mode.

You might, however, get in situations where there either is no major mode for the text you are editing or the major mode that exists doesn't support outline mode. In these situations, you need to tell outline mode yourself what a headline looks like and how to figure out the level of a given header if you want to use it.

> You might want to skip the rest of this section now, and continue with the section "Folding Text: A Sort of Categorized Outline." If you get in a situation like described before, make sure you come back!

Two different configuration options exist for telling Emacs about the outline structure. These include the variable `outline-regexp`, which is used to describe which lines are heading lines (and sometimes even the level of the given headline), and the variable `outline-level`, which must be set to a Lisp function which tells the level of a given header.

Defining Lisp functions is beyond the scope of this book; fortunately the default value for `outline-level` is very useful and does not need to be redefined in most cases. What it does is let the length of the text matched with `outline-regexp` determine the level on which the headline exists.

In most situations it is therefore enough to set the variable `outline-regexp` to a regular expression that matches more text the deeper a headline is located (see Hour 9, "Regular Expressions"). Three examples will be provided here to give you an idea how to write such a regular expression. All examples are for file formats for which an outline setup already exists. This is merely to give you good examples.

Example 1

In LaTeX there exist chapters, sections, subsections, and so on, written as `\chapter`, `\section`, `\subsection`, `\subsubsection`, and so on. As stated previously, the regular expression must match more text the more deeply a header is located. This gives us a problem, as the words *chapter* and *section* are equally long. The trick here is simply to write a regular expression that matches any character after *section*, as in Figure 15.5.

FIGURE 15.5

This regular expression matches headlines in LaTeX.

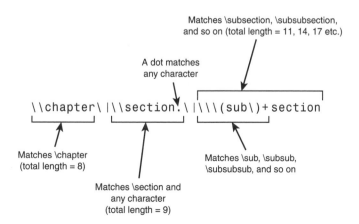

Matches \subsection, \subsubsection, and so on (total length = 11, 14, 17 etc.)

A dot matches any character

`\\chapter\|\\section.\|\\\(sub\)+section`

Matches \chapter (total length = 8)

Matches \section and any character (total length = 9)

Matches \sub, \subsub, \subsubsub, and so on

Note, in Figure 15.5, the trick is that the dot matches any character, and thus \section is more deeply nested than \chapter.

Example 2

In HTML, there are six header lines: <h1>, <h2>, <h3>, <h4>, <h5>, and <h6>, with <h1> as the topmost header line.

In this situation all header lines have the same length, but fortunately you can use the trick from Figure 15.5, which gives us the following regular expression:

<h1>\¦<h2>.\¦<h3>..\¦<h4>...\¦<h5>....\¦<h6>.....

The best—or at least the most beautiful—solution would be to identify lines with <h.> as header lines and then use the function outline-level to extract the number matches to get the level. This does work unless there is no character on the line to match the dots.

Example 3

The final example is from the C programming language. In C, there is no easy way to describe a function definition header line using a regular expression, so here you are in a bit of trouble. Fortunately the C mode contains several functions for indenting the code. This way, function definitions are indented at the lowest level. Statements within for loops are indented with more spaces than the for loop header and so on. Thus you can use the indentation to describe the level of a *header*. (It's not a header anymore, because every line is regarded as a header line, but with the outline functions it is now possible to hide the body of a for loop.)

The regular expression which could have been used in c mode is shown in Figure 15.6.

FIGURE 15.6

This regular expression is used to describe outline properties in C.

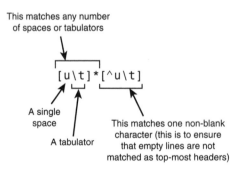

This regular expression might have been used in c mode, but another one was used that was more effective.

You have now seen three different examples of regular expressions for outline mode. You might see more examples by using igrep to search for `outline-regexp` in the Lisp files installed as part of your Emacs installation. (If you do not know where that is, search for files ending in `.el` on your hard disk.)

Using Outline or Narrowing in Two Different Views of the Same File

If you try to open the same buffer in two different windows, and afterward try to narrow it in two different ways, or try to create two different outlines, you will see that this is not possible. The reason for this is that both narrowing and the outline functions modify some characteristics of the buffer, which is independent of the fact that the buffer is shown in two different windows. Likewise you will see that it is not possible to mark in a buffer two different regions, which are shown in two different windows. The reason for this is that the mark (which is one end of the region) is shared between the windows.

A solution to these problems is to copy the buffer and use the copy for the outline and so on. Unfortunately this means that if you edit the one, you won't update the other. Emacs contains a nicer solution to this problem called *indirect buffers*. An indirect buffer is a copy of a buffer that has separate marks and other buffer characteristics but that ensures that an edit in one buffer is transferred to the other immediately.

Indirect buffers are unfortunately not yet part of XEmacs. This should change in later versions. So if you use XEmacs, you simply have to stick with the method of copying the content of the buffer to another one.

In `sams-lib.el` the function sams-make-buffer-copy exists. When this function is invoked, a new frame is created with an indirect buffer which is a copy of the current buffer.

If you get a copy of a buffer this way, you can use either outline or narrowing in two different views of the same file. Furthermore you can get two buffers with separate marks, so it is possible to get two different regions of the same file. This makes it possible to invoke `ediff-regions-linewise` on two regions in the same buffer (or what at least appears to be the same buffer).

> If you are using GNU Emacs 19 then you must use the library `noutline`
> instead of `outline` when you want to use indirect buffers. Simply press M-x
> `load-library` RET `noutline` RET to load the `noutline` library.
>
> The `noutline` library is an alternative implementation of the outline func-
> tions that works with indirect buffers. In GNU Emacs 20, this is no problem,
> because the `noutline` library, in fact, is the default for the outline functions.

Folding Text: A Sort of Categorized Outline

In the section "Configuring Outline," you saw an example of how to set up a regular
expression for using outline mode with the programming language C. (If you don't recall
this, it might be because it was in the section I offered for you to skip.)

The main drawback with this solution is that you are incapable of ordering the outline
that is dictated by the indentation of the text. What you might want to do is to group a
number of functions into one group which you could show or hide simultaneously. You
might in fact want this grouping at any level (for example, some statements of a function
might be grouped).

 For this purpose the library called folding exists. It is not part of the Emacs installation,
but it is located on the CD for this book (see Appendix A, "Installing Functions and
Packages from the CD," for an installation guide). In Figure 15.7 you can see a buffer
that has been folded.

Ordinary text that is not hidden   The folding prefix (this indicates that the text
(that is, text at the outermost level)   up to the matching ; ; } } } is in a fold)

FIGURE 15.7

A folded buffer.

A number of folded
entries (each line is
an folded entry)

More text that
is not hidden

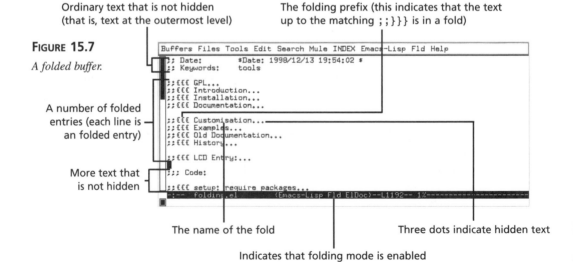

The name of the fold   Three dots indicate hidden text

Indicates that folding mode is enabled

15

Special markers in the text are required for folding to work. Each fold must start with a special mark and end in a special mark. This special mark depends on the major mode for the given buffer. This ensures that folding marks never interfere with the text of the buffer. After the opening mark comes a description of the fold. This is for your eyes only.

Don't get scared that you now have to learn a set of folding marks for each of your major modes. The library contains an menu item in which an entry called `foldify-region` exists. This function puts fold marks around a region for you. If there isn't support for a given major mode you can add it by using the function `fold-add-to-marks-list`.

In Figure 15.7, the special folding opening mark is `;;{{{` (two semicolons and three opening braces). As you can see in the mode-line, this buffer's major mode is `Emacs-Lisp`, which in fact uses the semicolon as comment characters. Thus to the Lisp interpreter that reads this file, the folding marks are merely comments.

Folds can nest; thus, it is possible to have subfolds within folds, like is the case in outline mode. Furthermore, as folds have explicit marks to end a fold, you can have text in a given fold after a subfold. This is impossible in outline. Think about how you would make some text part of a chapter, after a section in a book.

Folding Commands

When folding mode is started, an item called `Fld` is inserted into the menus, and the buffer is automatically folded, so you get an overview of it.

> To start playing with folding mode right away, load the library with the following command:
>
> `M-x load-file RET The folding.el file`
>
> Next read the file `folding.el` into Emacs (this file is written in folding mode), and start folding mode with this command:
>
> `M-x folding-mode RET`

Folding mode works much like outline mode. There are two major ways in which it is different:

- It does not contain as many functions for showing hiding text as outline mode does.

- It works together with narrowing that makes it possible to *enter a fold*, which means that only the text of this fold is shown.

Starting with the Showing and Hiding Functions

Folding mode contains the following functions for showing and hiding text:

- C-c @ C-w (fold-whole-buffer) and C-c @ C-o (fold-open-buffer)—These two functions fold the whole buffer (that is, hide the body of every fold, and show only the header of the topmost folds), and show the whole buffer respectively.

- C-c @ C-x (fold-hide) and C-c @ C-s (fold-show)—These are the functions that in the menus are called hide level and show level. These functions show or hide a given fold. When a fold is shown, its body text is shown and the heading lines of the subfolds are shown, but not their body lines or their subfolds.

- C-c @ C-y (fold-show-subtree)—This function shows all the content of a fold: That is, its body text and all its subfolds.

As previously mentioned, folding mode makes it possible to enter a fold, which means that the buffer is narrowed to the given fold. The body text of the fold is shown, but the content of its subfolds are hidden. You can furthermore enter subfolds, which narrow further down to show only the subfold. When you exit a subfold, the buffer is widened to show the fold in which the subfold was located or to show the whole buffer if the subfold is located at the outermost level.

Folds are entered with C-c @ > (fold-enter) and exited with C-c @ < (fold-exit). If you have entered subfolds within a given fold, all folds can be exited by pressing C-c @ C-t (fold-top-level).

Summary

You have now learned some valuable tools to get an overview of your documents. With narrowing, you can focus on only part of a buffer. As a side note I can inform you that it is frequently used behind your back. Mail and news readers and the info reader use it, for example.

Getting an outline of your document is often very valuable. It makes it much easier for you to get an impression of the overall document. It also represents an alternative to searching for information if you, for example, know you have a section somewhere but you can't remember its name.

If you get used to using the folding functions, you will find that your documents, programs, or whatever are much easier to read, by both yourself and others, when you haven't used your files for a long time.

Q&A

Q **Is it possible to narrow further in, when part of a buffer has already been narrowed?**

A Yes, simply do another narrowing. When you widen, however, you see the whole buffer, and not just the part from which you narrowed. Check the home page for this book. At the time you read this, I might have found a library, or have written one myself, for Emacs that makes it possible to widen back to the previous narrowing.

Q **I like the outline and folding functions a lot, but when I'm programming, I sometimes search for a function. I know it's in the given file, but I can't remember its name. Is there another way?**

A Yes. Two libraries do this: one for GNU Emacs and the other for XEmacs. Unfortunately neither of them can be used with both versions of Emacs. The library for GNU Emacs is called `imenu` (see Hour 18) while the library for XEmacs is called `func-menu`. Look in the files for installation descriptions. Both programs comes with the given Emacs as default.

Exercises

1. Load a large file and narrow to a small part of it. How does Emacs react when you try to go to the beginning or the end of the buffer?

2. What happens when you go to the end of the narrowed buffer and press `c-d`? Will you delete the text outside the narrowed region?

3. Find a file with text for C, C++, Java, LaTeX, or HTML and try out the outline functions.

4. How does searching work with outline?

5. If you mark text that contains hidden text (that is, the ellipsis) and copy it to another place, will the hidden content be copied too?

6. Try the folding mode. You can, for example, try it with the file `folding.el`.

7. How does searching works with folding?

HOUR 16

Interfacing with the System

This hour assumes a working knowledge of your operating system of choice, in which you will be able to leverage your operating system within Emacs's environment. Emacs can interact with other programs in a variety of ways, including

- Invoking Emacs as an editor from other programs
- Executing a program and viewing its output
- Running an interactive shell using Emacs to enhance the shell interface
- Running commands remotely on other machines
- Writing your own specialized system commands
- Editing directories
- Printing to system print queues

This wide range of options continues—Emacs has specialized interfaces—but there is not enough space to cover them all. For convenience in this hour,

I will assume you are running on UNIX. UNIX tools are available on Windows NT from different vendors and over the Internet, so examples can be replicated. In many cases, Emacs covers Windows, making it appear as though you are running on a UNIX machine.

Some system commands will not be covered. They include the specialized `grep` command, found in Hour 8, "Searching for Text in Multiple Files"; compilation and debugging, found in Hour 19, "Programming Utilities"; external spelling checkers, found in Hour 11, "Editing Utilities"; running diffs, found in Hour 14, "Finding Differences Between Files"; or sending email and news, found in Part V, "Mail and News."

Invocations

Aside from simply invoking Emacs with no parameters, there are several additional details you can use. For example, to edit a file, you can pass the filename to Emacs on the command line as a general argument. Passing the `--help` argument to Emacs provides you with a list of arguments that are valid. Some useful ones include `--no-windows` or `-nw` to run in a terminal, and `--no-init-file` or `-q` to suppress the reading in of your `~/.emacs` file.

You can even write shell scripts to invoke Emacs into specialized modes. The `-f` flag causes Emacs to run a specific function, `-l` causes it to load an additional Lisp file, and `--eval` permits the execution of arbitrary Lisp code. As a good example of the use of these flags, you can write a shell script to run Ediff on two files like this:

```
#!/bin/sh
emacs -q --eval "(ediff \"$1\" \"$2\" )"
```

Here, `-q` prevents loading potentially slow init files, and `--eval` executes your generated command.

> Different shells have different conventions for quoting characters and using argument substitution. Any such language can invoke Emacs in this way.

Some command-line programs, including mail, need to invoke an editor. They use the `EDITOR` environment variable. If this is not set, vi is typically used instead. Set the variable to the string `emacs` to invoke Emacs for your editing needs.

If you do not like the idea of starting a new Emacs every time some program wants to edit something, you are in luck. Emacs can be used as an editing server, allowing you to have a single Emacs invocation provide editing services to other applications. The first thing you want to do is run Emacs. Next, execute the command M-x server-start. The server-start command initializes the interface Emacs listens to while waiting for external editing requests.

Now that your server has been started, you can now move to a terminal window, and execute the program emacsclient. You can do that like this:

```
emacsclient ~/.emacs
```

You immediately see that Emacs brings that file into a buffer. You can edit this file to your heart's content. When you're finished, execute the server-edit command with the keybinding C-x #. When this is executed, Emacs switches to the next client file and the originating emacsclient invocation exits.

To automate this process, you can add the following line to your .emacs file

```
(start-server)
```

and, set your EDITOR environment variable to emacsclient. It might look like this for csh:

```
setenv EDITOR emacsclient
```

> Another more complex method of controlling a running Emacs is with a program called gnudoit, which can be found on the Internet and permits the running of arbitrary Lisp expressions.

Running Programs

Emacs can also be used to run commands and maintain the output in its buffers. You have already seen this with the M-x command in Hour 7, "Searching for Text in a Buffer." This technique is also used by Ediff for building its differences in Hour 14. There are several ways you can take advantage of this with some simple commands. The most obvious is the shell command bound to M-!. This prompts you for a command to run that depends on the operating system you are currently using.

On UNIX, the command you enter is executed through sh, the Borne shell, and any conventions allowed by it are permitted. Thus, on UNIX you can run a command and pipe it into another command as you would in a terminal program. The command entered is run synchronously.

Executing a command *synchronously* means that all processing for Emacs is put on hold until this new subprocess is completed. If you want to keep working in Emacs while a program is running, you will want to run it asynchronously.

When the program exits, the output is then displayed. If there is no output, a message is displayed stating so. If the output is one line long, it is put in the minibuffer. If there is lots of output, that output is displayed in the Shell Command Output buffer. This is quite handy when you need to do a simple task, such as perform command-line operations on a file or other details.

Another handy command is shell-command-on-region, which is bound to M-¦ (meta pipe). This command takes the current region (the area between point and the last mark) and uses it as the standard input of the command you type at the prompt. Output is handled in the same way as the shell command.

This command can do some nifty stuff. For example, you can uuencode a region and insert that buffer's contents into a mail message. Some other uses include piping a mail message through metamail or pushing command sequences in a text file through an interactive program.

Interactive Shells

Emacs can also run other programs asynchronously. So far you learned the synchronous commands, but you can also execute the command shell asynchronously with M-x shell. A new buffer appears, named Shell, in which all output from your default shell will go. Each additional call of M-x shell brings up a previously created shell when it is available.

You can create multiple shell buffers by renaming the Shell buffer to something else by using M-x rename-buffer and running M-x shell a second time.

Working with this shell is like working with a shell in a terminal, with one difference. You can navigate anywhere in the Shell buffer, and copy, paste, or use any other Emacs editing command. When you press Enter, the line that point is on is used as the command line and executed. When you are on a prompt, you can also use the key sequences M-n and M-p to navigate through the command history while sitting on a prompt.

This basic behavior is the lowest common denominator to a whole range of programs and is referred to as *comint*. Comint is a subsystem for running an interactive command line–based asynchronous process. Learning these basics then becomes invaluable for everything from the shell to remote logins to running debuggers.

Some common configuration elements for comint include the following:

- `comint-scroll-to-bottom-on-input`—Scroll to the end of the comint buffer when you type something.
- `comint-scroll-to-bottom-on-output`—Scroll to the end of the comint buffer when there is output from the subprocess.
- `comint-eol-on-send`—Move point to the end of the line before sending the input to the subprocess.
- `comint-process-echoes`—Different shells have different behaviors. If you get duplicate command-line output, or no command echoing at all, this variable might be set wrong.

In the Shell buffer, there are additional commands that can be used. Emacs performs command-line completion of filenames with the Tab key and tracks your current directory through your use of cd, pushd, and popd so that a find file (`C-x C-f`) defaults to the correct location.

> When you work with a comint buffer, it is important to remember that the asynchronous subprocess receives no input from Emacs until Enter is used. This is unlike a common shell where the shell receives the input and uses it to display characters.

In addition to running a simple shell under Emacs, you can also run shells remotely with the commands `M-x rlogin` and `M-x telnet`. These commands run rlogin and telnet respectively, and are based on comint. Both these commands behave as the shell does, with the exceptions that the startup requires the name of the machine to run on and that you will have to log in to that machine.

Terminal Emulation (Interactive Shells)

If you need better interaction with your subprocesses under Emacs, such as wanting to run Emacs on a remote machine, you are in luck. The command `M-x term` starts up a terminal buffer called terminal and offers to run a shell command of your choice. This terminal interprets the sequences used to control a typical terminal, and performs the appropriate display adjustments. This emulation is so good, you can run Emacs in terminal mode inside Emacs.

The greatest disadvantage to this is that you cannot take advantage of many of Emacs's default editing commands. All editing is provided solely from the program being run, no matter how inadequate that might be. Another side effect is that C-c is the only escape character. The important escape commands to remember are

- C-c C-c—Sends a C-c (interrupt) character to the subprocess
- C-c o—Switches to another window
- C-c b—Switches to another buffer
- C-c C-b—Shows the buffers display
- C-c k—Kills the terminal buffer

In fact, most C-x commands are replicated on C-c in the terminal. Type C-c C-h to get a list of all the commands bound under C-c.

> Use M-x shell in preference to M-x term unless terminal emulation is absolutely necessary. The advantages are well worth it.

Writing Your Own Commands to Execute Programs

Now that you are familiar with running different types of programs from Emacs, you might be interested in having a few specialized commands of your own to run. These commands could take care of running the program and even figuring out the command-line parameters for you.

For example, say you have a unique version control system which you work with regularly, and this system is different from the version control programs discussed in Hour 19. This system has the command checkout as a method for locking the file locally. What you most likely want is a command that runs checkout synchronously, and you want to make sure no errors occur.

To do this, you can create an example that serves as a template for almost any command you would like to bind. You start with the command call-process, a function that runs a synchronous subprocess. The parameters are PROGRAM, INPUT, OUTPUT, and DISPLAY, and command-line arguments follow. The program is a string representing the program to run (without arguments). INPUT specifies a stdin to use and OUTPUT represents the std-out. INPUT is either nil (no input) or a string representing the text to be sent to the subprocess. OUTPUT can be t, meaning the current buffer, or another buffer. DISPLAY means that the OUTPUT buffer is updated as new input is made available (even though you are calling your subprocess synchronously).

The next useful function you need to know is buffer-file-name, which returns the file-name of the current buffer. This saves you time when you run your program. You can now write your program, which will look like this:

```
(defun my-checkout ()
  "Check out the current buffer's file using our unique checkout
➥program."
  (interactive)
  (save-excursion
    (let ((cb (current-buffer)))
      (set-buffer (get-buffer-create "*TEMP*"))
      (call-process "checkout" nil t nil (buffer-file-name cb))
      ;; Perform error checking here
      )))
```

16

This forms the baseline for any program you might want to write to call external programs. One of the important things to do is have the output go into a temporary buffer for examination later. This is what the (set-buffer (get-buffer-create... line does. When your current buffer is now the temporary one, you can call your subprocess with the buffer you saved in cb. The let command locally binds cb to the value of (current-buffer) so you can use it when your current buffer is something different.

Now that you have run your program, you might want to extend it to do error checking. Let's say the checkout program outputs the string:

Gnarly error: You forgot to do something important.

After the comment referring to error checking, you would add the following code:

```
    (goto-char (point-min))
    (if (looking-at "Gnarly error:")
        (error (buffer-string)))
```

Here, the first line simply moves point to the beginning of the buffer. The next line checks the output to see whether there was a gnarly error or not. looking-at can take a regular expression as discussed in Hour 9, "Regular Expressions," but plain text works fine too. It returns *t* if there is a match. Finally, when there is an error, use the error command to report it with buffer-string as the text displayed in the minibuffer. Now that this is in your ~/.emacs file, you can run it whenever you want by typing M-x my-checkout Enter.

Now finish by showing this as a template for use by any command:

```
(defun my-<program> ()
  "Run <program> on the current buffer's file."
  (interactive)
  (save-excursion
    (let ((cb (current-buffer)))
```

```
        (set-buffer (get-buffer-create "*TEMP*"))
        (call-process "<program>" nil t nil (buffer-file-name cb)
➡ "<other parameters>")
        ;; Perform error checking here
        (goto-char (point-min))
        (if (looking-at "<error text regular expression>")
            (error (buffer-string)))
        )))
```

For more detail on how to write programs, be sure to read Hour 24, "Installing Emacs Add-Ons."

Editing Directories

There are also some special built-in commands that deal with the filesystem, such as M-x make-directory, M-x rename-file, and others. The easiest way to work with these commands is to use dired (*directory edi*tor). You can edit a directory with C-x d, which prompts you for a directory, though it is as easy to use find file (C-x C-f) and choose a directory instead of a file.

The resulting display is a listing as would be produced with the UNIX command ls -la. Each file is represented on one line with permissions, owner, and size. The sort order can be changed from alphabetized to date with the keystroke s. You can insert additional directories into the buffer by placing point on a line representing a directory (the first character in the permissions field is a d) with the keystroke i.

> Windows users also have the same display as UNIX users, although the ls command is not actually used and is internally emulated in Emacs.

There is an immense list of file operations that can be performed on files from this display. The commands allowed are broken into groups which are then bound to key patterns. In general, lowercase alphanumeric keys perform operations that do not affect the filesystem. Uppercase alphanumeric keys do perform operations that affect the filesystem. Another handy aspect is that almost all bindings are representative of the command to be executed. You can easily navigate up and down the listing with the spacebar and Delete key, respectively.

> The notable exception to the upper- and lowercase rule is that although lowercase d (delete file) only marks a file to be deleted, lowercase x (expunge) performs an actual filesystem deletion. To remove a file from the list without deleting it from the filesystem, use the kill lines command bound to k.

16

Before I list all the most useful commands available, it is important to discuss marking. When editing directories there two kinds of user-controllable marks. There are deletion marks, which are represented by a capital D in the first column. There is also a generic mark represented by an asterisk (*) in the first column. You set a deletion mark with d, and a regular mark with m. All marks can be removed with the unmark command bound to u, or with the unmark backwards command bound to Delete.

In general, operations that affect the filesystem work on the file under the cursor *unless* there are marks. When there are marks, the entire group of files are affected.

Some common operations to perform when editing a directory include the following:

- f or e—Edit the file under point
- v—View the current file
- d—Mark the current file for deletion
- g—Refresh the listing
- m—Mark the current file with a generic mark
- ~—Mark all backup files (files ending with ~) for deletion
- u—Unmark the current file
- M-=—Execute diff on this file with its backup

In addition to these commands, there are many extended mark commands bound behind the asterisk (*):

- *-m—Same as m, mark the current file
- *-u—Same as u, unmark the current file
- *-!—Unmark all files
- *-/—Mark directories with a generic mark
- *-@—Mark all symlinks with a generic mark
- *-*—Mark all executables with a generic mark

When you have successfully marked all your files, you can perform filesystem operations on them. When examining the list that follows, the *current file* is the file under the point or all files with a generic mark. It is not the file under the point and the generically marked files. Some of the most common are as follows:

- D—Immediately delete the current file
- C—Copy the current file to a new name or directory
- R—Rename the current file to a new name (single file) or move multiple files to a new directory
- M—Change the mode, or file permissions of the current file
- O—Change the owner of the current file
- X or !—Execute a program against the current file
- Z—Compress or decompress the current file
- +—Make a new directory

These commands do real things to your filesystem, so always be careful what your marks are set to, and be cautious while experimenting with them.

There are also commands bound under the % key that allow regular expression filtering. These commands match the ones already listed. For example, %-m marks all files matching a regular expression that you enter. %-C copies files. %-d flags files matching the regular expression for deletion. The only commands that don't quite match are %-u and %-l, which convert the current file or marked files into upper- and lowercase respectively.

When working with regular expressions, it is very important to remember that these are full-featured regular expressions as discussed in Hour 9 and not file expressions. Thus, if you enter foo*.ps, it will not match foofile.ps, but instead find foooootps (if such a file exists).

Printing

Another system interface Emacs has is the capability to print buffers. In general there are two ways to do this. The simplest way is with the lpr or print command. The commands M-x lpr-buffer and M-x lpr-region take the affected text and print them with the UNIX lpr command. The commands M-x print-buffer and M-x print-region print the affected text with lpr -p, meaning that plain-text headers will be added to the top of every page.

Both commands generate the text they want to print and execute a system command for printing, namely the lpr command. (lp on some systems). A side effect of this is that the variable lpr-switches can control additional command-line parameters to pass to the print command whenever you print a file. This command is a list; thus, if you want to specify a printer to send your output to, the command to add to your ~/.emacs file would look like this:

```
(setq lpr-switches '("-Potherprinter"))
```

If you wanted to add something else, such as -m to have the printer send your mail when the job is finished, the updated entry in your ~/.emacs file would look like this:

```
(setq lpr-switches '("-Potherprinter" "-m"))
```

With these commands you've covered the simple printing of plain text. Emacs also supports printing with PostScript. The PostScript printer has the advantage of enabling the printing of text attributes such as bold, italic, underline, and even color when available in hardware. The commands for printing with the PostScript driver are M-x ps-print-buffer, M-x ps-print-region. To enable the display of colors you can use the commands M-x ps-print-buffer-with-faces, and M-x ps-print-region-with-faces.

Each of these commands converts the buffer into PostScript, complete with page titles. If you don't want your files printed right away, or if you want to group them together, you can spool them, with commands such as M-x ps-spool-buffer, M-x ps-spool-region, M-x ps-spool-buffer-with-faces, and M-x ps-spool-region-with-faces. When you've spooled a few PostScript jobs together, you can print them with M-x ps-despool.

The PostScript print driver uses the lpr-switches and commands you learned earlier, so you don't have to do anything more to configure the printing of your file in PostScript. There are, however, many more configuration items available for the PostScript driver than for the plain text printing option. Some of these are as follows:

- ps-number-of-columns—The number of columns to display on a single page (default is 1).
- ps-zebra-stripes—Add gray bars alternating every three lines throughout the file (default is nil).
- ps-line-number—Add line numbers for the whole file if not nil (default is nil).
- ps-print-header—Display a header on the top of each page if not nil (default is t).
- ps-print-color-p—Is the printer capable of displaying color (default is nil)?

Some additional variables are useful in converting color displays, commonly found when using font lock in source code on color displays, into black and white. All the font-lock fonts are covered already, but you might want to add additional faces depending on your needs. The variables to customize for this are as follows:

- `ps-bold-faces`—These colored faces are represented on paper with bold type.
- `ps-italic-faces`—These colored faces are represented on paper with italic type.
- `ps-underlined-faces`—These colored faces are represented on paper as under-lined.

A given face can appear in multiple lists adopting multiple features.

Although the defaults when using the PostScript printing code are great for source code, it is not always desirable to print a header all the time. For example, you can use enriched mode if you want to print your text with the faces you've added, but without the header on every page. You can write your own commands to print files with the tweaks you want. In the preceding scenario, you might put something like this in your `~/.emacs` file.

```
(defun my-print ()
  "Postscript print the current buffer with faces, but without a header."
  (interactive)
  (let ((ps-print-header nil))
      (ps-print-buffer-with-faces)))
```

This creates the command `my-print` in your `~/.emacs` file which you can execute with the keystroke `M-x my-print` `Enter`. The way this program works is by overloading the value of `ps-print-header`, which controls the display of headers on pages with nil. While its value is nil, it prints the buffer with faces, but without page headers. When Emacs is finished printing, it reverts the value back to its original, so your future print-outs contain the headers. You can do this with any of the customizable values if you want to have special print commands that have different types of outputs.

Summary

It should now be clear that Emacs can support a vast array of system interactions, including running external programs synchronously, asynchronously, and interactively. In addition, Emacs has complete control over the filesystem with the capability to be a file manager that can move and manipulate files. You learned how to print from Emacs using the convenience functions at any level of detail that might be needed.

Lastly, it should now be possible to write simple programs that add commands into Emacs to perform specialized shell commands and specialized printing.

Q&A

Q I started Emacs with the -q switch, and now some commands are missing!

A You might have commands and keybindings in your local init file ~/.emacs which were not read. Make sure you know what your ~/.emacs file does.

Q I typed M-! my-command Enter, and now Emacs is not responding.

A Your command has not exited correctly. Type C-g twice to get back control.

Q My shell buffer has gotten *huge*! Doesn't Emacs limit the size of the buffer?

A It does, but the default size is 1024 lines. You can modify the variable comint-buffer-maximum-size in your .emacs file to any dimension you like.

Q I can't seem to delete a directory in dired. What did I do wrong?

A The directory is probably not empty. Edit that subdirectory and make sure it is empty by deleting the files in it first.

Exercises

1. Write a shell program to print a file in PostScript using Emacs.

2. Generate help text with M-x apropos, and uuencode it without using intermediate files.

3. Write a program in your ~/.emacs to run chmod on it to make it writable with the equivalent command line command chmod a+x <file>. When this is finished, make sure to call (revert-buffer t t) on it, which makes sure that the current buffer and filesystem are the same. Also make sure to (save-buffer) before doing this command!

4. Using dired, come up with a list of key sequences that would move all PostScript files (ending with .ps) from the current directory to a subdirectory named old if old does not yet exist.

5. Write a command to print a file with PostScript and zebra stripes.

16

PART IV
Specialized Editing

Hour

HOUR 17

Editing LaTeX/HTML Files

Although a text editor such as Emacs is most often used for writing and editing plain text, many people also use it to write specialized forms of text which are not intended to be read in their raw state. This sort of file, known as marked-up or tagged text, is intended to be interpreted by a separate program and then displayed in a form which is suitable for high-quality printing or viewing. The two most commonly used formats are HTML and LaTeX.

HTML files are the format in which Web pages on the WWW are written (as well as documentation for some software). LaTeX is a set of macros which makes Donald Knuth's TeX markup language easier to work with; after processing with the freely available TeX tools, the marked-up file is eventually transformed into a PostScript file which can be printed or viewed. When Emacs is used with these markup languages it becomes a sort of middle-ground between editors and word processors, with the advantage that control of the appearance of the output file is limited only by the amount of time you are willing to spend learning the many options available. In general TeX and LaTeX are preferable for long documents and academic papers, especially scientific, mathematical, and book-length works. HTML is increasingly being used for general documents not necessarily intended for the World Wide Web, but in comparison to TeX and LaTeX its formatting capabilities are limited.

HTML and Emacs

A common misconception is that HTML is a difficult and obscure programming language, used in its raw form only by skilled programmers. HTML, in fact, is merely a text markup language. The text in an HTML file is just like any other text; the only difference is that markup tags surround various words, paragraphs, and sections of the text. Tags are set off from the text in the document by angle brackets (< >). The tags are the instructions used by a Web browser to display text in specific ways. As an example, the tag which indicates a boldface word or phrase would look like this:

```
<b>This sentence would be shown in a Web browser in a bold font.</b>
```

Although many commercial HTML editors are available, most of them hide the actual structure and tags of the document and often create HTML files which are difficult to read with other tools. Tags can be cumbersome to type, but using them directly gives the writer maximum control of the HTML file's eventual appearance in a browser. Another approach to inserting tags is to make them easier to type rather than hiding them. Hotkeys and mouse-selected menu items can be used to insert tags, which are the methods used by Emacs.

With Emacs, you can cut or copy text from other files to include in your HTML file or browse directories on your computer's hard disk. You can even upload the completed HTML file to a directory on your Internet service provider's (ISP) machine.

GNU Emacs and XEmacs both come with specialized modes for writing HTML. Because the two Emacs variants have markedly different HTML modes, a separate section has been devoted to each.

With a little practice, writing HTML with Emacs can be quick and easy, and as a bonus you will become familiar with HTML rather than relying upon a program to know it for you.

The GNU Emacs HTML Mode

In an Emacs window, type C-x C-f and then type trial.html. Notice that two new menu names appear on the menubar, HTML and SGML. I'll discuss the SGML menu later; for now, click the HTML menu. You'll see the drop-down menu that appears in Figure 17.1. Many of the most commonly used tags can be selected with the mouse and inserted in your document.

FIGURE 17.1

Skeleton HTML file with HTML menu.

There is no point in repeatedly typing in the same basic HTML framework for every new file. In order to save time, I recommend loading a simple skeleton template file rather than creating an empty file. After editing this template file, simply save it under a new name (select Save Buffer As in the Files menu) and you will be able to use it again. A template file should look something like this:

```
<!DOCTYPE HTML PUBLIC "-//W3C//DTD HTML 3.2 Final//EN">
<html>
  <head>
    <title></title>
  </head>
  <body>
    <h1></h1>

  </body>
</html>
```

Type the previous lines and save the file, perhaps naming it `template.html`. Now you can fill in a title between the `<title>` tags; this appears in the title bar of the browser window. The remainder of the contents of your file should be between the two `<body>` tags. Notice that the second tag of each pair has a forward slash before the identifying name.

The main header of your file should be inserted between the <h1> tags. Subsidiary section and subsection headers are usually enclosed within <h2> or <h3> tags, which are also available from the menu. The menu is also available on UNIX-like systems by pressing the Ctrl key along with the right mouse button.

Probably the most frequently used tag is <p>, used at the beginning of each new paragraph. This particular tag is unusual in that a closing </p> tag isn't required, although putting one in won't cause problems. Because the paragraph tag is used so often, using the mouse to insert the tag from the menu can be distracting while typing. Fortunately all of the tags in the HTML menu have keybindings associated with them, such as C-c Enter for the paragraph tag. The keystrokes needed are listed in the menu as an aid to learning them.

Not appearing on the menu are several other HTML tags that have their own keystrokes. Type C-h m to split the Emacs window horizontally; the new lower half of the window now displays basic help for the active editing modes (as shown in Figure 17.2). Scroll to the bottom of the Help display to find other keybindings that can be used in your HTML files—for example, keystrokes for the smaller subsection headers such as <h6>.

FIGURE 17.2

Help window showing mode information.

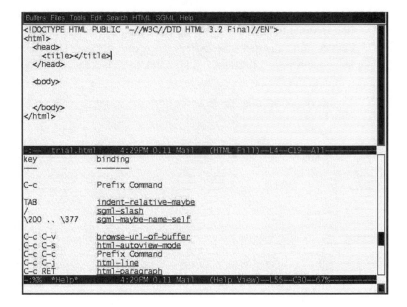

The commonly used character formatting tags such as <b> for bold, <i> for italic, and <u> for underlining don't appear on the HTML menu. These tags can be selected from the Edit, Text Properties, Face submenu, and they can also be accessed by typing M-g, which causes these choices to appear in the minibuffer. These commands are designed to work on selected regions.

Lists: Ordered and Unordered

The two varieties of lists used in HTML files are ordered and unordered. An ordered list has its items sequentially numbered, whereas an unordered list is just a list. Typing C-1-c C-1-c o inserts the following ordered list in your file:

```
<ol>
     <li>(the cursor will be left here)
</ol>
```

A list item is one of the individual members of a list. A browser indents the entire list to set it off from the remainder of the page. Each item in an unordered list is displayed with a bullet in front of it, which is either a large dot or a circle, depending on the browser. Items in an ordered list are prefixed with a number.

The list item tag <li> is like the paragraph tag in that it doesn't need a matching closing tag. Type a few words after the <li> tag and type C-c C-c i; the result looks like this:

```
<ol>
     <li>words you typed
     <li>another item
</ol>
```

There can be as many list items as you like. The only restriction is that they all have to be between the <ol> and </ol> tags. In a browser, the second example would look like this:

```
1.  words you typed
2.  another item
```

Unordered lists are just like ordered, but without the numbers before each item. Type C-c C-c-u for this type of list. Lists are displayed in a browser indented from the main text in order to set them apart.

External and Internal Links

One of the contributing factors to the explosive growth of the Internet is HTML's capability to reference external files with links. It's all done with a simple little tag containing the URL (uniform resource locator) of another HTML file, either a file on your machine or a file on a remote Internet site.

17

The URL is always between quotes, whereas the section just before the `</a>` end tag is actually visible when the file is viewed with a browser. Just type `C-c C-c h` and Emacs prompts you in the minibuffer for the URL. Type it in and your cursor ends up before the end tag, enabling you to type in the name for the link. A link looks something like this:

```
<a href "http://www.mcp.com>">[the cursor is placed here]</a>
```

Inline and Linked Images

What would a Web page be without images? For one thing, pages would load more quickly, but when used discreetly images can greatly enhance a Web page. There are several tags that are used to display images both inline (right on the page) and externally (as a hyperlink). The simplest one looks like this, which can be inserted by typing `C-l-c C-c i`:

```
<img src="another.gif">
```

 If your image is not in the same directory on the server as your HTML file, a path might have to be appended to the image's filename.

Not everyone browses the Web with a computer capable of displaying images well. Rather than using the bare image tag, as in the previous example, it's a good idea to use the `<img alt>` tag, which looks like this:

```
<img alt="Here's another photo!" src="another.gif">
```

Visitors to your page who, for whatever reasons, aren't displaying the images will at least see a short text description of the image, and the site will probably make more sense to them.

GNU Emacs's default HTML mode doesn't have a keybinding for this second tag, but it's easy enough to add the `alt=` section manually.

It's generally preferable (and courteous) to keep the size and number of inline images to a minimum. Larger images can be linked to your page with a hyperlink rather than inline with an `<img>` tag. This gives the visitor to your site the option of either clicking on the image link (if they really want to see it) or ignoring it.

To create an image link, first type `C-c C-c h`. You are prompted in the minibuffer for a URL, but in this case you don't need one. Just press Enter, and you see this in your file:

```
<a href "http://"></a>
```

Delete the `http://` characters between the quotes and insert the filename of your image.

Highlighting and Hiding Tags

Depending on which version of Emacs you have installed, the various tags and their contents might or might not be displayed in a combination of bold, italic, and colored fonts.

It takes a little work with Customize to set up a pleasing combination of highlighting colors that works with your default background and foreground colors, but it's worth the trouble if you will be working with tagged files such as HTML and LaTeX. All you need to do is click the Help menu, move the mouse cursor to Customize and select Browse Customization Groups. When the Customize Browser buffer opens, find Font Lock Highlighting Faces (in the Font Lock category, shown in Figure 17.3) and try some different color combinations.

FIGURE 17.3

Font-highlighting Customize buffer.

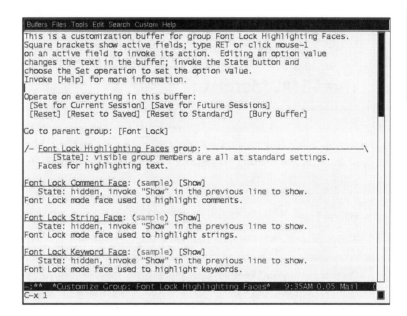

```
 Buffers Files Tools Edit Search Custom Help
This is a customization buffer for group Font Lock Highlighting Faces.
Square brackets show active fields; type RET or click mouse-1
on an active field to invoke its action.  Editing an option value
changes the text in the buffer; invoke the State button and
choose the Set operation to set the option value.
Invoke [Help] for more information.

Operate on everything in this buffer:
 [Set for Current Session] [Save for Future Sessions]
 [Reset] [Reset to Saved] [Reset to Standard]   [Bury Buffer]

Go to parent group: [Font Lock]

/- Font Lock Highlighting Faces group: ------------------------------\
      [State]: visible group members are all at standard settings.
    Faces for highlighting text.

Font Lock Comment Face: (sample) [Show]
    State: hidden, invoke "Show" in the previous line to show.
Font Lock mode face used to highlight comments.

Font Lock String Face: (sample) [Show]
    State: hidden, invoke "Show" in the previous line to show.
Font Lock mode face used to highlight strings.

Font Lock Keyword Face: (sample) [Show]
    State: hidden, invoke "Show" in the previous line to show.
Font Lock mode face used to highlight keywords.

-:**  *Customize Group: Font Lock Highlighting Faces*   9:35AM 0.05 Mail  (
C-x 1                                                                    ■
```

17

Another method to access and modify the relevant Customize settings is useful if you already know the name of the Customization group you want to affect. Just type M-x (customize-group). Remember that after typing M-x, any further commands appear in the minibuffer rather than in the main text area. The response from Emacs is Customize Group (Default Emacs). If you just type Enter at this point a Customization buffer appears with all groups listed under the broad category Emacs. Instead type font-lock, and just the font-lock customization settings appear. One of these is Global Font Lock Mode, along with the option to either toggle the setting on or off. Toggle it on, click State, and in the resulting menu select Save for Future Sessions. This action causes this particular setting to be saved in your .emacs initialization file, so that each time you start up Emacs it causes all files in formats recognized by Emacs to be *fontified*, which is Emacs jargon for syntax highlighting.

Viewing Your File

Writing HTML is much easier if the file can be periodically viewed in a browser such as Netscape, Lynx, or Internet Explorer.

This is a quick way to determine whether links are working correctly, and any mismatched or missing tags are glaringly obvious. The Emacs HTML mode provides a quick method to either send your file to a running browser or to start the browser with the file displayed. Whenever you have made several changes to a file, just click View Buffer Contents in the HTML menu and your file is visible in your browser. When the browser has loaded your file the display can be periodically updated by reloading the file, either using the Reload icon or the equivalent keystroke (Alt-R in Netscape).

The SGML Menu

Next to the HTML menu on the menubar is the SGML menu. SGML stands for *Standard Generalized Markup Language*, an international document standard. HTML is a smaller subset of SGML that was developed for use on the Internet. The only SGML menu item of immediate interest is Toggle Tag Visibility (as shown in Figure 17.4), which enables you to hide all of the angle-bracketed tags and view just the bare text. This is very useful in longer HTML documents; being able to review the text without the distracting tags can be a help while editing. The keystroke C-c Tab is another way to hide the tags.

The final, somewhat-cryptic item on this menu deserves at least a mention. Validate allows Emacs to call an external SGML parser that checks your file for correct HTML syntax. One of the commonly used parsers is James Clark's sgmls. Frankly, though, this is of limited use for beginners, because nearly all Web browsers are very lenient about bad HTML syntax and attempt to display just about anything between <html> tags. If you would like to pursue this further, a search on the Internet for SGML, James Clark, or sgmls will likely yield a bounty of avenues to follow.

FIGURE 17.4

The SGML menu.

Writing HTML with XEmacs

Much of the information in the previous GNU Emacs section also applies to XEmacs.

The maintainers of XEmacs have chosen to use psgml as the native XEmacs HTML mode. This is a complex package, originally written by Lennart Staflin and James Clark and subsequently adapted for XEmacs by Ben Wing, Bill Perry, and Steve Bauer. Parts of Nelson Minar's html-helper-mode have been incorporated into the HTML-specific portions of the code in the XEmacs version. You can access this mode at the following Web site: `http://www.santafe.edu/~nelson/tools/`

Using psgml-HTML

psgml's HTML mode is not as easy to use as the GNU Emacs HTML mode, but many more tags are supported. There are more menus (five in all), but the menus won't make much sense without first reading the Info help documentation (`C-h-i` summons the Info index). The basic tag-insertion functions aren't immediately evident, but clicking with the right mouse button shows a cascading menu of context-sensitive tag items. By *context-sensitive*, I mean that the only tags shown in the menu are those which are appropriate to the cursor position in the file. For example, if your cursor is below the second `</head>` tag the menu consists of a single item, Body, because that is the only appropriate tag for that place in the file.

But let's ignore the mouse menus for the time being. Learning the keybindings for the tags is more important, especially in this particular mode. In this mode, the equivalent tag keybindings aren't shown on the menus. The psgml Info file doesn't list them; most of this documentation is concerned with esoteric commands and functions used with other sorts of SGML files. Any time you're faced with an Emacs mode and need some quick information, typing C-h-m helps. If an HTML file is being edited, a window appears with a brief summary of psgml's HTML mode, followed by two full pages of keybindings. Information concerning other active modes (such as font-lock-mode and text-mode) also appears; just scroll down to the section beginning with HTML Mode.

This is a good opportunity to practice cutting and pasting. Type C-space at the beginning of the HTML mode section and scroll down to the end of the buffer (type M-> to get there quickly). When your cursor is at the end of the last line, type M-w, which copies the region you have marked with the two previous commands.

Now type C-x C-f. You are prompted for a filename in the minibuffer; type in a nonexistent mnemonic filename, perhaps something such as html-keys.txt. After the new empty buffer appears, type C-y and watch the HTML-mode section of the mode-help buffer appear in your buffer. I recommend printing out this file, because it is a great help in learning the keybindings for this particular HTML mode.

It is often useful to be able to tag a marked region or selection. This feature makes it possible to write a file in untagged normal text and go back through the file afterward and tag regions, effectively transforming a text file into an HTML file. Tagging marked selections is also handy when importing blocks of text from a text file into an HTML file.

Try it out by first marking an area of text, first using C-space to mark one end. Move the cursor to the other end of the region and type C-u followed by a keybinding for any of the HTML tags. For example, if an area of text is selected, typing C-u C-z q surrounds the area with the <blockquote> tags, which causes the area to be indented in from the rest of the text when a browser displays the file.

Using Emacs in Conjunction with HTML Editors

Every piece of software has strong and weak points. A commercial HTML editor often has useful facilities for precise image placement and color choices, but the actual text-editing powers in most cases is minimal. Many writers of HTML rough out the basic structure of a document in a commercial editor and load the file into a text editor such as Emacs in order to check the tagging and to be able to make use of a more versatile editing environment. This is also one way to learn new methods of using the HTML tags—by observing how the HTML editor applies them and adapting these techniques to your own HTML files.

Writing and Processing LaTeX

Why even bother to learn LaTeX when a word processor offers similar functionality without the bother of markup tags? For a short document such as a letter or memo, a word processor is often more convenient. However, keeping indexes, cross-references, and footnotes synchronized as a document is written can strain the capabilities of a word processor. This is where LaTeX styles and packages come into play. A TeX/LaTeX installation includes a wide variety of predefined styles and optional packages with many more available on the Internet. This enables a writer to concentrate on content, letting the TeX utilities perform the grunt work of constructing a document that is consistently formatted and professional looking.

17

Getting Started

You can create and edit LaTeX files with Emacs, but to process them you need a functional TeX installation. There are several TeX/LaTeX packages available for just about any operating system, some free and others which cost money. Linux users can install preconfigured packages which are included with most Linux distributions.

> Several packages are available for Windows that can be found on any CTAN archive site, such as ftp.cdrom.com (in the directory /pub/tex/ctan/ systems/win32). Also check the Windows NT Emacs FAQ on the CD-ROM.

Because the files required are large, many people purchase a TeX CD-ROM from a vendor such as Walnut Creek (see their Web site at http://www.cdrom.com).

Most TeX packages include ample documentation, often including the unprocessed LaTeX files; these files can be identified by their .tex suffix, and provide good examples for viewing and experimentation. A particularly useful introductory file is called essential.tex, available at CTAN mirrors such as ftp.cdrom.com; on that North American site it can be found in the directory /pub/tex/ctan/info/latex-essential. essential.tex (or any short LaTeX file) can be used to determine whether your TeX installation is configured properly. At a command prompt, type latex essential.tex; the result should be a file named essential.dvi. By processing this file you have verified that TeX is functional on your machine, and as a bonus you have a very readable and informative beginner's guide to LaTeX.

When you have verified that TeX works for you, load the original essential.tex file into an Emacs session. You should notice that a new menu, TeX, has appeared on the menubar (as shown in Figure 17.5). From this menu you can run the file through the TeX process, creating a DVI file and viewing the file with your DVI viewer. Type C-h-m; a window opens showing the various special keys which this TeX mode offers. Look over the essential.tex file; at the very beginning of this file (and scattered elsewhere) are lines which begin with a % character. These comments are ignored by the TeX parser and do not appear in the output file. Any line beginning with a backslash is a formatting command (or tag) for TeX. Notice the markup tags near the beginning of the file that set the document type and other variables. Scroll farther in the file and you see that paragraphs of the actual text content are relatively free of markup. A blank line signals a new paragraph just as in a word processor.

FIGURE 17.5

essential.tex *file*
with TeX menu.

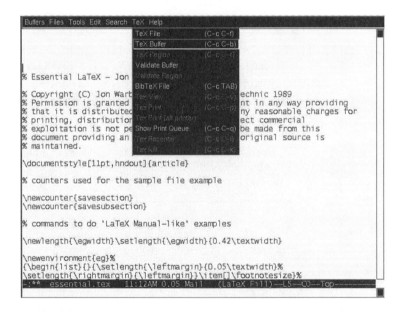

The default settings, such as the name of the DVI viewer and your printing commands, likely work out of the box on a Linux system.

> If you are running Windows you likely need to change the default settings. Under the Help menu, open the Customize submenu and click Browse Customization Groups. In the resulting Customize Browser window, scroll down to the WP category, click the + sign, and select the Tex Group. Inspect the available settings in the Tex Group buffer, including the subcategories which can be expanded, and change the settings so they correspond with your particular setup. Don't forget to Save For Future Sessions; if you don't, the changed settings are effective only during the current editing session. Click State to see the menu with the saving options.

As with HTML, basic document templates save time when you create a LaTeX file from scratch. essential.tex contains a simple template which can be copied into a new file for this purpose. If you do this, it's a good idea to make one change in the template. essential.tex was written in 1988, when LaTeX version 2.09 was current. Since then, LaTeX has been revised and improved (the current version is LaTeX2e). The essential.tex file uses the obsolete \documentstyle tag; this should be changed in your template to \documentclass.

AucTeX Installation and Basics

The GNU Emacs default TeX mode is useful, but you still have to type the majority of the markup tags. A separately maintained add-on package called AucTeX adds many convenient shortcuts for editing LaTeX files in Emacs. This package is included with XEmacs, but it works equally well with GNU Emacs. If you decide to spend much time writing LaTeX files, it's well worth the time spent obtaining and installing it.

If you use XEmacs, AucTeX should be already installed (but not necessarily configured). GNU Emacs users can obtain the latest version of the package from the WWW site http://sunsite.auc.dk/auctex/.

The source archive includes a makefile, which needs to be edited in order to adapt the installation to your needs (mainly setting paths, such as the location of your Emacs site-lisp directory and the TeX installation). Typing make install should first byte-compile the Lisp files, using Emacs in its noninteractive batch mode, and then install the files in a newly created auctex subdirectory of your site-lisp directory. The final steps are to edit the /site-lisp/auctex/tex.el file and copy the clearly marked sections that determine the paths to a new file, /site-lisp/tex-site.el. Edit this file so that it accurately reflects the actual locations of your TeX directory and your Emacs AucTeX directory. Then append to your .emacs file the following line:

```
(require 'tex-site)
```

17

The next time you start up Emacs and load a .tex file you see new items on the menubar. Instead of a single TeX menu, you see both a LaTeX and a Commands menu. Numerous commands are on these menus, most of which are relatively self-explanatory (read the AucTeX info files, which come with the distribution). As a demonstration of the convenience of this package, open a new empty LaTeX file called trial.tex, by typing C-x-C-f and, when prompted in the minibuffer, type trial.tex. AucTeX should be loaded automatically. Confirm this by seeing whether the two new items mentioned appear on the menubar. If AucTeX fails to load, make sure you have correctly modified your .emacs file, and recheck the settings in the new tex-site.el file.

Pull down the LaTeX menu, select Insert Environment (as shown in Figure 17.6), and choose the topmost of the three alphabetically arranged submenus. Select Document as the environment to be inserted into the file. The keybinding for Insert Environment is C-c C-e. When using this keybinding, you are prompted in the minibuffer for the type of environment with a default choice suggested.

FIGURE 17.6

Skeleton LaTeX buffer with LaTeX menu.

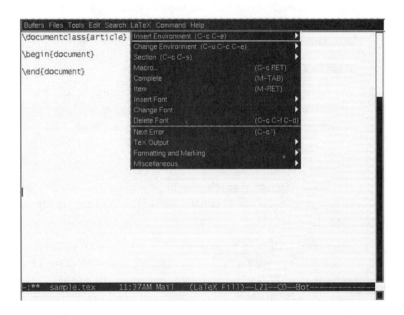

A environment in a LaTeX document is a set of tags surrounding an area of text that specifies how it should be formatted. In this case, the Document environment is the entire file. Every document needs to belong to one of several available document classes; the class can be book, letter, article, report, or slide.

Several characters have a special meaning to the TeX processor; in order to use them normally in a file, you need to *escape* them, which means prefixing them with a backslash. These characters are $, &, %, #, _, ~, ^, {, and }.

The backslash is an exception, in that typing \\ in your Emacs file won't show up as a literal backslash in the final output. \\ forces a new line. A literal backslash has to be written like this: $\backslash$.

Tags and Keys

AucTeX has a well-designed set of keybindings which simplify entering tags. For example, `C-c C-s` enters an appropriate section tag. You are prompted in the minibuffer for the type of section as well its name and label; the default choice offered for the type of section depends on the type of document you are editing. The label is used internally for cross references and indexing.

Various types of lists, both numbered and ordinary, are easily included in a LaTeX file. Look at the third submenu under LaTeX, Insert Environment; select Itemize and you should see this tagging in your file:

```
\begin{itemize}
\item
\end{itemize}
```

The cursor is placed right after \item, making it easy to type your item's content. Type a word or two and press `M-Enter`. A new item tag is inserted. The `enumerate` tag is a variation that sequentially numbers the items in the output. The numbers don't need to be included in the LaTeX file, because the TeX programs automatically put them in.

Another commonly used group of tags is used to change the font of a word or region. The keybindings for these tags all begin with `C-c C-f`:

`C-c C-f C b`	inserts the Bold tag
`C-c C-f C e`	inserts the Emphasize tag
`C-c C-f C t`	inserts the Typewriter tag (a monospaced like Courier)
`C-c C-f C c`	inserts the Small Caps tag (all capitalized in a small font)
`C-c C-f C f`	inserts the Sans Serif tag (a font like Helvetica)
`C-c C-f C I`	inserts the Italic tag
`C-c C-f C s`	inserts the Slanted tag (similar to italic)
`C-c C-f C r`	inserts the Roman tag (a font like Times New Roman)
`C-c C-f C a`	inserts the Calligraphic tag

17

Try typing one of the more commonly-used tags—C-c C-f C i, used for italic text. You see this in your buffer:

```
textit{}
```

Anything typed within the pair of curly braces of this tag is italicized in the final output.

The LaTeX menu can also be used for these tags. They can be found as submenus under the Insert Font, Change Font, and Delete Font items.

The Command Menu

Next to the LaTeX menu is the Command menu. Here you find commands for processing a LaTeX file from within Emacs. The most useful item on this menu when writing LaTeX files is LaTeX Interactive. Try it out either by loading a finished LaTeX file or by writing one yourself. Select LaTeX Interactive from the Command menu, and your Emacs window splits horizontally. The bottom half of the screen displays the verbose output of the TeX engine as it processes the file. It should complete successfully, as indicated by the statement Output written on *filename*.dvi (as shown in Figure 17.7).

FIGURE 17.7

LaTeX Interactive window shown below a LaTeX file buffer.

If any serious errors appear, the line number is indicated in the output window. AucTeX provides a convenient method of stepping through errors that might occur. An item in the LaTeX menu, Next Error, moves forward in the file to each successive error when you finish fixing the problem. C-c-' is the keyboard equivalent.

When you have processed the file and no errors are being reported, select View from the Command menu. A message appears in the minibuffer, showing you the command that is run if you press Enter. The default DVI viewer is xdvi; if yours has a different name, edit the command before pressing Enter. The name of the default viewer should be changed using Customize if you use AucTeX often.

Summary

This hour helps you learn to create your own HTML and LaTeX files using specialized modes that extend the Emacs editor. Each of these modes has a set of time-saving key-strokes that help you quickly insert tags into your text. These tags are a series of characters that are read by the text processor—either a Web browser for HTML or the TeX program for LaTeX. Pull-down menus are also provided for mouse-based insertion of tags and for sending the file to the text processor.

17

Q&A

Q What is the result of pressing the keys c-h-m?

A The window is split and the new half displays a Help buffer with documentation for the mode.

Q What is the text-formatting system upon which LaTeX relies?

A Donald Knuth's TeX system.

Q What is the outermost tag that defines the document class of a LaTeX file?

A This tag: \documentclass{*article*}, with *article* replaced by *book*, *letter*, or any other valid class.

Q What significance does the % character have in a LaTeX file?

A This is the comment character; anything after % anywhere in a line is ignored when the file is processed.

Q How do you step from one trouble spot in a LaTeX file to the next?

A Use the menu item Next Error or the keybinding c-c '.

Q How do you convert a LaTeX file into a DVI file from within Emacs?

A In the Command menu, select either LaTeX or LaTeX Interactive.

Exercises

1. Save an Internet HTML file from within a Web browser. Load the file into an Emacs session and make changes such as adding new tagged paragraphs or links. Then view the modified file in the browser and see what your changes really look like and whether the links work. Hint: save the file from a fairly plain Web page—one without frames, tables, or Java applets.

2. Open a plain text file with Emacs and type C-x C-w (Save As). When prompted in the minibuffer, save the file as a new file with the .html or .htm suffix. Now try to insert the proper tags so that the new file displays properly in a Web browser.

3. Try exercise 2 with LaTeX rather than HTML, using the same plain text file. Save the file using a name with the .tex suffix rather than the .html suffix. After you insert the necessary LaTeX tags, process it with TeX and view the DVI file with your viewer. Notice how the formatted output differs from the results of exercise 2.

HOUR 18

Editing C, C++, and Java Files

This hour assumes a good working knowledge of Java, C, C++, or Objective C. Working with a programming language such as Java or C in Emacs is like editing any other type of text file. The advantage is that for each language, there is a specialized programming mode which provides easy access to the following:

- Advanced language syntax navigation
- Indentation
- Extended editing modes
- Commenting
- C preprocessor management
- Advanced tag and file management

Java, C, C++, and Objective C, while different in many ways, have the same keybindings and language feature support. For convenience in this hour, generic features are discussed using examples in C unless the feature is available only for Java or C++.

Advanced C-Based Language Editing

When working with a C-based language, it is important to make sure that the buffer is in the correct mode. This should be handled automatically by Emacs, but if Emacs gets it wrong, you can run the command M-x c-mode for C code, M-x c++-mode for C++, M-x java-mode for Java code, or M-x objc-mode for Objective C. When you are in the correct mode, you can proceed to work with these languages more efficiently.

You have already been exposed to navigation and marking and deleting text based on some primitive constructs such as characters, lines, and words. In the C-based languages, there are even more advanced constructs that can be manipulated such as functions, lists, and syntactic expressions. It might seem like an impossibility to remember even more key sequences for navigation, but the keybindings are organized so they are easy to remember. For example, C-a is beginning of line, and M-a is beginning of sentence. Because a sentence doesn't make too much sense in C, M-a means beginning of command. This shows that control is used for geometric style units, and many Meta-key commands are used for items based on a language's syntax. Next, C-M-a means beginning of function. In this case, it moves the cursor to the opening { of your C function. By the same token, you can assume that M-e moves to the end of a command, and C-M-e moves to the end of a function definition.

Mixing familiar commands with these new commands in a table helps in remembering them:

Key	Control	Meta	Control-Meta
a, e	Beginning, end of line	Beginning, end of statement	Beginning, end of function
F, b	Forward, back character	Forward, back word	Forward, back syntactic expression
t	Transpose characters	Transpose words	Transpose syntactic expressions
k	Kill line	Kill sentence	Kill syntactic expression
n, p	Next, previous		Forward, back list
h		Mark paragraph	Mark function
l	Recenter on line		Recenter on function

It would seem logical during experimentation to extend other keys as well, such as Backspace or Delete for removal of syntactic expressions for a buffer. After all, Delete removes a character, and M-Delete deletes a word. Be warned that on some platforms Control-Alt-Delete runs system shutdown. Control-Alt-Backspace exits the XFree86 version of X Window, which is common under Linux.

One of the new navigation features introduced is the *syntactic expression*. A syntactic expression is a group of characters that represents some structure, including symbols, strings, comments, and lists. Text, such as words, can be syntactic expressions, but is often an element of a larger structure, such as a symbol. In a C language file, navigate over the symbol new_symbol using M-f and M-b. Now try it with C-M-f and C-M-b. When navigating words, the cursor will stop on the underscore (_) character, but not when navigating as a syntactic expression. Try navigating over code blocks, strings, and comments with these new commands as well.

Some other types of things Emacs knows about are all clumped under the syntactic expression when it comes to keybindings. A string that starts and ends with a double quote (") character represents the string. A character in C-based languages starts and ends with a single quote (') character, but Emacs treats these as strings as well. A comment in C starts with /* and ends with */. In C++ and Objective C, the additional comment start of //, which comments to the end of the line, is also known.

What is especially interesting about strings and comments is that, when the cursor is outside the bounds of these objects, they are treated as one large element, regardless of their contents. This permits the forward syntactic expression command to skip over them, even if they contain characters that would normally terminate the current syntactic expression. If, on the other hand, the cursor is in a string or comment, such elements as parentheses matching and moving over syntactic expressions work as if the string or comment were not there.

In command names under Emacs, a syntactic expression is referred to as a sexp.

When using apropos as discussed in Hour 10, "The Emacs Help System and Configuration System," you can get a list of all syntactic expression related functions using sexp as the search element.

18

The other useful language features Emacs knows about are lists. Because much of Emacs has been implemented in Lisp, a list-based language, this makes a lot of sense. In C-based languages, a list starts with an open parenthesis, brace, or bracket, and continues until a closing character. Fortunately, Emacs is smart enough to skip such characters that are in strings or comments, so there is no fear of errors while using navigation or editing keys.

A list is also classified as a syntactic expression, so you can use C-M-f and C-M-b to navigate over them, but using C-M-n and C-M-p has the advantage of skipping over all text between the cursor and the list and moves over the list as well. Another useful command is called down-list and is bound to C-M-d. This skips from the cursor position to the next available list and stops after the opening character. You can pass a universal argument of -1 to move backward to the previous list as well.

All the navigation commands introduced in this hour accept the universal argument. This argument (passed with C-u or C-M-—) lets you repeat a given operation or reverse it easily.

Automatic Indentation

One of the most powerful features of Emacs while editing C-based languages is its capability to indent code by pressing Tab. This can be the most distracting behavior for new Emacs users who have become accustomed to other editors, but it is, by far, a huge time saver in the long run. You will find that complete control over indentation is allowed so if the default style is unappealing or incorrect for your situation, it can be adjusted to suit your needs.

To start with, load up a file in C, C++, Objective C, or Java. Start at the beginning of a function or other element and press Tab. Continue pressing Tab on each line afterward. You will find that not only does it not matter where the cursor is on the line, but the line chooses a location and stays there instead of continually adding more spaces before the text. Try changing the indentation of the line by deleting or adding spaces at the beginning of the line, and press Tab again. The line shifts back to its desired location.

The first concern with automatic indentation is how to insert a Tab character when Tab is behaving in a nontraditional fashion. You can insert a Tab at any time by pressing C-q first, which will quote the next keystroke in directly. If you are entering a string literal, you should always use the \t character modifier instead of a literal Tab character.

I hope that you have now decided that this is the one true way of indenting and you're ready to move on to some serious code formatting. A common situation would be to wrap a block of code in a conditional, which requires indenting all lines that are wrapped. Although that is certainly simple to do with the Tab key, it is more appropriate to use the indent region command C-M-\ instead. The indent region command is quite handy with the specialized mark commands such as C-M-SPC (mark syntactic expression), C-M-h (mark function), or C-x h (mark whole buffer).

> On some Intel-based PCs, Control-Alt-Spacebar is the default keybinding for power-saving mode. This can be annoying at best; on some systems, this causes a no-questions-asked reboot which is no fun at all.

There are additional bindings available for indenting blocks of code without setting the mark. For example, if you want to reindent the contents of an if block, you can place the cursor before the opening { and press C-M-q, which indents the expression following the cursor. You can also use C-c C-q to indent all the lines in the current function.

So look at how you can handle your example. In typical Emacs fashion there are several ways to do it. To type this in logically, you'd probably start at the beginning of the code you need to conditionalize, and type

```
if(condition) {
```

You'd then want to go to the end of the code, and add in a } on a line by itself. This leaves all the old code indented incorrectly.

It would certainly be easy to use C-c C-q to reindent the entire function you are in, but that could take a long time for very long functions. It would also have been wise to leave a mark with C-SPC after typing the opening {, but you might have forgotten. You could always drop a mark, use backward syntactic expression C-M-b, and use the indent region command. Of course, if you moved back to the beginning, you could use the indent syntactic expression command C-M-q. As it turns out, the fastest way to do this without moving the cursor is to use the mark syntactic expression command with a negative argument and use indent region. As you learned earlier, C-u - and C-M-- are roughly equivalent in providing a negative argument. Next, C-M-SPC marks the block of code you entered. Now you can use indent region with C-M-\ and everything is as you want it.

> If you want to force very large amounts of code to be indented in a known amount, the rigid indentation function can be much faster. Try C-x Tab on a region with and without a universal argument to see how this works.

18

Indenting with Style

Despite the rigid indentation enforced while editing C-based language files, Emacs is not as tyrannical as one might think. If the default GNU editing style is either not to your liking or wrong due to corporate coding standards, you can change it to your heart's content.

First, you might want to try out some of the built-in styles. The set style command is available with `C-c .` or with the extended command `M-x c-set-style`. The most common styles are GNU, K&R, and, of course, the Java style. Each of these styles controls not only how individual commands are indented, but also how braces, switch statements, and other elements are handled.

Chances are that your preferences are covered in the several styles available by default. If your corporate environment demands a stringent pattern, however, you might need to create your own indentation style. This requires some work in your `.emacs` initialization file. Please refer to Hour 24, "Installing Emacs Add-Ons," for details on writing Lisp if the upcoming section is unclear.

The easiest way to create your own style is to find a style that is as close to what you want as you can find. This becomes the parent indentation style and minimizes the amount of work you need to do. Next, track those elements you don't like for reference. Are the braces spaced incorrectly between the opening command, and enclosing statements? Are your K&R function headers indented too much? Emacs wants to know.

Next, prepare to edit your configuration file found in `~/.emacs`. The command you add will look something like this:

```
(require 'cc-mode)
(c-add-style "my-style"
        '( "parent style"
           ( variable . value )
           ( c-offsets-alist .
           ( ( offset-name-1 . Offset )
             ( offset-name-2 . Offset ) ) )
         ) )
```

The text in the string `parent style` represents the style you found earlier while experimenting with the different indentation types. Everything not specified in the following section will be derived from this parent style saving you the time needed to enter it into your `.emacs` file.

All the elements in the list following the parent style is called an *alist*, which is short for *association list*. Each element of an alist is a *dotted pair*, meaning that it is a list with two elements of the form (KEY . DATA). KEY is some name used as reference, and DATA is the data associated with it. The key element of each association is a variable name, and its data is the value it will take. The variable `c-offsets-alist` is an alist describing how the language should be indented. The key is a symbol describing the syntactic content of the current C line. The data element of each association is how much to indent when this item is found.

Some common variables to set in your style are the following:

- `c-basic-offset`—The smallest unit of indentation in your style
- `c-backslash-column`—When adding \ characters to long macros, the desired column
- `c-offsets-alist`—The alist of symbols representing a C-based language's syntax, and the offsets associated with each

> All variables available in a style specification are also available as generic variables. This means you can use custom on them, or modify them directly in your `.emacs` file. Any such customization is overridden by the style you create.

18

The most important of these variables is most likely the `c-offsets-alist`. Each key for the C indent engine can be listed here, giving the ultimate control of the indentation engine. Some common syntactic elements you might want to change are the following:

- `statement`—A generic C command statement
- `statement-cont`—Continuation of a C statement that is longer than a single line
- `block-open`—When a code block unrelated to a control statement is started
- `substatement-open`—A code block below a control statement such as `if` or `for`

There are many more elements which you can access through Emacs's internal documentation for the variable `c-offsets-alist`. You can reference this by using the help command `C-h v c-offsets-alist RET`.

> All variables listed in a style can be accessed via Emacs's built-in help using `C-h v`, and the names of all the useful ones start with `c-.` making it easy to find what you need.

The data element for each syntax type you specify can be a number, representing the number of characters of indentation desired. If you want this element to line up under the previous element, a 0 is appropriate. You can also specify data as the symbol + or -, which specify one increment or decrement of c-basic-offset. ++ and -- mean that many increments of c-basic-offset. * and / mean one half of c-basic-offset.

If you need some syntactic element to always start at the first column, such as macros, an offset isn't appropriate because you want to use a constant. Unfortunately, the method of bringing text to the first column requires putting in a very large negative number. This effectively backs up the indentation until it cannot get any smaller.

If you are feeling exceptionally brave after finishing this book, you can also set the data element of a statement to a function. This function is described with Emacs's documentation for the variable c-offsets-alist. Such a function can provide near infinite control over all permutations of a given syntactic element. The default comment indentation data are functions, which is how such great comment indentations are made available.

Now that you have defined your own indentation style mode, you should apply it to all files that you edit so that you do not have to use the set style command C-c . every time. To do this, set the variable c-default-style to the string my-style in your .emacs file. The code would look like this:

```
(setq c-default-style "my-style")
```

Proactive Editing

The C-based language editing mode provides some additional editing modes beyond most other language editing modes. These include

- Auto new line
- Hungry delete

Each of these can be toggled easily or have their behaviors modified slightly. What both of these modes do is increase the amount of stuff Emacs does in certain situations. Auto new line automatically adds extra white space in certain situations, and hungry delete performs extra white space deletions.

Auto new line mode is toggled with the key sequence C-c C-a. When active, the major-mode string changes to include /a. Thus, if you are editing C, it reads C/a; if you are editing Java, it says Java/a. It could say /ha instead, and this means that auto new line mode is on at the same time as hungry delete mode.

When active, auto new line changes the behavior of the brace keys, semicolon, and comma. Whenever one of these is entered, Emacs adds a new line after it when appropriate. You can change the occurrences when this happens by examining the variable `c-hanging-semi&comma-criteria`. To do this you must be prepared to write a function that analyzes the current location and returns `'stop` to prevent a new line from being added or a non-nil value to cause a new line to appear. Please see Hour 24 for additional details on how to accomplish this.

Hungry delete takes the opposite approach. Where auto new line adds extra carriage returns, hungry delete removes as much white space as possible. To activate hungry delete, you can toggle it with `C-c C-d`, and a `/h` or `/ha` should be added to the mode description. To use hungry delete when it is active, all you have to do is press the Backspace key, and hungry delete remove as much white space as possible. White space deleted includes spaces, tab characters, and new lines. Using hungry delete could prove distracting to new users, but it can prove valuable in some situations where there is lots of pesky white space.

Much of what hungry delete does can be replicated through use of a few other built-in commands. For completeness, you can also use the function just-one-space, which is bound to `M-SPC`, and delete-blank-lines which is bound to `C-x C-o`. Unlike these functions, however, hungry delete remove all white spaces of both types.

These two modes complement each other well, so you can toggle them to both come on at the same time with `C-c C-t` command. When both are active, the mode name will have the string `/ha` appended.

If you would like these modes to be automatically activated whenever you enter a file containing a C-based language, you will need to update your `.emacs` file. To modify what happens when a C language file is loaded, write a function that turns on these modes. The functions to use are `c-toggle-auto-state`, `c-toggle-hungry-state`, and `c-toggle-auto-hungry-state`. Each of these functions takes a single numeric argument. To force the mode on, a 1 is used, and to force it off, a -1 is used; otherwise the mode is toggled.

You can do all this with a command in your `.emacs` file that looks like this:

```
(add-hook 'c-mode-hook (lambda () (c-toggle-auto-hungry-state 1)))
```

 Two packages are available that perform tasks similar to hungry delete, but for any language mode. One is called `greedy-delete.el`, and the other is `tinyeat.el`. Please see those files for details on their use.

Comment Acceleration

Emacs has several advanced commands that are useful when working with comments. You might have already noticed that comments in C are indented quite cleverly and wonder what more there could be. Emacs can manage the following comment basics for you:

- Text filling
- Creating new comments
- Removing comments

When working with large amounts of text in a comment, the built-in fill command seems a good choice, but there is actually a special fill comment command in the C menu which rearranges all the text in a comment so that it neatly fills the space available. This is very much like the fill paragraph command discussed earlier in Hour 12, "Visible Editing Utilities," but is designed especially for comments. If you do not have access to the menubar, you can invoke this function using the extended command `c-fill-paragraph` like this `M-x c-fill-paragraph RET`.

Emacs is also expert at adding new comments. There are two methods for doing this. The first is the indent-for-comment command which is bound to `M-;`. This is specially designed for dropping a new comment on the right side of the code. Not only does it move the cursor to a specified column and insert comment characters, it also takes an existing comment and moves it to the correct location. Try it out in some code to get the feel for what it does. Notice that if you use this command on a line with a lone closing brace, the comment appears directly after the closing brace. If you use this command on a line containing code, it moves out to some column regardless of the code line length.

When indenting comments for code, the location where Emacs places the comment is called the comment column. You can modify this by moving the cursor to the column you want, and using the set comment column command bound to `C-x ;`. The comment column is similar in nature to the fill column, but is specifically for your comments.

You can set the comment column in your `.emacs` file with a command like this:

```
(setq-default comment-column 70)
```

Here `70` is the column number for your comments.

Emacs defaults to a fill column of 70. Classically, printers, terminals, news media, and other things UNIX default to an 80-column area for fixed width fonts. Although Emacs lets you do whatever you want, it is advisable for readability purposes to stick within these bounds.

Emacs also has some comment commands for dealing with regions of code. The comment region command works in all language modes and has some clever properties. The need to comment out a region of code in C might seem unnecessary with preprocessor directives, but Emacs makes it easy: Mark the region you need commented out and use the comment region command bound to C-c C-c. Every line in C gets surrounded with its own /* and */ characters. In C++ and Java, each line is started with the // comment start.

If you want to remove the comment characters from your code in the future, you are in luck. Instead of having to remove all those characters yourself, you can pass the universal argument (with C-u) to the comment region command with C-u C-c C-c and have all those comment characters removed.

Navigating C Preprocessor Directives

When working with C, C++, and Objective C you will most likely encounter the C preprocessor. This preprocessor is the program that adds the #include commands that permit your source code to access prototypes from other source code files. It also includes #if, #ifdef, #else, and #endif commands. Although it is common to see these directives close together, they can be difficult to deal with when they cover wide blocks of code, providing compile-time configuration, or platform-specific details.

Emacs provides no fewer than three methods of viewing your directives. Fortunately, the basics of navigation are provided once by the default C mode. To begin, edit a file that contains some directives or add #ifdef #else #endif around some code where you can see all three elements. You will notice that the indenting engine knows to always bring these commands to the first column. Next, you can use the forward and backward conditional commands. Position the cursor at the beginning of the opening #if and use forward conditional command C-c C-n. Next try C-c C-p. This moves the cursor across the condition and skips across the #else directive.

> Notice the use of C-n and C-p with a C-c prefix. As you learned earlier, C-c prefixes mode specific commands, and C-n and C-p are used for navigating the Next and Previous lines. This should keep these commands easy to remember.

Next, if you are deep inside several nested conditionals, you can go up to the most-recently-entered conditional with the up conditional command bound to C-c C-u. Up conditional can also be reversed to move to the end of the current conditional with a negative argument. Thus, you can go to the #endif part with C-u - C-c C-u.

Viewing Code with Expanded Macros

Sometimes it is easier to understand source code with complex conditionals or macros if you can get a good view of what it would look like after it's been through the preprocessor. The first of several methods is provided in the default C mode with the macro expand region command bound to C-c C-e. This is the most robust of the many macro interpreters provided with Emacs; it calls the C preprocessor and collects its output for viewing. All macros, including macro functions, constants, and conditionals are all expanded out so nothing but the plain source code is left.

This command can be slow because it has to run an external process in which to interpret the code. It also has the disadvantage of showing the modified code in a separate buffer. Although this is the best you'll get for macros, there are two interpreters for preprocessor conditionals to use that mesh the display properties in your source code, with complete control of what code is shown or hidden.

A fancy conditional collapse program is called cpp after the C preprocessor. To start, run the program M-x cpp-highlight-buffer. This command brings up a control buffer with several buttons in it and highlights all the conditionals in the current buffer. Through this control buffer, you can specify background colors for different conditional results, and even mark sections read-only or hide them completely. The end result is a buffer with only the data you want and colors of your choosing marking the meaning of different code sections.

When the control buffer is active, use the middle mouse button (or both together if you have only two) on different bold buttons to make modifications. First, make sure you specify your background color on the Background section. Next, at the bottom is a list of macros. You can middle-click the True and False face and pick a special background for a conditional. Next, click Apply, and each element of the conditional disappears leaving only the code you requested behind. If you have a good selection of items, you can save the settings and load them back in later, applying them to other buffers as well.

If you run in a terminal and can't access the mouse, you can change any element by pressing the key enclosed in brackets ([ ]) near the field you want to change. For example, use b for the background or t to set the True face on a symbol.

Unfortunately, there is no way to remove all the highlighting colors from your buffer without going back to the cpp buffer and clicking, and rechoosing everything. You can kill the buffer and load it in again afterward, however.

The second preprocess collapsing program is called hideif. Unlike cpp, which has a control panel and lots of color options, hideif takes a different approach. To enable its features, you need to run the command M-x hide-ifdef-mode. When enabled, the string Ifdef should appear in the mode line and several new commands are made available on the prefix C-c @.

You can now move to different conditionals in your program and hide them quickly with the command C-c @ C-d, and you can bring them back with C-c @ C-s. This lets you control each individual occurrence of a conditional as you need it. If you want to have entire classifications of conditionals hidden, you need to specify some define lists. Unlike the cpp package, which has controls and fonts, hideif takes a little more effort to make it hide what you want and requires that you do some programming in your .emacs file to save configured information.

> When using hideif, hidden conditionals are still in the buffer and are merely invisible. It is possible to type new code into a hidden block without realizing it. To avoid this you can make the buffer read-only whenever something is hidden with C-c @ C-q.

If you want all conditionals in your buffer to be hidden at once, run the hide ifdefs command with C-c @ h to hide all conditionals. By default, it assumes that no macros have been defined. This causes everything to be hidden or have only the #else clause shown. If you want to see a specific hidden entry, you can either show it with C-c @ C-s or tell hide if that a given variable is to be defined.

If you have a conditional that looks like this

```
#ifdef HAVE_FUNCTION
    system_function(d);
#else
    local_system_function(d);
#endif
```

by default, the code between the #ifdef and #else is hidden with C-c @ h. To make all conditionals that depend on HAVE_FUNCTION appear, use C-c @ d. At the prompt, enter HAVE_FUNCTION. Now all conditionals depending on HAVE_FUNCTION will show the then clause, and not the else clause. To remove this definition, use C-c @ u and enter the variable you want removed, and all the hiding will be updated.

18

If you have a set of elements you always want defined in Emacs, you have to modify your .emacs file. Do this by adding a `hidif` mode hook. The entry in your .emacs file would look like the following:

```
(setq hide-ifdef-define-alist
      '( (list-name-1 HAVE_FUNC_1 HAVE_FUNC_2)
         (list-name-2 HAVE_HEADER_1) ) )
(add-hook 'hide-ifdef-mode-hook
           '(lambda () (hide-ifdef-use-define-alist 'list-name-2) ) )
```

The first `setq` creates a list of define groups. Each element of the `hide-ifdef-define-alist` starts with a list name. All elements after that are *symbols* whose names match that of the macro the conditionals are using. The hook then sets the default list to be `'list-name-2`. This is a symbol matching the names in the preceding alist. You can switch between these specified lists by using C-c @ U. At the prompt, type the name of the list you want to use, such as `list-name-1`. You can manage lists of this nature as well. For example, if you've used C-c @ d to define some symbols you like, use C-c @ D, and type a name for that list. This lasts only to the end of your session, however, so if you want it saved, you need to add it to your .emacs file yourself.

File and Tag Browsing

As mentioned in Hour 8, "Searching for Text in Multiple Files," when working with almost any language, it is possible to create a TAGS file and jump to the function or variable of your choosing with simple commands. Under GNU Emacs, another program that can be used to a similar end is called imenu. When you enter the command M-x imenu-add-menubar-index, a new menu item titled Index appears. Every element of this menu is a symbol representing some function or variable in your language. Choosing a menu item jumps you to that location in the buffer. If you want this added to all your C buffers, add the command imenu-add-menubar-index to your c-mode-hook, c++-mode-hook, or java-mode-hook.

In XEmacs, the functions provided by imenu are replaced with a package called func-menu. You need to load this package yourself with the command M-x load-library RET func-menu RET before installing the menu item with the command M-x fume-add-menubar-entry RET.

Another program useful for browsing tags based on a filesystem view is called Speedbar. To start this program, enter the Speedbar command M-x speedbar. A thin frame should appear next to your Emacs frame with a listing of the current directory. Almost everything in Speedbar can be clicked. To select an item, either click it with the second mouse button or double-click it with the first mouse button. Sometimes you can power-click something. This means to hold Shift down while clicking on the item. A power click is useful if the cached information you are displaying is stale.

 A version of Speedbar that works under Emacs and XEmacs has been included on the CD accompanying this book (see Figure 18.1). To use this program, follow the directions for installing an Emacs program on the CD-ROM and load it using M-x load-library RET speedbar RET.

FIGURE 18.1

Speedbar displaying tags for a source file in Emacs.

The first line contains a display of the full pathname. You can select any element of that directory to switch Speedbar's directory to that location. Each directory entry in the current directory appears with a <+> symbol next to it. You can open the directory in place by selecting the <+>. You can switch Speedbar's full path to that location by selecting the name.

Each file in the current directory that Emacs knows how to read will appear with a [+] next to it. Clicking on the filename switches the current buffer in the main frame to this file. Clicking on the [+] uses imenu to select all the tags in that file. Clicking on a tag group {+} token shows all that tags in that group. Clicking on a tag name jumps to that tag in the main Emacs frame. If the tags are stale or inaccurate because you have modified the source file, hold down Shift while clicking on the [+] to display the tags, and they are regenerated.

XEmacs users might find that they do not have imenu installed. In this case Speedbar uses etags to generate tag lists instead. This has the side effect of a slightly less robust tag generation scheme.

Speedbar attempts to display additional information about each file as well. A * next to a filename means that file has been checked out of a version control system such as RCS, or SCCS. A # next to a filename means that the C, C++, Objective C, or Java file has an up-to-date object file. A ! next to a file means that the source file has an object file, but that the source is newer than the object file.

Speedbar has many other options available by clicking with the third mouse button to get a menu. It can perform file operations and has specialized displays for other purposes. Play with the items to get a feel for the capabilities. Speedbar can be used with other programming languages as well.

Summary

When working with C, C++, Objective C, or Java, many of the same elements work across all four languages. Many of the lessons learned in this hour can be applied to other languages such as Pascal, Fortran, Python, and other more-esoteric programming languages. Emacs can enable many of these features through a syntax definition provided by each language. All the key sequences learned for navigation and comment management can be applied in almost any situation.

At the end of this hour, you should be able to easily identify and navigate across advanced syntactic expressions such as lists, symbols, and functions. It should also be straightforward for you to manage your comments and make your code format itself with the tough configuration issues saved in your .emacs configuration file.

You should also now know whether you like the proactive editing features such as hungry delete, auto newline, and the C preprocessor management modes, and how to enable them if they appeal to you.

Lastly, some tagging features have been covered, giving you a couple more methods of finding the code segments you want to work on more easily.

Q&A

Q **Emacs chooses tab characters when indenting my code. How do I make it use spaces?**

A Set the variable `indent-tabs-mode` to nil and tab characters will not be used during indentation.

Q **My Emacs doesn't know about `c-set-style`! What should I do?**

A The style feature of C editing mode was introduced in the late 19.3x series of Emacs. You need to upgrade to a newer version.

Q **Speedbar doesn't know how to tag my Java files. What can I do?**

A Some versions of XEmacs don't support Imenu. You need to install Imenu under XEmacs.

Exercises

1. Similar to the example given, you have if'd out a block of code and the cursor is at the end of the new block, so the code looks like this:

```
if(foo) {
    line1();
    line2();
    }
```

The cursor is at the end of the last line. You need to reindent the code in the `if` statement. This hour explained how to do this without moving the cursor. Come up with a way to do it with the least number of keystrokes without causing Emacs to reindent the entire function or buffer.

2. If you have a program with several preprocessor conditionals, write a hook for `hideif` that defines the correct values for your preprocessor symbols for two different platforms. Now load your source file and switch between these two virtual platforms.

18

Hour **19**

Programming Utilities

This hour assumes that you have a basic working knowledge of version control system concepts and compilers, as well as of make and debugging programs. In most cases, working with these systems in Emacs is similar to using them from the command line. The difference is that you never need to leave Emacs to do it. This hour covers the following:

- Version control systems
- Compiling programs
- Debugging programs

Careful use of all these features can improve your development for programs written in almost any language, including C/C++, Java, Assembler, and Perl.

Version Control Systems

If you do not have your source code in a version control system, consider using one of the free systems. If you have never used a version control system before, note that it enables you to keep revisions of your source code available, storing only differences. Such a system is ideal for verifying changes; it enables you to go backward through the change-logs to identify bugs that were introduced a long time ago.

If you want to use a version control system and have not done so before, check to see if you have RCS or SCCS installed. If neither of these systems is available, RCS is very easy to install. To enable your current source code directory for RCS, simply create an RCS directory. For SCCS, create an SCCS directory. For the purposes of this section, it is assumed that you are using RCS, unless it is otherwise specified.

Windows users who want to install either CVS or RCS should consult the NT Emacs FAQ. If you want to use Emacs with other control system versions, you will probably have to do some customizing.

If you want to use CVS, you need to read the manual for setting up a CVS repository. After these setups are complete, everything else can be done under Emacs, with the underlying implementation hidden.

The package pcl-cvs.el also handles CVS repository access, and might be preferable to the minimal support that is available by default. It is available on the CD in the back of this book.

Entering Code into the Repository

The first thing that you need to do with your source code is to enter it into the repository. To do so, load the source file that you want to enter, and then press C-x v i. This registers the file, which means that there is now a control file in the repository. After this is done, a string appears in the mode line. For RCS, this string is RCS:1.1. For CVS, it is CVS:1.1. For SCCS, it is simply SCCS.

After all your software is in the repository, several options become available. The first thing that you might notice is that all your source is now read-only. This protects you from modifying source at the filesystem level without first making sure that you are tracking your changes. To check a file out of the version control system, thereby locking the file, you use the same keystroke that is used to toggle the read-only buffer flag: C-x c-q. This sets a lock on the file, in addition to making a writable copy available. You can also use the key sequence C-x v v.

Now that you have access to your source file, you might want to add some headers to it. Version control headers allow RCS to put details into the source file, such as the version of the file or a change log. Emacs can automatically add headers for you if you are unsure what you want to add. Just put the cursor near the top header of your file and type C-x v h. The headers that are installed are dependent on the version control system that is in use.

Now it's time to decide if you like the changes you've made. To do so, you can use C-x v = to compare the current version with the last checked-in version. When the system command completes, the output of diff is displayed in a buffer named *vc-diff*. You can peruse this file at your leisure to determine if the changes you made are correct. If these changes are exceptionally complex, you can also use ediff to view the differences by choosing File with Revision from the Compare menu. See Hour 14, "Finding Differences Between Files," for details.

> The output from a version control diff is compatible with the patch program. Therefore, you can use Emacs and version control to easily create patches for a distributed development environment. When you are making a similar diff from the command line, use the -c command line argument to add context to a difference. The -u argument is also preferred by some authors to unify the new and old sections.

If you want to throw out the changes you've made, use C-x v u to revert to the last checked-in version. When you do this, everything that you've done since you last checked out the file is lost. If you want to keep your changes, use C-x C-q to toggle the read-only state again. Instead of making the toggle immediately, a new buffer, called *VC-log*, appears. After this buffer is up, you can enter comments that relate to the change you're about to make. If you can't remember all the changes that you made, you can use C-x v = again to bring back the difference buffer. Entering a good log is important. These commands, which can appear in the source code, are used to remind yourself—or others—about the changes you made.

If you have performed several check-ins already, you can use M-p and M-n to pull back log messages from previous check-ins. You can even use M-r and M-s to search forward or backward in the logs that you've previously entered to find just the right one. This makes it easy to check in multiple files with exactly the same log message. When you are done entering a log, press C-c C-c to commit your changes and save the log.

19

Even now, it is not too late to discard the changes you just made. The keystroke C-x v c cancels the last commitment that was made. It is usually unwise to cancel revisions, however, because the information is lost forever. Instead, just back the changes out and save under a new revision number. That way, it is always possible to get those changes back if they are needed in the future.

> The easiest way to back out a change is with the Compare File with Revision command that is found under File. This enables you to see what's going on and choose the parts that you need to rescue.

Querying the Repository

Now that you are familiar with the register, check-out, check-in cycle, it's time to learn about querying the repository. Everything that you might possibly want to know about the source code you've checked in can be found and displayed in Emacs. For example, the log message that was recently entered can be queried with C-x v l. This opens a *vc* buffer. In this log, you find information that is relevant to the system you are using, including the log messages.

The tool tinyrlog.el provides additional functionality to the log output. Download it from the CD-ROM and read its documentation for details.

You can also pull up old versions with C-x v ~. This prompts you for the version number that is to be referenced and saves it as *file~version~*. This enables you to make a patch against an old version of software—or accept patches on old versions of software—more easily. This is the same method that is used by the Compare File with Revision menu item.

When you are working on large software changes, sometimes it is difficult to keep track of the state of all the files. You can use Speedbar (introduced in Hour 18, "Editing C, C++, and Java Files"), which displays a * next to each file that is currently checked out. You can also get a directory listing that specifies all checked out files with C-x v d; at the prompt, enter the source directory or just press Enter. This listing is in dired mode, which is discussed in Hour 16, "Interfacing with the System." Unlike dired mode, there are special commands for performing batch operations. The character *v* is the version control prefix character, and the next character is the same as the one that is found under the C-x v prefix for files.

In a dired listing, the command v= generates a difference of the last check-in version, and vl generates a log. The command vv performs the next action that is appropriate for a file, such as beginning the check-in process. Each of these commands operates on the current file, or on all files that are marked using the *m* key. The g command refreshes the status of all the files that are committed in the repository, and the special mark command *l marks all the files that are locked by the user.

Therefore, while you are in VC-controlled dired mode, the sequence * l v v enables you to check in all the files that are currently locked. This makes it even easier to check in several files that all have the same comment. Other operations, such as such as reverting, work similarly against all marked files.

Eventually, it will be important to release the software. When this occurs, it is time to make a snapshot. You can make a snapshot directly from Emacs with C-x v s, which asks you for a name for your snapshot. This performs different actions, depending on the revision control software that you are using. In general, it tracks the name that you enter with a version number from each file. It is important when you do this to remember exactly which files went into the software release on which you are working.

If you make revisions after taking a snapshot, you can always get that snapshot back by retrieving it with C-x v r. After you have retrieved the snapshot, you can make branches and patches in your repository, easing your capability to service software that has been released.

If you are writing software that follows the GNU conventions of including a ChangeLog file, you can use Emacs to update a change log. A ChangeLog is a file that specifies changes made to the source code, and the times at which they were made. Using the command C-x v a causes Emacs to reference the repository log and generate the change log automatically. This can be a big time saver for authors of free software.

19

Compiling Programs

If you are authoring software in C, C++, or Java, it is important to know how to compile the software into a machine-usable program. For traditional software systems, this requires a compiler that is controlled by make, which includes the maintenance of a Makefile. For Java or Ada systems, the Makefile is not really necessary because the systems can provide their own commands for compilation and dependency management; however, a Makefile can be used to maintain other aspects of your system.

Regardless of the actual process, Emacs enables you to build your program, watch the output of the compilers, and to easily jump to error locations. If Emacs does not understand the errors that are produced by your compiler, it can be taught.

To compile a program under Emacs, use the `compile` command; type `M-x compile`. You are prompted for the shell command that is to be used to compile your program; the default is `make -k`. If you are not using `make`, just delete this text and replace it with the command that you need to make your program work. This command is remembered for the next time that you use `compile`. The `compile` command prompt is like any other prompt in Emacs in that it accepts `M-p` and `M-n` to move backward and forward through the `compile` command history.

Microsoft, for reasons known only in Redmond, named their make utility nmake. For ease in compiling programs with Visual C++, insert the following into your `.emacs` file.

```
; Compilation setup:
; Visual C++ Debug:
(setq compile-command '("nmake -f .mak" . 10))
; Visual C++ Release:
; (setq compile-command '("nmake -f .mak CFG=\"MyProject -
➥Win32 Release\"" . 10))
```

This prepares the compilation command default so that you are all set to edit in the name of your makefile just before you execute it.

I've provided you with two default compile commands: one for debug, one for release. If you program like I do, you will use the release one rarely. You can set the default compile command to the release version by evaluating the release version of the Lisp expression. Place the cursor at the end of the line and type `C-x C-e`.

After Emacs starts the compilation, a buffer titled `*compilation*` appears. The mode-line contains the string Compiling in all buffers to indicate that something is going on, even if you later hide the `*compilation*` buffer. When the compilation is finished, a message appears at the end of the buffer telling you the status, and the string Compiling disappears from the mode-line in all buffers. In the `*compilation*` buffer, the exit status of the compilation tells you how it went. A status of 0 indicates a successful compile.

To cause the `*compilation*` buffer to automatically scroll to the end of new output, set the variable compilation-scroll-output to t in your `~/.emacs` file as follows:

```
(setq compilation-scroll-output t)
```

You do not need to wait for the compilation to complete before you can do something else. You can easily continue editing, or even visit errors and warnings, while the compilation occurs asynchronously. If things get out of hand during the compilation, for example if a runaway process occurs or you have ludicrous amounts of errors, you can put the cursor in the compilation buffer and press C-c C-k to kill the compilation process.

When errors appear in the buffer, Emacs can parse them and bring up the offending code. You can make this happen in a couple ways. First, you can place the cursor on the error that you want and press Enter or C-c C-c. You can also click on the error with the middle mouse button. Any of these techniques enable you to choose a specific error; the file with the error is loaded, and the cursor is positioned on the offending line.

After you've fixed your first error, however, it is not always convenient to move back to the *compilation* buffer. The command next error is available in all buffers that are bound to C-x `. This command either starts with the first error or moves from the last error to which you went to the next consecutive error within any Emacs buffer. This makes it exceptionally convenient to move across all the errors that are produced by the compiler.

There are a few items available under the menu in a compile buffer as well. Recompile enables you to rerun the compile command using the same command as before. You can also jump to different errors, such as the first or previous error.

> You might have noticed that compiling a program is very similar to the grep command that is discussed in Hour 8, "Searching for Text in Multiple Files." compile and grep use the same system for running a subprocess and navigating between hits, which makes it easy to remember how to navigate using these different programs.

19

Minor Compilations

There are often situations in which the methods of compilation are inappropriate—or too little, too late. One such example involves building a program on a remote machine. You might want to edit your files locally using the virtual FTP filesystem that is covered in Hour 4, "Basic Editing," or you might be working in a *shell* buffer when the errors appear.

The case of the remote system is more interesting, so I'll cover that here. First, you can run a remote login program such as telnet or rlogin from a *shell* buffer, or you can just use the rlogin command, for example M-x rlogin. This enables you to run programs on the remote system and potentially run a compilation.

After a compilation has been started, you can turn on the compilation minor mode in the buffer, enabling the use of all the keystrokes that you learned earlier. To do this, type M-x compilation-minor-mode. You can now use C-c C-c to navigate to an error. Remote buffers such as rlogin are even smart enough to use the correct remote file name. You need to run the compilation-minor-mode command a second time to disable these features to regain use of C-c C-c as a cancel key and Enter for entering new commands in your shell.

Adding Compiler Parsing

Not all compiler error messages are created equal. Some compilers for new languages, or home-grown compilers in large corporations, might not have a recognizable format; therefore, Emacs cannot parse them. Fortunately, there is a method that can be used to teach Emacs about these elements. Performing these tasks requires a knowledge of the compiler and the errors it generates, in addition to some mastery of Hour 9, "Regular Expressions."

First, here's a look at a sample error message format. Pretend that your compiler makes the following error:

```
Error 51 on line 45 and column 23 of yourfile.c
```

Now that you have an error, you must create a regular expression to match it. Details on how to do this have already been covered, but in review, the expression "[0-9]+" finds a number, and "\\([0-9]+\\)" not only finds the number, but also tags it as a subexpression.

Therefore, an expression for finding and tagging the important elements for this error, with the added capability of finding warnings, looks similar to the following when it is coded in Lisp:

```
"\\(Error\\¦Warning\\) [0-9]+ on line \\([0-9]+\\) and \
     column \\([0-9]+\\) of \\(.*\\)$"
```

Now that you know how to create this expression, it's time to teach compile mode how to read it. You do this by modifying the variable compilation-error-regexp-alist. Each element of this list is also a list. The first element is the regular expression that you just created, followed by the tag of the file, the line number tag, and the column number tag. Unfortunately, you cannot just modify this variable in your .emacs file because you need to improve its value and the compilation package has not yet been loaded. You can easily get past this by adding the command

```
(require 'compile)
```

before your modification, but this can slow down the loading of Emacs. Instead, you want to add this expression into the main list in a hook. Because you don't want to have the expression loaded into the variable every time, use a function called `add-to-list`, which only adds something once. The end result follows:

```
(add-hook 'compilation-mode-hook
  (lambda ()
    (add-to-list 'compilation-error-regexp-alist
                 '("\\(Error\\¦Warning\\) [0-9]+ on line \
\\([0-9]+\\) and column \\([0-9]+\\) of \\(.*\\)$"
                 4 2 3)))
```

You can read the documentation that is associated with the variable `compilation-error-regexp-alist` for additional details on the format of this list in case your errors are even more complex.

Debugging Programs

After your program has been compiled, you might find runtime errors or anomalies and turn immediately to the debugger. All traditional UNIX debuggers are command-line–based; this makes them difficult to learn at first, but ideal for running under Emacs. This section assumes that you have at least a basic understanding of your system's debugger and the language you are attempting to debug.

Emacs has extensive knowledge of debuggers and the languages with which they work. To accommodate the vast array of debuggers for everything from C to Perl, a base called the Grand Unified Debugger was written. This provides the baseline for working with a debugger in Emacs. After you learn the basics of the Grand Unified Debugger, almost any language or system debugging tool can be used with ease.

To simplify this hour, I'll give examples that use gdb, the GNU Debugger. This debugger is widely available for almost any platform, and even has features that were designed especially for use under the Grand Unified Debugger.

First, make sure that you know where the program you want to debug is. Next, you might want to load a source file for the program so that the Grand Unified Debugger has a starting point, and so that you can be ready to put in a few break points. After you're ready, run one of the many debugger programs. For this example, the command is M-x gdb. On some commercial UNIX systems, you might be running dbx, sdb, or some other debugger. For Java, you run jdb, and for Perl, you run perldb.

After you choose your debugger, you are queried for a command line. You can pass any arguments to the debugger, but usually you just want to enter the name of the program that you want to debug. Pretend that you're working on a program called twiddle, the purpose of which is to adjust bits in a file. Therefore, you'll type in twiddle at the gdb prompt.

19

As soon as you press Enter, Emacs runs gdb in a subprocess. This mode is probably familiar to you because it is closely related to Shell mode, which is introduced in Hour 16. In this case, however, you have a (gdb) prompt, and gdb will have reported its success in loading the program and its symbol table.

You probably know that there are usually several ways to do any one thing. To begin, assume that there is a problem in the function twiddle_file, which loops over the file and twiddles its bits. At the (gdb) prompt you can type in break twi, where break is the command for setting a break point and twi is the first few characters of the function name. You can now use Tab completion to fill out the rest of the function name. This is true for any command in gdb that accesses a symbol of any kind, including print.

 In dbx, you can set a break point with the stop in command.

Now you have a break point in your function. You can now type run, followed by any needed parameters, to start your program under the debugger. When the program reaches twiddle_file it stops in the debugger; Emacs shows you file.c, which contains the twiddle_file function, and an overlay arrow appears next to the beginning of your functions.

You can now step through your program using some simple keys, instead of typing in debugger commands. Emacs knows which command is for which debugger, so you only have to remember the Emacs key sequence—not the more archaic commands. In almost all cases, a command has some keystroke associated with it, such as C-n. When the current buffer is the GUD buffer, prefix it with C-c to run it. If you are in a source file, prefix it with C-x C-a.

To use the next command, which walks over one command, press C-c C-n. To use the step command to step into a function, use C-c C-s. In either case, the overlay arrow is updated to the new location regardless of the file to which you moved. Another big advantage to using these keybindings is that the gdb buffer is not filled up with useless status messages. Instead, that information is filtered out completely, and the overlay arrow shows you the current state of the debugger. If your current buffer is the source code and not the debugger buffer, you can still use the next and step commands by using the C-x C-a prefix that was mentioned earlier. Therefore, C-x C-a C-n executes next, and C-x C-a C-s executes step.

You might find that you must step too much in the main loop of this function. If the bug in which you are interested is after this loop, move the cursor to a line of interest, and type C-x SPC; a break point is registered for that location. Now type C-x C-a C-r to cause the debugger to continue throughout the loop. When the debugger hits the new break point, it stops and updates the source buffers. If you want to get rid of this break point, you can use the C-x C-a C-d command to remove it.

Now that you are here, you might be interested to know what the values of some variables are. Did the file pointer get cleared correctly? How many characters have been scanned? Position the cursor over a variable name, and type C-x C-a C-p. This prints out the value of the item under the cursor. In C, it is even smart enough to pick up full structure elements or function call parameters.

In Figure 19.1, you can see that the cursor is on the variable unchanged. The resulting output of C-x C-a C-p, which prints the value under the cursor, is prefixed with $1 =, which simply indicates the first item you've printed.

FIGURE 19.1

Debugging twiddle_file *in* twiddle.c.

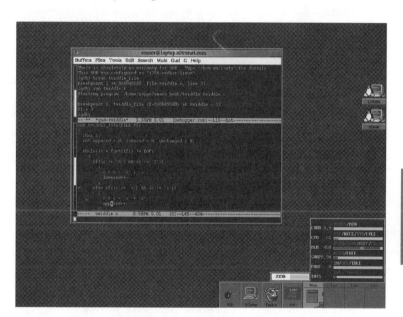

19

Are other stack layers at fault here? You can navigate up and down the stack with some quick keystrokes. In the gdb buffer, use C-c < to go up the stack and C-c > to go down. If you are still in the source buffer, use C-x C-a < and C-x C-a > to move up and down, respectively. After you've switched to that new stack frame, you can use the print command that you learned earlier to examine the variables in this stack frame as well.

It is obvious that all the basics of the debugger are covered with simple keystrokes. Any additional functionality that is provided by a debugger can still be accessed by just typing in the desired command as if you were on the command line, and not in Emacs at all. If any command you enter changes the current state of the stack, Emacs picks up on it and adjusts the currently displayed buffers to make sure that the area of interest is visible.

Because the commands you've just learned all work by sending a command string to the debugger and interpreting its output, it's possible to add new commands of your own creation if something is not covered by the basics. Doing so involves the same programmatic features that are used by the individual debugging modes such as gdb.

For example, say it is common for you to set watch points in gdb so that you can track changes in variable values. You can do this easily enough by just typing `watch <variable>` at the command line. Because you are in the mood to impress your friends, however, say you want to bind this to a key sequence. This requires some modification to your `.emacs` file. First, you know that you want to add a hook for gdb to add this binding. Next, you need to understand the Lisp function `gud-def`. This function takes four arguments, starting with the name that you want to give the Lisp function, followed by the string that is sent to the debugger, the keybinding, and some documentation. Call your function `my-watch`; the command is `watch <variable>`; and the key binding is `C-w`.

When you specify `C-w` as your key sequence, it really means that in the gud buffer, your new function is accessible through `C-c C-w` and from a source buffer as `C-x C-a C-w`.

When you are specifying the command to send to the debugger, specify that your preference is for the `<variable>` part of your command to be automatically filled in with the symbol under the cursor. To do this, replace `<variable>` with `%e`. `%e` is automatically replaced by GUD with the expression found under the cursor. Some other symbols that you can add to your string include `%f` for the filename, and `%l` for the current line number.

Now put all this information together to customize the gdb mode for all future sessions. Your `.emacs` now contains the following information:

```
(add-hook 'gdb-mode-hook
            (lambda ()
            (gud-def my-watch "watch %e"
                       "\C-w" "Watch my variables.")
              )
  )
```

After this is set up and gdb is restarted, you can use `C-x C-a C-w` in your source buffer to set watch points on the expression on which the cursor sits.

Summary

Emacs has been enabled to control all stages of the development process, from the most basic of functions to high-level functions such as debugging. You now know how to control all your sources within a version control system such as RCS, and how to provide detailed queries into the repository.

Not only is your code safe, but you can compile, you can fix compilation warnings, and you can debug your source code. After you fix the bugs, you can start the cycle over again without ever leaving Emacs. These diverse commands all work inside buffers, just as your source code is managed. This means that basic navigation within and between these three tasks is consistent.

Lastly, you are now familiar enough with the tools to make changes in their behavior to suit your specialized needs, taking advantage of the hooks and features that are provided to add unique functionality.

Q&A

Q **I don't want Emacs to automatically check files in and out. Instead, I want to corrupt my source code. How do I just toggle read-only mode?**

A `M-x toggle-read-only RET`

Q **I'm using *<esoteric versioning system here>*, which doesn't seem to be supported by Emacs. What can I do?**

A Some version control vendors provide Emacs programs on customer-accessible FTP sites. Check there first, and then ask on an Emacs help newsgroup such as `gnu.emacs.help`.

Q **My Makefile recurses into subdirectories, and Emacs keeps asking me for the full path to my source code! What do I do?**

A The GNU version of `make` prints out announcements when it changes directories, which Emacs can pick up on. Try using that version of `make` (`prep.mit.ai.edu`).

Q **I'm using dbx, and Emacs doesn't pull up the source code when it hits a break point. What am I doing wrong?**

A Not all dbx implementations are created equal. Some do not output the necessary information for Emacs to interpret. If all else fails, execute an `up` and `down` command.

19

Exercises

1. Add a new compiler error parser that matches the following:

   `PANIC: File foo.c is critically damaged on line 23!`

2. Write a "hello world" program in C, compile it, and step through it line by line without using a terminal window or even a `*Shell*` buffer.

3. Create a GUD command to display the details of a data type. This is the `ptype` command in gdb. To display the structure `Foo` in gdb, then, you type the command `ptype struct Foo`.

PART V
Mail and News

Hour

HOUR 20

Gnus Basics

I guess you already are using an email client and a news reader, right? And I guess that you're asking yourself, "Why should I take the time to learn a new email client and news reader?" Right?! The answer is simple; Gnus is without a doubt the best news reader available. Because Gnus is simply an extension to Emacs, you can use all of Emacs's features, including macros, incremental searching, and all the editing commands such as transposing and dynamic abbreviation. If you are not convinced, please think carefully about your normal mail clients and news readers, and ask yourself whether you have ever needed the power of Emacs.

The description of Gnus is split over two hours. This hour should give you enough knowledge to get up and running, and Hour 21, "Advanced Gnus," takes you farther and shows you some of the features that makes Gnus such a fantastic program. These include

- Using a database with information about people
- Ordering your group in topic
- A scoring mechanism with which you can let Gnus find the most interesting articles

In this hour the names of the functions invoked by the keys described are not listed. The reason for this is that the functions often have very long names, and I will tell you about many keybindings in these hours. Furthermore it is unlikely that any of these keybindings are changed (compared to the keybindings for the normal Emacs use).

At the moment I write this, the newest version of Gnus that these two hours describe is still being developed. This means that there might be some points that are not correct in the book. So please visit the book's home page at www.mcp.com, for a list of changes since this was written.

Windows does not come with a UNIX-style mail transport agent (MTA), and most Windows users get their mail from a remote Post Office Protocol (POP) server. To get your mail from a POP server, get the latest version of the EPOP3 package. For details, see the NT Emacs FAQ. Setup is straightforward. Read the file epop3mail.el for the details. Don't forget to prepend po: to your email address when you set it in your .emacs file.

```
(setq rmail-primary-inbox-list '("po:login@my.isp.com"))
```

If you want to see exactly what EPOP3 is doing, add this to your .emacs:

```
; debug tool:
(setq epop3-mail-debug t)
```

To handle attachments, see the FAQ for information on the metamail package.

Introducing Gnus

Gnus is a combined news and mail reader and, of course also a news and mail writer. At first glance, it might seem like a strange thing that Gnus does both, but the following lists of similarities and dissimilarities should make it clear that news and mail aren't that different.

The following are the similarities:

- Mail and news are both concerned with messages from one person to one or several others. Common for both types is that the message does not necessarily need to be read at once and sometimes does not even need to be answered.

- Mail and news can both be threaded; that is, you can write a letter (or post an article), someone can answer or comment on this, and you can later answer or comment on this letter again. This way a discussion might go on for a long time.

- Without proper organization, important information can get lost. With mail, this can happen if you have hundreds of unread letters and one of them is an important note from your boss. With news, this can happen if the number of articles posted every day is more than you are capable of handling and you don't have proper tools to help you out.

The following are the differences:

- Mail tends to be more personal than news (although this is not true for mailing lists).

- Mail is often directed to one person, whereas news is sent to a group without knowing anything about the receiver. (Again, this is not true for mailing lists.)

- The technologies and the terms used when sending mail and news are different. You, for example, talk about "sending a letter," whereas you "post an article."

It is important to study these items, because they list both why you should use the same tool for mail and news and some of the pitfalls you should be careful about. The major pitfall with using the same tool is that you might start projecting some of your habits from news reading onto mail reading, for example, the ease with which you can discard news.

The Gnus Interface

In Gnus you work in four different buffers. These buffers are as follows:

- The Group buffer—In the group buffer you get an overview of all your subscribed groups (see Figure 20.1). This includes newsgroups and mail folders. In fact you will seldom see a difference between news, mailing lists, and ordinary mail.

- The Summary buffer—You enter the summary buffer by pressing either the Spacebar or the Enter key on top of one of the groups in the Group buffer. The Summary buffer shows a summary of all the letters in the given group (see Figure 20.2). Often, you see only the unread letters, but you have control over that of course.

20

Name of the groups   Your incoming mail folder   Ordinary newsgroups

FIGURE 20.1

The Group buffer.

Number of articles
in the groups

A special group, with
information on getting
started with Gnus

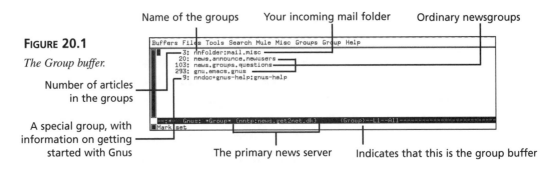

The primary news server   Indicates that this is the group buffer

The author of the message   The subject of the message

FIGURE 20.2

The Summary buffer.

A thread
(note the indentation)

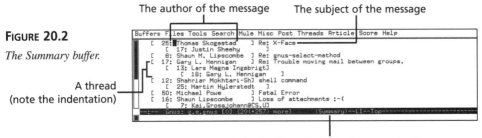

Indicates that this is the Summary buffer

- The Article buffer—Pressing the Enter key in the summary buffer shows you the content of the given letter or article, from now on referred to as the *message* (see Figure 20.3).

- The Message buffer—When you need to send a message, you are placed in a buffer where you can write the message (see Figure 20.4).

The current message shown in the Article buffer

The Summary buffer   The header of the message

FIGURE 20.3

*The Article buffer
(viewing messages).*

The Article buffer

The body of the message

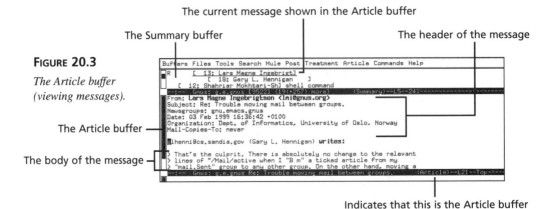

Indicates that this is the Article buffer

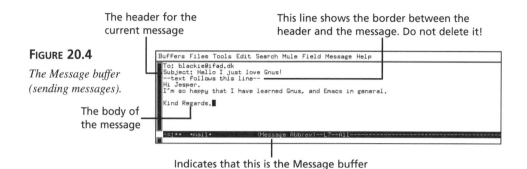

<figure>
The header for the current message

This line shows the border between the header and the message. Do not delete it!

FIGURE 20.4

The Message buffer (sending messages).

The body of the message

Indicates that this is the Message buffer
</figure>

The Way Gnus Works with Email

Gnus works a bit differently than other email programs (that is, other email programs not working in Emacs). When you receive a letter, Gnus copies this letter from your inbox to a special directory where only Gnus has access to it. This is to avoid all the problems that otherwise often are involved with two processes accessing the same files simultaneously, and also to make Gnus work faster.

The directory Gnus copies the file to can be chosen from one of the following:

- nnmbox—This is the standard mailbox used for incoming mail in UNIX. (This is several folders in one file.)

- nnfolder—This is like mbox, but each folder is kept in separate files.

- nnml—This is a format specific to Gnus. Each letter is located in a separate file. This is the fastest method, but uses many files. (The number of files on a hard disk is limited!)

- nnmh and nnbabyl—These are formats used in a few other (and much older) mail readers.

Each of these methods are often referred to as *mail backends*.

Setting Up Gnus

20

To get started with Gnus, you need to insert a few lines in your .Gnus file. The .Gnus file is located in the same place as your .emacs file and serves the same purpose as the .emacs file, with the one exception; the code written into the .Gnus file is configured specifically for Gnus.

You might be in a situation where you want to use Gnus for either news *or* mail, but not both. In that case, do one of the following:

- To make Gnus handle news, you must tell it which news server (or NNTP server) you would like to use. If you do not have a clue what this should be then start Gnus without configuring it and, if you are lucky, someone else already has configured this for you (for example, your system administrator). You should see the name of the news server in the modeline (refer to Figure 20.1).

- If you want Gnus to handle mail, you have to decide which mail backend you want to use. As a rule of thumb, you might chose nnfolder if you have large mail archives (with many letters that should last forever) or if you are very anxious about not burning any bridges and want to be able to get back to your old mail program. If, on the other hand, you subscribe to many mailing lists with a lot of mail arriving each day, you should probably use the nnml backend. It is possible to change the backend later! This is, however, beyond the scope of this book, so please refer to the Gnus reference manual.

Server and Backend

Given that the server you want to use is called news.somewhere.org and you want to use the nnfolder backend, you must insert one of the following into your .emacs file:

- Using Gnus only for news:

  ```
  (setq gnus-select-method '(nntp "news.somewhere.org"))
  ```

- Using Gnus only for mail:

  ```
  (setq gnus-select-method '(nnfolder ""))
  ```

- Using Gnus for news and for mail:

  ```
  (setq gnus-select-method '(nntp "news.somewhere.org"))
  (setq gnus-secondary-select-methods '((nnfolder "")))
  ```

Mail Source

If you want to read mail with Gnus, you have to tell Gnus about where it should fetch your mail from. There are three different ways Gnus can fetch mail for you:

- Using a spool file. In UNIX this is the most common way to retrieve mail (for example, from /var/spool/mail/*user-name*).

- Using a POP server. This is the easiest way for Windows users and is also often used by users who are reading their mail from an ISP.

- Fetching mail from a directory. This is used when you use an external program such as procmail to sort mail coming from a mailing lists into different files each belonging to one mailing list.

Each of the three methods have options describing the method, as can be seen in Table 20.1

TABLE 20.1 OPTIONS SPECIFYING WHERE TO FETCH MAIL

Option	Description
Reading Mail from a File	
path	The path to the file containing the mail.
Reading Mail from a POP Server	
server	This is the name of the server to fetch the mail from.
user	This is your username on the server.
password	This is your password on the server (if you haven't specified this, you will be prompted in the minibuffer).
Reading Mail from a Directory	
path	This is the directory in which the files are located.
suffix	This is the suffix for the files. You might, for example, ask procmail to deliver your letters in the Mail directory, and name them with the extension .procmail. Then Gnus reads in these and writes its own copies to the files without the .procmail extension. (Remember: Gnus reads the mail into a file of its very own).

Additional options exist for the POP mail-fetching method. These do, however, require customization beyond the scope of this book. See the Gnus reference manual if this doesn't work for you.

You can tell Gnus to read your mail from several different sources at the same time; for example, if you have your inbox in the ordinary spool directory and you also get mailing lists sorted into a directory, it is possible to get mail from both places. To specify where to get mail from, you must set the variable nnmail-spool-file. This variable is best described with an example:

```
(setq nnmail-spool-file '(
    (file :path "/var/spool/mail/blackie")
    (directory :path "/home/blackie/Mail" :suffix ".procmail")
    (pop :server "pop.mail.server" :user "Gnus-lover" :password "SeCrEt")
))
```

The first and last lines are simply some Lisp code that needs to be there. The three lines in the middle describe three different places to fetch mail from. The first is from a spool file; the second is from a directory where mail has been delivered into files ending in

20

.procmail. Finally, the third place is a POP server called pop.mail.server, where my username at the server is Gnus-lover, and my password is SeCrEt. Please note the colons in front of the options.

Installing the Mailboxes

When you have told Gnus where to fetch your mail and news, it's time to start Gnus for the first time. But before you do that, please ensure that you are online and that you have some mail in your inbox (given, of course, that you want to read mail with Gnus). To start Gnus, press M-x and type gnus. When Gnus has started up, it reads the information from your news server about which groups exist. The size of this information depends on the number of newsgroups your server offers (the size for my server is approximately 2MB). Don't worry; Gnus does not have to fetch this file each time it starts.

When Gnus has started, you will be subscribed to a few newsgroups, and your incoming mail folder is shown as a group called mail.misc. This can be seen in Figure 20.1.

If you, for some reason, should not be subscribed to your incoming mail boxes, press the caret (^). This brings you to a buffer like the one seen in Figure 20.5.

FIGURE 20.5

The Server buffer.

The mail backend   The primary news server

In this buffer you can see all your *servers* (that is, all the different places from which Gnus can fetch mail and news). If you press the Enter key on the backend you use for mail (nnfolder in Figure 20.5), you get to a buffer like the one seen in Figure 20.6. From this buffer you can subscribe to the mail groups available. (There might be several if you have told Emacs to read mail from a directory; in this case, each file in this directory reflects a mail group.) Subscribing to one of the groups is done by pressing u. (That is, *u* for *u*nsubscribe—the key is a toggle.)

FIGURE 20.6

This shows the mail group with the incoming messages.

Reading Mail and News

Now when you have set up Gnus for your personal account, it's time to start learning about Gnus. To start Gnus, press M-x and type either gnus or Gnus-no-server. The second method starts up Gnus without querying any of the news servers for news, but only the mail backends.

The first buffer you get to is the Group buffer. This buffer contains all the groups you are subscribed to. A subscribed group is one that Gnus should check for new messages in. The Group buffer can be seen in Figure 20.1. Each line represents a newsgroup or a mail folder. The first column indicates the number of unread messages in the given group. The second column states both the backend used and the name of the group. In most cases, however, you don't care about which backend is used for a given group. The lines that describe the groups can be customized as much as you want. Customization of the group line is described in the next hour.

Only groups containing new messages are listed. To see all subscribed groups (that is, those without new messages too), press L. To hide the groups without any messages, press l.

Gnus works with groups on four different levels: subscribed groups, unsubscribed groups, killed groups, and zombie groups. The difference between unsubscribed groups and killed groups is that Gnus still remembers which messages you have read in unsubscribed groups, which isn't the case for killed groups. When you press L, you also see the unsubscribed groups. Zombie groups are discussed in the next section.

Subscribe or Unsubscribe to Groups

When you start Gnus for the first time, you are subscribed to a few newsgroups, but as you surely know, there are many more available. (My news sources have almost 40,000 newsgroups!) To see a complete list of newsgroups, simply type A A. This exchanges the content of the Group buffer with a list of all newsgroups. Fortunately, this list is sorted, so it should be easy to get to the hierarchies you are interested in. If you are searching for a specific group, you can use the normal search functions of Emacs to get to the group you are looking for. (See Hour 7, "Searching for Text in a Buffer" for a reference of all the ways to search for text in a buffer.)

20

When you have found a group that you want to subscribe to, press u to subscribe to it. As mentioned previously, u is a toggle, so pressing u once again unsubscribes you from the group.

To get back to the ordinary group overview press 1 or L, as described earlier.

When you are in the Group Overview buffer, you can unsubscribe from any group there by pressing u when point is located on the given group. Unsubscribing might, however, not be what you want to do, because Gnus still keeps some information about the group when it is unsubscribed (as mentioned previously). If you really think that you are finished with a given group and do not expect to read it for a long time, you should instead kill the group. Killing a group is done by pressing C-k when point is located on the line listing the group.

> Killing a group is preferred to unsubscribing from it if you do not expect to read the group for a long time, because this makes Gnus start up much faster.

There also exists another way to subscribe to a group, which is to press U. This queries you in the minibuffer for the newsgroup to subscribe to.

Whenever Gnus starts up, it asks your servers for new groups that have come to existence since the last time you used Gnus. Any new group becomes a *zombie*. A zombie is a subscription level even lower than unsubscribed groups, but more alive than killed groups. You must explicitly subscribe to these zombie groups before they become part of your daily news repertoire (that is, you do not see them in the normal overview buffer). To see the list of zombie groups, press A z in the Group buffer. This takes you to a buffer from which you can subscribe to the zombie groups you want to read. When you have subscribed to the zombie groups of interest, you can delete the rest of them by pressing S z. This brings you back to your normal group overview.

> This also applies to mail groups read from directories, so if you use procmail to sort mail into several different files, and you have told Emacs to read these files from a directory, a new file in this directory does *not* show up in your Group buffer before you have subscribed to it from the zombie subscription buffer.

To ask Gnus to query the server for new messages in the groups, press g. This queries Gnus for new messages in all groups. If you want only to see whether there is any new email, press C-2 g. Finally if you want to search for new mail only in the current group, press M-g.

Reading the Articles

The previous section told you about subscribing and unsubscribing to groups, so finally it's time to learn how to read the actual messages. Pressing the Enter key on top of a group brings you to a Summary buffer, such as the one seen in Figure 20.2. From this Summary buffer you can get further on to the actual messages by pressing the Enter key on top of one of the messages, which splits the window in two and shows the message in one of the windows (refer to Figure 20.3).

If the text spans more than one window, you can switch to the window containing the message and use the normal movement commands to scroll through the text. An alternative is to stay in the Summary buffer, and use the Spacebar to scroll one page forward and the Delete key to scroll one page backward.

In the Summary buffer you can move up and down, as in any other buffer, but additional commands exist for traversing the threads. All these commands can be seen in the menu item called Threads.

As well as moving past a whole thread, you might also want to fold a thread, showing only the top of it. (This is equivalent to using outline mode, described in Hour 15, "Getting an Overview of a File"). Hiding all the threads in the Summary buffer is done by pressing T H. When you press Enter on top of on of the thread, the message at the top of the thread is shown, and the whole thread is once again shown. An example of folding all threads can be seen in Figure 20.7.

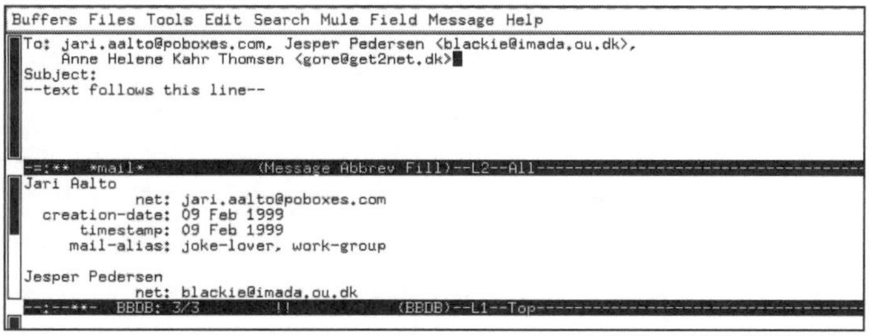

FIGURE 20.7

An ellipsis indicates that the thread has been folded.

20

Some people do not quote enough of a letter for you to understand the answer they give. In these situations it might be useful to see the message they answer to or comment on. The whole thread can't, however, be shown at a given time, due to the fact that you already might have read some of the messages earlier in the thread. By pressing ^ (that is, the caret) in the Summary buffer, you ask Gnus to query the server for the message previous message in the thread.

If the group contains any unread messages or any ticked messages (ticked messages are described in the next section), only the unread and ticked messages are shown in the Summary buffer when you enter it. To see all the messages, you must press C-u before you press the Enter key to enter the group (from the Group buffer). If on the other hand, the group has neither any unread articles nor any ticked ones, all the read articles in the group are shown when you enter the Summary buffer.

If you are located in the summary buffer, you can ask Gnus to query the server for new messages (and hide the ones you already have read) by pressing g. Likewise, you can ask Gnus to search for new messages and list all articles at the same time by pressing M-g.

Expiring Messages

Though it would be nice to keep messages infinitely, it seldom is possible. Both news-groups and your own incoming mailing lists need to be trimmed once in a while. The expiration is done based on the age of the messages. That is, messages can be deleted when they are older than a day or when they are older than 100 years (that depends solely on the news server or, in case of mail, on the mail group). There is nothing you can do about the expiring process at the news server, but you are responsible for config-uring the expiring process for your own mail groups.

Starting with newsgroups, as stated previously, there is nothing you can change about the expiring process for them. You might, however, once in a while see a message that you find valuable, and thus want to keep beyond the lifetime of the article in the news server. What you do in these cases is simply to press the asterisk key (*) on top of the article. This copies the message to your local hard disk and keeps it there until you press M-*, which tells Gnus to delete it from your local disk again. Articles marked with an asterisk are not shown when you enter the Summary buffer, unless you press C-u before pressing Enter to enter it. Later I get back to what it means to press the asterisk in a mail group.

Gnus treats mail messages like news articles in the interface. That is, when you have read a message, Gnus marks this message as read, but it does not delete it from disk immedi-ately; instead it expires the message later. Surprised? Well that is the way it works with news, right?

In fact, in the default setup of Gnus, mail is never deleted, unless you explicitly tell Gnus to do so.

To tell Gnus to delete a message, you must press E on top of the message. This tells Gnus that this message should be expired. When you leave the group, Gnus deletes all messages marked for expiring, if and only if they are older than a specified age (the default age is seven days).

Autoexpiring

It might be quite annoying to tell Gnus to mark messages as expirable for each message you have read; thus, it is possible to tell Gnus that messages should be marked as expirable instead of read whenever you have read a message or whenever you tell Gnus to catch up with the group (catching up is discussed shortly). This featured is called *autoexpiring*. Autoexpiring can be enabled based on the name of the group. This is done by forming a regular expression that matches the groups which you want autoexpiring enabled for. To enable autoexpiring for the groups junk-mail and dotfile-mailing-list, insert the following into your .Gnus file:

```
(setq gnus-auto-expirable-newsgroups
     "junk-mail\\¦dotfile-mailing-list")
```

To enable autoexpiring for all your mail groups instead, insert the following into your .Gnus file:

```
(setq gnus-auto-expirable-newsgroups "")
```

This is a regular expression that matches any group name.

> Though the name of the variable included the name *newsgroups*, this does only make sense for mail groups; you still don't have any control over when messages are expired on the news server.

20

Expiring Period

Whenever you leave a mail group, Gnus expires all messages marked for expiring that are older than a given age. This age can be set for all groups by setting the variable gnus-expiry-wait. Its value can be a number that states the number of days; the word immediate, which means that the messages should be expired as soon as possible (when the mail group is left); or the word never, which means that expiring should never be done. To tell Gnus to wait 31 days before expiring a message, insert the following into your .Gnus file:

```
(setq gnus-expiry-wait 31)
```

To tell Gnus to do expiring at once, insert the following into your .Gnus file:

```
(setq gnus-expiry-wait 'immediate)
```

You might, however, be in a situation where you want Gnus to expire mail at once in some groups, wait for a month in others, and finally never do expiring in a third set of groups. This can be achieved by setting the variable Gnus-expiry-wait-function to a function that determines the value based on the name of the group. The following is an example of such a function:

```
01: (setq nnmail-expiry-wait-function
02:        (lambda (group)
03:           (cond ((string= group "mail.private")
04:                   31)
05:                 ((string= group "mail.junk")
06:                  'immediate)
07:                 ((string= group "important")
08:                  'never)
09:                 (t
10:                  6))))
```

Mail in the group mail.private in line 3 should expire after 31 days, which is listed in line 4. Mail in the group mail.junk shown in line 5 should expire immediately (notice line 6). As shown in lines 7 and 8, mail in the group important should never expire. Finally, mail in any other group should expire after 6 days, which you can see in line 10.

You should be able to customize this without knowing much about Lisp. Be careful with the parentheses!

Deleting Mail at Once

In a few situations you might really want to get rid of a letter at once instead of waiting for it to expire. This might, for example, be the case if someone sends you a letter containing a 5MB attachment and your account doesn't allow you to have more than 5MB on your disk.

To delete the letter for good, press B DEL (that is, a capital b and the delete key). Emacs asks you with a yes/no question whether you really intend to delete the letter forever. In case you want to delete many letters, you can mark each letter by pressing # (that is, the pound sign or hash mark) on each letter, and then pressing B DEL. (This method is discussed in detail in the next hour.)

Using Marks in the Summary Buffer

A few different marks exist, with which you can change the status of a message. You have already seen the asterisk, which is used to copy an article from the news server to a local directory. Table 20.2 shows a list of the most important marks, their indication in the Summary buffer, and how to set them. The indication is shown in the first column of the Summary buffer.

TABLE 20.2 ARTICLE MARKS AND THEIR INDICATION IN THE SUMMARY BUFFER

Indication	Key Used to Set the Mark	Description of the Mark
!	!	The exclamation mark is used to tick an article. Ticked articles are shown together with unread articles, when ever you enter the summary buffer. Ticked articles are not expired in mail folders, but they are expired in news groups. To keep an article in a newsgroup, use the asterisk. Both the asterisk and the exclamation mark can be used at the same time.
* to In	*	The asterisk is used to make an article unexpirable as described in the beginning of this section. Articles marked with an asterisk are not shown when you enter the summary buffer. For newsgroups, it might be a good idea to use both the asterisk and the exclamation mark make an article visible all the time, and unexpirable. mail groups on the other hand, the asterisk is not necessary to make the article unexpirable (when the exclamation mark is used). In mail groups it might, on the other hand, be used to save articles that you do not want to see every time you enter the Summary buffer, but that you do not want to expire.
?	?	The question mark is like the exclamation mark, with the exception that the message is shown only when an unread successor exists. This is often used when you post an article on a newsgroup. In these cases, your message shows up whenever someone answers it or comments on a article that stems from your article.
E	E	Pressing E makes the article expirable. This is useful only if you do not use autoexpire.
R		An article is marked with a uppercase R whenever it is read, but not marked as expirable. (Remember: only mail messages can be marked as expirable.)
r	d	A lowercase r indicates that the article has not been read, but it has been marked as such (this can also happen when you catch up a group).

20

A few additional marks exist that are seen more seldom and are beyond the scope of this book. To erase all the marks for a message press M-u. This *marks* the article as unread (which is indicated by the absence of a mark).

Catching Up

When reading newsgroups or mailing lists (but *not* your incoming mail!) you might want to skip the rest of the messages in the group. This is called *catching up with the group*. Pressing c in the summary buffer or the group buffer catches up with the group by marking any unread messages as read. Two other very useful combinations for catching up with a group also exist only in the Summary buffer. These are M H, which catches up with all the messages before the one you are currently located at, and C-w, which catches up with all the messages between point and mark. The first of these (M H) is useful if you skim the subject of the messages, have to leave the group in the middle, and want to mark the messages you have skimmed so far as read.

Sending Mail and News

Now you have learned some of the ways you can read mail and news and a lot of the different options with which you can configure this process. So now it's finally time to learn how to send messages.

To send a new mail message, press m. (This works almost anywhere in Gnus). To post a new article press a. You must be in the group to which you want to send the message (that is, in the Summary buffer for the group or in the Message buffer for an article of the group). When you have pressed either m or a you are taken to a message buffer where you can write your letter or article. A Message buffer can be seen in Figure 20.4.

The first few lines are the header of the article. If you need to add an extra header line, you can simply do it by writing it (or you might find the appropriate header line from the field menu item). Thus if you, for example, need to insert a CC field, simply type CC: on a line by itself and type the email address you want to send a carbon copy to.

Do not delete the line that says

```
--text follows this line--
```

This line is used by Gnus to figure out where the headers end and where the body of the message starts (that is, where the text you are actually sending starts). The line is *not* shown in the message you send.

Posting a reply on a newsgroup is called *follow up*, whereas sending a reply to an email message is called *reply to*. You can also send a reply to an article in a newsgroup, but this is then interpreted as sending a reply to the author of the message (not as posting a follow up to the newsgroup!). Finally you can send a *wide reply* to a message. A wide reply is simply an email message that is sent to all the original recipients and the originator of the message you reply to (excluding any newsgroups).

When replying to a message, it is often useful to include the original message. Variants of each of the reply/follow up functions described exist that *yank* the original text before you are allowed to edit it. In the Post menu you can find all the functions described previously. To ensure that you send the message to the correct people, the functions are summarized in Table 20.3.

TABLE 20.3 FUNCTIONS FROM THE POST MENU USED TO REPLY TO OR FOLLOW UP ON A MESSAGE

Name	Location to Which the Message Is Sent
Follow up	The reply is posted to the newsgroup where the original message is located. If the article is not from a newsgroup, the message is replied to.
Reply	The reply is sent to the author of the message. This is true both for messages from a newsgroup and from a mail group
Wide Reply	The message is sent to everyone who received the message that you reply to, excluding any newsgroup. That is all email addresses listed in the header
receive your	reply, but no newsgroups.

Finally you might want to forward a letter to another person using either email or a newsgroup. This is achieved by the functions Forward Mail and Forward News.

Postponing Messages

Whenever you write a message, you might find that you do not have time to finish the letter until later. In these cases you simply press C-c C-d (in the Message buffer). This postpones the message. When you later want to continue the letter you must go to the group called Drafts. From this group you can continue editing the letter, send it, or throw it away. The available actions can be seen in the Draft menu available when you have selected this group.

20

If you cannot find this group, try to press g in the group buffer. The reason might be that the group hasn't been updated to reflect that it now contains your postponed message.

Keeping an Archive of Sent Messages

When you send a message, you often want to keep a copy of the letter for yourself. If you insert the following lines into your .Gnus file, Gnus automatically saves a copy to the file sent:

```
(setq gnus-message-archive-group "sent")
```

This mechanism is, however, very powerful. Insert the following line into your .Gnus file instead to get the outgoing messages saved in a group called sent-*year*-*month*:

```
(setq gnus-message-archive-group
   '((concat "sent-" (format-time-string "%Y-%B" (current-time)))))
```

Whenever you compose a new message, a header called Gcc is inserted with the name of the group to save to (see Figure 20.8). If you do not want the current message to be saved to this article, you can simply delete this line.

This line specifies where the message should be saved

FIGURE 20.8

Keeping an archive of sent messages.

The backend

The name of the group, in which this message is stored

If you want to save the letter to another folder, simply edit the line. If you want to save it to several, add extra names with a comma in between.

Incorporating Old Archives

If you have old mail archives in ordinary mbox format, you can simply copy these files to your ~/Mail/archive directory, and issue the command nnfolder-generate-active-file. If this, for one reason or another, should not make your old archives visible in the group buffer, go to the Server buffer as described in the section "Installing the Mailboxes" earlier this hour, and subscribe the groups from the server called nnfolder+archive.

Sending Attachments

Sending attachments with Gnus is quite easy. Simply press `C-c C-a`. Gnus then asks you for the following things in the minibuffer:

- The filename—Type the filename to attach. This is Emacs! Of course you have file completion available.

- The content-type—This describes the type of the file you send. This is to help the mail reader that should read this message. (If you do not know what this is, press Enter to accept the default suggestion from Gnus.)

- A comment—Finally you can add a comment to the file you send.

Summary

You have now been introduced to the world's most powerful mail and news reader, and believe me, I have only scratched the surface. To give you an idea of how complex and customizable Gnus is, the number of pages in the reference manual might give you a hint. The reference manual for Emacs is 500 pages long, whereas the reference manual for Gnus is almost 400 pages long!

Fortunately, you are not finished with Gnus yet. This hour has told you the basic things about Gnus. The next hour goes a step deeper and teaches you some of the more exotic commands. This includes using a database with Gnus, searching for messages, and splitting incoming mail.

Q&A

Q **Is it possible to change the backend later, if I find that the backend I have chosen does not fit me?**

A Yes. In the next hour the `doc` backend is described. Using this backend you can copy your messages from one group to another.

Q **Is it possible to ask Gnus not to show the backend name in the Group buffer?**

A Yes, this is described in the next hour.

Q **When I'm writing a message, I would like to use auto-fill mode. How do I do that?**

A You can enable auto-fill mode as usual by pressing `M-x` and typing `auto-fill-mode`, but I guess you are asking how you can enable it by default, right? Okay, insert the following into your `.Gnus` file:

```
(add-hook 'message-setup-hook 'turn-on-auto-fill)
```

20

Q **Okay, I followed your advice about starting auto-fill mode. It's behaving strangely, though. When I type a line and it is broken, it inserts a greater-than sign (>) at the beginning of the line. Why?! (I might add that this happens only when I reply to a letter.)**

A The reason for this is that adaptive filling (see Hour 12, "Visible Editing Utilities") thinks that the line is an item, due to the special symbol (the > sign) that is used to quote the letter you are replying to. There are two different solutions to this problem:

- You can leave a blank line after the text you reply to
- You can insert the line

```
(sams-gnus-filling)
```

This starts auto filling in the message buffer, but disables adaptive filling when sending replies.

Exercises

1. Subscribe to the groups called `gnu.emacs.help`, `comp.emacs`, and `comp.emacs.xemacs`.

2. See whether you can find a newsgroup called `test` in your area. For example, if you live in Germany, you might find a group called `de.test`.

3. When you have found such a group and you have ensured that the group is merely to send test messages, subscribe to it, and try to post a message to it.

4. Set up the expiring mechanism the way you like it. You might try to use the immediately expiring period to see what gets expired.

5. Send a letter to me. My email address is `blackie@ifad.dk`. But please include a header called `X-Postcard:`. (You do that like you add a To: field.). This way I can set up a procmail filter that sorts your mail into a folder I can read whenever I have time. Please also include the text "Postcard" in the subject (in case the other method fails). As the body of the letter you might send me any comment you have on the book.

6. If you succeed in sending me the letter I'll let procmail send you an automatically generated answer back. Read it with Gnus. (Don't delete it; you'll need it in the exercises of the next hour.)

HOUR 21

Advanced Gnus

Are you ready to see why I constantly hail Gnus as being the most powerful mail and news reader? In this hour you will see some of the really cool things one can do with Gnus. These include

- Scoring—This is a mechanism with which you can tell Gnus about authors you think say interesting things, and about subjects that you very much dislike, and that you think messages longer than 100 lines are way out.

- Sorting mail—Gnus can sort all your incoming mail into different groups for you.

- Limiting—If you search for a message from someone, it is useful to ask Gnus to show messages sent only from this person.

This hour also helps you customize some of the minor things that can be annoying if they don't work the way you want them to. Hey, this is Emacs—almost everything can be customized!

Customizing the Group Buffer

Start with the Group buffer. In this section you will see how you can organize your mail groups into topics, how you can customize the group line to show only the information you are interested in, and how you may make Gnus sort your incoming mail into a set of groups.

Topics

After you learn how to subscribe to groups and you find out how easy it is to make Gnus find the messages in a group that are of special interest to you, you will suddenly find that you are subscribed to 20 different newsgroups, and perhaps as many mailing lists.

The problem then is to find the group you want to read messages from. Fortunately, there's a solution in Gnus to this problem—*topic*. Topic is like a directory structure where each topic can contain a number of groups and subtopics. Furthermore you can fold topics so their content is hidden. This can be seen in Figure 21.1. (Note that this is from my personal setup, and I've changed the group lines; you will shortly learn how to do that.)

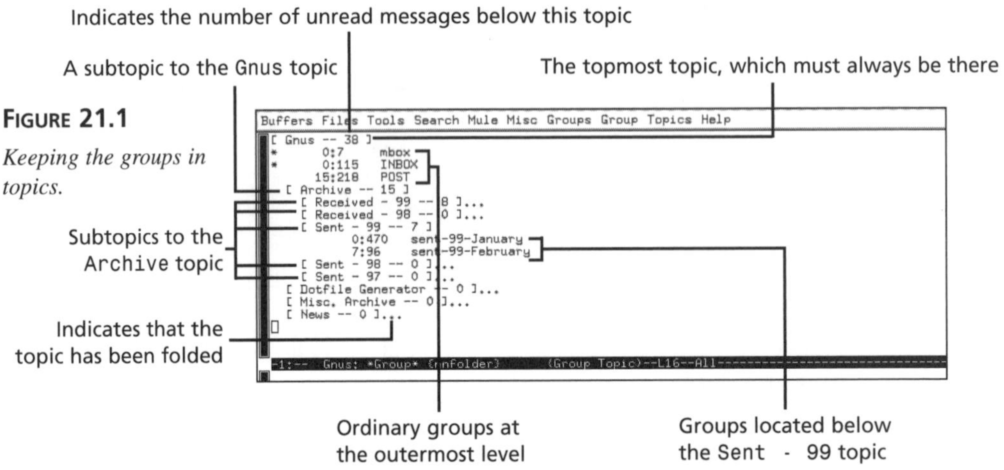

Indicates the number of unread messages below this topic

A subtopic to the Gnus topic   The topmost topic, which must always be there

FIGURE 21.1

Keeping the groups in topics.

Subtopics to the
Archive topic

Indicates that the
topic has been folded

Ordinary groups at   Groups located below
the outermost level   the Sent - 99 topic

All the topic commands are available from the Topics menu item, but before you can do anything with topics, you need to enable topics, which you do by pressing t.

Now you can add new topics by pressing T n. Gnus queries you in the minibuffer for the name of the topic, and inserts it as the last element under the topic, which point currently is within. If this is not the correct location for the topic, you can move it to another location by killing it with c-k and pasting it in at another location with c-y.

If you paste a topic at the end of another topic, it will be located at the same level as the other topic. If your intention was that it should have been a subtopic of this other topic, simply press the Tab key, which pushes the topic one level down. This can be seen in Figures 21.2 and 21.3.

FIGURE 21.2

Using the Tab key—before.

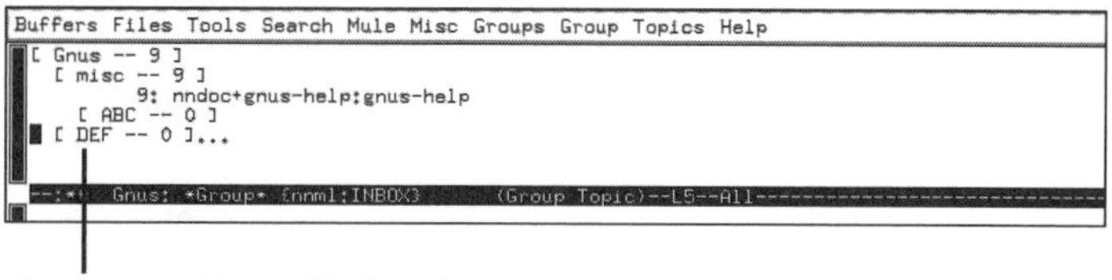

The topic DEF has just been pasted in at this location.

FIGURE 21.3

Pressing the Tab key brings DEF to the same level as ABC. Pressing Tab once more brings it to a subitem to ABC.

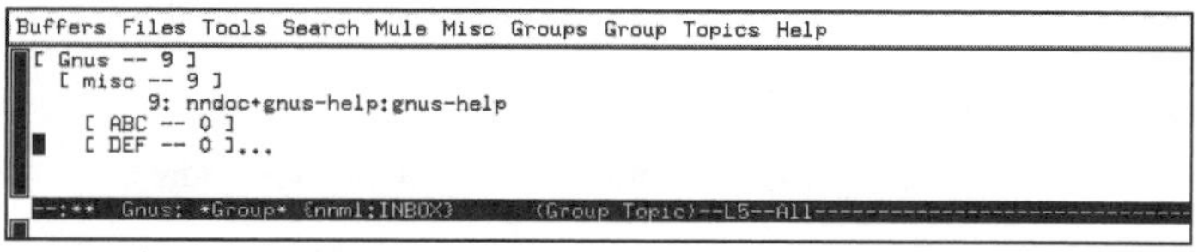

There are a few different ways to move groups around, but the easiest way is simply to kill them with C-k and then paste them in again at another location using C-y. You can kill several groups after each other. The order in which they are pasted in is in the reverse order they have been killed—that is, the last one killed is the first one pasted in.

You can collapse and expand topics by pressing the Enter key when point is on top of them, or by pressing the second mouse button upon them.

Once you have set up topics, you always want to have them enabled, right? You can achieve this by inserting the following into your .Gnus file:

```
(add-hook 'gnus-group-mode-hook 'gnus-topic-mode)
```

Additional Servers

Gnus has a few additional servers, called doc-server and virtual-server. There is no need for you to think about these features as servers in general, but you will see them listed as servers in different places in Gnus, so it is convenient for you to know.

doc-server

The doc-server is used to tell Gnus to read a file as a group. This is convenient if you have an old mailbox that you just want to peek into. To create a doc-group, type G-f. Gnus now asks you for the name of the file and creates a group from this file.

21

If you want to copy any of the messages from this file to any of your existing groups, then you can press B c. Gnus then asks you for the group to copy this message to. You can also mark a number of messages by pressing # and copy them all in one go.

If, on the other hand, you want the messages handled as if they have just arrived, press B r. This might be of interest if you have set Gnus up to sort your incoming mail into several different groups (this is discussed in the section "Sorting Incoming Mail Using Gnus").

When you are finished with the group, kill it using C-k.

The Virtual Server

Sometimes different newsgroups exist that more or less cover the same topic, or it might at least seem so from your point of view. Examples of this include

- comp.emacs and gnu.emacs.help
- alt.fan.depeche-mode and alt.music.depeche-mode

The existence of two groups might have the following disadvantages to you:

- You have to read and manage two groups. This is, however, not a big issue, because you could expect twice as many messages if there were one common group.
- If someone posts a question to both groups, it can be answered separately in each of the groups. This means that you have to go to both groups to see an answer. This is worse than it sounds! For each thread of answers, you have to get into context before you can read the answers. Getting into context means that you have to understand the question. With answers located in both groups, you have to get into context twice, which can give you a substantial amount of overhead.

The solution to this problem is to merge the two groups into one group. This is done using a virtual group.

Creating a Virtual Group Containing comp.emacs and gnu.emacs.help

This task shows you how to create a virtual group with the messages from comp.emacs and gnu.emacs.help. Follow these steps:

1. Subscribe to the two groups as usual.
2. Create a virtual group by pressing G V. Gnus now asks for the name of the group. Call it Emacs. Now a virtual group exists, but it does not contain any messages, because no groups are attached to it.

▼

▼   3. Move point to each of the two Emacs groups, and for each of them press G v.
        Gnus now asks you which virtual group the current group should be attached to.
        Type the name you gave it previously.

     4. Now a virtual group exists. It contains all the messages from both groups, and you
        will never see that it is not one group, but in fact two. The two original groups are,
        however, also still visible. To remove them, you must unsubscribe them, but *not*
        kill them. That is press u when point is on the original groups.

     The same method may also be used to join your outgoing and incoming mail groups
     together to one, where you can see both the letters you sent and the letters which you
▲   received.

     There is one caveat with virtual groups, which is that when you want to post a new mes-
     sage to one of the groups that the virtual group contains, you have to go to the original
     groups and post the message from there. This, however, doesn't apply to followups to the
     messages in the groups.

Customizing the Group Line

The group lines (those showing a group in the Group buffer), the topic lines, and the
summary lines (those showing the messages in the Summary buffer) can all be configured. This way you can make Gnus include just the information you care about. If you,
for example, do not want to see the select method (for example, nnfolder:), you can
configure the group line not to show this. Likewise you might want to know how many
messages a given group contains—that is, not only the number of unread messages
(which is the default), but the total number of messages.

The group line is configured using the variable gnus-group-line-format. This variable
must have a string assigned to it that shows the information you want. In this string you
can include placeholders, each of which are expanded to show information about the
group in question. The placeholders are specified with a percent character (%), and a
character specifying which placeholder it is. The default value of the group line can be
seen in Figure 21.4.

All the specifics available for this variable can be seen in the description of the variable.
That is, press C-h v (describe-variable) and type gnus-group-line-format. If you do
not want to see the select method, but only the name of the group, you can insert the following into your .Gnus file:

```
(setq Gnus-group-line-format "%M%S%p%P%5y: %(%G%)%l\n")
```

21

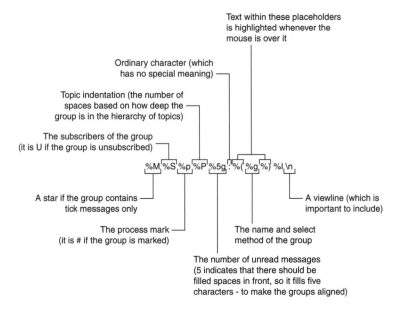

FIGURE 21.4

The default value of the group-line-format variable.

Sorting Incoming Mail Using Gnus

Whenever Gnus finds new mail, it moves it to a location that is private for Gnus. During this mail transferring, Gnus can also sort the mail into several different groups. This is useful if you are subscribed to a number of mailing lists and do not care to use the time to set up an external program to sort mail for you (such as procmail).

The configuration of mail sorting is done with the variable nnmail-split-methods. The following is a configuration where mail is split in three different groups:

```
(setq nnmail-split-methods '(
  ("debian-devel" "^To:.*debian-devel@lists.debian.org")
  ("postcard" "^Subject:.*Postcard:")
  ("Miscellaneous" "")
))
```

The previous code is a Lisp expression, but you should be able to figure out how to use it without knowing anything about Lisp. The three lines in the middle are the ones that say which mail should go where. Each line must start and end with a parenthesis. Between the parentheses, two strings limited by quotation marks are listed. The first string names the mail folder that mail should be put in if the regular expression, given as the second string, matches.

The regular expression of the last line should *always* be the empty string to ensure that there always is at least one regular expression that matches. The letter is always placed in the group associated with the first regular expression that matches the letter. Thus each letter is always located in only one group!

Gnus can in fact do more powerful mail sorting than the previous example indicates, but in case you need more power, I suggest that you use a tool, such as procmail, developed specifically for this task.

> If you want to use procmail, it might be a good idea to use The Dotfile Generator to configure the `.procmailrc` file. This file specifies how procmail should sort the mail. Information about The Dotfile Generator is available from its home page, located at `http://www.imada.ou.dk/~blackie/` `dotfile/`. Just in case you're wondering, I'm the author of The Dotfile Generator and the procmail module for it.

Using a Database with Gnus

When communicating with lots of people using email and news, it can often be either difficult to remember the email address of a person, or to remember who a person is, when you see a message from him. This can be solved by using a database with information about people.

BBDB (Insidious Big Brother Database) is such a database. It can work together with Gnus to let you search for an email address when filling out the To field, for example. It also pops up with the information from the database about a person when you load a message from him.

To make BBDB work together with Gnus, you need to insert the following lines into your `.Gnus` file:

```
(require 'bbdb)
(bbdb-initialize)
(add-hook 'gnus-startup-hook 'bbdb-insinuate-gnus)
(add-hook 'gnus-startup-hook 'bbdb-insinuate-message)
(add-hook 'message-setup-hook 'bbdb-define-all-aliases)
(sams-bind-alias-tabs-in-gnus)
```

Inserting Entries into BBDB

The database is worthless as long as there is nothing in it, so I'll start out by showing how to insert entries into the database.

21

The easiest way to insert an entry for a person into BBDB is to press : (colon) in the Summary buffer when a message from him is the selected one. If the person is in the database already, nothing happens; otherwise, Emacs asks you if you want to insert him into the database.

Sometimes you might also want to add a note on the entry. That might be a comment on who this guy is. This can be done by pressing ; (semicolon). If the person is not in the database, he will first be inserted.

Whenever Gnus is about to show a message for a person in the database, a window with the BBDB entry is shown, as can be seen in Figure 21.5.

FIGURE 21.5

The BBDB window.

The date when this entry was inserted into the database

The date when this entry was most recently edited

The notes field inserted by pressing ;

The figure after the slash is the total number of entries in the database

The BBDB window

If you do not have a message from the person you want to insert into the database, you can press M-x and type bbdb-create. Emacs then asks you a number of questions about the person's name, net-address (email address), postal address, and phone number.

Editing an Entry

Editing the entry for a person is quiet easy. First you have to switch to the BBDB buffer. If the buffer is not onscreen or does not contain the entry you want to edit, press M-x and type bbdb to find and display the entry.

If you want to edit an existing field, press e on top of the field. If you want to add a new field instead, press C-o. A few fields are special to BBDB, and you should seldom need to add new ones, but you are perfectly allowed to. As in many other places, completion is available when you tell BBDB which field you want to add.

Finally, deleting a field is done by pressing d on top of it. Pressing d on top of the name field means to delete the whole entry in the database.

Selecting an Address from the Database

What you really need a database for is to look up an email address, given a person's given name, right? Using BBDB, this is especially simple—just type part of his name and then type M-TAB. If the name matches several persons, then a BBBD window is shown, where you can see the possible matches, and eventually select one.

Mail Aliases (Local Mailing Lists)

In some circumstances it is useful to send a letter to several people, such as co-workers, people who have a common interest with you, or people who appreciate getting a joke sent to them from you.

BBDB can help you set up such a *mailing list*. This is done by adding a mail alias to each of the entries for the persons for this mailing list, as the following tasks shows.

> Because the words *mailing list* make people think about a public mailing list where you can send a letter and from which your letter is sent to a number of people, the topic in the rest of this section be referenced to as *mail aliases* (which it also is in the BBDB documentation).

▲ To Do

Creating a List of Email Addresses

Follow these steps to learn how to set up a mail alias using BBDB:

1. Find a good name for your mailing alias. This might for example be *joke-lovers*, *work-group*, or *depeche-fans*.

2. Find the BBDB entry for a person who should be on this list. You can use the command bbdb or bbdb-name to search for her.

3. Switch to the BBDB buffer and press C-o. This makes Emacs ask for the name of the field to add.

4. Type mail-alias and press Enter. The very first time you add a mail alias, it is not possible to complete the name, but it is subsequent times. The first time BBDB also complains that it doesn't know this field, and asks you if you want to add it. You do!

5. Now type the name you found in step 1.

▼ 6. Repeat steps 2-5 for each of the people who should be on this list.

21

▼ Well that's it! Given that you have a line in your `.Gnus` file that says (`sams-bind-alias-tabs-in-gnus`), all should work fine. You can define as many aliases for a person as you
▲ want. In these cases, simply separate each alias with a comma.

When you want to send mail to the your newly created mail alias, type the name of the list and press M-TAB as you would do with any ordinary mail address. This can be seen in Figures 21.6 and 21.7.

FIGURE 21.6

Mail buffer just before pressing M-TAB to expand the mail alias joke-lover.

FIGURE 21.7

Mail buffer just after having pressed M-TAB.

Mail addresses for the persons matching the alias *joke-lover*

The definition of the alias

The BBDB buffer shows all the persons who match this mail alias

 There is one pitfall with these mail aliases. You can't autocomplete their names! In the example in Figures 21.6 and 21.7, you can't just type *joke-* and press M-TAB; you need to type the name in full, and press M-TAB.

Additional Summary Commands

It is in the Summary buffer that you can see all the messages for a given group. The number of messages can range from a few in your default mailbox to several thousand in very active newsgroups or in your archives. It is therefore quite important that you ask Gnus to help you find the messages you are interested in. Gnus can help you in several different ways, as this section shows you.

Searching Through All Your Messages

By pressing M-s or M-r in the Summary buffer, you can search through all the messages in the given group—that is, through the bodies of all the messages in the given group. C-s and C-r in this buffer are used to search the content of the Summary buffer.

Sorting Your Messages

Besides showing the messages as threads, Gnus can also sort the messages by the order of arrival, by author, by subject, or by a few other means. When using this feature, you should most likely disable threading, which is done by pressing C-M-t, because otherwise only the topmost message in the thread is used when sorting. The rest of the messages just come along with the topmost one. There is one exception to this rule, which is that sorting by score is a good idea to do when threads is enabled, because this means that the threads with the highest scores are shown first. All the sorting functions is available from the Misc menu in the sum entry called Sort.

Limiting the View

If you are searching for a message from a given person, it might still be hard to find, if a hundred messages from him reside next to hundreds of other messages in the given buffer. A solution to this problem is to limit the view to show only the messages from him and then continue the search for the given message from there on. When you have only messages from him shown, you can continue limiting the search to messages sent within the last year, for example, and finally simply search through the rest of the messages using M-s as described previously.

The menu item Misc, Mark Limit contains all the functions for limiting the Summary buffer. These functions include functions for limiting to subject, author, and age for example.

When you have limited the set of messages to a given subset in the Summary buffer and are finished with this limit, you might want to see all the messages from the Summary buffer again. This is achieved using the element called Pop Limit in the menu. This works much like narrowing described in Hour 15, "Getting an Overview of a File," where you can narrow and later widen. There is one difference, though! Using narrowing, you can narrow down several times, but only widen once, which shows you the whole buffer again. In contrast, in Gnus you can use Pop Limit as many times as you limit.

If you need to limit to something special, then you can get a long way by setting process marks on the messages that you want to limit to and then use the function Misc, Mark Limit, Articles.

21

Process marks can be set by pressing # when point is on a message. Process marks can be removed by pressing M-#. Finally, there are many different functions for setting process marks in the menu item Misc, Process Mark. In this menu, you find functions for setting process marks in a region or based on a regular expression.

Customizing the Summary Line

In the section "Customizing the Group Line," you saw that it is possible to customize the group line. Likewise it is possible to customize the Summary line, which shows the author, score, and subject for a given message. This line is configured the same way that the group line was configured.

One of the problems with the current Summary line format is that it is not very informative when you look at groups containing messages you sent (for example, your archive of sent messages). The reason for that is that the summary line shows the author of the messages, but all of the messages are from you and you know that already. If you make an addition similar to the following into your .Gnus file, this problem will be solved:

```
(setq gnus-ignored-from-addresses "blackie@ifad.dk")
(setq gnus-extra-headers '(To Newsgroup))
(setq nnmail-extra-headers gnus-extra-headers)
(setq gnus-summary-line-format "%U%R%z %4i %([%4L: %-25,25f]%) %I%s\n")
(setq gnus-summary-same-subject "-¦¦-")
```

Besides solving this problem, this addition makes the summary line much more readable when many levels of threads are shown. You can see for yourself in Figure 21.8.

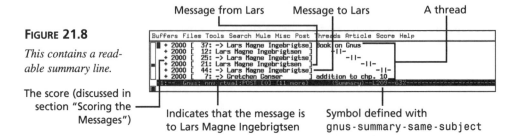

FIGURE 21.8

This contains a readable summary line.

The score (discussed in section "Scoring the Messages")

Indicates that the message is to Lars Magne Ingebrigtsen

Symbol defined with gnus-summary-same-subject

For the addition to work, you should replace blackie@ifad.dk with your own email address. (This is, in fact, a regular expression, so the dot should have been escaped for this to be completely accurate). In Figure 21.9 you can see a description of the most interesting element from the previous formatting expression.

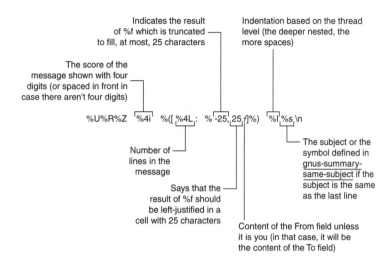

FIGURE 21.9

The formatting expression used to format the summary line.

Scoring

When subscribed to high-volume newsgroups or mailing lists, you will quickly find that your days simply are too short to read through all the messages. What you need is a slave who can read all the messages and then show you the most interesting messages. You might argue here that it is very difficult to get good slaves nowadays, but you are wrong! The slaves nowadays are called computers! People often tend to forget that.

Using the scoring system in Gnus, you can tell your slave to find the messages that are of special interest to you. This is done by telling Gnus to score each messages based on a set of rules, and then show you only the messages above a given score, or asking it to sort the messages based on their score.

The score rules can be arbitrarily complex, but the simple ones discussed in this hour will do in most cases. The simple rules include the following:

- Whenever Lars Ingebrigtsen says something, then I'd better listen, so score all his messages high.

- There is this very irritating person who asks stupid and rude questions all the time, so give his messages a negative score. A negative score means that I'm less interested in his messages than messages that haven't gotten a score at all.

- I just love hearing about scoring on the Gnus mailing list, so add a positive score to all messages with the word *score* in their subject.

21

- Whenever someone answers one of my messages to a list, then I'd better pay attention. Add a positive score to messages that stem from one of mine.
- This thread is interesting (or boring), so score all messages in this thread with a positive (or negative) score.

Scoring the Messages

You configure your scoring from the summary buffer. To add a score, select Increase Score from the Score menu. To lower the score, select Lower Score from the Score menu. The scoring is done based on the current message.

By default, 1000 points are added or subtracted by these commands, but you can change that by pressing Escape, typing the number, and then selecting the commands from the Score menu.

When you have selected a score function, Gnus asks you what part of the message you want to score on. The idea is that the current message should be a template for scoring other messages. The question is What part of the current message should be used as the template? The author? The subject? Messages from the thread?

To this question, you can answer one of the following things (press ? to show you which key to press to get a given match):

- Match the From field (press **a**)—This changes the score on all messages from the author of the given message.
- Match the Subject field (press **s**)—This changes the score on all messages with the same subject. Later, you will see that you can change this statement to *all messages with approximately the same subject*.
- Match the date of the message (press **d**)—This changes the score of all messages sent on the same day as the current one, all messages sent before the current one, or all messages sent after the current one. (Gnus asks you whichever it is.)
- Match followup to messages from a given person (press **f**)—Using this match type you can tell Gnus to change the score for all messages that are responses to a message from the author of the current message. You can, for example, use this to increase the score of all responses to messages sent by you.
- Match subbranches of the thread rooted at the given message (press **t**)—If you see an interesting message or a thread that is lengthy and not of interest to you, then you can use this scoring method to change the score of all messages that stem from the current message.

More ways to match text exist. For a complete list, please see the Gnus reference manual.

When you tell Gnus which part to match, it asks you how to match it. For the date match type it suggests *before*, *on the same day*, and *after*. All the others described previously are matched as strings, and the following matching patterns exist:

- Exact string match—When a message is matched against your formula, then it matches only if the string from the message matches exactly. For example, if you have said that you want to increase the score when a message is from "Jesper Pedersen <blackie@ifad.dk", then this will not match "Jesper Pedersen <blackie@imada.ou.dk", due to the changed domain.

- Substring match—Using substring matches, you can specify a string that should be part of the string to match. This way you can, for example, score on the string .edu depending on how much you like mail from universities.

- Regular expression match—With this match type you are allowed to type in a regular expression that should match.

- Fuzzy matching—From the reference manual: "It's so fuzzy that there's not even a definition of what fuzziness means." This matching type matches the two strings, after it has removed *noise*. Noise is defined as extra spaces, parenthetical remarks, and so on.

Finally Gnus will ask you which type of scoring this should be. You have two choices:

- Permanent scoring—This means that the score exists forever (in contrast to *temporary scoring*). This is used to score people you know as being competent. This could, for example, be Lars Magne Ingebrigtsen, the maintainer of Gnus, or Richard Stallman, the author of Emacs.

- Temporary scoring—To avoid the tables with scoring information growing huge, you may specify that a scoring is to be regarded as temporary. This means that if it hasn't been used for a week, it will be deleted. This might be a good idea when scoring on a thread, for example.

When you have scored an message, the scoring takes effect when you enter the Summary buffer next time. If this is not good enough for you, you can select Rescore Buffer from the Score menu, and press C-M-t twice (which disables and then again enables threading, or the other way around if threading is not enabled).

21

Scoring Using BBDB

It can be very useful to let BBDB help you score persons. This is done by adding the following to your .Gnus file:

```
(setq bbdb/gnus-score-default 2000)
(setq gnus-score-find-score-files-function '(gnus-score-find-bnews
➥bbdb/gnus-score))
```

2000 is the default value which is added to a message's score if the message is from a person in the BBDB database.

For each person in the database, you can also specify the score separately. This is done by adding a field called gnus-score (see the section "Inserting Entries into BBDB").

Using the Score Information

Now that you have scored your messages, it would be nice to use this information, right? There are a number of things you can do:

- You can make Gnus show the score in the Summary buffer, as can be seen in Figures 21.7 and 21.8. By default only a plus is shown if the message's score is above zero and a minus if the score is below zero.
- By default all messages that have a negative score are marked as read.
- You can tell Gnus to sort your messages with respect to the score, as you saw in the previous section. If you want to do that by default, insert the following into your .Gnus file:

```
(setq gnus-thread-sort-functions
      '(gnus-thread-sort-by-number
        gnus-thread-sort-by-total-score))
```

Scoring Individual Groups

Normally the score information is kept separate for each group you are subscribed to. That is, when you score on an author in one group, then this author's score is not affected in the other groups.

You can, however, tell Gnus to add scores to the file all.SCORE. This score then affects all groups. This is done by selecting the item Switch Current Score File from the Score menu and typing all.SCORE when Emacs asks for a filename. (You should be able to make a macro that does this.)

By pressing `M-i a I` or `M-i a L` you raise or lower the score, respectively, in the global file instead of the score file local for the group.

These keybindings might not be that easy to remember, so if you insert the following into your `.Gnus` file, then you can press `C-S-i` or `C-S-l` instead to raise or lower the score in the global kill file.

```
(sams-define-score-bindings)
```

Summary

This is the end of your journey through the most-powerful news and mail reader in the world. If you miss a feature in Gnus, there is a great likelihood that the reason is that it just hasn't been covered in this relatively small introduction. Examples of features left out are off-line news reading, scoring using world wide score files, message duplication suppression, and customization on a per-group basis. I strongly suggest that you take a deep look into the Gnus manual once you are used to the material in this hour. You will find many interesting features not described here.

Q&A

Q I don't think I can see the major difference between the matching methods for strings, that is *exact match*, *substring match*, and *fuzzy match*. When should I use which?

A A rule of thumb that I use is

- Use exact match or substring match for email addresses.
- Use fuzzy match for subjects
- Use exact matches when covering message IDs (for example, when matching threads)

Q How do I delete a score I've made?

A I don't think there are any easier ways than editing the file with the score. You may do that by selecting Edit Current Score File from the Score menu. This file is in a syntax that resembles Lisp, but you should be okay if you delete an equal number of opening and closing braces. When you are finished, press `C-c C-c` to exit.

21

Exercises

1. Arrange all your messages in topics.

2. Develop a group line that shows the total number of messages in the group, including read messages, and the group's description.

3. Create a macro that increases the score of the current thread.

4. Using the letter you received from me when doing the exercises in the previous hour, insert my name into your database, and set the score for me to 5000. (I'm important, you know.)

5. Using *limits*, search for a message in one of your huge mail folders.

PART VI
Advanced Emacs

Hour

Appendix

HOUR 22

Learning Lisp Basics

Emacs is extended using a variant of Lisp called Emacs Lisp, or *elisp* for short. Emacs can be extended almost limitlessly using elisp. Think about dired, discussed in Hour 16, "Interfacing with the System". dired has very little in common with the original task of Emacs, namely editing text files; still, dired is built purely on Emacs, written using only Lisp.

You also use elisp yourself, when configuring minor things in your `.emacs` file. You can, for example, see Lisp expressions such as the following in the `.emacs` file:

```
(setq next-line-add-newlines nil)
```

The focus in this hour is on customizing Emacs using your `.emacs` file, not on topics specific to writing larger extensions. This hour teaches you enough about Lisp to understand and edit your `.emacs` file. You should not, however, expect to be able to build larger extensions to Emacs, such as dired.

This hour assumes no knowledge of programming, so if you have never programmed a single line of code before, you should still get through. The hour does, however, draw parallels to other programming languages to make it easier for those who have programmed before.

The Purpose of Lisp

You might very well ask yourself Why do I need such a complex system as Lisp to configure things in the `.emacs` file? The answer is simple: This is to give you enough power to do whatever you want! An example might clarify my point.

Imagine that you had only a very simple syntax with which you could configure things in your `.emacs` file. The syntax could for example resemble

```
option1: value1
option2: value2
option3: value3
...
```

How would you, using this syntax, tell Emacs that an option should have one value in one major mode, and another value in another major mode? You might suggest that you make sections in the configuration file for each major mode like:

```
major-mode1:
option1: value1
option2: value2
option3: value3
...

major-mode2:
...
```

Okay...how would you then avoid having to specify the same value twice for all major modes, if the value was mode independent? How would you specify a value based on both major and minor mode? one based on the computer you were logged in to? the capabilities of your monitor? the major/minor modes? whether you use GNU Emacs or XEmacs? whether you use version 19 or version 20? and on and on....

If you have a good answer to this question, I'll bet that your answer is a full-blown programming language. Lisp *is* a full-blown programming language, so why reinvent the wheel?

Evaluation in Lisp

In a programming language such as C or Pascal, you would write the addition of three numbers with subsequent assignments to a variable in the following way:

```
a := 10 + 20 + 30
```

In Lisp this is written like

```
(setq a (+ 10 (+ 20 30)))
```

The syntax is different, but what is done is, in fact, the same.

The reason for the difference in syntax is that Lisp is a much older language than Pascal. Parsing the preceding Pascal expression was very expensive in the ancient days when Lisp was invented; furthermore, the methods you know today for parsing weren't invented at that time.

The Lisp expression is evaluated from the inside out. That is, first the numbers 20 and 30 are added and the result, 50, is added to 10. Finally, the result of this is assigned to the variable named a.

The preceding statement couldn't be more wrong, but it's a nice way to think about it! What actually happens is that the Lisp interpreter sees the outermost parentheses and concludes that this is something for it to evaluate. The first element of this list is regarded as a function, and the remaining elements are regarded as arguments to this function. Before the Lisp interpreter executes the function, all its arguments are evaluated. In this round of evaluation, the result of 10+20+30 is calculated.

Values in Lisp

Several different values, of course, exist in Lisp. These values are now explained using a real-life example where a need for such values exists.

Booleans

In many situations there are two possible values for a given configuration option. The option can often be stated as a yes/no question. An example might be: "Do you want a blank line inserted if you ask Emacs to move point to the next line, when you already are located at the last line of the buffer?" The value to an answer of the preceding question is a truth value, either true or false (true represents the answer *yes*, and false represents *no*, in the given example).

The value *true* is in Lisp represented using the character t, and false is represented using nil. The reason for this strange convention is merely one of historical reasons. Thus telling Emacs that it should insert a blank line is done using the line

```
(setq next-line-add-newlines t)
```

whereas telling Emacs not to insert a blank line is done by inserting the line

```
(setq next-line-add-newlines nil)
```

Numbers

Numbers are also a value type needed in Emacs. Examples of the use of numbers include the number of backups to keep, the number of characters to indent when programming C, and the maximum size of buffers to fontify with font-lock mode. Numbers are specified as is.

String

Strings are used in Emacs in many different situations. Most of these situations are when programming Lisp. Examples of these might be a string of text to search for, a message sent to the user, and names of different things such as buffers, files, and bookmarks. When customizing things in your .emacs file, you often use strings for directory or filenames and regular expressions. String are represented by placing quotation marks around the string. An example is

```
(setq abbrev-file-name "/home/blackie/Abbreviations")
```

If the string contains a backslash, you need to escape it. Thus the regular expression that matches the word ".Emacs" (that is, a period, the letter E, and so on) looks like "\.Emacs" (the period needs to be escaped otherwise it would mean any single character). To insert this regular expression into a string, you need to escape the backslash, and the result is thus "\\.Emacs".

Symbols

In Emacs, a data type called *symbols* exists. The difference between a symbol and a string is too technical if you are not a programmer, so in this case you might think about symbols as another way of writing a string.

Symbols are written by putting a single quotation mark in front of the name as in 'do-backup.

If you are a programmer, this is the difference between a symbol and a string. A *symbol* is an object that can be compared to another object in constant time. Emacs can, for example, answer whether 'aaaab is equal to 'aaaaac in constant time. On the other hand for Emacs to compare the strings "aaaab" and "aaaaac", it needs to compare the first character and, if these are the same, it must compare the second character, and so on. Thus the time it takes to compare two strings is equal to the length of the strings.

Lists

You often need to list a number of values. Examples of this include

- A list of directories for Emacs to search for template files
- A list of indexes counted from the beginning of the line, where a tab stop should exist
- A list of split methods as seen in Hour 21, "Advanced Gnus"

Lists are specified by listing each of the elements within a pair of parentheses, the outermost list must be prefixed with a quote, as discussed later in this hour. The following are examples of lists:

```
1. (setq tab-stop-list '(2 4 6 8 10 12 14 16 18 20))
2. (setq template-default-directories
        '("~/Templates" "/usr/local/Templates"))
3. (setq nnmail-split-methods '(
        ("debian-devel" "^To:.*debian-devel@lists.debian.org")
        ("postcard" "^Subject:.*Postcard:")
        ("Miscellaneous" "")))
```

The first example is a list of numbers, and the second is a list of strings. The third example is a list of lists. Each of these lists contain two elements that are strings.

The list must be prefixed with a quote, otherwise the Lisp interpreter thinks that the first element of the list is a function for it to execute, and the rest of the elements are arguments to the function. Thus if you write

```
(setq a (+ 1 2))
```

then the Lisp interpreter assigns the value 3 to the variable a. If, on the other hand, you write

```
(setq a '(+ 1 2))
```

the list with three elements, namely the symbol + as the first element, 1 as the second, and 2 as the third, is assigned to the variable.

Association Lists (alist)

An association list is a map from a key to a value. An example of this data type is `auto-mode-alist`, which is a variable that describes which major mode to start based on the filename. A regular expression describing properties for the filename is the key, whereas the name of the major-mode is the value. A key/value pair is listed like a list, with the exception that a period is inserted in between. This can be seen from the following example:

```
(setq auto-mode-alist '(
  ("\\.gnus$" . emacs-lisp-mode)
  ("\\.py$" . python-mode)
  ("\\.c\\'" . c-mode)
  ("\\.h\\'" . c-mode)
  ("[Mm]akefile" . makefile-mode)
))
```

To be completely accurate, the preceding code is a list, in which each individual element is itself a list (although it is a special kind of list).

Operations on Lists

Often you do not want to create a new list, but rather modify an existing one. An example of this is the list of directories where Emacs searches for Lisp files. You do not want to replace the existing list of directories whenever you have an additional directory for Emacs to look in. Instead you want to tell Emacs to look in the directories it is used to and your new directory.

Whether your new element should be added to the front of the list or the end of the list depends on what your intentions are. In the example, adding the directory to the front of the list means that Lisp files in your new directory take precedence over the others. That is, if a Lisp file exists both in your new directory and in one of the directories from the original set of directories, Emacs uses the one from your new directory. Likewise, if you add your directory to the end of the list, a file from your directory only is used, if it is in none of the other directories.

Inserting in the Front of a List

Adding an element to the front of the list is done using the function cons. This function takes an element to add and a list, and returns a new list as a result. Thus, to add the directory called ~/Lisp-files, you should insert the following into your .emacs file:

```
(setq load-path (cons "~/Lisp-files" load-path))
```

The code says that the string ~/Lisp-files should be inserted at the front of the list contained in the variable load-path. The result should be inserted into the variable load-path again. (This way the variable load-path is updated.) The parenthesis in front of the word cons tells Lisp that cons is a function it should execute. This is discussed later.

To insert two elements in front of the variable load-path, you can write something like:

```
(setq load-path
   (cons "~/Lisp-files/Major-modes"
       (cons "~/Lisp-files/Minor-modes" load-path)))
```

To read the previous example, you must read from the inside out. First the string `~/Lisp-files/Minor-modes` is inserted in the front of the list from the variable `load-path`. This results in a new list. Next the string `~/Lisp-files/Major-modes` is inserted in the front of the just-made list, and this new list is finally inserted into the variable `load-path`.

Inserting at the End of a List

Inserting elements at the end of the list is done by forming a list and appending this newly formed list to the end of the original list. Thus you do not insert an element to the end of a list.

> Lists are implemented by having a pointer to the front of the list. Adding an element to the front of the list is done in constant time, but inserting an element to the end of a list takes time equal to the length of the list. Forcing you to append a list of elements to a list rather than simply insert at the end several times makes you aware of the time it takes.

Thus to insert the two directories to the end of the list, insert the following into your `.emacs` file:

```
(setq load-path (append load-path '("~/Lisp-files/Major-modes"
                                    "~/Lisp-files/Minor-modes")))
```

Assigning Variables

A variable is a container that can hold a value for later retrieval. You have already seen numerous examples of variables: `load-path`, `next-line-add-newlines`, and `abbrev-file-name` to name a few.

Some of the variables can be made buffer-local. That is, their values are different from buffer to buffer. This has the advantage that different major modes can configure Emacs in specific ways. A good example of this are the variables `comment-start` and `comment-end`. These variables are used by the filling commands (see Hour 12, "Visible Editing Utilities," for a description of these commands).

When a major mode is started in a given buffer, it makes these two variables buffer-local and sets them to their specific values for the given major mode. Making the variables buffer-local ensures that the variable is configured only for the given buffer and that the variable is not changed in any of the other buffers, which might be in a different major mode.

When a variable is made buffer-local, changes made to it in the given buffer only have an effect in that buffer, not in any of the other buffers. Still a global variable might exist that all the other buffers share (including new ones).

Some variables can be made buffer-local in such a way that new buffers created get a local copy of it. The copy they get is initialized from a default value. An example of such a variable is `fill-column`. Depending on your intention and whether the variable is buffer-local or not you can use either `setq` or `setq-default`. The possible combinations is shown in Table 22.1.

TABLE 22.1 FUNCTIONS TO USE TO SET VARIABLES (SETQ OR SETQ-DEFAULT)

Intention	Set Global Value	Set Local Value
The variable is not buffer-local	This is the most common situation. Here you can simply use `setq`. You can, however, also use the function `setq-default`. Thus, it is possible to use this function all the time, when you want to set the global value for a variable.	In this situation, the variable is not a buffer-local value. To make a buffer-local variable, you must use the function `make-local-variable`. Given that it is the variable `next-line-add-newlines`, which you want to make buffer-local and set to nil, use this code: `(make-local-variable 'next-line-add newlines)` `(setq next-line-add newlines nil)`
The variable is buffer-local	To set the global value for a buffer-local variable, you must use the function `setq-default`.	To set a local value for a buffer-local buffer simply use the function `setq`. To set a variable local for a given buffer, you must either press M-: and execute the commands described previously, or insert the command in a *hook* (hooks are described in Hour 24, "Installing Emacs Add-Ons"). In short, hooks are commands executed when a major mode, for example, starts.

If you, for example, want to set the global value for the variable `fill-column`, you must use `setq-default`, because this variable is buffer-local.

Configuring Options for a Single File

Some configurations might be local to a given file rather than a given major mode. Examples of these kinds of configurations are

- Files used to save abbreviations in. You can have a file in which you have some specific abbreviations that you want defined only for that file. These can be obtained by setting the variable `abbrev-file-name` local for the given file.

- The language used to spell-check a given file. This is very useful if your default dictionary is English, but you now and then need to spell-check a file in another language—for example, Danish.

- If you need special keybindings for a given file. You might need to insert some text over and over again in the given file. Then you can record a number of macros and save them to a file and finally bind the macros to easy-to-reach keys (maybe overriding the default keybinding, which you would otherwise use often).

This can be obtained by inserting a few lines at the bottom of the given file. These look like

```
01   /* Local Variables:  */
02   /* variable1: value1 */
03   /* variable2: value2 */
04   /* End:              */
```

In line 1, `Local Variables:` and `End:` must be there as is, to ensure that Emacs recognizes these lines as instructions to it. Also in line 1, notice the slashes and asterisks. All the lines must start and end with the same text as this line. These are the comment characters for a C file. `variable1` in line 2 is the name of the variable. And the value for this variable is `value1`, also shown in line 2.

The following is an example where the abbreviation file and the fill-column are set: in a HTML file (enclose a comment in `<!--` and `-->`).

```
<!-- Local Variables: -->
<!-- fill-column: 100 -->
<!-- abbrev-file-name: "~/WWW/.abbrevs" -->
<!-- End: -->
```

Executing Code

In the previous examples, loading a file was also mentioned as one of the things you could do with this feature. In general, any kind of Lisp code can be executed. Simply insert a line starting with `eval:` and include the Lisp expression after that, as can be seen in the following example:

```
<!-- Local Variables: -->
<!-- fill-column: 100 -->
<!-- eval: (load-file "~/Emacs/Macros/chapter-macros.el") -->
<!-- End: -->
```

The function `load-file` reads in a Lisp file and evaluates it.

Now that you have learned this feature, please think carefully before you insert text such as the preceding in your files, especially if someone else is supposed to edit the files too. If your configuration is a matter of personal taste, it might be a better idea to customize the options using hooks on major modes instead.

When Emacs loads a file with local variables, it asks whether you really want this region evaluated. This is to avoid reading in someone else's file, where the file contains code in the eval section that does something you do not like (such as erasing your hard disk). You can ask Emacs to skip this security check if you never edit other people's files. This is done by inserting the following line into your `.emacs` file:

```
(setq enable-local-eval t)
```

Function Definitions

A function is a collection of commands that is given a name. When the function is executed, each command is executed in turn. You have already seen numerous functions—namely those that you can invoke by pressing M-x and typing a name (which in fact is the function name).

Functions can take a number of arguments. These arguments are used to configure the behavior of the function. An example is the function that is used to switch to another window (called `other-window` and bound to C-x o). This function takes an argument that tells it how many windows to skip and which direction to move.

The functions you need to write to configure Emacs do not require any arguments, but it's worth it for you to know the existence of arguments, because some of the functions you need to invoke require arguments. You have already seen how to invoke a function, but I haven't been concrete about that matter until now.

A function is invoked by typing its name at the first position within a set of parentheses. The elements at the subsequent positions are arguments to the function. Thus to invoke `other-window` with an argument of `-1`, use `(other-window -1)`.

The following is an example of a function that switches buffer in the backward direction:

```
01  (defun my-switch-buffer ()
02    "Like switch-buffer but in the opposite direction"
03    (interactive "")
04    (other-window -1)
05  )
```

In line 1 of this code, defun is a keyword to indicate a function definition. my-switch-buffer is the name of the new function. The parentheses in line 1 contain the arguments to the function (none in this case). Line 2 provides an optional description of the function (see it with C-h f). And (interactive "") in line 3 is an interactive specification.

The interactive specification is used to tell Emacs that the function can be invoked by pressing M-x and typing its name, or by binding it to a key. Without this line you can call the function only from within another function or from a hook. The string given as argument defines how Emacs should obtain the argument to the function, when it is called interactively. But as this function takes no arguments, this string is empty.

With the previous function in your .emacs file you can now press M-x and type my-switch-buffer, or bind the function to a key.

It is beyond the scope of this book to tell you the whole story about function definitions, so I'll focus on what you really need to know in order to configure Emacs. You need to define functions that you can attach to hooks. Hook functions do not need an interactive part and take no arguments. As an example of a hook function, the following is a function that turns on auto-fill mode and sets the fill column to 100:

```
(defun my-auto-fill-hook-function ()
  (setq fill-column 100)
  (turn-on-auto-fill)
)
```

This function can now be added to the hook for c-mode (called c-mode-hook) with the following code:

```
(add-hook 'c-mode-hook 'my-auto-fill-hook-function)
```

Hooks are discussed in more detail in Hour 24.

 Please note the quote in front of my-auto-fill-hook-function; without this quote Lisp thinks that my-auto-fill-hook-function is a variable that it needs to find a value for in its dictionary. With the quote, Lisp knows that you are stating a name of a function.

Anonymous Functions

With the previous method for defining hooks, you often find that you need a new name for a function, with the only reason that the function needs a name is so that you can give it to the add-hook declaration. With an anonymous function you can save time and avoid having to find a name for the function. Anonymous functions are defined with the keyword lambda instead of the keyword defun, as can be seen in the following example:

```
(add-hook 'c-mode-hook
  (lambda ()
    (setq fill-column 100)
    (turn-on-auto-fill)
))
```

> If you think that the lambda function is an extra complexity, you might be right. I told you about lambda functions only because you most likely will see the preceding method as the preferred one in many other sources.
>
> Lambda functions are in fact very powerful when you use Lisp for writing real programs—that is, in contrast to configuring minor things in Emacs.

Organization of Your Configurations

When you start to configure Emacs, you should find that your .emacs file grows large. For readability you should split it into several files. I suggest that you create a directory called Emacs and two subdirectories within it: Extensions and Configurations. In the Extensions directory you can place all the Lisp files with extensions that you find on, for example, the CD. In the Configurations directory, you can keep a number of different configuration files, all of which are split from your original .emacs file.

Your .emacs file can be split into the following:

- emacs-std.el—This file is for the standard Emacs options. This includes next-line-add-newlines, auto-mode-alist, and the like.
- bindings.el—This file includes the keybindings for your Emacs setup. This might be a copy of the file usr/share/emacs-lisp/refcard/refcard.el from the CD.
- macros.el—This file can contain all the macros you have developed.
- modes.el—This file can contain configurations for the different major modes that you use, such as c-mode, html-mode, and text-mode.
- extensions.el—This file can contain configurations for the different extensions you use. The larger ones of them can even be put in a file by themselves.

Your .emacs file needs not contain more lines than the following:

```
(setq load-path
  (cons "~/Emacs/Configurations"
    (cons "~/Emacs/Extensions" load-path)))
(load "emacs-std")
(load "bindings")
```

```
(load "macros")
(load "modes")
(load "extensions")
```

Byte-Compiling Files

Emacs can byte-compile your Lisp files, which makes them run faster. This is done using the function `byte-compile-file` or `byte-recompile-directory`. You should byte-compile both your configuration files and the extensions you use.

> If you use different versions of Emacs or you use both GNU Emacs and XEmacs, you should not byte-compile your files, because the byte-compiled files are incompatible from one version to the other.

Byte-Compiling a Directory

Follow these steps to learn how to byte-compile all the files in a directory:

1. If you want Emacs to unconditionally compile all your uncompiled files, press `C-0` (Ctrl-zero); otherwise, press `C-u`. Next, press `M-x`, type `byte-recompile-directory`, and finally press `RET`.

2. Emacs asks for a directory name. If you want your entire Lisp file compiled, give it the root directory name (that is, `~/Emacs` in a configuration as described earlier this hour); otherwise, give it the name of the directory in which the Lisp files are located (that might be `~/Emacs/Configurations`).

▲   These steps create a `.elc` file from each of your `.el` files.

Summary

This hour does not tell you all you need to know to write an extension to Emacs. It also hasn't told you enough to make the simplest functions in Emacs to manipulate your text. But that was not the intention. It has, however, succeeded in telling you enough about Lisp that you now understand most of what is going on in your `.emacs` file.

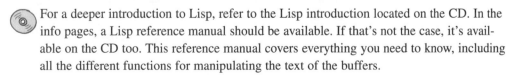

For a deeper introduction to Lisp, refer to the Lisp introduction located on the CD. In the info pages, a Lisp reference manual should be available. If that's not the case, it's available on the CD too. This reference manual covers everything you need to know, including all the different functions for manipulating the text of the buffers.

Q&A

Q Why does Emacs use Lisp as the extension language? Isn't that an ancient programming language?

A Yes and no. Lisp is an old language—that is correct. It was developed back in the '60s, but it is still a very powerful language. Furthermore, it would require huge amounts of work to rewrite all the existing extensions already written for Emacs to another language, and the value of this would be limited.

Q Why do I need to escape a backlash in strings?

A In strings, a backslash is used as a control character. Thus \n specifies a newline, for example. An ordinary backslash is written as two backslashes in order to escape it in the string. If you need to escape it in the regular expression too, you need four backslashes. These four backslashes are translated to two after the expansion in the string, and these two are translated to one after the expansion in the regular expression. Don't worry; you'll get used to it.

Q Is there any way I can see whether a given variable is buffer-local by default?

A First you might try to read the documentation for the variable (by pressing C-h v). The documentation often mentions whether the variable is buffer-local. If that doesn't say anything, try pressing M-x and type set-variable, press Enter, and type the variable's name and value. When you finish that, look at the description of the variable again. If it is buffer-local, the description mentions both a local value and a global value.

Q When should I use a quote (') in front of a variable or function name?

A You should use a quote in front of the name when you want to specify a function or variable name. You should not use a quote when specifying the value of the function or variable.

Exercises

1. Try to design an alternative to Lisp, with which you can do all the possible configurations you can think of.

2. Take a look into your .emacs file and classify your variables in the categories described in the section named "Values in Lisp".

3. See if you can think of a smarter way to append an element to the front of a list, other than doing

```
(cons val1 (cons val2 (cons val2 ... (cons val42
➥original-list) ... )))
```

4. Order your configurations from your `.emacs` files as described in the section named "Organization of Your Configurations" and byte-compile the files (given that you only use one version and flavor of Emacs).

22

Hour **23**

Binding Keys and Creating Menus

Emacs is a peculiar editor in the sense that it lets you configure everything in your sight: programming modes, syntax highlighting (the color of the buffer's text), external process communication, timers, calendars, appointments, and even your keyboard layout and installed menus. Default Emacs installation comes with a lot of shortcut command keybindings preconfigured. You can find out how many preset commands there are by calling C-h m (describe-bindings). Figure 23.1 shows the first of nearly 600 possible commands.

The command C-h m (describe-bindings) lists all known bindings that are active in the current buffer. Before you go farther, you must define some terms that you use from now on. A keypress represents an input event to Emacs. An input event can be a single character, a function key, a keypad key, mouse button click, mouse dragging, and so on.

FIGURE 23.1

Output of describe-bindings.

Keyboard Modifiers

Did you know that one of the acronyms invented for *Emacs* is *E*scape, *M*eta, *A*lt, *C*ontrol, *S*hift?

This leads us to talk about the modifiers that you can apply to the events. Emacs has several modifiers, but not all keyboards support the modifier keys Emacs can accept:

- Meta-modifier can be generated by the Esc key and Alt key. In Win32 the variable `w32-alt-is-meta` controls whether the Alt key produce Meta-modifier. It does that in the standard installation and the default value of `w32-alt-is-meta` is t. When you press Esc, the minibuffer at the bottom reads ESC, signaling that Emacs has captured the Esc-event and is waiting for more keys to be pressed. This is later interpreted as Meta, but it is possible that in some keyboard configurations the Esc key is interpreted as escape-modifier instead of Meta-modifier.
- Alt-modifier is generated by the Alt key.
- Control-modifier is generated the Ctrl key.
- Shift-modifier is generated by the Shift key.
- Hyper-modifier exists on some keyboards.
- Super-modifier exists on some keyboards.

Notice that both Esc and Alt can generate the Meta-modifier and in some keyboards, typically in UNIX, you might have an Alt key, but to configure it to generate an Alt-modifier is sometimes a pretty hard job. Contact your system administrator or someone who knows how to configure keyboard layout under X using programs such as xmodmap(1)—the standard keymap control program—or xkeycaps(1)—which can be found easily with, for example, the AltaVista search engine. Check also the Linux Keyboard-and-Console-HOWTO document at `sunsite.sunc.edu`.

So you have input events and modifiers mapped to them so that you can press Alt and the character "a" to generate the key sequence Alt-a. You can also make more complex key sequences if you press and hold Ctrl, press and hold Alt, press and hold Shift, and hit "a" to generate a key sequence that reads M-C-a near the bottom of window. Notice that the Alt key here is known as the Meta-modifier. It could also read A-C-a in a different keyboard.

Keyboard and Events

23

In addition to your modifier and character keys, there are function keys, the keypad set, and possibly other keys on the keyboard. These keys don't generate characters, but named events. For example, the function keys and keypad keys generate event names:

```
f1,f2,f3 .. f20 kp-1, kp-2, ... kp-9, kp-add, kp-enter, kp-substract,
➥kp-multiply, kp-divide
```

Mouse and Events

You can best work with Emacs if you own a three-button mouse. These buttons have been named from left to right in the order of appearance: mouse-1, mouse-2, mouse-3, and sometimes even mouse-4, if you have a four-button mouse. What if you have only two buttons? Well, the missing mouse-3 is emulated by pressing mouse-1 and mouse-2 simultaneously. You have to practice this for some time to do it smoothly. Take your time and adjust your mouse software as needed if the simultaneous keypress timing is not suitable for you.

In XEmacs the mouse events have different names, for example, Emacs mouse-1 event is labeled button1up in XEmacs. Refer to XEmacs documentation for more complete description of the mouse event names.

Key Sequences and Keymaps

A key sequence is the input packet that Emacs interprets as a whole. The key sequence is associated to some action through keymap. A keymap in Emacs is stored in a Lisp variable, which is traditionally named so that it ends in the suffix -keymap. The most basic predefined keymaps in Emacs are the following: global-map, esc-map, mode-specific-map, ctl-x-map, ctl-x-4-map, ctl-x-5-map.

The first one, global-map, contains key definitions that are available everywhere in Emacs. Normal keyboard characters *a* and *b*, and other character keys, such as Enter (which generates ASCII code 10) and the Tab key (which generates ASCII code 9) are defined in this map.

The esc-map is part of the global-map and handles all key sequences that are started with Esc key.

The mode-specific-map is part of the global-map and handles all the key sequences started with the C-c key. This is the keymap that Emacs has specifically reserved for extension packages and for user keybindings.

The ctl-x-map is the keymap under which C-x-derived key sequences are interpreted. This keymap is the heart of the Emacs, because most of the Emacs functions have been buried under the C-x key.

The ctl-x-map includes two more submaps: ctl-x-4-map, where you find "other window" commands, and ctl-x-5-map, which contains frame-handling commands.

Prefix Key Accesses Submap

A key sequence that leads to the submap—such as C-x, C-c, C-x 4, C-x 5—is called prefix key. A prefix can be a single key or combination of characters, modifiers, and named events (complex key sequence).

Let's take a look what prefix is in your Emacs: Press C-h b (describe-bindings) and look for lines that read *Prefix Command*. To make skimming the long listing easier, adjust it to show only the lines matching the word *prefix* like this:

1. Switch to the Help window. If modeline reads %%, call C-x C-q to toggle the buffer's read-only flag to the off position. Proceed when modeline reads --.

2. Position the cursor at the top of the window.

3. Call the command M-x delete-non-matching-lines RET prefix RET.

> Traditionally the Help key has been C-h, but in other programs the f1 key established the position to access the help system. Emacs followed this tradition and added f1 key to mean the same as C-h.

The exact listing depends on your configured Emacs, but Figure 23.2 is an example of what you can expect.

FIGURE 23.2

List of prefix keys.

There are several defined prefix keys that lead to further submaps, which is indicated by the wording *Prefix command*. From here you can query the defined keys in a particular keymap with the key sequence <PREFIX-KEY> followed by C-h. For example, to peek at what keys are defined in ctl-x-4-map, press C-x 4 C-h. The listing shows us several commands in that submap (see Figure 23.3).

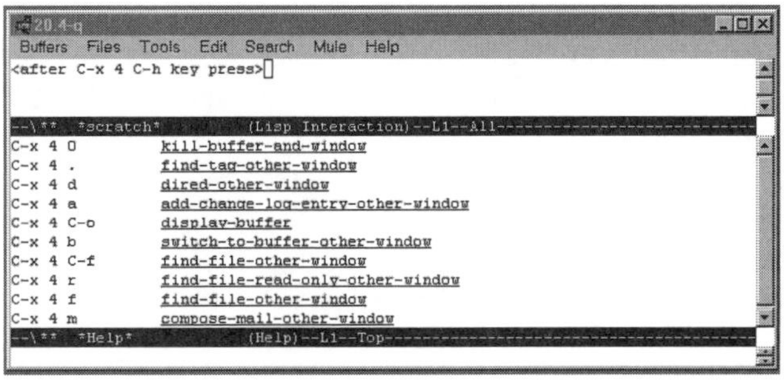

FIGURE 23.3

Keybindings in ctl-x-4-map.

Prefix Argument

A prefix argument carries extra information to the command behind key sequence. It is an additional parameter that makes the command work differently than without a parameter. Take a closer look at key *a*, with C-h a:

```
(self-insert-command N)
```

This command can accept the additional argument N (count), so how do you send it? The keys C-u (universal-argument) and Esc followed by a numeric value have been assigned to be used for a prefix argument. The C-u can be distinguished from the Esc prefix key, but that depends on the command if it wants to do that. C-u can be taken as C-u (raw prefix argument '(4) in Lisp), but can also be interpreted to map to value 4 or a multiple of it. If you press C-u C-u, it can be counted as 4×4 = 16 (raw value would be '(16) in Lisp). The self-insert-command interprets C-u as 4, so if you press C-u a; you would get *a* repeated four times. Not very useful? Well, let's draw some straight lines. Try C-u C-u C-u = and you get 64 equal characters on the screen. You could have done that with the Esc prefix key too by pressing Esc followed by number keys *6* and *4* plus the equals sign (=). Want to delete all lines to the end of buffer? Use C-u C-u C-u C-u C-k, which sends 4×4×4×4 (256) kill-line commands.

It is also possible to pass negative prefix arguments to commands. The plain minus sign is sent with key sequence C-u - followed by <command>. That did not request four dashes, if you thought that it would draw a small separator on the screen. Emacs reserves the minus sign for the negative prefix, because that's the only way to pass signed values. If you want to pass numeric negative values, you can add a number: C-u - 2 would pass -2 to a <command>.

> C-u does not multiply when it is used for negative prefixes.

You can find a use for negative arguments, for example, when you adjust indentation. First, draw a region, then call C-u C-x Tab (indent-rigidly) to push selected lines four spaces forward. To unindent the text, first select a region or recall the previous region with C-x C-x (exchange-point-and-mark), then call C-u - 4 C-x Tab. This is same command except that you used -4 instead of the positive value 4.

Major Modes and Keymaps

As you learned earlier, the global-map rules everywhere and inside it there can be more keymaps and submap definitions. There are many modes in Emacs, such as text-mode, mail-mode, message-mode, c++-mode, sh-mode, dired-mode, tar-mode, that need special keybindings to serve the mode's needs. How does a mode take over a global-map that is always present? It defines its own keymap and overrides the global-map with it. The dired-mode can now take control of all your regular keys such as *a*, *b*, and *c* and make it easier to use the mode.

Only one major mode can be active at the time. C++ editing mode (c++-mode), for example, is one major mode that remaps your global-map keys with its own keymap. In C++ the key mappings are mostly designed to help you position your code, to indent braces { and }, or to indent your current line when you hit the Tab key.

Each major mode keymap is named by using the mode's name and adding a suffix -keymap to it. The major mode name is the command that turns on the major mode—for example, M-x text-mode, M-x c++-, and so on. The keymap for each mode is named respectively text-mode-map and c++-mode-map.

Major Mode Hook and Mode Keymaps

You can't use the major mode keymaps right away. The only keymaps that are immediately available in Emacs are those mentioned in the "Key Sequences and Keymaps" section earlier this hour, which were part of the global-map. Remember that global-map was always present and defined.

The major mode's keymap does not exist until the major mode has been loaded and it has defined and initialized the keymap. If you have vanilla Emacs and you try to access c++-mode-map, Emacs rings a bell and tells you that "Symbol's value as variable is void: c++-mode-map."

```
;; See if C-c C-c binding is defined in c++-mode-map
(lookup-key c++-mode-map "\C-c\C-c")   ;; --> Signals error
```

The right moment to access a mode's keymap is when the mode gets turned on. At that point, mode initializes itself and runs a MODE-hook for user customizations. C++ mode runs c++-mode-hook, text mode runs text-mode-hook, and so on. The following is a solution to handle mode's keybinding settings in separate functions:

```
(add-hook 'c++-mode-hook 'my-c++-mode-hook)

(defun my-c++-mode-hook ()
   (define-key c++-mode-map [(f4)] 'c-indent-function))
```

This Lisp code says that call function my-c++-mode-hook is used when C++ mode is turned on, and key f4 defines the run command c-indent-function.

Minor Modes and Keymaps

There can be only one major mode active in a buffer, but it is possible to have any number of accompanying minor modes running parallel to major mode. For example, minor modes font-lock-mode and lazy-lock-mode can run at the same time as the major mode c++-mode. These two minor modes highlight your current program so that function names, language keywords, type definitions, and so on get a distinct coloring.

Minor modes can have keymaps that override the major mode's keymap. If you have modes (A-major) and minor modes X Y Z shown in the modeline, and if they all define key C-c C-c, the leftmost minor mode sweeps the board.

Minor Mode Hook and Mode Keymap

While all major modes have a MAJOR-hook, it is not always the case with minor modes. For example font-lock-mode is a minor mode and it runs font-lock-mode-hook. lazy-lock-mode is also a minor mode, but it does not have and thus doesn't run lazy-lock-mode-hook.

You have to examine each minor mode to see if it supports a MODE-hook, where you can add minor mode keybinding customizations or other minor mode setup code. Use C-h v <MODE-NAME + Tab> to find your information on variables defined by minor mode. If you can complete a variable name with the Tab key to end with -hook suffix, the mode (whether it's major or minor) does have its own hook.

Clearing Keybinding in Keymaps

To define and modify key settings in Emacs, you have to write some Lisp code. Suppose you want to disable an Emacs keybinding that you find disturbing. Do you find yourself mistakenly hitting C-z and iconifying Emacs accidentally from time to time? Me too, so here is the Lisp command that makes the C-z binding go away:

```
;; C-x runs Emacs command iconify-or-deiconify-frame
 (define-key global-map [(control z)] nil)
```

Creating Custom Keymaps in Global-Map

Let's return to that C-z binding. Suppose you still have the default binding which you can restore with the following:

```
(global-set-key [(control z)] 'iconify-or-deiconify-frame)
```

You can't assign C-z-derived keys, such as if you try to add these new bindings:

```
;;  Signals error:
;;  "Key sequence control a uses invalid prefix characters"
(global-set-key [(control z) (p)] 'print-buffer)
(global-set-key [(control z) (P)] 'print-region)
```

Why not? Because the C-z key has already been taken by iconify-or-deiconify-frame. To be able to press keys *after* C-z, the key must be made a prefix key first. You make one by clearing the key as you did earlier:

```
(define-key global-map [(control z)] nil)
```

Now C-z has no definition, so you can use it as a prefix key and bind more keys after it:

```
(global-set-key [(control z) (p)] 'print-buffer)
(global-set-key [(control z) (P)] 'print-region)
```

If you look at the listing C-z C-h, you see that Emacs has made a submap that is accessed via C-z (see Figure 23.4).

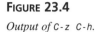

FIGURE 23.4

Output of C-z C-h.

Know Your Environment

Before you leap into defining custom keybindings, you have to find out what kind of key sequence Emacs thinks you pressed.

Running Emacs in an X Window system is different from running Emacs in console mode. The console mode can be started with the -nw (no window) command-line switch or you might be running it already inside a vt100 tty or equivalent terminal. Be prepared that console Emacs can't use the same bindings as the X Window version. Here is a comparison minitable for Ctrl-<key> combinations in both environments. Notice that this listing might be different in the terminal where you're running the Emacs:

Keypress	-nw	*Windowed*
Ctrl-right	Esc O C	C-right
Ctrl-left	Esc O D	C-left
Ctrl-up	Esc O A	C-up
Ctrl-down	Esc O B	C-down
Ctrl-RET	RET	C-return <<bold
Shift-RET	RET	S-return <<bold

Look closely at the last rows: In a nonwindowed environment the Shift and Ctrl modifiers are not recognized for these keys, whereas Ctrl-a and Shift-a are. In the nonwindowed Emacs, the cursor keys are recognized as a combination of separate characters. The cursor keys appear in this case under the Esc O prefix key.

Finding the Key Sequence Syntax

The most convenient way to find out the key sequence syntax is to press the keys and recall the input with command C-h l (view-lossage). Follow these steps:

1. Press the *x* key three times.

2. Press a key sequence, say Ctrl-Alt-a.

3. Press the *x* key three times.

4. Recall the view-lossage with `C-h l`.

The output of the buffer contains the key sequence syntax that you can use. Look for text in the buffer that looks like the following:

```
x x x M-C-a x x x C-h l
```

Between the x's you see the key sequence. The Emacs keybinding syntax for this sequence is

```
(global-set-key [(meta control a)] 'beginning-of-defun) ;; Go to function
```

The syntax is written inside [ ]. The parentheses () close a single key sequence and each M and C have been converted to lowercase `meta` and `control` modifier names. This universal keybinding syntax works between a variety of Emacs and XEmacs platforms.

How about mouse keybindings? They can be found as easily as the keyboard bindings. Try pressing `Ctrl-Alt-mouse-1` and `Ctrl-Alt-mouse-2` and check the results from `C-h l` buffer:

```
C-M-down-mouse-1 C-M-down-mouse-2
```

These key sequences can be bound to conveniently scroll your current buffer:

```
(global-set-key [(control meta mouse-1)] 'scroll-up)     ;; Like Page down
➥key
(global-set-key [(control meta mouse-2)] 'scroll-down)   ;; Like Page up
➥key
```

Look at more examples. You want to bind `Ctrl-F1`:

```
;;   C-h l reads:  C-f1, so here is the binding
(global-set-key [(control f1)] 'shell)
```

Or maybe bring up a diary with `Ctrl-Alt-d`. Pay attention to the meta modifier; which was produced by this keyboard:

```
;; C-h l reads: M-C-d; which was useless down-list command
(global-set-key [(meta control ?d)] 'diary)
```

In some other keyboards the previous example could read as the following:

```
;; C-h l output reads: A-C-d
(global-set-key [(alt control ?d)] 'diary)
```

The compile command doesn't seem to have a default keybinding, so let's map it to Alt-f12:

```
;; C-h l output reads: M-f12
(global-set-key [(meta f12)] 'compile)
```

What if you map Esc-mouse-1 to run command imenu, which brings up a function summary in programming modes? Pay attention that mouse buttons generate multiple events and you need only the button press event, which is mouse-1. Also note that Esc is part of the ASCII code table and can be represented with ?\e escape code. You use that and not the "escape" event name:

```
;; C-h l output reads: escape down-mouse-1 mouse-1
(global-set-key [(?\e mouse-1)] 'compile)
```

Recording and Running a Macro with Easier Keybindings

One of the handiest features in Emacs is the capability to record keyboard activities and play them back later. The macros are suitable for ad hoc tasks where you have a repeated editing task in the buffer. The Emacs default macro keybindings C-x (and C-x) have been assigned to uncomfortable key sequences, so let's remap them to faster keys:

```
(global-set-key [(control ?\()] 'start-kbd-macro)
(global-set-key [(control ?\))] 'end-kbd-macro)
(global-set-key [(control ?\=)] [ja1]'call-last-kbd-macro)
```

You picked three close keys from the top row and assigned them to macro commands: Hold down Ctrl-Shift-8 (choose the *8* that's in the top row of the keyboard) and you can start recording a macro. Hold down Ctrl-Shift-9 (choose the *9* the top row) to stop recording the macro. Finally press Ctrl-Shift-0 to play the recorded macro.

You see something new in this global-set-key Lisp call. When you map keys, Emacs can interpret normal ASCII characters as usual with (Ctrl-a), but if you map something outside of regular ASCII range, you have to use Emacs character syntax, where a character is denoted with a question mark. [(Ctrl-a)] can be represented with [(Ctrl-?a)] and with [(Ctrl-?\a)] syntaxes. That extra backslash means "take the next character literally."

Keep in mind which are your ASCII keys in the keyboard and which are named events. Emacs doesn't always do the thinking for you. For example, what if you want to map Meta-space to a filename completing command? Press Meta-Space and recall the presentation from C-h l and it tells you:

escape SPC

But that's not what you should bind. First, a space is ASCII code 32 or " " and, second, the Meta keys could have been your Esc or Alt key. If you try to bind the key directly from copying the C-h l syntax, it goes wrong:

```
;; With autoload we tell Emacs that 'comint-dynamic-complete
;; command comes from package "comint".
(autoload 'comint-dynamic-complete "comint" nil t)
(global-set-key [(escape SPC)] 'comint-dynamic-complete)
--> Signals error "two bases given in one event"
```

Instead, write the call this way: first the modifier and then the ASCII code. Space is not a named event although Emacs seemed to show the key that way. Be careful that you preserve space after backslash:

```
(global-set-key [(meta ?\ )] 'comint-dynamic-complete)
```

Passing Arguments to Commands

You have only seen how single functions can be bound to keys; but what if you want to always pass a certain prefix argument to the function? Take, for example, C++ mode and commenting. Go to an empty buffer and call M-x c++-mode. The mode line indicator shows that your major mode is "(C++)". To peek at the mode's bindings, press key sequence C-h m (describe-mode) and find comment-region, which is bound to key C-c C-c. Follow these steps:

1. Type two lines of text into the buffer.
2. Draw a region over those lines.
3. Press C-c C-c to comment the region.

The next question is how you uncomment the region. Examine what the comment-region function definition says with C-h k C-c C-c. I've included only some relevant lines from that description below:

```
(comment-region BEG END &optional ARG)
...
With just C-u prefix arg, uncomment each line in region.
```

The need to pass C-u argument to the C-c C-c key sequence might not look like much trouble, but it soon starts to be when you work with the code longer. And it would be nice if you wouldn't have to stress your pinky to access C-c C-c in a long editing session. Let's move the comment and uncomment commands to function keys f5 and f6, which are more easily accessible. Recall the previously mentioned C++ setting example and add couple of new Lisp lines to it:

```
(add-hook 'c++-mode-hook 'my-c++-mode-hook)

(defun my-c++-mode-hook ()
 (define-key c++-mode-map [(f4)] 'c-indent-function)
 (define-key c++-mode-map [(f5)] 'comment-region)
 (define-key c++-mode-map [(f6)] (definteractive (comment-region '(4))))
 )
```

The macro definteractive is not part of the default Emacs command set, but you can find it from the CD by loading sams-lib.el. You attached your first customized function call into key. definteractive declares an anonymous function at point with the body containing a call to comment region with argument '(4), which is the Lisp representation for the C-u prefix argument. The function key F6 now always calls function comment-region with prefix C-u and you don't have to type it as in the original c++-mode-map binding C-u C-c C-c. Commenting and uncommenting a region is only two keypresses away!

Making Personal Keybindings

The cursor keys have only the default command bindings next-line (down), previous-line (up), forward-char (right), and backward-char (left) and they are waiting for you to make them more productive. You have many modifiers that can be attached to these keys.

First, Emacs doesn't have a slide bar that would scroll a window horizontally and the default bindings C-x < and C-x > are pretty useless for buffers that have many long lines. You can't bear to type C-x < and C-x > after a few minutes when you are trying to see to the end of the line that is out of the visible screen area. Try these:

```
(global-set-key [(control meta left)] (sams-definteractive (scroll-right
➥10)))
(global-set-key [(alt control left)](sams-definteractive (scroll-right
➥10)))
```

Adjusting the scrolling direction with cursor keys is easy while you hold down the Alt and Ctrl keys. If you have looked closely at the C-h b keybinding listing, you'll have found out that the scrolling keys have already been bound to C-prior (Ctrl Page up) and C-next (Ctrl Page down). Somehow I find it more intuitive if these keys are bound to commands that take me to the beginning and to the end of buffer:

23

```
(global-set-key [(control select)]      'end-of-buffer)
(global-set-key [(control prior)]       'beginning-of-buffer)
```

Now when you page up and down, keys scroll one window at a time. Adding a Ctrl modifier makes them leap to the buffer's bounds to the beginning and to the end.

I also find that I am unintentionally typing the Home and End keys, so let's map them to something else. The following remappings are very handy in programming modes where the Home key positions the cursor to the beginning of a function and the End key to the end of a function.

```
(global-set-key [(home)]    'beginning-of-defun)
(global-set-key [(end)]     'end-of-defun)
```

Defining the keys into global-map works because the programming modes seldom, if ever, define the keys Home and End, so the keybinding is looked at from the upper level, from the global-map. (For example, C++ mode only partially overrides keys in the global-map. Recall the C-c prefix key in C++ mode from the previous sections.)

Summary

Keymaps in Emacs are the primary instrument for controlling Emacs. They are the launching board of all the default and used commands. Although nearly 600 predefined keybindings are already available when you start Emacs, that's only the tip of the iceberg of the total user-callable commands that you can find with C-h a-. (command-apropos followed by regexp character dot).

The Recipe to successfully written keybindings is to follow these rules:

- Consult the C-h l buffer frequently when you start customizing your Emacs keyboard.
- Use only the universal [()] notation.
- Keep in mind that Emacs started in nonwindowed mode (-nw) or in nonwindowed environment (tty) does not know all the named events. Check your binding with C-h l in -nw Emacs too if you need ultimate portability.

Happy experimenting!

Q&A

Q How do you know whether a command interprets the C-u argument as raw C-u '(4) or the number 4?

A   You don't. The implementation is transparent to the user. Only if the documentation of the command mentions specifically key C-u, you know that passing Esc 4 is differentiated from the C-u keypress. If there is no mention about the C-u key, you can safely assume that C-u is interpreted as any other numeric argument.

Q You said that I can't print four dashes with key sequence C-u, because the dash is interpreted as a negative prefix. Ho do you know that?

A   See the global map C-h b and find the line that reads "C-- negative-argument". Note: The notation C-- means that C- starts a key sequence and is followed by dash. Pay attention to digit-argument lines that mean numeric prefix values that can be passed to commands.

Q Do you know when you would use ?\a or plain a syntax in keybinding commands

A   The normal ASCII codes that you can print to the screen don't usually need the escaped notation, but in practice you should escape all characters that are nonalphanumeric. For example, although parentheses are normally printable characters, the parentheses are heavily used in Lisp; if you write [(meta ?))], it won't be parsed correctly and you'll have to use ?\). Ctrl characters must also be defined with syntaxes ?\C-c and ?\t.

Q I have seen the binding \C-i. What's that?

A   It's your Tab key, which can be written as \t or \C-i.

Exercises

1. Find out the name of the keymap that C-h accesses.

2. Find out the commands in the C-h keymap.

3. Can you find the keymap for fundamental-mode? Find from the Emacs info pages why the fundamental-mode is so limited. (See C-h i and search for "fundamental.*mode".)

4. Suppose you are already accustomed to the Emacs way of asking for help with C-h prefix key and you want to take the f1 key to another use. How do you bind the key f1 to call the command copy-region-as-kill?

Hour **24**

Installing Emacs Add-Ons

Emacs was designed to be extended by its users, and extend it they have.
Over the years, numerous add-ons (also known as modes) have been written,
which add features and adapt the editor to new circumstances. There is even
a Usenet newsgroup (news://gnu.emacs.sources) to which people post
new extensions for the Emacs community to try out. Knowing how to install
a new mode is an essential Emacs skill and, as this hour demonstrates, it
doesn't need to be a difficult task.

Simple and Complex Add-Ons

All Emacs add-ons are text files that are written in the Lisp programming
language, but extensive Lisp knowledge isn't necessary for you to use and
customize them. Some add-on modes are just a single file, whereas others
are made up of several files that work together. There is a certain format that
nearly all add-ons follow: At the top of the file, before the actual Lisp code
begins, there is a section that is commented out, with each line beginning
with one or more semicolons. This section is ignored by Emacs when the

file is loaded. Here you can find the instructions for loading and customizing the file or files. A larger add-on, which is made up of several files, often has a README or INSTALL file included, which contains the necessary information.

Installing an Add-On

Emacs is designed in such a way that new add-ons can be easily installed. Further steps are needed for you to make use of them. Various types of lines are added to the .emacs startup file, which either load an add-on for the duration of the session or make it available when it is needed.

Location and Paths

When Emacs is first installed, an empty directory is created just for add-on modes. It's called the site-lisp directory, and its location varies depending on which operating system you use. If you install many Emacs extensions, this directory can become crowded, making it difficult to keep track of what add-ons have been installed. This is especially true when large multifile packages, such as the W3 Web browser or AucTeX, are installed. One method of organizing the files is to keep them in separate directories and tell Emacs where they are. A statement in your .emacs file such as

```
(setq load-path (cons directory load-path))
```

causes Emacs to look for files to load in your new directory before searching the standard Emacs Lisp directories. If you prefer that Emacs search its native directories first, use the following statement instead:

```
(setq load-path (append load-path (list directory)))
```

The first of these examples is used when a newer version of a default Emacs mode has been installed and you want it to be used instead the default mode.

A Sample Installation

 The easiest way to understand how this works is to copy one of the add-on files that is on the CD-ROM to your site-lisp directory. Cyclebuffer.el is a short file that is used here as an example (see Figure 24.1). Open the file with Emacs, and then look for the commented-out section near the top of the file.

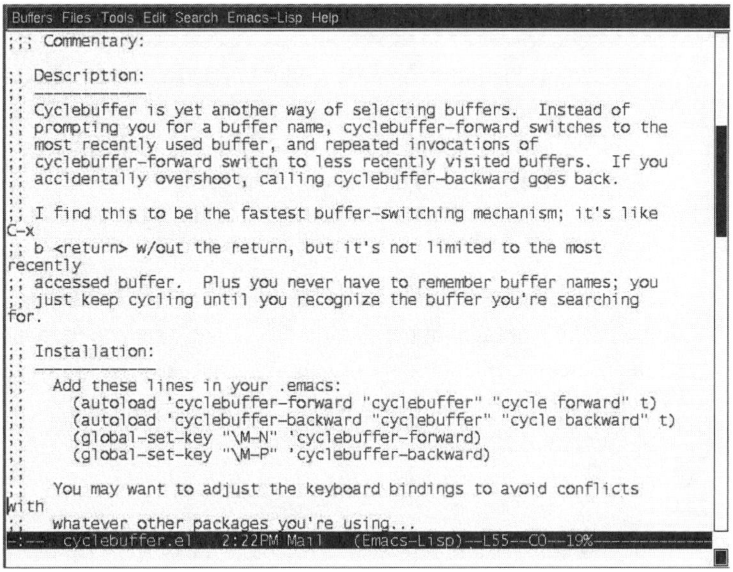

FIGURE 24.1

*Cyclebuffer.el
commentary.*

```
 Buffers Files Tools Edit Search Emacs-Lisp Help
;;; Commentary:
;; Description:
;; ----------
;; Cyclebuffer is yet another way of selecting buffers.  Instead of
;; prompting you for a buffer name, cyclebuffer-forward switches to the
;; most recently used buffer, and repeated invocations of
;; cyclebuffer-forward switch to less recently visited buffers.  If you
;; accidentally overshoot, calling cyclebuffer-backward goes back.
;;
;; I find this to be the fastest buffer-switching mechanism; it's like
C-x
;; b <return> w/out the return, but it's not limited to the most
recently
;; accessed buffer.  Plus you never have to remember buffer names; you
;; just keep cycling until you recognize the buffer you're searching
for.
;;
;; Installation:
;; ----------
;;    Add these lines in your .emacs:
;;      (autoload 'cyclebuffer-forward "cyclebuffer" "cycle forward" t)
;;      (autoload 'cyclebuffer-backward "cyclebuffer" "cycle backward" t)
;;      (global-set-key "\M-N" 'cyclebuffer-forward)
;;      (global-set-key "\M-P" 'cyclebuffer-backward)
;;
;;    You may want to adjust the keyboard bindings to avoid conflicts
with
;;    whatever other packages you're using...
-:--  cyclebuffer.el   2:22PM Mail    (Emacs-Lisp)--L55--C0---19%-----
```

24

You can skip the very first part because in most cases it contains licensing information. The information that you need is normally in a section that begins with Commentary:. A brief description of the mode's purpose is usually followed by lines that are to be inserted into your .emacs file; in this case, you see the following four lines:

```
(autoload 'cyclebuffer-forward "cyclebuffer" "cycle forward" t)
(autoload 'cyclebuffer-backward "cyclebuffer" "cycle backward" t)
(global-set-key "\M-N" 'cyclebuffer-forward)
(global-set-key "\M-P" 'cyclebuffer-backward)
```

If you copy these lines directly from the file on the CD-ROM, be sure to delete the semicolons at the beginning of each line; otherwise Emacs ignores them when it is loading the .emacs file.

After you have copied the file into a directory on your load-path and added the required lines to your .emacs file, you are ready to try the new mode. Save your .emacs file, and then type M-x load-file. When you are prompted in the minibuffer, type ~/.emacs; this causes Emacs to reread the file. Next, load several files. When you type either M-P or M-N, cyclebuffer is automatically loaded and you can use the keybindings to quickly cycle through the available buffers.

Loading Techniques

Autoloading is the most common method of activating an add-on mode. This method is very efficient because the actual Lisp code is not loaded until the functions in the mode are actually needed. When Emacs starts up and reads your .emacs file, it deals with autoload statements (such as the two in the preceding example) not by loading the Lisp file, but by remembering the name of the file in case it is needed during the editing session.

There are some Emacs add-ons that are intended to be activated when Emacs starts and remain active throughout the session. The load-library function loads a Lisp file, and a similar function called require loads a file only if it hasn't already been loaded. These two statements are used as follows:

```
(load-library 'name)
```

```
(require 'name)
```

In the preceding examples, name is the filename of the Lisp file without the .el or .elc extension.

Another function that you will occasionally encounter is provide. provide is used when you need to make a specific feature in a Lisp file available. The statement looks similar to the following:

```
(provide 'name)
```

Filenames and Interpreters

Many modes are designed to work with files that normally have a particular filename suffix. For example, Python source files usually have the suffix .py, so it makes sense for these files to be edited in python-mode.

Some add-ons need a line that tells Emacs to associate filenames that have a certain suffix with a particular mode. A line similar to the following

```
(setq auto-mode-alist (cons '("\\.chp?$" . text-mode)auto-mode-alist))
```

causes any files with the suffix .chp to be automatically edited in text-mode. auto-mode-alist is a list that is automatically loaded when Emacs starts up. This list tells the editor which mode to use for files with various suffixes. A statement such as the previous example adds a new item to this internal list.

Similar to `auto-mode-alist` is `interpreter-mode-alist`. This is an internal list of command interpreters that are to be associated with executable scripts. These scripts often have the name of the interpreter in the first line, prefixed by `#!`. When Emacs loads a file with this type of first line, it attempts to use the major mode that is associated with the name of the interpreter, as in the following example:

```
(setq interpreter-mode-alist (cons '"tash" . sh-mode)auto-mode-alist))
```

This line causes shell scripts that are intended for the (imaginary) `tash` command shell to be automatically opened in sh-mode, which is a mode that is used for all shell scripts.

The contents of either of these lists can be viewed by typing `C-h v`, which is a request for help with Emacs variables. When you are prompted in the minibuffer, type either `auto-mode` or `interpreter-mode`, and then press the Tab key, which completes the variable name. A Help window appears, displaying the contents of the requested list.

Any of the preceding statements can be suggested by a particular add-on mode. After you have added the needed lines to your `.emacs` file, reload the file as described previously. Now you can use the new mode.

Controlling Options

Many add-ons have options that can be set or changed. Newer add-on packages often have a Customize interface, which is the easiest method. Otherwise, you set the user-configurable options by including statements in your `.emacs` file. The Commentary section of the add-on Lisp file contains examples of the `.emacs` lines that are needed to change these options. In this section you can also find the mode's location in the Customize menu.

Hooks

Hooks are often provided for add-on Lisp files. Hooks are aptly named—they are functions that an Emacs process can "hook" into in order for a user to change the default behavior. An example might make this clearer:

```
(add-hook 'text-mode-hook 'turn-on-auto-fill)
```

By default, Emacs doesn't automatically wrap lines in text- mode. Adding the preceding lines to your `.emacs` file causes the function `turn-on-auto-fill` to be automatically loaded along with text-mode. When this hook is active, lines are automatically wrapped as you type. To try out a hook without including it in your `.emacs` file, type the line (complete with parentheses) into the Scratch buffer and then type C-x C-e, which is the keybinding for Evaluate LastS-Expression. The hook is then active until you exit Emacs.

Hooks are also used when you want to load two modes simultaneously. For example, if you want outline-minor-mode to be loaded along with AucTeX when you are editing TeX files, the following line is needed in your .emacs file:

```
(add-hook 'LaTeX-mode-hook '(lambda () (outline-minor-mode1)))
```

Using the lambda statement is a method of creating a nameless function (see Hour 22, "Learning Lisp Basics"); in this case, it causes outline-minor-mode to be loaded along with AucTeX's LaTeX mode. You didn't need to use lambda in the earlier examples because turn-on-auto-fill is already a function, whereas outline-minor-mode is a mode. In order for outline-minor-mode to be used in an add-hook statement, it is necessary to wrap it in a function definition.

Hooks can also be used to choose between several available options. CC-mode is a major mode that is used for editing C and C++ source-code files. The mode can be set to use one of several different coding styles with the following statement:

```
(add-hook 'c-mode-hook
         '(lambda ()
            (c-set-style "gnu")))
```

Many modes have their own built-in hooks, which you normally don't want to disable. The add-hook statement leaves existing hooks active while adding an additional hook.

Binding Keys With Hooks

Hook statements are often used to change the keybindings of a mode, most of which have predefined keymaps. Everyone has different editing habits and needs, so the most convenient and comfortable keys differ from user to user. Using mode-hooks ensures that the new keybindings only take effect when the particular mode is in use. Following are some examples:

```
(add-hook 'notes-mode-hook
  '(lambda ()
    (define-key notes-mode-map [f5] 'notes-follow-prev-link)
    (define-key notes-mode-map [f6] 'notes-follow-next-link)))
```

This example changes two multiple-key bindings to an adjacent pair of unused function keys. This speeds up two often-used commands in notes-mode. This mode is briefly described at the end of the hour:

```
(setq mail-mode-hook
  '(lambda ()
```

```
(define-key mail-mode-map "\C-cm" 'mail-send-and-exit)
(define-key mail-mode-map "\C-cc" 'mail-cc)
('turn-on-auto-fill)
(setq fill-column 65)))
```

In this example, two keybindings have been changed to shorter key sequences, auto-fill has been turned on, and the fill column has been narrowed to 65. Mail-mode doesn't have a predefined hook, so the `setq` statement is used to create one. Any mail-mode hook statements that follow this one in the `.emacs` file can use the `add-hook` function rather than `setq`.

Some add-ons have special provisions for changing the keybindings. For example, Folding-mode includes a function called `fold-default-keys-function`, which simplifies the alteration of keybindings. A function such as this in your `.emacs` file changes just one of the keybindings:

```
defun my-fold-bind-keys ()
 "My favorite fold key settings"
 ;;  - I want the default ones, but I want fold-whole-buffer and
 ;;    fold-open-buffer to be close together, instead of the
 ;;    default
 ;;  - read them all.
 ;;
 (fold-default-keys)
 ;;  - first disable old bind and define new one.
 ;;
 (define-key folding-mode-map "\C-c\C-w" nil)
 (define-key folding-mode-map "\C-c\C-p" 'fold-whole-buffer)
 )
```

This function first sets the keymap to the default with the `(fold-default-keys)` statement. Next, the default keybinding for `fold-whole-buffer` is disabled and a new binding (`C-c C-p`) is substituted.

The following line assigns the new `my-fold-bind-keys` function as the new default:

```
setq fold-default-keys-function 'my-fold-bind-keys)
```

Adapting Functions

There is another way to modify existing functions without using hooks, and without modifying the function itself. The advice tool is a part of Emacs that enables the user to insert a short statement in the `.emacs` file, which in effect gives advice to a function in order to change its behavior. This is similar to using hooks, but the advice utility is more flexible and open-ended.

Following is an example in which the default action of the `switch-to-buffer` function (normally called with the keybinding `C-x b`) is changed. If this advice is activated, the `switch-to-buffer` function no longer creates a new and empty buffer if the filename in the minibuffer refers to a nonexistent file; instead, the question *filename does not exist, create?* appears, giving the user a choice of whether to create a new buffer:

```
(defadvice switch-to-buffer (around confirm-non-existing-buffers activate)
  "Switch to non-existing buffers only upon confirmation."
  (interactive "BSwitch to buffer: ")
  (if (or (get-buffer (ad-get-arg 0))
          (y-or-n-p (format "`%s' does not exist, create? "(ad-get-arg
➥0))))
      ad-do-it))
```

Included in `sams-lib.el` is a utility that uses advice to set up an ongoing monitor of the hooks that are active in an Emacs session. To use this tracing utility, first make sure that `sam-libs.el` is being loaded from your `.emacs` file, and that the library is in your site-lisp directory or elsewhere on your load-path. The following line in the `.emacs` file loads the library:

```
(require 'sams-lib)
```

To activate the trace function, type `M-x sams-trace-hooks`. This code causes every instance of hook activation to generate a message in the minibuffer. This can be useful when you are trying new `add-hook` statements. You probably don't want this running all the time; to disable the monitoring, type the following command: `M-x sams-stop-trace`.

Exhaustive documentation and tutorials for the advice utility can be found at the beginning of the `advice.el` file, which is a part of every recent Emacs distribution.

Any time you edit your `.emacs` file, it is possible to accidentally leave out a parenthesis or to make a typographical error. When you start up Emacs it tries to load the `.emacs` file; if there are any errors, you see the following message in the minibuffer: `Error in init file`. Emacs won't load the remainder of the file, so whatever customizations you have made following the error in the file are ignored. One way to avoid this is to select any new lines that you have added and run `Evaluate Region`, which is a command that can be executed from the Emacs-Lisp menu. This enables you to spot the error early and correct it.

It's also a good idea to keep a copy of a functional `.emacs` file in another directory as a backup.

> If you want a new add-on to run as quickly as possible, don't forget to byte-compile the file or files. Just open the file in an Emacs session, and then select Byte-compile This File in the Emacs-Lisp menu. A new file with the extension `.elc` is created. Emacs uses these byte-compiled files rather than the `.el` files, if they exist.

> If you have installed several Emacs add-ons, there are probably some that you find more useful than others. If you decide that you don't need an add-on, it's advisable to disable it in your `.emacs` file. Just comment out the lines that load the package. Modes that don't get used waste memory and cause Emacs to start up slowly, especially if they are loaded with `load-library` rather than `autoload`.

24

A Sampling of Emacs Packages

In this section, several of the numerous Emacs add-ons are described. Some of the package developers have set up Web sites with introductory documentation and access information; other packages are available from public FTP servers.

Tiny-Tools

 Jari Aalto has written an enormous collection of miscellaneous Emacs modes, which he calls Tiny-Tools. There are many specialized modes in this package; there is also a wealth of documentation concerning the modes. Several lengthy text files, which discuss general Emacs configuration and usage, are also included. Tiny-Tools is available on this book's CD-ROM, even though it's an ongoing project and a more recent version might be available on the Internet. The following HTML file provides a general introduction with many links:

```
http://www.netforward.com/poboxes/?jari.aalto
```

Cyclebuffer.el

 Cyclebuffer.el provides an alternative to the standard buffer-switching behavior. Rather than typing `C-x b` and then typing in a buffer name (or pressing Enter if the last-visited buffer is what you want), this add-on enables you to quickly and easily cycle through all the existing buffers. You can find this file on the CD-ROM that is included with this book.

X-Symbol

X-Symbol, which is a ground-breaking package for XEmacs, adds semi-WYSIWYG capabilities to LaTeX, HTML, and other tag-based formatting modes. Instead of special symbol and graphics-inclusion tags, the actual symbol or scaled-down graphics image is displayed in the buffer. The package is available at the following Web site:

```
http://www.dfki.uni-sb.de/~burt/x-symbol
```

The Big Brother Database (BBDB)

The Big Brother Database (BBDB) is a highly-evolved address-book/database with hooks that allow it to cooperate with any of the Emacs mail readers. It can be found at the following home page:

```
http://pweb.netcom.com/~simmonmt/bbdb/index.html
```

Session.el

Session.el is a desktop-saving utility. It keeps track of recently opened files and the point and mark positions within them, as well as of recently-killed text blocks. Under XEmacs, new File submenus are provided to access these tracked items. The home Web site is

```
http://www.fmi.uni-passau.de/~wedler/session/
```

Htmlize.el

Htmlize.el is an ingenious package that can transform a font-locked HTML file buffer into an HTML file. The new file, when it is displayed with recent Netscape versions (such as 4.5), looks almost exactly like the Emacs display (including background color and font-lock colors). The latest version can be found at

```
http://jagor.srce.hr/~hniksic/htmlize.el
```

Dictionary Mode

Dictionary Mode is an Emacs interface to the freely available DICT dictionary databases. The mode enables the user to click on a word in a buffer and see the definitions (including clickable links to related words) in a new window. Keybindings are also provided. The latest version can be found at

```
http://www.in-berlin.de/User/myrkr/dictionary.html
```

VM

VM is another mail package, which some people prefer over tormail (the default) or Gnus. This is a user-configurable email interface that includes support for dealing with mailing list message digests. Although VM has some problems with GNU Emacs versions later than 20.0, these will be fixed when 20.4 is released. It works fine with XEmacs. The VM FTP site is as follows:

```
ftp://ftp.uu.net/networking/mail/vm/
```

Noah Friedman's Modes

Noah Friedman has written many interesting modes, all of which are described at

```
http://homepage6.lcs.mit.edu/users/friedman/software/emacs-lisp/index.html
```

Hm—html-menus

Hm—html-menus is an alternative HTML-editing package with many features and tag keybindings. The home site is

```
http://www.tnt.uni-hannover.de/~muenkel/software/own/hm—html-menus/
overview.html
```

Speedbar

Speedbar is a utility that creates a separate narrow window that contains lists of files (such as source files in a programming project) or locations within a file (such as nodes in an Info file). Speedbar is configurable via Customize. The Speedbar FTP site is as follows:

```
ftp://ftp.ultranet.com/pub/zappo/
```

Follow Mode

Follow Mode is used with an Emacs frame that is split vertically (that is, with two side-by-side windows). The two windows are linked, with the same file shown in each window. When one window is scrolled, the other follows it, enabling you to see twice as much of the file's contents at one time and to scroll both windows simultaneously. Follow Mode is particularly useful if you have a large screen. The latest release (and a demonstration of the mode) can be found at one of Anders Lindgren's Web pages:

```
http://www.csd.uu.se/~andersl/follow.shtml
```

24

Mailcrypt

Mailcrypt is an Emacs interface to the PGP and GPG keyed encryption utilities. Hooks for interaction with any of the Emacs mail and news readers are included. The Mailcrypt home page is at

```
http://www.nb.net/~linux/software/mailcrypt.html
```

Notes-mode

Notes-mode is a note-taking and indexing utility. Although it was designed for academic notes, it is also useful for organizing and cross-referencing a variety of notes and to-do lists. The notes are automatically time-stamped and indexed. Notes-mode needs a working Perl installation. The home-page is

```
http://gost.isi.edu/~johnh/SOFTWARE/NOTES_MODE/index.html
```

vi-dot.el

vi-dot.el is a mode that gives Emacs users the capability to use one of the most useful vi editor commands: repeating the previous command with a single keystroke. vi-dot.el, as well as many other interesting modes, can be found on Will Mengarini's home page:

```
http://www.eskimo.com/~seldon
```

Summary

This hour showed you how to install many of the add-on Emacs modes. Procedures for customizing modes were outlined. Several add-ons were described, and Internet links to the sources listed. Emacs by itself is a powerful editor, but using these add-ons enables you to tailor it to your needs (even though you never need all the available extensions). Try several of them, and eventually you will find a few that suit your editing style—and you will end up with a customized editor that, in effect, you have designed yourself.

Q&A

Q What function is used to create a mode-hook when the hook isn't provided by the mode?

A The setq function.

Q Can more than one add-hook statement for the same mode be used in the .emacs file?

A Yes, new hooks can be added at any time.

Q What effect does byte-compiling a Lisp file have?

A A byte-compiled Lisp file is more compact and loads faster, but in this form it is no longer readable as a text file.

Q What is the difference between autoloading a file and loading it with `load-library`?

A An autoloaded file isn't actually loaded until it is needed, whereas a file loaded with `load-library` is loaded into memory from the start.

Q What happens when a file is loaded with `require`?

A The `require` function only loads a file if it hasn't already been loaded.

Exercises

1. Investigate the modes that come with Emacs, many of which aren't activated by default. Select one of these and then edit your `.emacs` file so that it will function. Try changing some of the default keybindings using the `add-hook` function.

2. Create a new directory and copy some add-on modes to it. Add the directory's path to your load-path, and then try to use the modes.

24

APPENDIX **A**

Installing Functions and Packages from the CD

`sams-lib.el`

The custom functions described in this book are included in `sams-lib.el`, which is located in the `/opt/share/emacs-lisp/sams/sams-lib.el` directory on the CD.

Run Macro on Region

The function `sams-apply-macro-on-region` is an alternative to the standard Emacs function `apply-macro-to-region-lines`. It is described in Hour 12, "Visible Editing Utilities."

Cycle Marks

Cycle Mark functions (`cm-save-pointcm-rotate`) are used to mark and rotate locations in a buffer. They are described in Hour 8, "Searching for Text in Multiple Files."

igrep.el

This package is a frontend to grep, and includes functions to recursively search for text
in files that are in a whole directory structure. The package is described in Hour 8. You
can also find it in Kevin Rodger's /opt/share/emacs-lisp/users/kevinr/igrep.el
directory on the CD.

To use this package, insert the following lines to your .emacs file.

```
;;;;;;;;;;;;;;;;;;;;;;;;;;;;;;;;;;;;;;;;;;;;;;;;;;;;;;;;;;;;;;; the igrep
➡package
;;;;;;;;;;;;;;;;;;;;;;;;;;;;;;;;;;;;;;;;;;;;;;;;;;;;;;;;;;;;;;;;;;;;;;;;;;
(autoload (function igrep) "igrep"
"*Run `grep` PROGRAM to match EXPRESSION in FILES..." t)
(autoload (function igrep-find) "igrep"
"*Run `grep` via `find`..." t)
(autoload (function dired-do-igrep) "igrep"
"*Run `grep` on the marked (or next prefix ARG) files." t)
(autoload (function dired-do-igrep-find) "igrep"
"*Run `grep` via `find` on the marked (or next prefix ARG) directories."
➡t)
(autoload (function grep) "igrep"
"*Run `grep` PROGRAM to match EXPRESSION in FILES..." t)
(autoload (function egrep) "igrep" "*Run `egrep`..." t)
(autoload (function fgrep) "igrep" "*Run `fgrep`..." t)
(autoload (function agrep) "igrep" "*Run `agrep`..." t)
(autoload (function grep-find) "igrep" "*Run `grep` via `find`..." t)
(autoload (function egrep-find) "igrep" "*Run `egrep` via `find`..." t)
(autoload (function fgrep-find) "igrep" "*Run `fgrep` via `find`..." t)
(autoload (function agrep-find) "igrep" "*Run `agrep` via `find`..." t)
(autoload (function dired-do-grep) "igrep"
"*Run `grep` on the marked (or next prefix ARG) files." t)
(autoload (function dired-do-grep-find) "igrep"
"*Run `grep` via `find` on the marked (or next prefix ARG) directories."
➡t)
```

If you use GNU Emacs version 19, you also need to install the package cust-stub.el.

cust-stub.el

Packages that require custom.el do not work with Emacs versions prior to 20.x.
cust-stub.el is an emulation package for custom.el, and you can find it in Noah
Friedman's /opt/share/emacs-lisp/users/noah/cust-stub.el directory.

To use it instead of custom.el, add the following setup to your Emacs:

```
(eval-and-compile
(if (< emacs-major-version 20)
(require 'cust-setup)))
```

folding.el

In Hour 14, "Finding Differences Between Files," package folding is described. It is an alternative to outline-mode for programming languages. You can find it in Anders Lindgren's `/opt/share/emacs-lisp/users/andersl/folding.el` directory.

To install it, copy the file `folding.el` to your load path, and insert one of the following into your Emacs file:

```
(load "folding" 'nomessage 'noerror) (folding-mode-add-find-file-hook)
```

or

```
(autoload 'folding-mode "folding" "Folding mode" t) </pre>
```

The first line will allow Emacs to investigate if a file is written for folding-mode. This requires that the package be loaded at startup, which may add time to the Emacs startup time. If, on the other hand, you seldom use folding-mode then you may use the second line of code listed. To enable folding-mode in this case, you need to start it by typing M-x folding-mode RET.

If you are used to outline-mode, you may ask folding-mode to use keybindings that are like those for outline-mode. You can do this by inserting the following into the `.emacs` file:

```
(setq fold-default-keys-function 'fold-bind-outline-compatible-keys)
➡</pre>
```

If you would like a prefix other than C-c @ for the folding commands, you may set the variable `folding-mode-key-prefix`, such as in the following example:

```
(setq folding-mode-key-prefix [(control o)]) </pre>
```

A

pager.el

The pager package is described in Hour 4, "Basic Editing." It is a convenient way to scroll the display. You find it in Mikael Sjoumldin's `/opt/share/emacs-lisp/users/mikael/pager.el` directory.

It contains two groups of functions:

- Alternatives to the page up/page down functions. These alternatives preserve the location of point: If a number of pages up have been issued, the same number of pages down are issued (that is, it returns to the same location as it started out from).
- Functions for scrolling the window, but keeping the point at the same location of the window.

To install it, place the package in your lisp directory, and insert the following lines into your .emacs file:

```
(require 'pager)
(global-set-key [(control v)]       'pager-page-down) (global-set-key
[(next)]                 'pager-page-down) (global-set-key [(meta v)]
    'pager-page-up) (global-set-key [(prior)]            'pager-page-up)
  (global-set-key [(meta up)]     'pager-row-up) (global-set-key
[(meta kp-8)]  'pager-row-up) (global-set-key [(meta down)]  'pager-
row-down) (global-set-key [(meta kp-2)]  'pager-row-down) </pre>
```

template.el

In Hour 4, the package template by Christoph Wedler is discussed. To install it, copy the template.el file from the lisp subdirectory to your lisp directory. Create the directory ~/lib/templates and copy the files from the templates subdirectory to this one, or create your own in this directory. You can find it under the /opt/share/emacs-lisp/packages/ directory.

Insert the following to your .emacs file to make it do its job:

```
(require 'template)
(template-initialize)
```

For further example of its use, you may wish to look at the examples in the examples subdirectory.

flyspell.el

In Hour 11, "Editing Utilities," flyspell.el by Manuel Serrano is introduced. The on-the-fly spell-checking is described. This facility is located in the package flyspell.el. You can find it in the /opt/share/emacs-lisp/other/ directory. To install it, copy it to your lisp directory, and insert the following into your .emacs file:

```
(autoload 'flyspell-mode "flyspell" "On-the-fly spelling checking" t)
(autoload 'global-flyspell-mode "flyspell" "On-the-fly spelling" t)
</pre>
```

To enable it, press `M-x` and type `flyspell-mode`. If you want it enabled all the time (that is, in all your buffers), you may insert the following into your `.emacs` file:

```
(global-flyspell-mode)
```

To use `flyspell.el` under XEmacs, you need to copy `ispell.el` from the CD to either your `lisp` directory or to the installation directory of XEmacs.

bbdb.el

BBDB is a rolodex-like database program for GNU Emacs. BBDB stands for Insidious Big Brother Database. It provides the following features:

- Integration with mail and news readers, with little or no interaction by the user
- Listing all records that match a regular expression
- Listing all records that match a regular expression in a particular field (such as, "company" or "notes")

To use it, add the following code to your Emacs:

```
(require 'bbdb)
(bbdb-initialize 'gnus 'message)
(add-hook 'gnus-startup-hook 'bbdb-insinuate-gnus)
(bbdb-insinuate-message)
```

There have been reported problems with 2.00 that `bbdb-initialize` does not work if you byte compile BBDB. This problem may have been corrected in the latest version of BBDB.

A

INDEX

Other Related Titles

Linux Unleashed, 3rd Ed.
Tim Parker
0-672-31372-3
$39.99 US/$57.95 CAN

Linux Complete Command Reference
Red Hat
0-672-31104-6
$49.99 US/$70.95 CAN

Sams Teach Yourself UNIX in 10 Minutes
William Ray
0-672-31523-8
$12.99 US/$18.95 CAN

Sams Teach Yourself Windows NT Server 4 in 21 Days
Peter Davis
0-672-31555-6
$29.99 US/$42.95 CAN

Sams Teach Yourself Microsoft Exchange Server 5.5 in 21 Days
Jason vanValkenburgh
0-672-31525-4
$39.99 US/$57.95 CAN

Sams Teach Yourself HTML 4 in 24 Hours, 3rd Ed.
Dick Oliver
0-672-31369-3
$19.99 US/$28.95 CAN

UNIX Unleashed, 3rd Edition
Robin Burk
0-672-31411-8
$49.99 US/$71.95 CAN

Windows 98 Unleashed
Paul McFedries
0-672-31235-2
$34.99 US/$50.95 CAN

Sams Teach Yourself Windows 98 in 24 Hours
Greg Perry
0-672-31223-9
$19.99 US/$28.95 CAN

Sams Teach Yourself C++ in 21 Days
Jesse Liberty
0-672-31515-7
$29.99 US/$42.95 CAN

Sams Teach Yourself C in 21 Days, 4th Ed.
Peter Aitken
0-672-31069-4
$29.99 US/$42.95 CAN

How to Use Linux
Bill Ball
0-672-31545-9
$29.99 US/$42.95 CAN

Red Hat Linux Unleashed, 3rd Ed.
Bill Ball
0-672-31410-x
$39.99 US/$57.95 CAN

STY Linux in 10 Minutes.
John Ray
0-672-31524-6
$12.99 US/$18.95 CAN

www.samspublishing.com

All prices are subject to change.

Get FREE books and more...when you register this book online for our Personal Bookshelf Program

http://register.samspublishing.com/

SAMS

GNU GENERAL PUBLIC LICENSE

Version 2, June 1991

Copyright ® 1989, 1991 Free Software Foundation, Inc.

675 Mass Ave, Cambridge, MA 02139, USA

Everyone is permitted to copy and distribute verbatim copies of this license document, but changing it is not allowed.

Preamble

The licenses for most software are designed to take away your freedom to share and change it. By contrast, the GNU General Public License is intended to guarantee your freedom to share and change free software—to make sure the software is free for all its users. This General Public License applies to most of the Free Software Foundation's software and to any other program whose authors commit to using it. (Some other Free Software Foundation software is covered by the GNU Library General Public License instead.) You can apply it to your programs, too.

When we speak of free software, we are referring to freedom, not price. Our General Public Licenses are designed to make sure that you have the freedom to distribute copies of free software (and charge for this service if you wish), that you receive source code or can get it if you want it, that you can change the software or use pieces of it in new free programs; and that you know you can do these things.

To protect your rights, we need to make restrictions that forbid anyone to deny you these rights or to ask you to surrender the rights. These restrictions translate to certain responsibilities for you if you distribute copies of the software, or if you modify it.

For example, if you distribute copies of such a program, whether gratis or for a fee, you must give the recipients all the rights that you have. You must make sure that they, too, receive or can get the source code. And you must show them these terms so they know their rights.

We protect your rights with two steps: (1) copyright the software, and (2) offer you this license which gives you legal permission to copy, distribute and/or modify the software.

Also, for each author's protection and ours, we want to make certain that everyone understands that there is no warranty for this free software. If the software is modified by someone else and passed on, we want its recipients to know that what they have is not the original, so that any problems introduced by others will not reflect on the original authors' reputations.

Finally, any free program is threatened constantly by software patents. We wish to avoid the danger that redistributors of a free program will individually obtain patent licenses, in effect making the program proprietary. To prevent this, we have made it clear that any patent must be licensed for everyone's free use or not licensed at all.

The precise terms and conditions for copying, distribution and modification follow.

GNU General Public License

Terms and Conditions for Copying, Distribution and Modification

0. This License applies to any program or other work which contains a notice placed by the copyright holder saying it may be distributed under the terms of this General Public License. The "Program", below, refers to any such program or work, and a "work based on the Program" means either the Program or any derivative work under copyright law: that is to say, a work containing the Program or a portion of it, either verbatim or with modifications and/or translated into another language. (Hereinafter, translation is included without limitation in the term "modification".) Each licensee is addressed as "you".

   Activities other than copying, distribution and modification are not covered by this License; they are outside its scope. The act of running the Program is not restricted, and the output from the Program is covered only if its contents constitute a work based on the Program (independent of having been made by running the Program). Whether that is true depends on what the Program does.

1. You may copy and distribute verbatim copies of the Program's source code as you receive it, in any medium, provided that you conspicuously and appropriately publish on each copy an appropriate copyright notice and disclaimer of warranty; keep intact all the notices that refer to this License and to the absence of any warranty; and give any other recipients of the Program a copy of this License along with the Program.

   You may charge a fee for the physical act of transferring a copy, and you may at your option offer warranty protection in exchange for a fee.

2. You may modify your copy or copies of the Program or any portion of it, thus forming a work based on the Program, and copy and distribute such modifications or work under the terms of Section 1 above, provided that you also meet all of these conditions:

   a) You must cause the modified files to carry prominent notices stating that you changed the files and the date of any change.

   b) You must cause any work that you distribute or publish, that in whole or in part contains or is derived from the Program or any part thereof, to be licensed as a whole at no charge to all third parties under the terms of this License.

   c) If the modified program normally reads commands interactively when run, you must cause it, when started running for such interactive use in the most ordinary way, to print or display an announcement including an appropriate copyright notice and a notice that there is no warranty (or else, saying that you provide a warranty) and that users may redistribute the program under these conditions, and telling the user how to view a copy of this License. (Exception: if the Program itself is interactive but does not normally print such an announcement, your work based on the Program is not required to print an announcement.)

These requirements apply to the modified work as a whole. If identifiable sections of that work are not derived from the Program, and can be reasonably considered independent and separate works in themselves, then this License, and its terms, do not apply to those sections when you distribute them as separate works. But when you distribute the same sections as part of a whole which is a work based on the Program, the distribution of the whole must be on the terms of this License, whose permissions for other licensees extend to the entire whole, and thus to each and every part regardless of who wrote it.

Thus, it is not the intent of this section to claim rights or contest your rights to work written entirely by you; rather, the intent is to exercise the right to control the distribution of derivative or collective works based on the Program.

In addition, mere aggregation of another work not based on the Program with the Program (or with a work based on the Program) on a volume of a storage or distribution medium does not bring the other work under the scope of this License.

3. You may copy and distribute the Program (or a work based on it, under Section 2) in object code or executable form under the terms of Sections 1 and 2 above provided that you also do one of the following:

   a) Accompany it with the complete corresponding machine-readable source code, which must be distributed under the terms of Sections 1 and 2 above on a medium customarily used for software interchange; or,

   b) Accompany it with a written offer, valid for at least three years, to give any third party, for a charge no more than your cost of physically performing source distribution, a complete machine-readable copy of the corresponding source code, to be distributed under the terms of Sections 1 and 2 above on a medium customarily used for software interchange; or,

   c) Accompany it with the information you received as to the offer to distribute corresponding source code. (This alternative is allowed only for noncommercial distribution and only if you received the program in object code or executable form with such an offer, in accord with Subsection b above.)

The source code for a work means the preferred form of the work for making modifications to it. For an executable work, complete source code means all the source code for all modules it contains, plus any associated interface definition files, plus the scripts used to control compilation and installation of the executable. However, as a special exception, the source code distributed need not include anything that is normally distributed (in either source or binary form) with the major components (compiler, kernel, and so on) of the operating system on which the executable runs, unless that component itself accompanies the executable.

If distribution of executable or object code is made by offering access to copy from a designated place, then offering equivalent access to copy the source code from the same place counts as distribution of the source code, even though third parties are not compelled to copy the source along with the object code.

4. You may not copy, modify, sublicense, or distribute the Program except as expressly provided under this License. Any attempt otherwise to copy, modify, sublicense or distribute the Program is void, and

will automatically terminate your rights under this License. However, parties who have received copies, or rights, from you under this License will not have their licenses terminated so long as such parties remain in full compliance.

5. You are not required to accept this License, since you have not signed it. However, nothing else grants you permission to modify or distribute the Program or its derivative works. These actions are prohibited by law if you do not accept this License. Therefore, by modifying or distributing the Program (or any work based on the Program), you indicate your acceptance of this License to do so, and all its terms and conditions for copying, distributing or modifying the Program or works based on it.

6. Each time you redistribute the Program (or any work based on the Program), the recipient automatically receives a license from the original licensor to copy, distribute or modify the Program subject to these terms and conditions. You may not impose any further restrictions on the recipients' exercise of the rights granted herein. You are not responsible for enforcing compliance by third parties to this License.

7. If, as a consequence of a court judgment or allegation of patent infringement or for any other reason (not limited to patent issues), conditions are imposed on you (whether by court order, agreement or otherwise) that contradict the conditions of this License, they do not excuse you from the conditions of this License. If you cannot distribute so as to satisfy simultaneously your obligations under this License and any other pertinent obligations, then as a consequence you may not distribute the Program at all. For example, if a patent license would not permit

    royalty-free redistribution of the Program by all those who receive copies directly or indirectly through you, then the only way you could satisfy both it and this License would be to refrain entirely from distribution of the Program.

    If any portion of this section is held invalid or unenforceable under any particular circumstance, the balance of the section is intended to apply and the section as a whole is intended to apply in other circumstances.

    It is not the purpose of this section to induce you to infringe any patents or other property right claims or to contest validity of any such claims; this section has the sole purpose of protecting the integrity of the free software distribution system, which is implemented by public license practices. Many people have made generous contributions to the wide range of software distributed through that system in reliance on consistent application of that system; it is up to the author/donor to decide if he or she is willing to distribute software through any other system and a licensee cannot impose that choice.

    This section is intended to make thoroughly clear what is believed to be a consequence of the rest of this License.

8. If the distribution and/or use of the Program is restricted in certain countries either by patents or by copyrighted interfaces, the original copyright holder who places the Program under this License may add an explicit geographical distribution limitation excluding those countries, so that distribution is permitted only in or among countries not thus excluded. In such case, this License incorporates the limitation as if written in the body of this License.

9. The Free Software Foundation may publish revised and/or new versions of the General Public License from time to time. Such new versions will be similar in spirit to the present version, but may differ in detail to address new problems or concerns.

Each version is given a distinguishing version number. If the Program specifies a version number of this License which applies to it and "any later version", you have the option of following the terms and conditions either of that version or of any later version published by the Free Software Foundation. If the Program does not specify a version number of this License, you may choose any version ever published by the Free Software Foundation.

10. If you wish to incorporate parts of the Program into other free programs whose distribution conditions are different, write to the author to ask for permission. For software which is copyrighted by the Free Software Foundation, write to the Free Software Foundation; we sometimes make exceptions for this. Our decision will be guided by the two goals of preserving the free status of all derivatives of our free software and of promoting the sharing and reuse of software generally.

NO WARRANTY

11. BECAUSE THE PROGRAM IS LICENSED FREE OF CHARGE, THERE IS NO WARRANTY FOR THE PROGRAM, TO THE EXTENT PERMITTED BY APPLICABLE LAW. EXCEPT WHEN OTHERWISE STATED IN WRITING THE COPYRIGHT HOLDERS AND/OR OTHER PARTIES PROVIDE THE PROGRAM "AS IS" WITHOUT WARRANTY OF ANY KIND, EITHER EXPRESSED OR IMPLIED, INCLUDING, BUT NOT LIMITED TO, THE IMPLIED WARRANTIES OF MERCHANTABILITY AND FITNESS FOR A PARTICULAR PURPOSE. THE ENTIRE RISK AS TO THE QUALITY AND PERFORMANCE OF THE PROGRAM IS WITH YOU. SHOULD THE PROGRAM PROVE DEFECTIVE, YOU ASSUME THE COST OF ALL NECESSARY SERVICING, REPAIR OR CORRECTION.

12. IN NO EVENT UNLESS REQUIRED BY APPLICABLE LAW OR AGREED TO IN WRITING WILL ANY COPYRIGHT HOLDER, OR ANY OTHER PARTY WHO MAY MODIFY AND/OR REDISTRIBUTE THE PROGRAM AS PERMITTED ABOVE, BE LIABLE TO YOU FOR DAMAGES, INCLUDING ANY GENERAL, SPECIAL, INCIDENTAL OR CONSEQUENTIAL DAMAGES ARISING OUT OF THE USE OR INABILITY TO USE THE PROGRAM (INCLUDING BUT NOT LIMITED TO LOSS OF DATA OR DATA BEING RENDERED INACCURATE OR LOSSES SUSTAINED BY YOU OR THIRD PARTIES OR A FAILURE OF THE PROGRAM TO OPERATE WITH ANY OTHER PROGRAMS), EVEN IF SUCH HOLDER OR OTHER PARTY HAS BEEN ADVISED OF THE POSSIBILITY OF SUCH DAMAGES.

END OF TERMS AND CONDITIONS

Appendix: How to Apply These Terms to Your New Programs

If you develop a new program, and you want it to be of the greatest possible use to the public, the best way to achieve this is to make it free software which everyone can redistribute and change under these terms.

To do so, attach the following notices to the program. It is safest to attach them to the start of each source file to most effectively convey the exclusion of warranty; and each file should have at least the "copyright" line and a pointer to where the full notice is found.

> <one line to give the program's name and a brief idea of what it does.>
>
> Copyright (C) 19yy <name of author>
>
> This program is free software; you can redistribute it and/or modify it under the terms of the GNU General Public License as published by the Free Software Foundation; either version 2 of the License, or (at your option) any later version.
>
> This program is distributed in the hope that it will be useful, but WITHOUT ANY WARRANTY; without even the implied warranty of MERCHANTABILITY or FITNESS FOR A PARTICULAR PURPOSE. See the GNU General Public License for more details.
>
> You should have received a copy of the GNU General Public License along with this program; if not, write to the Free Software Foundation, Inc., 675 Mass Ave, Cambridge, MA 02139, USA.

Also add information on how to contact you by electronic and paper mail.

If the program is interactive, make it output a short notice like this when it starts in an interactive mode:

> Gnomovision version 69, Copyright (C) 19yy name of author
>
> Gnomovision comes with ABSOLUTELY NO WARRANTY; for details type "show w".

This is free software, and you are welcome to redistribute it under certain conditions; type "show c" for details.

The hypothetical commands "show w" and "show c" should show the appropriate parts of the General Public License. Of course, the commands you use may be called something other than "show w" and "show c"; they could even be mouse-clicks or menu items—whatever suits your program.

You should also get your employer (if you work as a programmer) or your school, if any, to sign a "copyright disclaimer" for the program, if necessary. Here is a sample; alter the names:

> Yoyodyne, Inc., hereby disclaims all copyright interest in the program "Gnomovision" (which makes passes at compilers) written by James Hacker.
>
> <signature of Ty Coon>, 1 April 1989
>
> Ty Coon, President of Vice

This General Public License does not permit incorporating your program into proprietary programs. If your program is a subroutine library, you may consider it more useful to permit linking proprietary applications with the library. If this is what you want to do, use the GNU Library General Public License instead of this License.